The Principles of
Moral and
Political
Philosophy

WILLIAM PALEY

The Principles of
Moral and
Political
Philosophy

William Paley

FOREWORD BY

D. L. Le MAHIEU

Liberty Fund

INDIANAPOLIS

This book is published by Liberty Fund, Inc., a foundation
established to encourage study of the ideal of a society of free and
responsible individuals.

The cuneiform inscription that serves as our logo and as the design
motif for our endpapers is the earliest-known written appearance
of the word "freedom" (*amagi*), or "liberty." It is taken from
a clay document written about 2300 B.C. in the Sumerian
city-state of Lagash.

06 05 04 03 02 C 5 4 3 2 I
06 05 04 03 02 P 5 4 3 2 I

Library of Congress Cataloging-in-Publication Data
Paley, William, 1743–1805.
The principles of moral and political philosophy / William Paley ;
foreword by D. L. Le Mahieu.
p.   cm.
Includes bibliographical references and index.
ISBN 0-86597-380-6 (hbk.: alk. paper)—ISBN 0-86597-381-4 (pbk.: alk. paper)
I. Utilitarianism. 2. Ethics. 3. Political science—Philosophy. I. Title.
B1382.P23 P73 2002
171'.5—dc21
2002029650

Liberty Fund, Inc.
8335 Allison Pointe Trail, Suite 300
Indianapolis, Indiana 46250–1684

Contents

BOOK III
RELATIVE DUTIES

Part I
Of Relative Duties Which Are Determinate

BOOK IV

DUTIES TO OURSELVES

BOOK V

DUTIES TOWARDS GOD

BOOK VI
ELEMENTS OF POLITICAL KNOWLEDGE

Foreword

WILLIAM PALEY'S *Principles of Moral and Political Philosophy*, first published in 1785, played a seminal role in the dissemination of utilitarianism in England. Adopted as an integral part of the curriculum at Cambridge University, the *Principles* helped shape the political thinking of England's intellectual elite well into the nineteenth century. "It has laid the foundation of the Moral Philosophy of many hundreds—probably thousands—of Youth while under a course of training designed to qualify them for being afterwards the Moral instructors of Millions," Archbishop Whately wrote in 1859; "such a work therefore cannot fail to exercise a very considerable and extensive influence on the Minds of successive generations." As late as 1933, John Maynard Keynes called Paley's *Principles* "an immortal book."[1]

Paley's political philosophy remains difficult to classify, especially by modern standards. His theological utilitarianism helped buttress the formation of classical liberalism, the most important political ideology to emerge from the Enlightenment. Yet his *Principles* also contains passages that mesh comfortably with traditional eighteenth-century aristocratic paternalism, a philosophy

---

1. Richard Whately, ed., *Paley's Moral Philosophy: With Annotations* (London, 1859), iii; John Maynard Keynes, *Essays in Biography* (London: Macmillan, 1933), 108n. On Paley's influence at Cambridge, see Martha McMackin Garland, *Cambridge Before Darwin: The Ideal of a Liberal Education, 1800–1860* (Cambridge: Cambridge University Press, 1980), 52–69; and Peter Searby, *A History of the University of Cambridge*, vol. 3, *1750–1870* (Cambridge: Cambridge University Press, 1997), 295–313. Paley was much less influential at Oxford. See M. G. Brock and M. C. Curthoys, eds., *The History of the University of Oxford*, vol. 6, *Nineteenth Century Oxford, Part I* (Oxford: Clarendon, 1997), 210.

frequently antagonistic to liberalism. Then too, despite his published opposition to the French Revolution, some considered Paley sympathetic to radicalism, a charge that may have affected his clerical advancement. Paley vivified the gross inequalities of the distribution of property; he condemned the slave trade; he proposed a graduated income tax that appealed to Tom Paine. In 1802, the *Anti-Jacobin Review* noted that from Paley "the most determined Jacobin might find a justification of his principles, and a sanction for his conduct."[2] Though radicals during the 1790s never claimed Paley as an ally, his iconoclasm remained appealing to many commentators. Paley wrote during a transitional era of rapidly evolving civic discourse when traditional political labels proved inadequate and emerging ideological designations had yet to be fully formed.[3]

Paley's *Principles* might best be placed within the context of his life and writings. William Paley was born in Peterborough in 1743, the son of a vicar who two years later became the headmaster of Giggleswick in Yorkshire. At sixteen, Paley entered Christ's College, Cambridge, where he distinguished himself as a student, graduating as Senior Wrangler in 1763. Three years later, he was elected to a fellowship at Christ's, where he lectured on metaphysics, moral philosophy, and the Greek Testament. It was from these lectures that Paley rapidly gained the reputation as one of Cambridge's most engaging teachers. He often challenged the complacent assumptions of his undergraduates, himself advocating a position so extreme that his students were forced to clarify their own opinions in relation to it. Paley's classroom notes, now preserved in the British Library, reveal that he based an enormous

2. Quoted in A. M. C. Waterman, "A Cambridge 'Via Media' in Late Georgian Anglicanism," *Journal of Ecclesiastical History*, 42, no. 3 (1991): 423.

3. James J. Sack, *From Jacobite to Conservative: Reaction and Orthodoxy in Britain, c. 1760–1832* (Cambridge: Cambridge University Press, 1993), 3–4.

amount of his later philosophy on his Cambridge teaching. As in his lectures, the *Principles* began with general observations on ethics, then proceeded directly into considerations of particular obligations such as the responsibilities of marriage, the nature of contracts, and the evils of fornication and drunkenness. Paley's great strengths as a writer—clear organization, lucid prose, striking examples—evolved from his years as an instructor of undergraduates.[4]

At Cambridge, Paley associated himself with Latitudinarians that included John Law, Richard Watson, and John Jebb. Law became Paley's closest friend and a valuable contact for Paley's career in the church. Watson rose to a minor bishopric, but was blocked from further advancement within the church by his outspoken views. Jebb eventually advocated politically radical views that Paley disavowed, though not at the cost of their friendship. This group shared a number of beliefs at Cambridge: they advocated a natural religion grounded upon the argument from design for the existence of God; they accepted a theologically informed utilitarian definition of virtue; and they endorsed an open and tolerant marketplace of ideas. As reformers, they also frequently disagreed among themselves. At one point on a particularly contentious issue, Paley noted flippantly that he "could not afford to keep a conscience," a remark that would haunt his reputation.[5]

---

4. D. L. Le Mahieu, *The Mind of William Paley: A Philosopher and His Age* (Lincoln: University of Nebraska Press, 1976), esp. chapter one. My analysis of Paley draws upon this earlier work. For Paley's life, see also M. L. Clarke, *Paley: Evidences for the Man* (London: SPCK, 1974).

5. Le Mahieu, 10–19. Paley's remark can be found in George Wilson Meadley, *Memoirs of William Paley, D.D.*, 2nd ed. (Edinburgh: A. Constable, 1810), 89. For Cambridge during this period, see John Gascoigne, *Cambridge in the Age of Enlightenment: Science, Religion, and Politics from the Restoration to the French Revolution* (Cambridge: Cambridge University Press, 1989), esp. 126–34, 195–211, 236–47.

Paley left Cambridge in 1776 and married Jane Hewitt, who would bear him eight children. He spent the remainder of his life as a clergyman, first in Appleby and Dalston for six years; then in Carlisle from 1782 to 1795 where he became archdeacon; finally in Durham and Lincoln from 1795 until his death in 1805. Like other eighteenth-century divines, he derived his income from a number of livings. Although he never experienced the poverty of some lesser clergy, he attained genuine affluence only when he was translated to the lucrative rectorship of Bishop-Wearmouth in 1795. The daily routine of his existence varied little after Cambridge. He discharged his clerical duties conscientiously; he involved himself in the domestic chores of raising a family; he devoted himself to his writings. In 1790, five years after the *Principles*, he published his most original study, *Horae Paulinae*, an exegesis of certain "undesigned coincidences" in the Acts and letters of Paul. In 1794, he completed his analysis of revealed religion with the *Evidences of Christianity*, a masterful example of Christian apologetics that earned him a variety of honors, including a Doctorate of Divinity from Cambridge. The *Evidences* also became part of the Cambridge curriculum and retained its defenders through the nineteenth century. In 1802, he published his *Natural Theology*, the cornerstone of his philosophic thought. The "following discussion alone was wanted to make up my works into a system," he wrote in the preface. "The public now have before them the evidences of Natural Religion, the evidences of Revealed Religion, and an account of the duties that result from both."[6]

Within the context of his life and thought, then, the *Principles* eventually became part of a coherent philosophic system that Paley synthesized from the Enlightenment in England and bequeathed

6. William Paley, *The Works of William Paley, D.D*, vol. 5, *Natural Theology*, ed. Edmund Paley (London, 1825), xix.

as undergraduate texts to the nineteenth century. As part of this system, Paley's ethics and politics, like his biblical criticism, were intimately related to his natural theology. The logical problems and underlying assumptions of the teleological argument for the existence of God provided a conceptual framework which Paley used with systematic thoroughness when he confronted the difficult task of building a system of ethics. The link between morals and theology, like that between natural and revealed religion, lay in a series of interconnecting analogies; it was from his observations of *telos* in natural phenomena—the adaptation of means to ends for beneficent purposes—that he derived his notion of utility and the conviction that God willed human happiness.

Like many Enlightenment moralists, Paley asserted that ethical statements reflected the emotional and intellectual proclivities of the moral agent. Deriving his notion of the good from Locke's epistemology, Paley argued that man's basic instinct was to seek pleasure and to avoid pain. As a Christian, he disassociated himself from vulgar notions of hedonism, providing a variety of reasons why happiness did not consist in sensual pleasures. More positively, he offered a specific definition of happiness, whose cardinal tenet emphasized "engagement," a notion that curiously prefigured Christian existentialism. To Paley, happiness consisted in living by a standard that was self-imposed and self-realized. It was self-imposed because the choice of activity remained radically individual. Unlike the phenomena of nature, which God created with a specific purpose, each person chose their own purpose in life, their final cause. Yet, as in nature where God adapted the various mechanisms of the eye for the purpose of seeing, each person must individually adapt themselves to their chosen end. Christianity, through its promise of an afterlife, offered an incentive to meaningful engagement matched by no other activity. The eternal bliss guaranteed to the faithful provided the best hope of continued pleasure after death. The notion of Christian engagement thereby dovetailed conveniently into Paley's general theory of value.

Paley defined moral virtue as "the doing good to mankind, in obedience to the will of God, and for the sake of everlasting happiness." In a single stroke, he thus encompassed the subject, rule, and motive of the moral life. To Paley, the undeniable demands of self-interest coincided rather than conflicted with the needs of society: one unselfishly contributed to the common good for the selfish purpose of achieving the pleasures of heaven and avoiding the pains of hell. For this reason, he has been called a theological utilitarian. Although he admitted that a future life remained strictly an article of faith, it provided his ethics with a powerful moral sanction. Secular utilitarians would dismiss the Christian motive for moral behavior, but found that the reconstruction of ethics without traditional sanctions was difficult to execute.

To Paley, as to thinkers before him, God's will could be found either in Scripture or nature, either in revealed or natural religion. In nature the purpose of each contrivance was not to harm a creature, and since God created all things, it followed that the Deity was benevolent. The argument's major premise encompassed a negative; that is, Paley demonstrated that evil was not the purpose of the contrivance. But behind the negative lay a positive assertion that constituted the thrust of the discussion; the adaptation of means to ends in all natural phenomena promoted the happiness of the creature. By analogy, Paley concluded that it was the utility of any moral rule alone which determined obligation, and he compressed this moral rule into a simple epigram: "Whatever is expedient, is right." Unfortunately, this notion of expediency would be misunderstood, even by his sympathetic readers. Of course "expedient" could mean "convenient" or "politic" as opposed to "just" or "right." For Paley, however, the controversial term was intended to convey moral suitability that was appropriately adjusted to specific goals, not unlike the relationship between means and ends in nature's contrivances. Once again, God's designs set the standard for moral deliberation.

The sources of Paley's theological utilitarianism have generally been traced to ethicists such as John Gay, Daniel Waterland, and Abraham Tucker. Although Paley's knowledge of Waterland remains conjectural, he certainly read Gay, whose short treatise on ethics appeared in 1731 as a preface to a work edited by Edmund Law, Paley's early patron and the father of his closest friend. Paley followed Gay in his definition of virtue, his psychological egoism, and in a number of minor points, though Paley tended to be less deterministic than the more mechanistic Gay. Gay's brief essay influenced both David Hartley, popular among early Romantics, and Abraham Tucker, who under the pseudonym Edmund Search, published his massive *The Light of Nature Pursued* between 1768 and 1778. Paley commends the work in his preface, but his debt proved less comprehensive than sometimes assumed. To be sure, Paley followed the general prescriptions of Tucker's theological utilitarianism, but the vast mass of Tucker's ponderous work finds no parallel in the *Principles.* In fact, on specific points, Paley borrowed heavily from the Cambridge divine Thomas Rutherforth who, because of a private feud, he never acknowledged.[7]

The theological utilitarians rejected the notion of a moral sense, arguing with Locke that nothing could be innate to the mind. Yet moral sense ethicists such as Shaftesbury, Hutcheson, and Adam Smith also drew upon the teleological categories of natural religion for their analysis. Natural religion provided the moral sense school with an ethical standard and a methodology that guided their reasoning. Though substantial and intractable differences separated the moral sense school from theological

7. Le Mahieu, 123–24.

utilitarians, both sought in ethics what they detected in God's creation. In an era noted for satire and bitter polemic, moralists
argued their differences with mutual respect precisely because they
operated within a shared intellectual framework. Paley distilled
fundamental elements of this consensus into his moral and political thought.[8]

Yet, as Paley himself asserted, he was more than a "mere compiler." He devoted the largest portion of his *Principles* to an
extended analysis of individuals' specific rights and their duties to
themselves, their society, and to God. This discussion, which consumes almost half the book, contains the bulk of his practical
advice on such topics as business contracts, probate, legal oaths,
and the duties of prayer. It also includes one of the most famous
and original passages in all of Paley's works. The pigeon analogy
demonstrated that Paley was painfully aware of the human ex-
ploitation that accompanied the institution of private property.
Ninety-nine toiled relentlessly for the benefit of one, often a
"madman" or a "fool." Wrenched from context, the analogy was
perhaps the most radical declaration against property in the
Enlightenment, though its explicit anti-aristocratic bias was not
without parallel in Paley's ethical thought. He often emphasized
virtues that could be practiced by rich and poor alike. His definition of happiness embodied strong elements of egalitarianism and
reflected the New Testament's prejudice against wealth and privilege. Indeed, Paley saved some of his most scathing indictments for
the idle preoccupations of the leisure class.

Yet Paley never sought to challenge landed wealth or to reform
radically the institution of private property. A cautious though not
always predictable realist, he valued social order. Immediately
following the analogy, he endorsed the standard justifications for

8. Ibid., 124–30.

private property and sanctioned philosophically the moral right of unlimited possessive individualism. He also justified the institution of property on the basis of its expediency for society. Property increased productivity and eliminated civil struggles over owner-ship. Despite its inequities, it contributed to social well-being. Unlike some apologists, Paley acknowledged the affective force of radical criticism and turned it to his own use. The parable of the pigeons, striking in its stark perception of human depravity, served as a rhetorical device to initiate a dialectical argument with his readers, much as he had done with his students at Cambridge.

He was less paradoxical when it came to charity. To Paley, individuals labored under a strong obligation to relieve the distress of the poor, since all land was once held in common, the private possession of no single person or state. Though eschewing the primitive communism of the early Christians, he also rejected the customary excuses why wealthy citizens refused to help the poor. Charity promoted their happiness and served the larger designs of God. Like earlier natural theologians such as John Ray and William Derham, Paley related the emotion of pity to the unfath-omable wisdom of a great Creator. God created within human nature feelings of empathy intended to ease suffering. Though in the *Natural Theology* Paley accepted a more Malthusian approach concerning the dispossessed, both the *Principles* and his sermons emphasized the traditional Christian obligations toward the poor.[9]

Like other Enlightenment theorists, Paley initiated his analysis of politics by discussing the origins of political society. Once establish the rationale of political groupings, it was reasoned, and the rights and duties of both the citizen and the government would

9. On Paley and the poor, see Thomas A. Horne, "'The Poor Have a Claim Founded in the Law of Nature': William Paley and the Rights of the Poor," *Journal of the History of Philosophy*, 23, no. 1 (1985): 51–70.

follow, like postulates from a theorem. This preoccupation with origins, which never pretended to be historical, had its counterpart in ethics where, as in Locke, moral problems were grounded in epistemology, ethics thereby becoming rooted in human psychology. The central precepts of the utilitarians liberated them from the awkward fiction of the social contract that, by the late eighteenth century, had sustained damaging criticism. Paley rejected the social contract for two reasons: He questioned its historical reliability, arguing that only in America had there been anything resembling a gathering of free individuals to plan a future government. More important, he repudiated the notion that political obligations passed from one generation to another without the knowledge or consent of the governed. As a theologian whose writings often implicitly challenged Original Sin, Paley mistrusted legal fictions. If, as Locke suggested, humans were born a *tabula rasa*, they could not be bound by ahistorical obligations.

In place of a social contract, Paley traced the origin of government to the gradual extension of the family unit into a protective military organization. He argued that the first governments were probably monarchies, though he stressed that this development carried with it no current rights or obligations. His natural history of civil society thus resembled those in vogue among Scottish philosophers, and forecast in embryonic form the anthropological studies of the late nineteenth century. Paley approached the issue of political obligation by analyzing how, in fact, governments controlled their citizens. Since the physical strength of any nation resided in the governed, the question became why major revolutions were not more frequent and minor revolts more violent. Writing four years before the French Revolution, Paley considered a number of possibilities, including the notion that the governed obeyed from prejudice and prescription. If, to Edmund Burke, the notion of prescription embodied almost mystic overtones, Paley described it simply as the habit of obedience, reinforced by self-interest and rational calculation. He opposed such developments as the formation of "combinations" or trade unions, because he knew that, when organized, the general population might discover its own considerable strength. For all his authentic concerns for the poor, Paley still regarded them as politically unpredictable and potentially dangerous.

For Paley, the moral basis of political obligation resided in the same standard that animated his ethics, "the Will of God as Collected from Expediency." Just as in nature where each part of a contrivance contributed to the efficient functioning of the whole, so in politics individuals needed to fit their own abilities to the happiness of the larger society. Conversely, a government remained legitimate only as long as it served effectively its constituents and therefore, as in Locke, the right of resistance became critical. To Paley such a right could be determined by careful calculation. He listed the factors to be evaluated, arguing that the larger social interest bound its individual parts. As in his analysis of evil in his *Natural Theology*, no exception disproved a general rule. Just as teeth were not contrived to ache, so also political subjects were not intended to revolt—even though occasionally teeth ached and subjects revolted. The rebellion in America, sympathetically assessed by Burke, stirred uneasy feelings in Paley, who found it difficult to comprehend the intense passions of political movements. He argued that discontented groups ought to act like rational individuals.

Like Paine, Paley recognized that the British constitution consisted of precedents fabricated by individuals and thereby subject to periodic revision. As a human artifact constructed over time, it nevertheless resembled nature in its concern for the happiness of its subjects. Paley endorsed the conventional notion found

in Montesquieu and others that the British constitution was a net-
work of checks and balances. Each component served its own
purpose while contributing to the functioning of the whole. To
such trusted themes, Paley added a discussion of crown patronage
as an integral element of the balanced constitution. Paley claimed
that without an extensive system of patronage the king would eventually relinquish his political leverage over the House of Commons. The *Principles* was published only four years after the famous
Dunning resolution which challenged the increasing power of the
monarchy and only three years after the movement for economical
reform eliminated the more egregious governmental sinecures.
Though Paley refused to defend all forms of patronage, he recognized that the future lay with the House of Commons, not the
monarchy.

Yet Paley opposed immediate electoral reform in part because
he feared its unintended consequences. Ever since the protracted
controversy over John Wilkes, reformers sought some alteration of
the franchise. Although the younger Pitt, a Tory, introduced
reform bills in the 1780s, it would be almost fifty years before the
Reform Bill of 1832 extended the vote. Paley believed that Parliament should represent only the landed and moneyed interests of
society. He rejected the notion that individuals possessed a natural
right to vote, adding in a footnote that if such a right existed,
women should vote as well. Though he defended the buying of
seats as an effective means of introducing talent into the legislature,
he condemned electoral bribery. Above all, he feared that comprehensive reform might lead unintentionally to mob rule. A balanced
constitution could not survive the transference of power to those
who lacked a stake in the system. This fear of democracy molded
his opposition to the French Revolution, during which he repub-
lished his chapter on the British constitution as a separate pamphlet to be distributed among the poor. Paley's antagonism to the

events in France became part of a larger ideological discourse that helped the British power structure withstand the revolutionary currents of the 1790s.[10]

The *Principles* also addressed other issues of concern to the British elites. Since the mid-eighteenth century, efforts to reform the complex, and often brutally ineffective, system of penal law had attracted wide attention. In 1750, for example, the novelist Henry Fielding published a work that explored the problem of crime and was flattered when, a few years later, a committee appointed by the House of Commons recommended acceptance of some of his suggestions. In 1771, William Eden published his *Principles of Penal Law* which, influenced by Montesquieu and Beccaria, argued that the severity of punishment, including the death penalty, rarely deterred crime. It was during this same period, of course, that Bentham began his long campaign to revise the English legal code.[11] Like Bentham and others, Paley considered the function of punishment to be essentially didactic: it sought to prevent crime rather than simply penalize it.

Yet, unlike Bentham, Paley refused to condemn the British legal system as archaic and corrupt. In one of the most remarkable passages in the *Principles*, he defended the death penalty for the stealing of horses and sheep. He noted that juries rarely enforced such draconian penalties that, he argued, frightened potential thieves from committing such crimes. Though he acknowledged that the certainty rather than the severity of punishment proved

10. For this discourse, see, among others, Ian R. Christie, *Stress and Stability in Late Eighteenth-Century Britain* (Oxford: Clarendon Press, 1984), and Thomas Philip Schofield, "Conservative Political Thought in Britain in Response to the French Revolution," *The Historical Journal*, 29, no.3 (1986): 601–22.

11. Leon Radzinowicz, *A History of English Criminal Law and Its Administration from 1750*, vol. 1 (London: Stevens and Sons, 1948), 301–449. On Fielding, see Martin C. Battestin, *Henry Fielding: A Life* (London: Routledge, 1989), 459–80.

the most effective deterrence, he remained deeply impressed by the efficacy of fear in reforming criminals. He argued against public executions, however, pointing out how they coarsened the honest citizenry. Paley considered his reflections on criminal law entirely consistent with his utilitarianism even though his analysis proved anathema to other reformers.

Paley also justified the practices of the church by an appeal to utility. Unlike William Warburton, who appealed to Divine Providence to defend church-state relations in England, Paley showed how existing hierarchies served society as a whole. The church preserved and communicated religious knowledge among the various social classes, while providing strong incentives for talented individuals to join the clergy. If, for the most part, these notions reinforced existing practices, Paley's views on religious toleration proved more controversial. He distinguished between partial toleration, where Dissenters could worship but not hold public office, and complete toleration, where all religious practitioners enjoyed the same civil rights. Reflecting the Latitudinarian views of his Cambridge friends, many of whom had protested the imposed uniformity of the Thirty-nine Articles, Paley advocated complete toleration. To Paley, as to Locke before him and Mill later on, toleration invigorated debate within the public sphere.

Paley's political thought demonstrated that utilitarianism need not be a radical doctrine. Unlike Bentham, whose invocation of utility constantly revealed the inadequacies and irrationalities of existing practices, Paley employed the notion to justify the *status quo*. In politics and ethics, Paley remained a theorist who, as in his natural theology, judged a practice by how well means were adapted to ends. Unlike his discontented contemporaries, he saw only successes; whether in the British constitution with its unique pattern of checks and balances, or in the legal code with its inconsistent enforcement of the death penalty. Paley sought the rationale of existing practices in the *Principles,* just as later, in the *Reflections,* Burke would demonstrate the usefulness of tradition. Both placed the burden of proof on those who innovated radically rather than reformed gradually.

The influence of the *Principles* on nineteenth-century thought often involved paradoxes and unintended consequences, a fate that would not have astonished Paley. His theological utilitarianism contributed to an ideological climate that made Bentham's ideas more palatable to respectable opinion. Yet the standard contrast between the cautious Paley and the radical Bentham sometimes obscures as much as it reveals. Paley's emphasis on individual autonomy in his definition of virtue and moral obligation meshed more comfortably with the political axioms of liberal reformers in the nineteenth century than Bentham's frequent authoritarian reliance on government legislation to create social happiness.[12] Moreover, Paley's utilitarianism, despite its Christian themes, contributed powerfully to the secularization of political theory in Britain.[13] In a variety of ways, including in his *Natural Theology* where he revised some of his earlier ideas, Paley became an important component of what A. M. C. Waterman has called "Christian Political Economy" in the early nineteenth century.[14] The complex evolution of nineteenth-century liberalism and conservatism involved a number of ideological crosscurrents. Paley's *Principles* became a protean source of ideas for thinkers and politicians of diverse allegiances.

12. James E. Crimmins, "Religion, Utility and Politics: Bentham versus Paley," in James E. Crimmins, ed., *Religion, Secularization and Political Thought: Thomas Hobbes to J. S. Mill* (London: Routledge, 1989), 130–52.

13. Robert Hole, *Pulpits, Politics and Public Order in England, 1760–1832* (Cambridge: Cambridge University Press, 1989), 73–81.

14. A. M. C. Waterman, *Revolution, Economics and Religion: Christian Political Economy, 1798–1833* (Cambridge: Cambridge University Press, 1991).

The book also sustained bitter criticism from both the Evangelicals and the Romantics. In 1789, for example, Thomas Gisborne condemned Paley's notion of expediency as morally pernicious. The concept, he wrote, could not be found in the Bible; it led to rationalizations about personal responsibilities; its consequences could not be predicted.[15] Other Evangelical writers such as William Wilberforce also condemned the notion of expediency as self-serving and materialistic.[16] The Romantics, like the Evangelicals, substituted an ethic of inward conscience and spiritual obligation for the calculating moral system of Paley. Both viewed the English empiricists as shallow optimists incapable of penetrating the mysteries of the human spirit. Samuel Taylor Coleridge condemned Paley's ethics as "the anarchy of morals" and a "debasing slavery to the outward senses." Such strong language was not unusual among the Romantic critics of the archdeacon. William Hazlitt labeled the *Principles* "a disgrace to the national character" and saved some of his most savage denunciations for Paley himself.[17]

Hostility to the *Principles* extended to respected dons at Cambridge itself. At Kings, the ascendancy of Charles Simeon meant that Evangelical distrust of Paley began filtering through to undergraduates, while at Sidney Sussex the master Edward Pearson published in 1800 a critique of both the Evangelicals and Paley. Though some defenders such as Latham Wainewright rallied to Paley's aid, the influence of the *Principles* sustained its most

15. Thomas Gisborne, *The Principles of Moral Philosophy Investigated, and Briefly Applied to the Constitution of Civil Society* (London: B. White, 1789), 33–34, 200.

16. Le Mahieu, 156–57. On the Evangelicals during this period, see Boyd Hilton, *The Age of Atonement: The Influence of Evangelicalism on Social and Economic Thought, 1795–1865* (Oxford: Clarendon Press, 1988).

17. Samuel Taylor Coleridge, *The Complete Works of Samuel Taylor Coleridge*, 5 vols. (New York, 1884), 1:158, 193n, 263; 2:296. Hazlitt quoted in Herschel Baker, *William Hazlitt* (Cambridge: Harvard University Press, 1962), 14.

effective criticism during the 1830s when two influential dons, Adam Sedgwick and William Whewell, warned against the dangers of utilitarian ethics. Sedgwick vehemently protested against Paley's rejection of the moral sense, while Whewell, the Knightsbridge Professor of Moral Philosophy, argued that Paley's thinking contributed to the ethical confusions of the age. Both of these early Victorians believed that morals implied duty, struggle, and a constant distrust of the senses. Although the *Principles* would remain on the reading lists of some colleges far into the nineteenth century, its practical influence waned during the 1830s.[18]

For readers today, the *Principles* offers insights into a complex era of intellectual history. As part of a coherent system of thought, Paley's moral and political philosophy demonstrates how a late eighteenth-century divine accommodated the secular impulses of the Enlightenment for religious purposes. Paley's synthesis would not survive the Darwinian redescription of the natural world, but his desire to reconcile science and religion drew upon traditions not yet extinguished. His specific version of theological utilitarianism finds no converts today, but his prescriptions for the good life transcend the historical context which produced them. Paley's strengths as a writer may still surprise readers in the twenty-first century.

D. L. Le Mahieu
Lake Forest College

18. Le Mahieu, 158–62. For Whewell and Paley, see James P. Henderson, *Early Mathematical Economics: William Whewell and the British Case* (Lanham, Md.: Rowman & Littlefield, 1996), 84–85.

Select Bibliography

Barker, Ernest. *Traditions of Civility*, pp. 193–262. Cambridge: Cambridge University Press, 1948. An old but still useful discussion of Paley's life and thought.

Clarke, M. L. *Paley: Evidences for the Man*. London: SPCK, 1974. A solid biography.

Hole, Robert. *Pulpits, Politics and Public Order in England, 1760–1832*. Cambridge: Cambridge University Press, 1989. A highly informative study of religion and political thought during this period.

Le Mahieu, D. L. *The Mind of William Paley: A Philosopher and His Age*. Lincoln: University of Nebraska Press, 1976.

Paley, William. *The Works of William Paley, D.D.* 7 volumes. Edited by Edmund Paley. London: C. and J. Rivington, 1825. The best of the many editions of Paley. Includes an important account of his life by his son, the editor.

Waterman, A. M. C. *Revolution, Economics and Religion: Christian Political Economy, 1798–1833*. Cambridge: Cambridge University Press, 1991. Makes a complex and important argument about the evolution of thought during this era.

To
The Right Reverend
Edmund Law, D.D.
Lord Bishop of Carlisle

MY LORD,

Had the obligations which I owe to your Lordship's kindness been much less, or much fewer, than they are; had personal gratitude left any place in my mind for deliberation or for inquiry; in selecting a name which every reader might confess to be prefixed with propriety to a work, that, in many of its parts, bears no obscure relation to the general principles of natural and revealed religion, I should have found myself directed by many considerations to that of the Bishop of Carlisle. A long life spent in the most interesting of all human pursuits—the investigation of moral and religious truth, in constant and unwearied endeavours to advance the discovery, communication, and success, of both; a life so occupied, and arrived at that period which renders every life venerable, commands respect by a title which no virtuous mind will dispute, which no mind sensible of the importance of these studies to the supreme concernments of mankind will not rejoice to see acknowledged. Whatever difference, or whatever opposition, some who peruse your Lordship's writings may perceive between your conclusions and their own, the good and wise of all persuasions will revere that industry, which has for its object the illustration or defence of our common Christianity. Your Lordship's researches have never lost sight of one purpose, namely, to recover the simplicity of the

Gospel from beneath that load of unauthorised additions, which the ignorance of some ages, and the learning of others, the superstition of weak, and the craft of designing men, have (unhappily for its interest) heaped upon it. And this purpose, I am convinced, was dictated by the purest motive; by a firm, and, I think, a just opinion, that whatever renders religion more rational, renders it more credible; that he who, by a diligent and faithful examination of the original records, dismisses from the system one article which contradicts the apprehension, the experience, or the reasoning of mankind, does more towards recommending the belief, and, with the belief, the influence of Christianity, to the understandings and consciences of serious inquirers, and through them to universal reception and authority, than can be effected by a thousand contenders for creeds and ordinances of human establishment.

When the doctrine of Transubstantiation had taken possession of the Christian world, it was not without the industry of learned men that it came at length to be discovered, that no such doctrine was contained in the New Testament. But had those excellent persons done nothing more by their discovery than abolished an innocent superstition, or changed some directions in the ceremonial of public worship, they had merited little of that veneration, with which the gratitude of Protestant Churches remembers their services. What they did for mankind was this: they exonerated Christianity of a weight which sunk it. If indolence or timidity had checked these exertions, or suppressed the fruit and publication of these inquiries, is it too much to affirm, that infidelity would at this day have been universal?

I do not mean, my Lord, by the mention of this example, to insinuate that any popular opinion which your Lordship may have encountered ought to be compared with Transubstantiation, or that the assurance with which we reject that extravagant absurdity is attainable in the controversies in which your Lordship has been engaged; but I mean, by calling to mind those great reformers of the public faith, to observe, or rather to express my own persuasion, that to restore the purity, is most effectually to promote the progress of Christianity; and that the same virtuous motive which has sanctified their labours, suggested yours. At a time when some men appear not to perceive any good, and others to suspect an evil tendency, in that spirit of examination and research which is gone forth in Christian countries, this testimony is become due, not only to the probity of your Lordship's views, but to the general cause of intellectual and religious liberty.

That your Lordship's life may be prolonged in health and honour; that it may continue to afford an instructive proof, how serene and easy old age can be made by the memory of important and well-intended labours, by the possession of public and deserved esteem, by the presence of many grateful relatives; above all, by the resources of religion, by an unshaken confidence in the designs of a "faithful Creator," and a settled trust in the truth and in the promises of Christianity; is the fervent prayer of,

My Lord,
Your Lordship's dutiful,
Most obliged,
And most devoted servant,
William Paley

Carlisle,
Feb. 10, 1785

Preface

IN THE treatises that I have met with upon the subject of *morals*, I appear to myself to have remarked the following imperfections—either that the principle was erroneous, or that it was indistinctly explained, or that the rules deduced from it were not sufficiently adapted to real life and to actual situations. The writings of Grotius, and the larger work of Puffendorff, are of too *forensic* a cast, too much mixed up with civil law and with the jurisprudence of Germany, to answer precisely the design of a system of ethics—the direction of private consciences in the general conduct of human life. Perhaps, indeed, they are not to be regarded as institutes of morality calculated to instruct an individual in his duty, so much as a species of law-books and law-authorities, suited to the practice of those courts of justice, whose decisions are regulated by general principles of natural equity, in conjunction with the maxims of the Roman code; of which kind, I understand, there are many upon the Continent. To which may be added, concerning both these authors, that they are more occupied in describing the rights and usages of independent communities than is necessary in a work which professes not to adjust the correspondence of nations, but to delineate the offices of domestic life. The profusion also of classical quotations with which many of their pages abound seems to me a fault from which it will not be easy to excuse them. If these extracts be intended as decorations of style, the composition is overloaded with ornaments of one kind. To any thing more than ornament they can make no claim. To propose them as serious arguments, gravely to attempt to establish or fortify a moral duty by the testimony of a Greek or Roman poet, is to trifle with the attention of the reader, or rather to take it off from all just principles of reasoning in morals.

Of our own writers in this branch of philosophy, I find none that I think perfectly free from the three objections which I have stated. There is likewise a fourth property observable almost in all of them, namely, that they divide too much the law of Nature from the precepts of Revelation; some authors industriously declining the mention of Scripture authorities, as belonging to a different province; and others reserving them for a separate volume: which appears to me much the same defect, as if a commentator on the laws of England should content himself with stating upon each head the common law of the land, without taking any notice of acts of parliament; or should choose to give his readers the common law in one book, and the statute law in another. "When the obligations of morality are taught," says a pious and celebrated writer, "let the sanctions of Christianity never be forgotten; by which it will be shown that they give strength and lustre to each other: religion will appear to be the voice of reason, and morality will be the will of God."*

The *manner* also in which modern writers have treated of subjects of morality is, in my judgement, liable to much exception. It has become of late a fashion to deliver moral institutes in strings or series of detached propositions, without subjoining a continued argument or regular dissertation to any of them. This sententious apophthegmatising style, by crowding propositions and paragraphs too fast upon the mind, and by carrying the eye of the reader from subject to subject in too quick a succession, gains not a sufficient hold upon the attention to leave either the memory furnished, or the understanding satisfied. However useful a syllabus of topics or a series of propositions may be in the hands of a lecturer, or as a guide to a student, who is supposed to consult other books,

---

*Preface to "The Preceptor," by Dr. Johnson.

or to institute upon each subject researches of his own, the method is by no means convenient for ordinary readers; because few readers are such *thinkers* as to want only a hint to set their thoughts at work upon; or such as will pause and tarry at every proposition, till they have traced out its dependency, proof, relation, and consequences, before they permit themselves to step on to another. A respectable writer of this class* has comprised his doctrine of slavery in the three following propositions:

"No one is born a slave; because every one is born with all his original rights."

"No one can become a slave; because no one from being a person can, in the language of the Roman law, become a thing, or subject of property."

"The supposed property of the master in the slave, therefore, is matter of usurpation, not of right."

It may be possible to deduce from these few adages such a theory of the primitive rights of human nature, as will evince the illegality of slavery: but surely an author requires too much of his reader, when he expects him to make these deductions for himself; or to supply, perhaps from some remote chapter of the same treatise, the several proofs and explanations which are necessary to render the meaning and truth of these assertions intelligible.

There is a fault, the opposite of this, which some moralists who have adopted a different, and I think a better plan of composition, have not always been careful to avoid; namely, the dwelling upon verbal and elementary distinctions, with a labour and prolixity proportioned much more to the subtlety of the question than to its value and importance in the prosecution of the subject. A writer upon the law of nature,† whose explications in every part of philosophy,

---

*Dr. Ferguson, author of "Institutes of Moral Philosophy"; 1767.
†Dr. Rutherforth, author of "Institutes of Natural Law."

though always diffuse, are often very successful, has employed three long sections in endeavouring to prove that "permissions are not laws." The discussion of this controversy, however essential it might be to dialectic precision, was certainly not necessary to the progress of a work designed to describe the duties and obligations of civil life. The reader becomes impatient when he is detained by disquisitions which have no other object than the settling of terms and phrases; and, what is worse, they for whose use such books are chiefly intended will not be persuaded to read them at all.

I am led to propose these strictures, not by any propensity to depreciate the labours of my predecessors, much less to invite a comparison between the merits of their performances and my own; but solely by the consideration, that when a writer offers a book to the public, upon a subject on which the public are already in possession of many others, he is bound by a kind of literary justice to inform his readers, distinctly and specifically, what it is he professes to supply and what he expects to improve. The imperfections above enumerated are those which I have endeavoured to avoid or remedy. Of the execution, the reader must judge: but this was the design.

Concerning the *principle* of morals it would be premature to speak: but concerning the manner of unfolding and explaining that principle, I have somewhat which I wish to be remarked. An experience of nine years in the office of a public tutor in one of the universities, and in that department of education to which these chapters relate, afforded me frequent occasions to observe, that in discoursing to young minds upon topics of morality, it required much more pains to make them perceive the difficulty than to understand the solution; that, unless the subject was so drawn up to a point as to exhibit the full force of an objection, or the exact place of a doubt, before any explanation was entered upon—in other words, unless some curiosity was excited before it was attempted to be satisfied, the labour of the teacher was lost. When information was not desired, it was seldom, I found, retained. I have made this observation my guide in the following work: that is, upon each occasion I have endeavoured, before I suffered myself to proceed in the disquisition, to put the reader in complete possession of the question; and to do it in the way that I thought most likely to stir up his own doubts and solicitude about it.

In pursuing the principle of morals through the detail of cases to which it is applicable, I have had in view to accommodate both the choice of the subjects and the manner of handling them to the situations which arise in the life of an inhabitant of this country in these times. This is the thing that I think to be principally wanting in former treatises; and perhaps the chief advantage which will be found in mine. I have examined no doubts, I have discussed no obscurities, I have encountered no errors, I have adverted to no controversies, but what I have seen actually to exist. If some of the questions treated of appear to a more instructed reader minute or puerile, I desire such reader to be assured that I have found them occasions of difficulty to young minds; and what I have observed in young minds, I should expect to meet with in all who approach these subjects for the first time. Upon each article of human duty, I have combined with the conclusion of reason the declarations of Scripture, when they are to be had, as of co-ordinate authority, and as both terminating in the same sanctions.

In the manner of the work, I have endeavoured so to attemper the opposite plans above animadverted upon, as that the reader may not accuse me either of too much haste, or too much delay. I have bestowed upon each subject enough of dissertation to give a body and substance to the chapter in which it is treated of, as well as coherence and perspicuity: on the other hand, I have seldom, I hope, exercised the patience of the reader by the length and prolixity of my essays, or disappointed that patience at last by the tenuity and unimportance of the conclusion.

There are two particulars in the following work, for which it may be thought necessary that I should offer some excuse. The first of which is, that I have scarcely ever referred to any other book; or mentioned the name of the author whose thoughts, and sometimes, possibly, whose very expressions, I have adopted. My method of writing has constantly been this; to extract what I could from my own stores and my own reflections in the first place; to put down that, and afterwards to consult upon each subject such readings as fell in my way; which order, I am convinced, is the only one whereby any person can keep his thoughts from sliding into other men's trains. The effect of such a plan upon the production itself will be, that, whilst some parts in matter or manner may be new, others will be little else than a repetition of the old. I make no pretensions to perfect originality: I claim to be something more than a mere compiler. Much, no doubt, is borrowed; but the fact is, that the notes for this work having been prepared for some years, and such things having been from time to time inserted in them as appeared to me worth preserving, and such insertions made commonly without the name of the author from whom they were taken, I should, at this time, have found a difficulty in recovering those names with sufficient exactness to be able to render to every man his own. Nor, to speak the truth, did it appear to me worth while to repeat the search merely for this purpose. When authorities are relied upon, names must be produced: when a discovery has been made in science, it may be unjust to borrow the invention without acknowledging the author. But in an argumentative treatise, and upon a subject which allows no place for discovery or invention, properly so called; and in which all that can belong to a writer is his mode of reasoning, or his judgement of probabilities; I should have thought it superfluous, had it been easier to me than it was, to have interrupted my text, or crowded my margin, with references to every author whose sentiments I have made use of. There is, however, one work to which I owe so much, that it would be ungrateful not to confess the obligation: I mean the writings of the late Abraham Tucker, Esq. part of which were published by himself, and the remainder since his death, under the title of "The Light of Nature pursued, by Edward Search, Esq." I have found in this writer more original thinking and observation upon the several subjects that he has taken in hand than in any other, not to say, than in all others put together. His talent also for illustration is unrivalled. But his thoughts are diffused through a long, various, and irregular work. I shall account it no mean praise, if I have been sometimes able to dispose into method, to collect into heads and articles, or to exhibit in more compact and tangible masses, what, in that otherwise excellent performance, is spread over too much surface.

The next circumstance for which some apology may be expected is the joining of moral and political philosophy together, or the addition of a book of politics to a system of ethics. Against this objection, if it be made one, I might defend myself by the example of many approved writers, who have treated *de officiis hominis et civis*, or, as some choose to express it, "of the rights and obligations of man, in his individual and social capacity," in the same book. I might allege, also, that the part a member of the commonwealth shall take in political contentions, the vote he shall give, the counsels he shall approve, the support he shall afford, or the opposition he shall make, to any system of public measures— is as much a question of personal duty, as much concerns the conscience of the individual who deliberates, as the determination of any doubt which relates to the conduct of private life: that consequently political philosophy is, properly speaking, a continuation of moral philosophy; or rather indeed a part of it, supposing moral philosophy to have for its aim the information of the human conscience in every deliberation that is likely to come before it. I might avail myself of these excuses, if I wanted them; but the vindication upon which I rely is the following: In stating the principle of morals, the reader will observe that I have employed some industry in explaining the theory, and showing the necessity of *general rules;* without the full and constant consideration of which, I am persuaded that no system of moral philosophy can be satisfactory or consistent. This foundation being laid, or rather this habit being formed, the discussion of political subjects, to which, more than to almost any other, general rules are applicable, became clear and easy. Whereas, had these topics been assigned to a distinct work, it would have been necessary to have repeated the same rudiments, to have established over again the same principles, as those which we had already exemplified, and rendered familiar to the reader, in the former parts of this. In a word, if there appear to any one too great a diversity, or too wide a distance, between the subjects treated of in the course of the present volume, let him be reminded, that the doctrine of general rules pervades and connects the whole.

It may not be improper, however, to admonish the reader, that, under the name of *politics,* he is not to look for those occasional controversies, which the occurrences of the present day, or any temporary situation of public affairs, may excite; and most of which, if not beneath the dignity, it is beside the purpose, of a philosophical institution to advert to. He will perceive that the several disquisitions are framed with a reference to the condition of this country, and of this government: but it seemed to me to belong to the design of a work like the following, not so much to discuss each altercated point with the particularity of a political pamphlet upon the subject, as to deliver those universal principles, and to exhibit that mode and train of reasoning in politics, by the due application of which every man might be enabled to attain to just conclusions of his own. I am not ignorant of an objection that has been advanced against all abstract speculations concerning the

origin, principle, or limitation of civil authority; namely, that such
speculations possess little or no influence upon the conduct either
of the state or of the subject, of the governors or the governed; nor
are attended with any useful consequences to either: that in times
of tranquillity they are not wanted; in times of confusion they are
never heard. This representation, however, in my opinion, is not
just. Times of tumult, it is true, are not the times to learn; but the
choice which men make of their side and party, in the most critical
occasions of the commonwealth, may nevertheless depend upon
the lessons they have received, the books they have read, and the
opinions they have imbibed, in seasons of leisure and quietness.
Some judicious persons, who were present at Geneva during the
troubles which lately convulsed that city, thought they perceived,
in the contentions there carrying on, the operation of that political theory, which the writings of Rousseau, and the unbounded
esteem in which these writings are holden by his countrymen, had
diffused amongst the people. Throughout the political disputes
that have within these few years taken place in Great Britain, in her
sister-kingdom, and in her foreign dependencies, it was impossible
not to observe in the language of party, in the resolutions of public meetings, in debate, in conversation, in the general strain of
those fugitive and diurnal addresses to the public which such occasions call forth, the prevalency of those ideas of civil authority
which are displayed in the works of Mr. Locke. The credit of that
great name, the courage and liberality of his principles, the skill
and clearness with which his arguments are proposed, no less than
the weight of the arguments themselves, have given a reputation
and currency to his opinions, of which I am persuaded, in any
unsettled state of public affairs, the influence would be felt. As this
is not a place for examining the truth or tendency of these doctrines, I would not be understood by what I have said to express any
judgement concerning either. I mean only to remark, that such

doctrines are not without effect; and that it is of *practical* importance to have the principles from which the obligations of social
union, and the extent of civil obedience, are derived, rightly
explained, and well understood. Indeed, as far as I have observed,
in political, beyond all other subjects, where men are without some
fundamental and scientific principles to resort to, they are liable to
have their understandings played upon by cant phrases and
unmeaning terms, of which every party in every country possesses
a vocabulary. We appear astonished when we see the multitude led
away by sounds; but we should remember that, if sounds work miracles, it is always upon ignorance. The influence of names is in
exact proportion to the want of knowledge.

These are the observations with which I have judged it expedient to prepare the attention of my reader. Concerning the personal
motives which engaged me in the following attempt, it is not necessary that I say much; the nature of my academical situation, a
great deal of leisure since my retirement from it, the recommendation of an honoured and excellent friend, the authority of the venerable prelate to whom these labours are inscribed, the not perceiving in what way I could employ my time or talents better, and
my disapprobation, in literary men, of that fastidious indolence
which sits still because it disdains to do *little*, were the considerations that directed my thoughts to this design. Nor have I
repented of the undertaking. Whatever be the fate or reception of
this work, it owes its author nothing. In sickness and in health I
have found in it that which can alone alleviate the one, or give
enjoyment to the other—occupation and engagement.

The Principles of
Moral and
Political
Philosophy

Book I
Preliminary Considerations

Chapter 1
DEFINITION AND USE OF THE SCIENCE

Moral Philosophy, Morality, Ethics, Casuistry, Natural Law, mean all the same thing; namely, *that science which teaches men their duty and the reasons of it.*

The use of such a study depends upon this, that, without it, the rules of life, by which men are ordinarily governed, oftentimes mislead them, through a defect either in the rule, or in the application.

These rules are, the Law of Honour, the Law of the Land, and the Scriptures.

Chapter 2
THE LAW OF HONOUR

The Law of Honour is a system of rules constructed by people of fashion, and calculated to facilitate their intercourse with one another; and for no other purpose.

Consequently, nothing is adverted to by the Law of Honour, but what tends to incommode this intercourse.

Hence this law only prescribes and regulates the duties *betwixt equals;* omitting such as relate to the Supreme Being, as well as those which we owe to our inferiors.

For which reason, profaneness, neglect of public worship or private devotion, cruelty to servants, rigorous treatment of tenants or other dependants, want of charity to the poor, injuries done to tradesmen by insolvency or delay of payment, with numberless examples of the same kind, are accounted no breaches of honour; because a man is not a less agreeable companion for these vices, nor the worse to deal with, in those concerns which are usually transacted between one gentleman and another.

Again; the Law of Honour, being constituted by men occupied in the pursuit of pleasure, and for the mutual conveniency of such men, will be found, as might be expected from the character and design of the law-makers, to be, in most instances, favourable to the licentious indulgence of the natural passions.

Thus it allows of fornication, adultery, drunkenness, prodigality, duelling, and of revenge in the extreme; and lays no stress upon the virtues opposite to these.

Chapter 3
THE LAW OF THE LAND

That part of mankind, who are beneath the Law of Honour, often make the Law of the Land their rule of life; that is, they are satisfied with themselves, so long as they do or omit nothing, for the doing or omitting of which the law can punish them.

Whereas every system of human laws, considered as a rule of life, labours under the two following defects:

I. Human laws omit many duties, as not objects of compulsion; such as piety to God, bounty to the poor, forgiveness of injuries, education of children, gratitude to benefactors.

The law never speaks but to command, nor commands but where it can compel; consequently those duties, which by their nature must be *voluntary*, are left out of the statute-book, as lying beyond the reach of its operation and authority.

II. Human laws permit, or, which is the same thing, suffer to go unpunished, many crimes, because they are incapable of being defined by any previous description. Of which nature are luxury, prodigality, partiality in voting at those elections in which the qualifications of the candidate ought to determine the success, caprice in the disposition of men's fortunes at their death, disrespect to parents, and a multitude of similar examples.

For, this is the alternative: either the law must define beforehand and with precision the offences which it punishes; or it must be left to the *discretion* of the magistrate, to determine upon each particular accusation, whether it constitute that offence which the law designed to punish, or not; which is, in effect, leaving to the magistrate to punish or not to punish, at his pleasure, the individual who is brought before him; which is just so much tyranny. Where, therefore, as in the instances above-mentioned, the distinction between right and wrong is of too subtile or of too secret a nature to be ascertained by any preconcerted language, the law of most countries, especially of free states, rather than commit the liberty of the subject to the discretion of the magistrate, leaves men in such cases to themselves.

Chapter 4
THE SCRIPTURES

Whoever expects to find in the Scriptures a specific direction for every moral doubt that arises, looks for more than he will meet with. And to what a magnitude such a detail of particular precepts would have enlarged the sacred volume, may be partly understood from the following consideration: The laws of this country, including the acts of the legislature, and the decisions of our supreme courts of justice, are not contained in fewer than fifty folio volumes; and yet it is not once in ten attempts that you can find the case you look for, in any law-book whatever: to say nothing of those numerous points of conduct, concerning which the law professes not to prescribe or determine any thing. Had then the same particularity, which obtains in human laws so far as they go, been attempted in the Scriptures, throughout the whole extent of morality, it is manifest they would have been by much too bulky to be either read or circulated; or rather, as St. John says, "even the world itself could not contain the books that should be written."

Morality is taught in Scripture in this wise. General rules are laid down, of piety, justice, benevolence, and purity: such as, worshipping God in spirit and in truth; doing as we would be done by; loving our neighbour as ourself; forgiving others, as we expect forgiveness from God; that mercy is better than sacrifice; that not that which entereth into a man (nor, by parity of reason, any ceremonial pollutions), but that which proceedeth from the heart, defileth him. These rules are occasionally illustrated, either by *fictitious examples*, as in the parable of the good Samaritan; and of the cruel servant, who refused to his fellow-servant that indulgence and compassion which his master had shown to him: *or in instances which actually presented themselves*, as in Christ's reproof of his disciples at the Samaritan village; his praise of the poor widow, who cast in her last mite; his censure of the Pharisees who chose out the chief rooms, and of the tradition, whereby they evaded the command to sustain their indigent parents: *or, lastly, in the resolution of questions, which those who were about our Saviour proposed to him*; as his answer to the young man who asked him, "What lack I yet?" and to the honest scribe, who had found out, even in that age and country, that "to love God and his neighbour, was more than all whole burnt-offerings and sacrifice."

And this is in truth the way in which all practical sciences are taught, as Arithmetic, Grammar, Navigation, and the like. Rules are laid down, and examples are subjoined: not that these examples are the cases, much less all the cases, which will actually occur; but by way only of explaining the principle of the rule, and as so many specimens of the method of applying it. The chief difference is, that the examples in Scripture are not annexed to the rules with the didactic regularity to which we are now-a-days accustomed, but delivered dispersedly, as particular occasions suggested them; which gave them, however (especially to those who heard them, and were present to the occasions which produced them), an energy and persuasion, much beyond what the same or any instances would have appeared with, in their places in a system.

Besides this, the Scriptures commonly presuppose in the persons to whom they speak, a knowledge of the principles of natural justice; and are employed not so much to teach *new* rules of morality, as to enforce the practice of it by *new* sanctions, and by a *greater certainty*; which last seems to be the proper business of a revelation from God, and what was most wanted.

Thus the "unjust, covenant-breakers, and extortioners," are condemned in Scripture, supposing it known, or leaving it, where it admits of doubt, to moralists to determine, what injustice, extortion, or breach of covenant, are.

The above considerations are intended to prove that the Scriptures do not supersede the use of the science of which we profess to treat, and at the same time to acquit them of any charge of imperfection or insufficiency on that account.

Chapter 5
THE MORAL SENSE

"The father of *Caius Toranius* had been proscribed by the triumvirate. *Caius Toranius,* coming over to the interests of that party, discovered to the officers, who were in pursuit of his father's life, the place where he concealed himself, and gave them withal a description, by which they might distinguish his person, when they found him. The old man, more anxious for the safety and fortunes of his son, than about the little that might remain of his own life, began immediately to inquire of the officers who seized him, whether his son was well, whether he had done his duty to the satisfaction of his generals. 'That son (replied one of the officers), so dear to thy affections, betrayed thee to us; by his information thou art apprehended, and diest.' The officer with this, struck a poniard to his heart, and the unhappy parent fell, not so much affected by his fate, as by the means to which he owed it."*

Now the question is, whether, if this story were related to the wild boy caught some years ago in the woods of Hanover, or to a savage without experience, and without instruction, cut off in his infancy from all intercourse with his species, and, consequently, under no possible influence of example, authority, education, sympathy, or habit; whether, I say, such a one would feel, upon the

---

*"Caius Toranius triumvirûm partes secutus, proscripti patris sui praetorii et ornati viri latebras, aetatem, notasque corporis, quibus agnosci posset, centurionibus edidit, qui eum persecuti sunt. Senex de filii magis vitâ et incrementis, quam de reliquo spiritu suo sollicitus, an incolumis esset, et an imperatoribus satisfaceret, interrogare eos coepit. E quibus unus: 'Ab illo,' inquit, 'quem tantopere diligis, demonstratus nostro ministerio, filii indicio occideris:' protinusque pectus ejus gladio trajecit. Collapsus itaque est infelix, auctore caedis, quam ipsâ caede, miserior."

VALER. MAX. lib. ix. cap. 11.

relation, any degree of *that sentiment of disapprobation of Toranius's conduct* which we feel, or not?

They who maintain the existence of a moral sense; of innate maxims; of a natural conscience; that the love of virtue and hatred of vice are instinctive; or the perception of right and wrong intuitive; (all which are only different ways of expressing the same opinion), affirm that he would.

They who deny the existence of a moral sense, &c. affirm that he would not.

And upon this, issue is joined.

As the experiment has never been made, and, from the difficulty of procuring a subject (not to mention the impossibility of proposing the question to him, if we had one), is never likely to be made, what would be the event, can only be judged of from probable reasons.

They who contend for the affirmative, observe, that we approve examples of generosity, gratitude, fidelity, &c. and condemn the contrary, instantly, without deliberation, without having any interest of our own concerned in them, oft-times without being conscious of, or able to give any reason for, our approbation: that this approbation is uniform and universal, the same sorts of conduct being approved or disapproved in all ages and countries of the world—circumstances, say they, which strongly indicate the operation of an instinct or moral sense.

On the other hand, answers have been given to most of these arguments, by the patrons of the opposite system: and,

First, as to the *uniformity* above alleged, they controvert the fact. They remark, from authentic accounts of historians and travellers, that there is scarcely a single vice which, in some age or country of the world, has not been countenanced by public opinion: that in one country, it is esteemed an office of piety in children to sustain their aged parents; in another, to despatch them out of the way: that suicide, in one age of the world, has been heroism, is in another felony: that theft, which is punished by most laws, by the laws of Sparta was not unfrequently rewarded: that the promiscuous commerce of the sexes, although condemned by the regulations and censure of all civilised nations, is practised by the savages of the tropical regions without reserve, compunction, or disgrace: that crimes, of which it is no longer permitted us even to speak, have had their advocates amongst the sages of very renowned times: that, if an inhabitant of the polished nations of Europe be delighted with the appearance, wherever he meets with it, of happiness, tranquillity, and comfort, a wild American is no less diverted with the writhings and contortions of a victim at the stake: that even amongst ourselves, and in the present improved state of moral knowledge, we are far from a perfect consent in our opinions or feelings: that you shall hear duelling alternately reprobated and applauded, according to the sex, age, or station, of the person you converse with: that the forgiveness of injuries and insults is accounted by one sort of people magnanimity, by another meanness: that in the above instances, and perhaps in most others, moral approbation follows the fashions and institutions of the country we live in; which fashions also and institutions themselves have grown out of the exigencies, the climate, situation, or local circumstances of the country; or have been set up by the authority of an arbitrary chieftain, or the unaccountable caprice of the multitude—all which, they observe, looks very little like the steady hand and indelible characters of Nature. But,

Secondly, because, after these exceptions and abatements, it cannot be denied but that some sorts of actions command and receive the esteem of mankind *more* than others; and that the approbation of them is general though not universal: as to this, they say, that the general approbation of virtue, even in instances where we have no interest of our own to induce us to it, may be accounted for, without the assistance of a moral sense; thus:

"Having experienced, in some instance, a particular conduct to be beneficial to ourselves, or observed that it would be so, a sentiment of approbation rises up in our minds; which sentiment afterwards accompanies the idea or mention of the same conduct, although the private advantage which first excited it no longer exist."

And this continuance of the passion, after the reason of it has ceased, is nothing more, say they, than what happens in other cases; especially in the love of money, which is in no person so eager, as it is oftentimes found to be in a rich old miser, without family to provide for, or friend to oblige by it, and to whom consequently it is no longer (and he may be sensible of it too) of any real use or value; yet is this man as much overjoyed with gain, and mortified by losses, as he was the first day he opened his shop, and when his very subsistence depended upon his success in it.

By these means the custom of approving certain actions *commenced:* and when once such a custom hath got footing in the world, it is no difficult thing to explain how it is transmitted and continued; for *then* the greatest part of those who approve of virtue, approve of it from authority, by imitation, and from a habit of approving such and such actions, inculcated in early youth, and receiving, as men grow up, continual accessions of strength and vigour, from censure and encouragement, from the books they read, the conversations they hear, the current application of epithets, the general turn of language, and the various other causes by which it universally comes to pass, that a society of men, touched in the feeblest degree with the same passion, soon communicate to one another a great degree of it.* This is the case with most of us at present; and is the cause also, that

* "From instances of popular tumults, seditions, factions, panics, and of all passions which are shared with a multitude, we may learn the influence of society, in exciting and supporting any emotion; while the most ungovernable disorders are raised, we find, by that means, from the slightest and most frivolous occasions. He must be more or less than man, who kindles not in the common blaze. What wonder then, that moral sentiments are found of such influence in life, though springing from principles, which may appear, at first sight, somewhat small and delicate?"—*Hume's Inquiry concerning the Principles of Morals,* Sect. ix. p. 326.

the *process of association*, described in the last paragraph but one, is little now either perceived or wanted.

Amongst the causes assigned for the continuance and diffusion of the same moral sentiments amongst mankind, we have mentioned *imitation*. The efficacy of this principle is most observable in children: indeed, if there be any thing in them, which deserves the name of an *instinct*, it is their *propensity to imitation*. Now there is nothing which children imitate or apply more readily than expressions of affection and aversion, of approbation, hatred, resentment, and the like; and when these passions and expressions are once connected, which they soon will be by the same association which unites words with their ideas, the passion will follow the expression, and attach upon the object to which the child has been accustomed to apply the epithet. In a word, when almost every thing else is learned by *imitation*, can we wonder to find the same cause concerned in the generation of our moral sentiments?

Another considerable objection to the system of moral instincts is this, that there are no maxims in the science which can well be deemed *innate*, as none perhaps can be assigned, which are absolutely and universally *true;* in other words, which do not *bend* to circumstances. Veracity, which seems, if any be, a natural duty, is *excused* in many cases towards an enemy, a thief, or a madman. The obligation of promises, which is a first principle in morality, depends upon the circumstances under which they were made; they may have been unlawful, or become so since, or inconsistent with former promises, or erroneous, or extorted; under all which cases, instances may be suggested, where the obligation to perform the promise would be very dubious; and so of most other general rules, when they come to be actually applied.

An argument has been also proposed on the same side of the question, of this kind. Together with the instinct, there must have been implanted, it is said, a clear and precise idea of the object upon which it was to attach. The instinct and the idea of the object are inseparable even in imagination, and as necessarily accompany each other as any correlative ideas whatever: that is, in plainer terms, if we be prompted by nature to the approbation of particular actions, we must have received also from nature a distinct conception of the action we are thus prompted to approve; which we certainly have not received.

But as this argument bears alike against all instincts, and against their existence in brutes as well as in men, it will hardly, I suppose, produce conviction, though it may be difficult to find an answer to it.

Upon the whole, it seems to me, either that there exist no such instincts as compose what is called the moral sense, or that they are not now to be distinguished from prejudices and habits; on which account they cannot be depended upon in moral reasoning: I mean that it is not a safe way of arguing, to assume certain principles as so many dictates, impulses, and instincts of nature, and then to draw conclusions from these principles, as to the rectitude or wrongness of actions, independent of the tendency of such actions, or of any other consideration whatever.

Aristotle lays down, as a fundamental and self-evident maxim, that nature intended barbarians to be slaves; and proceeds to deduce from this maxim a train of conclusions, calculated to justify the policy which then prevailed. And I question whether the same maxim be not still self-evident to the company of merchants trading to the coast of Africa.

Nothing is so soon made, as a maxim; and it appears from the example of Aristotle, that authority and convenience, education, prejudice, and general practice, have no small share in the making of them; and that the laws of custom are very apt to be mistaken for the order of nature.

For which reason, I suspect, that a system of morality, built upon instincts, will only find out reasons and excuses for opinions and practices already established—will seldom correct or reform either.

But further, suppose we admit the existence of these instincts; what, it may be asked, is their authority? No man, you say, can act in deliberate opposition to them, without a secret remorse of conscience. But this remorse may be borne with: and if the sinner choose to bear with it, for the sake of the pleasure or the profit which he expects from his wickedness; or finds the pleasure of the sin to exceed the remorse of conscience, of which he alone is the judge, and concerning which, when he feels them both together, he can hardly be mistaken, the moral-instinct man, so far as I can understand, has nothing more to offer.

For if he allege that these instincts are so many indications of the will of God, and consequently presages of what we are to look for hereafter; this, I answer, is to resort to a rule and a motive ulterior to the instincts themselves, and at which rule and motive we shall by-and-by arrive by a surer road—I say *surer*, so long as there remains a controversy whether there be any instinctive maxims at all; or any difficulty in ascertaining what maxims are instinctive.

This celebrated question therefore becomes in our system a question of pure curiosity; and as such, we dismiss it to the determination of those who are more inquisitive, than we are concerned to be, about the natural history and constitution of the human species.

Chapter 6
HUMAN HAPPINESS

THE word *happy* is a relative term: that is, when we call a man happy, we mean that he is happier than some others, with whom we compare him; than the generality of others; or than he himself was in some other situation: thus, speaking of one who has just com-passed the object of a long pursuit, "Now," we say, "he is happy"; and in a like comparative sense, compared, that is, with the general lot of mankind, we call a man happy who possesses health and competency.

In strictness, any condition may be denominated happy, in which the amount or aggregate of pleasure exceeds that of pain; and the degree of happiness depends upon the quantity of this excess.

And the greatest quantity of it ordinarily attainable in human life, is what we mean by happiness, when we inquire or pronounce what human happiness consists in.*

* If any *positive* signification, distinct from what we mean by pleasure, can be affixed to the term "happiness," I should take it to denote a certain state of the nervous system in that part of the human frame in which we feel joy and grief, passions and affections. Whether this part be the heart, which the turn of most languages would lead us to believe, or the diaphragm, as Buffon, or the upper orifice of the stomach, as Van Helmont thought; or rather be a kind of fine net-work, lining the whole region of the praecordia, as others have imagined; it is possible, not only that each painful sensation may violently shake and disturb the fibres at the time, but that a series of such may at length so derange the very texture of the system, as to produce a perpetual irritation, which will show itself by fretfulness, impatience, and restlessness. It is possible also, on the other hand, that a succession of pleasurable sensations may have such an effect upon this subtile organization, as to cause the fibres to relax, and return into their place and order, and thereby to recover, or, if not lost, to preserve, that harmonious conformation which gives to the mind its sense of complacency and satisfaction. This state may be denominated happiness, and is so far distinguishable from pleasure, that it does not refer to any particular object of enjoyment, or consist, like pleasure, in the gratification of one or more of the senses, but is rather the secondary effect which such objects and gratifications produce upon the nervous system, or the state in which they leave it. These conjectures belong not, however, to our province. The comparative sense, in which we have explained the term Happiness, is more popular, and is sufficient for the purpose of the present chapter.

In which inquiry I will omit much usual declamation on the dignity and capacity of our nature; the superiority of the soul to the body, of the rational to the animal part of our constitution; upon the worthiness, refinement, and delicacy, of some satisfactions, or the meanness, grossness, and sensuality, of others; because I hold that pleasures differ in nothing, but in continuance and intensity: from a just computation of which, confirmed by what we observe of the apparent cheerfulness, tranquillity, and contentment, of men of different tastes, tempers, stations, and pursuits, every question concerning human happiness must receive its decision.

It will be our business to show, if we can,

I. What Human Happiness does not consist in:

II. What it does consist in.

FIRST, then, Happiness does not consist in the pleasures of sense, in whatever profusion or variety they be enjoyed. By the pleasures of sense, I mean, as well the animal gratifications of eating, drinking, and that by which the species is continued, as the more refined pleasures of music, painting, architecture, gardening, splendid shows, theatric exhibitions; and the pleasures, lastly, of active sports, as of hunting, shooting, fishing, &c. For,

1st, These pleasures continue but a little while at a time. This is true of them all, especially of the grosser sort of them. Laying aside the preparation and the expectation, and computing strictly the actual sensation, we shall be surprised to find how inconsiderable a portion of our time they occupy, how few hours in the four-and-twenty they are able to fill up.

2dly, These pleasures, by repetition, lose their relish.

It is a property of the machine, for which we know no remedy, that the organs, by which we perceive pleasure, are blunted and benumbed by being frequently exercised in the same way. There is hardly any one who has not found the difference between a gratification, when new, and when familiar; or any pleasure which does not become indifferent as it grows habitual.

3dly, The eagerness for high and intense delights takes away the relish from all others: and as such delights fall rarely in our way, the greater part of our time becomes, from this cause, empty and uneasy.

There is hardly any delusion by which men are greater sufferers in their happiness, than by their expecting too much from what is called pleasure; that is, from those intense delights, which vulgarly engross the name of pleasure. The very expectation spoils them. When they do come, we are often engaged in taking pains to persuade ourselves how much we are pleased, rather than enjoying any pleasure which springs naturally out of the object. And whenever we depend upon being vastly delighted, we always go home secretly grieved at missing our aim. Likewise, as has been observed just now, when this humour of being prodigiously delighted has once taken hold of the imagination, it hinders us from providing for, or acquiescing in, those gently soothing engagements, the due variety and succession of which are the only things that supply a vein or continued stream of happiness.

What I have been able to observe of that part of mankind, whose professed pursuit is pleasure, and who are withheld in the pursuit by no restraints of fortune, or scruples of conscience, corresponds sufficiently with this account. I have commonly remarked in such men, a restless and inextinguishable passion for variety; a great part of their time to be vacant, and so much of it irksome; and that, with whatever eagerness and expectation they set out, they become, by degrees, fastidious in their choice of pleasure, languid in the enjoyment, yet miserable under the want of it.

The truth seems to be, that there is a limit at which these pleasures soon arrive, and from which they ever afterwards decline. They are by necessity of short duration, as the organs cannot hold on their emotions beyond a certain length of time; and if you endeavour to compensate for this imperfection in their nature by the frequency with which you repeat them, you suffer more than you gain, by the fatigue of the faculties, and the diminution of sensibility.

We have said nothing in this account of the loss of opportunities, or the decay of faculties, which, whenever they happen, leave the voluptuary destitute and desperate; teased by desires that can never be gratified, and the memory of pleasures which must return no more.

It will also be allowed by those who have experienced it, and perhaps by those alone, that pleasure which is purchased by the encumbrance of our fortune, is purchased too dear; the pleasure never compensating for the perpetual irritation of embarrassed circumstances.

These pleasures, after all, have their value; and as the young are always too eager in their pursuit of them, the old are sometimes too remiss, that is, too studious of their ease, to be at the pains for them which they really deserve.

SECONDLY; Neither does happiness consist in an exemption from pain, labour, care, business, suspense, molestation, and "those evils which are without"; such a state being usually attended, not with ease, but with depression of spirits, a tastelessness in all our ideas, imaginary anxieties, and the whole train of hypochondriacal affections.

For which reason, the expectations of those, who retire from their shops and counting-houses, to enjoy the remainder of their days in leisure and tranquillity, are seldom answered by the effect; much less of such, as, in a fit of chagrin, shut themselves up in cloisters and hermitages, or quit the world, and their stations in it, for solitude and repose.

Where there exists a known external cause of uneasiness, the cause may be removed, and the uneasiness will cease. But those imaginary distresses which men feel for want of real ones (and which are equally tormenting, and so far equally real), as they depend upon no single or assignable subject of uneasiness, admit oftentimes of no application of relief.

Hence a moderate pain, upon which the attention may fasten and spend itself, is to many a refreshment: as a fit of the gout will sometimes cure the spleen. And the same of any less violent agitation of the mind, as a literary controversy, a law-suit, a contested election, and, above all, gaming; the passion for which, in men of fortune and liberal minds, is only to be accounted for on this principle.

THIRDLY; Neither does happiness consist in greatness, rank, or elevated station.

Were it true that all superiority afforded pleasure, it would follow, that by how much we were the greater, that is, the more persons we were superior to, in the same proportion, so far as depended upon this cause, we should be the happier; but so it is, that no superiority yields any satisfaction, save that which we possess or obtain over those with whom we immediately compare ourselves. The shepherd perceives no pleasure in his superiority over his dog; the farmer, in his superiority over the shepherd; the lord, in his superiority over the farmer; nor the king, lastly, in his superiority over the lord. Superiority, where there is no competition, is seldom contemplated; what most men are quite unconscious of.

But if the same shepherd can run, fight, or wrestle, better than the peasants of his village; if the farmer can show better cattle, if he keep a better horse, or be supposed to have a longer purse, than any farmer in the hundred; if the lord have more interest in an election, greater favour at court, a better house, or larger estate, than any nobleman in the county; if the king possess a more extensive territory, a more powerful fleet or army, a more splendid establishment, more loyal subjects, or more weight and authority in adjusting the affairs of nations, than any prince in Europe; in all these cases, the parties feel an actual satisfaction in their superiority.

Now the conclusion that follows from hence is this; that the pleasures of ambition, which are supposed to be peculiar to high stations, are in reality common to all conditions. The farrier who shoes a horse better, and who is in greater request for his skill, than any man within ten miles of him, possesses, for all that I can see, the delight of distinction and of excelling, as truly and substantially as the statesman, the soldier, and the scholar, who have filled Europe with the reputation of their wisdom, their valour, or their knowledge.

No superiority appears to be of any account, but superiority over a rival. This, it is manifest, may exist wherever rivalships do; and rivalships fall out amongst men of all ranks and degrees. The object of emulation, the dignity or magnitude of this object, makes no difference: as it is not what either possesses that constitutes the pleasure, but what one possesses more than the other.

Philosophy smiles at the contempt with which the rich and great speak of the petty strifes and competitions of the poor; not reflecting that these strifes and competitions are just as reasonable as their own, and the pleasure, which success affords, the same.

Our position is, that happiness does not consist in greatness. And this position we make out by showing, that even what are supposed to be the peculiar advantages of greatness, the pleasures of ambition and superiority, are in reality common to all conditions. But whether the pursuits of ambition be ever wise, whether they contribute more to the happiness or misery of the pursuers, is a different question; and a question concerning which we may be allowed to entertain great doubt. The pleasure of success is exquisite; so also is the anxiety of the pursuit, and the pain of disappointment—and what is the worst part of the account, the pleasure is shortlived. We soon cease to look back upon those whom we have left behind; new contests are engaged in, new prospects unfold themselves; a succession of struggles is kept up, whilst there is a rival left within the compass of our views and profession; and when there is none, the pleasure with the pursuit is at an end.

II. We have seen what happiness does not consist in. We are next to consider in what it does consist.

In the conduct of life, the great matter is, to know beforehand, what will please us, and what pleasure will hold out. So far as we know this, our choice will be justified by the event. And this knowledge is more scarce and difficult than at first sight it may seem to be: for sometimes, pleasures, which are wonderfully alluring and flattering in the prospect, turn out in the possession extremely insipid; or do not hold out as we expected: at other times, pleasures start up which never entered into our calculation; and which we might have missed of by not foreseeing: whence we have reason to believe, that we actually do miss of many pleasures from the same cause. I say, to know "beforehand"; for, after the experiment is tried, it is commonly impracticable to retreat or change; beside that shifting and changing is apt to generate a habit of restlessness, which is destructive of the happiness of every condition.

By the reason of the original diversity of taste, capacity, and constitution, observable in the human species, and the still greater variety, which habit and fashion have introduced in these particulars, it is impossible to propose any plan of happiness, which will succeed to all, or any method of life which is universally eligible or practicable.

All that can be said is, that there remains a presumption in favour of those conditions of life, in which men generally appear most cheerful and contented. For though the apparent happiness of mankind be not always a true measure of their real happiness, it is the best measure we have.

Taking this for my guide, I am inclined to believe that happiness consists,

I. In the exercise of the social affections.

Those persons commonly possess good spirits, who have about them many objects of affection and endearment, as wife, children, kindred, friends. And to the want of these may be imputed the peevishness of monks, and of such as lead a monastic life.

Of the same nature with the indulgence of our domestic affections, and equally refreshing to the spirits, is the pleasure which results from acts of bounty and beneficence, exercised either in giving money, or in imparting to those who want it the assistance of our skill and profession.

Another main article of human happiness is,

II. The exercise of our faculties, either of body or mind, in the pursuit of some engaging end.

It seems to be true, that no plenitude of present gratifications can make the possessor happy for a continuance, unless he have something in reserve—something to hope for, and look forward to. This I conclude to be the case, from comparing the alacrity and spirits of men who are engaged in any pursuit which interests them, with the dejection and *ennui* of almost all, who are either born to so much that they want nothing more, or who have *used up* their satisfactions too soon, and drained the sources of them.

It is this intolerable vacuity of mind, which carries the rich and great to the horse-course and the gaming-table; and often engages them in contests and pursuits, of which the success bears no proportion to the solicitude and expense with which it is sought. An election for a disputed borough shall cost the parties twenty or thirty thousand pounds each—to say nothing of the anxiety, humiliation, and fatigue, of the canvass; when, a seat in the house of commons, of exactly the same value, may be had for a tenth part of the money, and with no trouble. I do not mention this, to blame the rich and great (perhaps they cannot do better), but in confirmation of what I have advanced.

Hope, which thus appears to be of so much importance to our happiness, is of two kinds—where there is something to be done towards attaining the object of our hope, and where there is nothing to be done. The first alone is of any value; the latter being apt to corrupt into impatience, having no power but to sit still and wait, which soon grows tiresome.

The doctrine delivered under this head, may be readily admitted; but how to provide ourselves with a succession of pleasurable engagements is the difficulty. This requires two things: judgement in the choice of *ends* adapted to our opportunities; and a command of imagination, so as to be able, when the judgement has made choice of an end, to transfer a pleasure to the *means:* after which, the end may be forgotten as soon as we will.

Hence those pleasures are most valuable, not which are most exquisite in the fruition, but which are most productive of engagement and activity in the pursuit.

A man who is in earnest in his endeavours after the happiness of a future state, has, in this respect, an advantage over all the world: for, he has constantly before his eyes an object of supreme importance, productive of perpetual engagement and activity, and of which the pursuit (which can be said of no pursuit besides) lasts him to his life's end. Yet even he must have many ends, besides the *far end;* but then they will conduct to that, be subordinate, and in some way or other capable of being referred to that, and derive their satisfaction, or an addition of satisfaction, from that.

Engagement is every thing: the more significant, however, our engagements are, the better: such as the planning of laws, institutions, manufactures, charities, improvements, public works; and the endeavouring, by our interest, address, solicitations, and activity, to carry them into effect; or, upon a smaller scale, the procuring of a maintenance and fortune for our families by a course of industry and application to our callings, which forms and gives motion to the common occupations of life; training up a child; prosecuting a scheme for his future establishment; making ourselves masters of a language or a science; improving or managing an estate; labouring after a piece of preferment; and lastly, *any* engagement, which is innocent, is better than none; as the writing of a book, the building of a house, the laying out of a garden, the digging of a fish-pond—even the raising of a cucumber or a tulip.

Whilst our minds are taken up with the objects or business before us, we are commonly happy, whatever the object or business be; when the mind is *absent*, and the thoughts are wandering to something else than what is passing in the place in which we are, we are often miserable.

III. Happiness depends upon the prudent constitution of the habits.

The art in which the secret of human happiness in a great measure consists, is to *set* the habits in such a manner, that every change may be a change for the better. The habits themselves are much the same; for, whatever is made habitual, becomes smooth, and easy, and nearly indifferent. The return to an old habit is likewise easy, whatever the habit be. Therefore the advantage is with those habits which allow of an indulgence in the deviation from them. The luxurious receive no greater pleasure from their dainties, than the peasant does from his bread and cheese: but the peasant, whenever he goes abroad, finds a feast; whereas the epicure must be well entertained, to escape disgust. Those who spend every day at cards, and those who go every day to plough, pass their time much alike: intent upon what they are about, wanting nothing, regretting nothing, they are both for the time in a state of ease: but then, whatever suspends the occupation of the card-player, distresses him; whereas to the labourer, every interruption is a refreshment: and this appears in the different effects that Sunday produces upon the two, which proves a day of recreation to the one, but a lamentable burthen to the other. The man who has learned to live alone, feels his spirits enlivened whenever he enters into company, and takes his leave without regret; another, who has long been accustomed to a crowd, or continual succession of company, experiences in company no elevation of spirits, nor any greater satisfaction, than what the man of a retired life finds in his chimney-corner. So far their conditions are equal; but let a change of place, fortune, or situation, separate the companion from his circle, his visitors, his club, common-room, or coffee-house; and the difference and advantage in the choice and constitution of the two habits will show itself. Solitude comes to the one, clothed with melancholy; to the other, it brings liberty and quiet. You will see the one fretful and restless, at a loss how to dispose of his time, till the hour come round when he may forget himself in bed; the other easy and satisfied, taking up his book or his pipe, as soon as he finds himself alone; ready to admit any little amusement that casts up, or to turn his hands and attention to the first business that presents itself; or content, without either, to sit still, and let his train of thought glide indolently through his brain, without much use, perhaps, or pleasure, but without *hankering* after any thing better, and without irritation. A reader, who has inured himself to books of science and argumentation, if a novel, a well-written pamphlet, an article of news, a narrative of a curious voyage, or a journal of a traveller, fall in his way, sits down to the repast with relish; enjoys his entertainment while it lasts, and can return, when it is over, to his graver reading, without distaste. Another, with whom nothing will go down but works of humour and pleasantry, or whose curiosity must be interested by perpetual novelty, will consume a bookseller's window in half a forenoon: during which time he is rather in search of diversion than diverted; and as books to his taste are few, and short, and rapidly read over, the stock is soon exhausted, when he is left without resource from this principal supply of harmless amusement.

So far as circumstances of fortune conduce to happiness, it is not the income, which any man possesses, but the increase of income, that affords the pleasure. Two persons, of whom one begins with a hundred, and advances his income to a thousand pounds a year, and the other sets off with a thousand, and dwindles down to a hundred, may, in the course of their time, have the receipt and spending of the same sum of money: yet their satisfaction, so far as fortune is concerned in it, will be very different; the series and sum total of their incomes being the same, it makes a wide difference at which end they begin.

IV. Happiness consists in health.

By health I understand, as well freedom from bodily distempers, as that tranquillity, firmness, and alacrity of mind, which we call good spirits; and which may properly enough be included in our notion of health, as depending commonly upon the same causes, and yielding to the same management, as our bodily constitution.

Health, in this sense, is the one thing needful. Therefore no pains, expense, self-denial, or restraint, to which we subject ourselves for the sake of health, is too much. Whether it require us to relinquish lucrative situations, to abstain from favourite indulgences, to control intemperate passions, or undergo tedious regimens; whatever difficulties it lays us under, a man, who pursues his happiness rationally and resolutely, will be content to submit.

When we are in perfect health and spirits, we feel in ourselves a happiness independent of any particular outward gratification whatever, and of which we can give no account. This is an enjoyment which the Deity has annexed to life; and it probably constitutes, in a great measure, the happiness of infants and brutes, especially of the lower and sedentary orders of animals, as of oysters, periwinkles, and the like; for which I have sometimes been at a loss to find out amusement.

The above account of human happiness will justify the two following conclusions, which, although found in most books of morality, have seldom, I think, been supported by any sufficient reasons:

FIRST, that happiness is pretty equally distributed amongst the different orders of civil society:

SECONDLY, that vice has no advantage over virtue, even with respect to this world's happiness.

Chapter 7
VIRTUE

Virtue is "*the doing good to mankind, in obedience to the will of God, and for the sake of everlasting happiness.*"

According to which definition, "the good of mankind" is the subject; the "will of God," the rule; and "everlasting happiness," the motive, of human virtue.

Virtue has been divided by some moralists into *benevolence, prudence, fortitude*, and *temperance. Benevolence* proposes good ends; *prudence* suggests the best means of attaining them; *fortitude* enables us to encounter the difficulties, dangers, and discouragements, which stand in our way in the pursuit of these ends; *temperance* repels and overcomes the passions that obstruct it. *Benevolence*, for instance, prompts us to undertake the cause of an oppressed orphan; *prudence* suggests the best means of going about it; *fortitude* enables us to confront the danger, and bear up against the loss, disgrace, or repulse, that may attend our undertaking; and *temperance* keeps under the love of money, of ease, or amusement, which might divert us from it.

Virtue is distinguished by others into two branches only, *prudence* and *benevolence: prudence*, attentive to our own interest; *benevolence*, to that of our fellow-creatures: both directed to the same end, the increase of happiness in nature; and taking equal concern in the future as in the present.

The four CARDINAL virtues are, *prudence, fortitude, temperance*, and *justice*.

But the division of virtue, to which we are in modern times most accustomed, is into duties—

Towards *God;* as piety, reverence, resignation, gratitude, &c.

Towards *other men* (or relative duties); as justice, charity, fidelity, loyalty, &c.

Towards *ourselves;* as chastity, sobriety, temperance, preservation of life, care of health, &c.

More of these distinctions have been proposed, which it is not worth while to set down.

———

I shall proceed to state a few observations, which relate to the general regulation of human conduct; unconnected indeed with each other, but very worthy of attention; and which fall as properly under the title of this chapter as of any future one.

I. Mankind act more from habit than reflection.

It is on few only and great occasions that men deliberate at all; on fewer still, that they institute any thing like a regular inquiry into the moral rectitude or depravity of what they are about to do; or wait for the result of it. We are for the most part determined at once; and by an impulse, which is the effect and energy of pre-established habits. And this constitution seems well adapted to the exigencies of human life, and to the imbecility of our moral principle. In the current occasions and rapid opportunities of life, there is often-times little leisure for reflection; and were there more, a man, who has to reason about his duty, when the temptation to transgress it is upon him, is almost sure to reason himself into an error.

If we are in so great a degree passive under our habits; Where, it is asked, is the exercise of virtue, the guilt of vice, or any use of moral and religious knowledge? I answer, In the *forming and contracting* of these habits.

And hence results a rule of life of considerable importance, *viz.* that many things are to be done and abstained from, solely for the sake of habit. We will explain ourselves by an example or two. A beggar, with the appearance of extreme distress, asks our charity. If we come to argue the matter, whether the distress be real, whether it be not brought upon himself, whether it be of public advantage to admit such application, whether it be not to encourage idleness and vagrancy, whether it may not invite impostors to our doors, whether the money can be well spared, or might not be better applied; when these considerations are put together, it may appear very doubtful, whether we ought or ought not to give any thing. But when we reflect, that the misery before our eyes excites our pity, whether we will or not; that it is of the utmost consequence to us to cultivate this tenderness of mind; that it is a quality, cherished by indulgence, and soon stifled by opposition; when this, I say, is considered, a wise man will do that for his own sake, which he would have hesitated to do for the petitioner's; he will give way to his compassion, rather than offer violence to a habit of so much general use.

A man of confirmed good habits, will act in the same manner without any consideration at all.

This may serve for one instance; another is the following. A man has been brought up from his infancy with a dread of lying. An occasion presents itself where, at the expense of a little veracity, he may divert his company, set off his own wit with advantage, attract the notice and engage the partiality of all about him. This is not a small temptation. And when he looks at the other side of the question, he sees no mischief that can ensue from this liberty, no slander of any man's reputation, no prejudice likely to arise to any man's interest. Where there nothing further to be considered, it would be difficult to show why a man under such circumstances might not indulge his humour. But when he reflects that his scruples about lying have hitherto preserved him free from this vice; that occasions like the present will return, where the inducement may be equally strong, but the indulgence much less innocent; that his scruples will wear away by a few transgressions, and leave him subject to one of the meanest and most pernicious of all bad habits—a habit of lying, whenever it will serve his turn: when all this, I say, is considered, a wise man will forego the present, or a much greater pleasure, rather than lay the foundation of a character so vicious and contemptible.

From what has been said, may be explained also the nature of *habitual* virtue. By the definition of virtue, placed at the beginning of this chapter, it appears, that the good of mankind is the subject, the will of God the rule, and everlasting happiness the motive and end, of all virtue. Yet, in fact, a man shall perform many an act of virtue, without having either the good of mankind, the will of God, or everlasting happiness in his thought. How is this to be understood? In the same manner as that a man may be a very good servant, without being conscious, at every turn, of a particular regard to his master's will, or of an express attention to his master's interest: indeed, your best old servants are of this sort: but then he must have served for a length of time under the actual direction of these motives, to bring it to this: in which service, his merit and virtue consist.

There are *habits*, not only of drinking, swearing, and lying, and of some other things, which are commonly acknowledged to be habits, and called so; but of every modification of action, speech, and thought. Man is a bundle of habits.

There are habits of industry, attention, vigilance, advertency; of a prompt obedience to the judgement occurring, or of yielding to the first impulse of passion; of extending our views to the future, or of resting upon the present; of apprehending, methodising, reasoning; of indolence and dilatoriness; of vanity, self-conceit, melancholy, partiality; of fretfulness, suspicion, captiousness, censoriousness; of pride, ambition, covetousness; of over-reaching, intriguing, projecting: in a word, there is not a quality or function, either of body or mind, which does not feel the influence of this great law of animated nature.

II. The Christian religion hath not ascertained the precise quantity of virtue necessary to salvation.

This has been made an objection to Christianity; but without reason. For as all revelation, however imparted originally, must be transmitted by the ordinary vehicle of language, it behoves those who make the objection to show that any form of words could be devised, that might express this *quantity;* or that it is possible to constitute a standard of moral attainments, accommodated to the almost infinite diversity which subsists in the capacities and opportunities of different men.

It seems most agreeable to our conceptions of justice, and is consonant enough to the language of Scripture,* to suppose, that there

---

*"He which soweth sparingly, shall reap also sparingly; and he which soweth bountifully, shall reap also bountifully." 2 Cor. ix. 6. "And that servant which knew his Lord's will, and prepared not himself, neither did according to his will, shall be beaten with many stripes; but he that knew not, shall be beaten with few stripes." Luke xii. 47, 48. "Whosoever shall give you a cup of water to drink in my name, because ye belong to Christ; verily I say unto you, he shall not lose his reward;" to wit, intimating that there is in reserve a proportionable reward for even the smallest act of virtue. Mark ix. 41. See also the parable of the pounds, Luke xix. 16, &c.; where he whose pound had gained ten pounds, was placed over ten cities; and he whose pound had gained five pounds, was placed over five cities.

are prepared for us rewards and punishments, of all possible degrees, from the most exalted happiness down to extreme misery; so that "our labour is never in vain"; whatever advancement we make in virtue, we procure a proportionable accession of future happiness; as, on the other hand, every accumulation of vice is the "treasuring up so much wrath against the day of wrath." It has been said, that it can never be a just oeconomy of Providence, to admit one part of mankind into heaven, and condemn the other to hell; since there must be very little to choose, between the worst man who is received into heaven, and the best who is excluded. And how know we, it might be answered, but that there may be as little to choose in the conditions?

Without entering into a detail of Scripture morality, which would anticipate our subject, the following general positions may be advanced, I think, with safety.

1. That a state of happiness is not to be expected by those who are conscious of no moral or religious rule: I mean those who cannot with truth say, that they have been prompted to one action, or withholden from one gratification, by any regard to virtue or religion, either immediate or habitual.

There needs no other proof of this, than the consideration, that a brute would be as proper an object of reward as such a man, and that, if the case were so, the penal sanctions of religion could have no place. For, whom would you punish, if you make such a one as this happy?—or rather indeed religion itself, both natural and revealed, would cease to have either use or authority.

2. That a state of happiness is not to be expected by those, who reserve to themselves the habitual practice of any one sin, or neglect of one known duty.

Because, no obedience can proceed upon proper motives, which is not universal, that is, which is not directed to every command of God alike, as they all stand upon the same authority.

Because such an allowance would in effect amount to a toleration of every vice in the world.

And because the strain of Scripture language excludes any such hope. When our *duties* are recited, they are put *collectively*, that is, as all and every one of them required in the Christian character. "*Add* to your faith virtue, and to virtue knowledge, and to knowledge temperance, and to temperance patience, and to patience godliness, and to godliness brotherly kindness, and to brotherly kindness charity."* On the other hand, when *vices* are enumerated, they are put *disjunctively*, that is, as separately and severally excluding the sinner from heaven. "*Neither* fornicators, nor idolaters, nor adulterers, nor effeminate, nor abusers of themselves with mankind, nor thieves, nor covetous, nor drunkards, nor revilers, nor extortioners, shall inherit the kingdom of heaven."†

Those texts of Scripture, which seem to lean a contrary way, as that "charity shall cover the multitude of sins";‡ that "he which converteth a sinner from the error of his way, shall hide a multitude of sins";§ cannot, I think, for the reasons above mentioned, be extended to sins deliberately, habitually, and obstinately persisted in.

3. That a state of mere unprofitableness will not go unpunished.

This is expressly laid down by Christ, in the parable of the talents, which supersedes all further reasoning upon the subject. "Then he which had received one talent, came and said, Lord, I knew thee that thou art an austere man, reaping where thou hast not sown, and gathering where thou hast not strawed: and I was afraid, and hid thy talent in the earth; lo, there thou hast that is thine. His lord answered and said unto him, Thou wicked and *slothful* servant, thou knewest, (or, knewest thou?) that I reap where I sowed not, and gather where I have not strawed; thou oughtest therefore to have put my money to the exchangers, and

---

* 2 Pet. i. 5, 6, 7.
† 1 Cor. vi. 9, 10.
‡ 1 Pet. iv. 8.
§ James v. 20.

then at my coming I should have received mine own with usury. Take therefore the talent from him, and give it unto him which hath ten talents; for unto every one that hath shall be given, and he shall have abundance; but from him that hath not, shall be taken away even that which he hath: *and cast ye the unprofitable servant into outer darkness, there shall be weeping and gnashing of teeth.*"*

III. In every question of conduct, where one side is doubtful, and the other side safe; we are bound to take the safe side.

This is best explained by an instance; and I know of none more to our purpose than that of suicide. Suppose, for example's sake, that it appear doubtful to a reasoner upon the subject, whether he may lawfully destroy himself. He can have no doubt, that it is lawful for him to let it alone. Here therefore is a case, in which one side is doubtful, and the other side safe. By virtue therefore of our rule, he is bound to pursue the safe side, that is, to forbear from offering violence to himself, whilst a doubt remains upon his mind concerning the lawfulness of suicide.

It is *prudent*, you allow, to take the safe side. But our observation means something more. We assert that the action concerning which we doubt, whatever it may be in itself, or to another, would, in *us*, whilst this doubt remains upon our minds, be certainly sinful. The case is expressly so adjudged by St. Paul, with whose authority we will for the present rest contented. "I know and am persuaded by the Lord Jesus, that there is nothing unclean of itself; but *to him that esteemeth any thing to be unclean, to him it is unclean.* Happy is he that condemneth not himself in that thing which he alloweth; and he that doubteth, is damned (*condemned*) if he eat, for whatsoever is not of faith (*i.e.* not done with a full persuasion of the lawfulness of it) is sin."†

*Matt. xxv. 24, &c.
†Rom. xiv. 14, 22, 23.

Book II
Moral Obligation

―――――

Chapter 1
THE QUESTION *WHY AM I OBLIGED TO KEEP MY WORD?* CONSIDERED

Why am I obliged to keep my word?

Because it is right, says one. Because it is agreeable to the fitness of things, says another. Because it is conformable to reason and nature, says a third. Because it is conformable to truth, says a fourth. Because it promotes the public good, says a fifth. Because it is required by the will of God, concludes a sixth.

Upon which different accounts, two things are observable:

FIRST, that they all ultimately coincide.

The fitness of things, means their fitness to produce happiness: the nature of things, means that actual constitution of the world, by which some things, as such and such actions, for example, produce happiness, and others misery; reason is the principle, by which we discover or judge of this constitution: truth is this judgement expressed or drawn out into propositions. So that it necessarily comes to pass, that what promotes the public happiness, or happiness on the whole, is agreeable to the fitness of things, to nature, to reason, and to truth: and such (as will appear by and by) is the Divine character, that what promotes the general happiness, is required by the will of God; and what has all the above properties, must needs be *right;* for, right means no more than conformity to the rule we go by, whatever that rule be.

And this is the reason that moralists, from whatever different principles they set out, commonly meet in their conclusions; that is, they enjoin the same conduct, prescribe the same rules of duty, and, with a few exceptions, deliver upon dubious cases the same determinations.

SECONDLY, it is to be observed, that these answers all leave the matter *short;* for the inquirer may turn round upon his teacher with a second question, in which he will expect to be satisfied, namely, *Why* am I obliged to do what is right; to act agreeably to the fitness of things; to conform to reason, nature, or truth; to promote the public good, or to obey the will of God?

The proper method of conducting the inquiry is, FIRST, to examine what we mean, when we say a man is *obliged* to do any thing; and THEN to show *why* he is obliged to do the thing which we have proposed as an example, namely, "to keep his word."

Chapter 2
WHAT WE MEAN WHEN WE SAY A MAN IS *OBLIGED* TO DO A THING

A man is said to be *obliged, "when he is urged by a violent motive resulting from the command of another."*

I. "The motive must be violent." If a person, who has done me some little service, or has a small place in his disposal, ask me upon some occasion for my vote, I may possibly give it to him, from a motive of gratitude or expectation: but I should hardly say that I was *obliged* to give it him; because the inducement does not rise high enough. Whereas if a father or a master, any great benefactor, or one on whom my fortune depends, require my vote, I give it him of course: and my answer to all who ask me why I voted so and so, is, that my father or my master *obliged* me; that I had received so many favours from, or had so great a dependence upon, such a one, that I was *obliged* to vote as he directed me.

Secondly, "It must result from the command of another." Offer a man a gratuity for doing any thing, for seizing, for example, an offender, he is not *obliged* by your offer to do it; nor would he say he is; though he may be *induced, persuaded, prevailed upon, tempted.* If a magistrate or the man's immediate superior command it, he considers himself as *obliged* to comply, though possibly he would lose less by a refusal in this case, than in the former.

I will not undertake to say that the words *obligation* and *obliged* are used uniformly in this sense, or always with this distinction: nor is it possible to tie down popular phrases to any constant signification: but wherever the motive is violent enough, and coupled with the idea of command, authority, law, or the will of a superior, there, I take it, we always reckon ourselves to be *obliged.*

And from this account of obligation it follows, that we can be obliged to nothing, but what we ourselves are to gain or lose something by: for nothing else can be a "violent motive" to us. As we should not be obliged to obey the laws, or the magistrate, unless rewards or punishments, pleasure or pain, somehow or other, depended upon our obedience; so neither should we, without the same reason, be obliged to do what is right, to practise virtue, or to obey the commands of God.

Chapter 3
The Question, *Why Am I Obliged to Keep My Word?* Resumed

Let it be remembered, that to be *obliged*, is "to be urged by a violent motive, resulting from the command of another."

And then let it be asked, Why am I *obliged* to keep my word? and the answer will be, "Because I am urged to do so by a violent motive" (namely, the expectation of being after this life rewarded, if I do, or punished for it, if I do not), "resulting from the command of another" (namely, of God).

This solution goes to the bottom of the subject, as no further question can reasonably be asked.

Therefore, private happiness is our motive, and the will of God our rule.

When I first turned my thoughts to moral speculations, an air of mystery seemed to hang over the whole subject; which arose, I believe, from hence—that I supposed, with many authors whom I had read, that to be *obliged* to do a thing, was very different from being *induced* only to do it; and that the obligation to practise virtue, to do what is right, just, &c. was quite another thing, and of another kind, than the obligation which a soldier is under to obey his officer, a servant his master; or any of the civil and ordinary obligations of human life. Whereas, from what has been said it appears, that moral obligation is like all other obligations; and that *obligation* is nothing more than an *inducement* of sufficient strength, and resulting, in some way, from the command of another.

There is always understood to be a difference between an act of *prudence* and an act of *duty*. Thus, if I distrust a man who owed me a sum of money, I should reckon it an act of prudence to get another person bound with him; but I should hardly call it an act of duty. On the other hand, it would be thought a very unusual and loose kind of language, to say, that, as I had made such a promise, it was *prudent* to perform it: or that, as my friend, when he went abroad, placed a box of jewels in my hands, it would be *prudent* in me to preserve it for him till he returned.

Now, in what, you will ask, does the difference consist? inasmuch, as, according to our account of the matter, both in the one case and the other, in acts of duty as well as acts of prudence, we consider solely what we ourselves shall gain or lose by the act.

The difference, and the only difference, is this; that, in the one case, we consider what we shall gain or lose in the present world; in the other case, we consider also what we shall gain or lose in the world to come.

They who would establish a system of morality, independent of a future state, must look out for some different idea of moral obligation; unless they can show that virtue conducts the possessor to certain happiness in this life, or to a much greater share of it than he could attain by a different behaviour.

To us there are two great questions:

I. Will there be after this life any distribution of rewards and punishments at all?

II. If there be, what actions will be rewarded, and what will be punished?

The first question comprises the credibility of the Christian Religion, together with the presumptive proofs of a future retribution from the light of nature. The second question comprises the province of morality. Both questions are too much for one work. The affirmative therefore of the first, although we confess that it is the foundation upon which the whole fabric rests, must in this treatise be taken for granted.

Chapter 4
THE WILL OF GOD

As the will of God is our rule; to inquire what is our duty, or what we are obliged to do, in any instance, is, in effect, to inquire what is the will of God in that instance? which consequently becomes the whole business of morality.

Now there are two methods of coming at the will of God on any point:

I. By his express declarations, when they are to be had, and which must be sought for in Scripture.

II. By what we can discover of his designs and disposition from his works; or, as we usually call it, the light of nature.

———————

And here we may observe the absurdity of separating natural and revealed religion from each other. The object of both is the same—to discover the will of God—and, provided we do but discover it, it matters nothing by what means.

An ambassador, judging by what he knows of his sovereign's disposition, and arguing from what he has observed of his conduct, or is acquainted with of his designs, may take his measures in many cases with safety, and presume with great probability how his master would have him act on most occasions that arise: but if he have his commission and instructions in his pocket, it would be strange not to look into them. He will be directed by both rules: when his instructions are clear and positive, there is an end to all further deliberation (unless indeed he suspect their authenticity): where his instructions are silent or dubious, he will endeavour to supply or explain them, by what he has been able to collect from other quarters of his master's general inclination or intentions.

Mr. Hume, in his fourth Appendix to his Principles of Morals, has been pleased to complain of the modern scheme of uniting Ethics with the Christian Theology. They who find themselves disposed to join in this complaint, will do well to observe what Mr. Hume himself has been able to make of morality without this union. And for that purpose, let them read the second part of the ninth section of the above essay; which part contains the practical application of the whole treatise—a treatise which Mr. Hume declares to be "incomparably the best he ever wrote." When they have read it over, let them consider, whether any motives there proposed are likely to be found sufficient to withhold men from the gratification of lust, revenge, envy, ambition, avarice; or to prevent the existence of these passions. Unless they rise up from this celebrated essay, with stronger impressions upon their minds than it ever left upon mine, they will acknowledge the necessity of additional sanctions. But the necessity of these sanctions is not now the question. If they be *in fact established*, if the rewards and punishments held forth in the Gospel will actually come to pass, they *must* be considered. Such as reject the Christian Religion, are to make the best shift they can to build up a system, and lay the foundation of morality, without it. But it appears to me a great inconsistency in those who receive Christianity, and expect something to come of it, to endeavour to keep all such expectations out of sight in their reasonings concerning human duty.

The method of coming at the will of God, concerning any action, by the light of nature, is to inquire into "the tendency of the action to promote or diminish the general happiness." This rule proceeds upon the presumption, that God Almighty wills and wishes the happiness of his creatures; and, consequently, that those actions, which promote that will and wish, must be agreeable to him; and the contrary.

As this presumption is the foundation of our whole system, it becomes necessary to explain the reasons upon which it rests.

Chapter 5
THE DIVINE BENEVOLENCE

When God created the human species, either he wished their happiness, or he wished their misery, or he was indifferent and unconcerned about both.

If he had wished our misery, he might have made sure of his purpose, by forming our senses to be so many sores and pains to us, as they are now instruments of gratification and enjoyment: or by placing us amidst objects so ill-suited to our perceptions, as to have continually offended us, instead of ministering to our refreshment and delight. He might have made, for example, every thing we tasted, bitter; every thing we saw, loathsome; every thing we touched, a sting; every smell a stench; and every sound a discord.

If he had been indifferent about our happiness or misery, we must impute to our good fortune (as all design by this supposition is excluded) both the capacity of our senses to receive pleasure, and the supply of external objects fitted to produce it. But either of these (and still more both of them) being too much to be attributed to accident, nothing remains but the first supposition, that God, when he created the human species, wished their happiness; and made for them the provision which he has made, with that view, and for that purpose.

The same argument may be proposed in different terms, thus: Contrivance proves design: and the predominant tendency of the contrivance indicates the disposition of the designer. The world abounds with contrivances: and all the contrivances which we are acquainted with, are directed to beneficial purposes. Evil, no doubt, exists; but is never, that we can perceive, the object of contrivance. Teeth are contrived to eat, not to ache; their aching now and then, is incidental to the contrivance, perhaps inseparable from it: or even, if you will, let it be called a defect in the contrivance; but it is not the *object* of it. This is a distinction which well deserves to be attended to. In describing implements of husbandry, you would hardly say of the sickle, that it is made to cut the reaper's fingers, though, from the construction of the instrument, and the manner of using it, this mischief often happens. But if you had occasion to describe instruments of torture or execution, This engine, you would say, is to extend the sinews; this to dislocate the joints; this to break the bones; this to scorch the soles of the feet. Here, pain and misery are the very *objects* of the contrivance. Now, nothing of this sort is to be found in the works of nature. We never discover a train of contrivance to bring about an evil purpose. No anatomist ever discovered a system of organization calculated to produce pain and disease; or, in explaining the parts of the human body, ever said, This is to irritate; this to inflame; this duct is to convey the gravel to the kidneys; this gland to secrete the humour which forms the gout: if by chance he come at a part of which he knows not the use, the most he can say is, that it is useless: no one ever suspects that it is put there to incommode, to annoy, or to torment. Since then God hath called forth his consummate wisdom to contrive and provide for our happiness, and the world appears to have been constituted with this design at first; so long as this constitution is upholden by him, we must in reason suppose the same design to continue.

The contemplation of universal nature rather bewilders the mind than affects it. There is always a bright spot in the prospect, upon which the eye rests; a single example, perhaps, by which each man finds himself more *convinced* than by all others put together. I seem, for my own part, to see the benevolence of the Deity more clearly in the pleasures of very young children, than in any thing in the world. The pleasures of grown persons may be reckoned partly of their own procuring; especially if there has been any industry, or contrivance, or pursuit, to come at them; or if they are founded, like music, painting, &c. upon any qualification of their own acquiring. But the pleasures of a healthy infant are so manifestly provided for it by *another*, and the benevolence of the provision is so unquestionable, that every child I see at its sport, affords to my mind a kind of sensible evidence of the finger of God, and of the disposition which directs it.

But the example, which strikes each man most strongly, is the true example for him: and hardly two minds hit upon the same; which shows the abundance of such examples about us.

We conclude, therefore, that God wills and wishes the happiness of his creatures. And this conclusion being once established, we are at liberty to go on with the rule built upon it, namely, "that the method of coming at the will of God, concerning any action, by the light of nature, is to inquire into the tendency of that action to promote or diminish the general happiness."

Chapter 6
UTILITY

So then actions are to be estimated by their tendency.* Whatever is expedient, is right. It is the utility of any moral rule alone, which constitutes the obligation of it.

But to all this there seems a plain objection, *viz.* that many actions are useful, which no man in his senses will allow to be right. There are occasions, in which the hand of the assassin would be very useful. The present possessor of some great estate employs his influence and fortune, to annoy, corrupt, or oppress, all about him. His estate would devolve, by his death, to a successor of an opposite character. It is useful, therefore, to despatch such a one as soon as possible out of the way; as the neighbourhood will exchange

---

*Actions in the abstract are right or wrong, according to their *tendency;* the agent is virtuous or vicious, according to his *design.* Thus, if the question be, Whether relieving common beggars be right or wrong? we inquire into the *tendency* of such a conduct to the public advantage or inconvenience. If the question be, Whether a man remarkable for this sort of bounty is to be esteemed virtuous for that reason? we inquire into his *design,* whether his liberality sprang from charity or from ostentation? It is evident that our concern is with actions in the abstract.

thereby a pernicious tyrant for a wise and generous benefactor. It might be useful to rob a miser, and give the money to the poor; as the money, no doubt, would produce more happiness, by being laid out in food and clothing for half a dozen distressed families, than by continuing locked up in a miser's chest. It may be useful to get possession of a place, a piece of preferment, or of a seat in parliament, by bribery or false swearing: as by means of them we may serve the public more effectually than in our private station. What then shall we say? Must we admit these actions to be right, which would be to justify assassination, plunder, and perjury; or must we give up our principle, that the criterion of right is utility?

It is not necessary to do either.

The true answer is this; that these actions, after all, are not useful, and for that reason, and that alone, are not right.

To see this point perfectly, it must be observed that the bad consequences of actions are twofold, *particular* and *general.*

The particular bad consequence of an action, is the mischief which that single action directly and immediately occasions.

The general bad consequence is, the violation of some necessary or useful *general* rule.

Thus, the particular bad consequence of the assassination above described, is the fright and pain which the deceased underwent; the loss he suffered of life, which is as valuable to a bad man, as to a good one, or more so; the prejudice and affliction, of which his death was the occasion, to his family, friends, and dependants.

The general bad consequence is the violation of this necessary general rule, that no man be put to death for his crimes but by public authority.

Although, therefore, such an action have no particular bad consequences, or greater particular good consequences, yet it is not useful, by reason of the general consequence, which is of more importance, and which is evil. And the same of the other two instances, and of a million more which might be mentioned.

But as this solution supposes, that the moral government of the world must proceed by general rules, it remains that we show the necessity of this.

Chapter 7
THE NECESSITY OF GENERAL RULES

You cannot permit one action and forbid another, without showing a difference between them. Consequently, the same sort of actions must be generally permitted or generally forbidden. Where, therefore, the general permission of them would be pernicious, it becomes necessary to lay down and support the rule which generally forbids them.

Thus, to return once more to the case of the assassin. The assassin knocked the rich villain on the head, because he thought him better out of the way than in it. If you allow this excuse in the present instance, you must allow it to all who act in the same manner, and from the said motive; that is, you must allow every man to kill any one he meets, whom he thinks noxious or useless; which, in the event, would be to commit every man's life and safety to the spleen, fury, and fanaticism, of his neighbour—a disposition of affairs which would soon fill the world with misery and confusion; and ere long put an end to human society, if not to the human species.

The necessity of general rules in human government is apparent: but whether the same necessity subsist in the Divine oeconomy, in that distribution of rewards and punishments to which a moralist looks forward, may be doubted.

I answer, that general rules are necessary to every moral government: and by moral government I mean any dispensation, whose object is to influence the conduct of reasonable creatures.

For if, of two actions perfectly similar, one be punished, and the other be rewarded or forgiven, which is the consequence of rejecting general rules, the subjects of such a dispensation would no longer know either what to expect or how to act. Rewards and punishments would cease to be such—would become accidents. Like the stroke of a thunderbolt, or the discovery of a mine, like a blank or a benefit-ticket in a lottery, they would occasion pain or pleasure when they happened; but, following in no known order, from any particular course of action, they could have no previous influence or effect upon the conduct.

An attention to general rules, therefore, is included in the very idea of reward and punishment. Consequently, whatever reason there is to expect future reward and punishment at the hand of God, there is the same reason to believe, that he will proceed in the distribution of it by general rules.

━━━━━━━━

Before we prosecute the consideration of general consequences any further, it may be proper to anticipate a reflection, which will be apt enough to suggest itself, in the progress of our argument.

As the general consequence of an action, upon which so much of the guilt of a bad action depends, consists in the *example;* it should seem, that if the action be done with perfect secrecy, so as to furnish no bad example, that part of the guilt drops off. In the case of suicide, for instance, if a man can so manage matters, as to take away his own life, without being known or suspected to have done so, he is not chargeable with any mischief from the example; nor does his punishment seem necessary, in order to save the authority of any general rule.

In the first place, those who reason in this manner do not observe, that they are setting up a general rule, of all others the least to be endured; namely, that secrecy, whenever secrecy is practicable, will justify any action.

Were such a rule admitted, for instance, in the case above produced; is there not reason to fear that people would be *disappearing*
perpetually?

In the next place, I would wish them to be well satisfied about
the points proposed in the following queries:

1. Whether the Scriptures do not teach us to expect that, at the
general judgement of the world, the most secret actions will be
brought to light?*

2. For what purpose can this be, but to make them the objects
of reward and punishment?

3. Whether, being so brought to light, they will not fall under
the operation of those equal and impartial rules, by which God will
deal with his creatures?

They will then become examples, whatever they be now; and
require the same treatment from the judge and governor of the
moral world, as if they had been detected from the first.

Chapter 8
THE CONSIDERATION OF GENERAL
CONSEQUENCES PURSUED

The general consequence of any action may be estimated, by asking what would be the consequence, if the same sort of actions
were generally permitted. But suppose they were, and a thousand
such actions perpetrated under this permission; is it just to charge
a single action with the collected guilt and mischief of the whole

---

*"In the day when God shall judge the secrets of men by Jesus Christ." Rom.
xi. 16. "Judge nothing before the time, until the Lord come, who will bring to
light the hidden things of darkness, and will make manifest the counsels of the
heart." 1 Cor. iv. 5.

thousand? I answer, that the reason for prohibiting and punishing an action (and this reason may be called the *guilt* of the action, if you please) will always be in proportion to the whole mischief that would arise from the general impunity and toleration of actions of the same sort.

"Whatever is expedient is right." But then it must be expedient on the whole, at the long run, in all its effects collateral and remote, as well as in those which are immediate and direct; as it is obvious, that, in computing consequences, it makes no difference in what way or at what distance they ensue.

To impress this doctrine on the minds of young readers, and to teach them to extend their views beyond the immediate mischief of a crime, I shall here subjoin a string of instances, in which the particular consequence is comparatively insignificant; and where the malignity of the crime, and the severity with which human laws pursue it, is almost entirely founded upon the general consequence.

The particular consequence of coining is, the loss of a guinea, or of half a guinea, to the person who receives the counterfeit money: the general consequence (by which I mean the consequence that would ensue, if the same practice were generally permitted) is, to abolish the use of money.

The particular consequence of forgery is, a damage of twenty or thirty pounds to the man who accepts the forged bill: the general consequence is, the stoppage of paper-currency.

The particular consequence of sheep-stealing, or horse-stealing, is a loss to the owner, to the amount of the value of the sheep or horse stolen: the general consequence is, that the land could not be occupied, nor the market supplied, with this kind of stock.

The particular consequence of breaking into a house empty of inhabitants, is, the loss of a pair of silver candlesticks, or a few spoons: the general consequence is, that nobody could leave their house empty.

The particular consequence of smuggling may be a deduction from the national fund too minute for computation: the general consequence is, the destruction of one entire branch of public revenue; a proportionable increase of the burthen upon other branches; and the ruin of all fair and open trade in the article smuggled.

The particular consequence of an officer's breaking his parole is, the loss of a prisoner, who was possibly not worth keeping: the general consequence is, that this mitigation of captivity would be refused to all others.

And what proves incontestably the superior importance of general consequences is, that crimes are the same, and treated in the same manner, though the particular consequence be very different. The crime and fate of the house-breaker is the same, whether his booty be five pounds or fifty. And the reason is, that the general consequence is the same.

The want of this distinction between particular and general consequences, or rather, the not sufficiently attending to the latter, is the cause of that perplexity which we meet with in ancient moralists. On the one hand, they were sensible of the absurdity of pronouncing actions good or evil, without regard to the good or evil they produced. On the other hand, they were startled at the conclusions to which a steady adherence to consequences seemed sometimes to conduct them. To relieve this difficulty, they contrived the τὸ πρεπον, or the *honestum*, by which terms they meant to constitute a measure of right, distinct from utility. Whilst the *utile* served them, that is, whilst it corresponded with their habitual notions of the rectitude of actions, they went by *it*. When they fell in with such cases as those mentioned in the sixth chapter, they took leave of their guide, and resorted to the *honestum*. The only account they could give of the matter was, that these actions might be useful; but, because they were not at the same time *honesta*, they were by no means to be deemed just or right.

From the principles delivered in this and the two preceding chapters, a maxim may be explained, which is in every man's mouth, and in most men's without meaning, *viz.* "not to do evil, that good may come": that is, let us not violate a general rule, for the sake of any particular good consequence we may expect. Which is for the most part a salutary caution, the advantage seldom compensating for the violation of the rule. Strictly speaking, that cannot be "evil," from which "good comes"; but in this way, and with a view to the distinction between particular and general consequences, it may.

We will conclude this subject of *consequences* with the following reflection. A man may imagine, that any action of his, with respect to the public, must be inconsiderable: so also is the agent. If his crime produce but a small effect upon the *universal* interest, his punishment or destruction bears a small proportion to the sum of happiness and misery in the creation.

Chapter 9
OF RIGHT

Right and obligation are reciprocal; that is, wherever there is a right in one person, there is a corresponding obligation upon others. If one man has a "right" to an estate; others are "obliged" to abstain from it—If parents have a "right" to reverence from their children; children are "obliged" to reverence their parents— and so in all other instances.

Now, because moral *obligation* depends, as we have seen, upon the will of God; *right*, which is correlative to it, must depend upon the same. Right therefore signifies, *consistency with the will of God.*

But if the Divine will determine the distinction of right and wrong, what else is it but an identical proposition, to say of God, that he acts *right?* or how is it possible to conceive even that he should act *wrong?* Yet these assertions are intelligible and significant. The case is this: By virtue of the two principles, that God wills the happiness of his creatures, and that the will of God is the measure of right and wrong, we arrive at certain conclusions; which conclusions become rules; and we soon learn to pronounce actions right or wrong, according as they agree or disagree with our rules, without looking any further: and when the habit is once established of stopping at the rules, we can go back and compare with these rules even the Divine conduct itself; and yet it may be true (only not observed by us at the time) that the rules themselves are deduced from the Divine will.

Right is a quality of persons or of actions.

Of persons; as when we say, such a one has a "right" to this estate; parents have a "right" to reverence from their children; the king to allegiance from his subjects; masters have a "right" to their servants' labour; a man has not a "right" over his own life.

Of actions; as in such expressions as the following: it is "right" to punish murder with death; his behaviour on that occasion was "right"; it is not "right" to send an unfortunate debtor to gaol; he did or acted "right," who gave up his place, rather than vote against his judgement.

In this latter set of expressions, you may substitute the definition of right above given, for the term itself: *e.g.* it is "consistent with the will of God" to punish murder with death; his behaviour on that occasion was "consistent with the will of God"; it is not "consistent with the will of God" to send an unfortunate debtor to gaol; he did, or acted, "consistently with the will of God," who gave up his place rather than vote against his judgement.

In the former set, you must vary the construction a little, when you introduce the definition instead of the term. Such a one has a "right" to this estate, that is, it is "consistent with the will of God" that such a one should have it; parents have a "right" to reverence from their children, that is, it is "consistent with the will of God" that children should reverence their parents; and the same of the rest.

Chapter 10
THE DIVISION OF RIGHTS

Rights, when applied to persons, are
>Natural or adventitious:
>Alienable or unalienable:
>Perfect or imperfect.

I. Rights are natural or adventitious.

Natural rights are such as would belong to a man, although there subsisted in the world no civil government whatever.

Adventitious rights are such as would not.

Natural rights are, a man's right to his life, limbs, and liberty; his right to the produce of his personal labour; to the use, in common with others, of air, light, water. If a thousand different persons, from a thousand different corners of the world, were cast together upon a desert island, they would from the first be every one entitled to these rights.

Adventitious rights are, the right of a king over his subjects; of a general over his soldiers; of a judge over the life and liberty of a prisoner; a right to elect or appoint magistrates, to impose taxes, decide disputes, direct the descent or disposition of property; a right, in a word, in any one man, or particular body of men, to make laws and regulations for the rest. For none of these rights would exist in the newly inhabited island.

And here it will be asked, how adventitious rights are created; or, which is the same thing, how any new rights can accrue from the establishment of civil society; as rights of all kinds, we remember, depend upon the will of God, and civil society is but the ordinance and institution of man? For the solution of this difficulty, we must return to our first principles. God wills the happiness of mankind; and the existence of civil society, as conducive to that happiness. Consequently, many things, which are useful for the support of civil society in general, or for the conduct and conservation of particular societies already established, are, for that reason, "consistent with the will of God," or "right," which, without that reason, *i.e.* without the establishment of civil society, would not have been so.

From whence also it appears, that adventitious rights, though immediately derived from human appointment, are not, for that reason, less sacred than natural rights, nor the obligation to respect them less cogent. They both ultimately rely upon the same authority, the will of God. Such a man claims a right to a particular estate. He can show, it is true, nothing for his right, but a rule of the civil community to which he belongs; and this rule may be arbitrary, capricious, and absurd. Notwithstanding all this, there would be the same sin in dispossessing the man of his estate by craft or violence, as if it had been assigned to him, like the partition of the country amongst the twelve tribes, by the immediate designation and appointment of Heaven.

II. Rights are alienable or unalienable.

Which terms explain themselves.

The right we have to most of those things which we call property, as houses, lands, money, &c. is alienable.

The right of a prince over his people, of a husband over his wife, of a master over his servant, is generally and naturally unalienable.

The distinction depends upon the mode of acquiring the right. If the right originate from a contract, and be limited to the *person* by the express terms of the contract, or by the common interpretation of such contracts (which is equivalent to an express stipulation), or by a *personal condition* annexed to the right; then it is unalienable. In all other cases it is alienable.

The right to civil liberty is alienable; though in the vehemence of men's zeal for it, and the language of some political remonstrances, it has often been pronounced to be an unalienable right. The true reason why mankind hold in detestation the memory of those who have sold their liberty to a tyrant, is, that, together with their own, they sold commonly, or endangered, the liberty of others; which certainly they had no right to dispose of.

III. Rights are perfect or imperfect.

Perfect rights may be asserted by force, or, what in civil society comes into the place of private force, by course of law.

Imperfect rights may not.

Examples of perfect rights.—A man's right to his life, person, house; for, if these be attacked, he may repel the attacked by instant violence, or punish the aggressor by law: a man's right to his estate, furniture, clothes, money, and to all ordinary articles of property; for, if they be injuriously taken from him, he may compel the author of the injury to make restitution or satisfaction.

Examples of imperfect rights.—In elections or appointments to offices, where the qualifications are prescribed, the best qualified candidate has a right to success; yet, if he be rejected, he has no remedy. He can neither seize the office by force, nor obtain redress at law; his right therefore is imperfect. A poor neighbour has a right to relief; yet if it be refused him, he must not extort it. A benefactor has a right to returns of gratitude from the person he has obliged; yet, if he meet with none, he must acquiesce. Children have a right to affection and education from their parents; and parents, on their part, to duty and reverence from their children; yet, if these rights be on either side withholden, there is no compulsion by which they can be enforced.

It may be at first view difficult to apprehend how a person should have a right to a thing, and yet have no right to use the means necessary to obtain it. This difficulty, like most others in morality, is resolvable into the necessity of general rules. The reader recollects, that a person is said to have a "right" to a thing, when it is "consistent with the will of God" that he should possess it. So that the question is reduced to this: How it comes to pass that it should be consistent with the will of God that a person should possess a thing, and yet not be consistent with the same will that he should use force to obtain it? The answer is, that by reason of the indeterminateness, either of the object, or of the circumstances of the right, the permission of force in this case would, in its consequence, lead to the permission of force in other cases, where there existed no right at all. The candidate above described has, no doubt, a right to success; but his right depends upon his qualifications, for instance, upon his comparative virtue, learning, &c.; there must be somebody therefore to compare them. The existence, degree, and respective importance, of these qualifications, are all indeterminate: there must be somebody therefore to determine them. To allow the candidate to demand success by force, is to make him the judge of his own qualifications. You cannot do this but you must make all other candidates the same; which would open a door to demands without number, reason, or right. In like manner, a poor man has a right to relief from the rich; but the mode, season, and quantum of that relief, who shall contribute to it, or how much, are not ascertained. Yet these points must be ascertained, before a claim to relief can be prosecuted by force. For, to allow the poor to ascertain them for themselves, would be to expose property to so many of these claims, that it would lose its value, or rather its nature, that is, cease indeed to be property. The same observation holds of all other cases of imperfect rights; not to mention, that in the instances of gratitude, affection, reverence, and the like, force is excluded by the very idea of the duty, which must be voluntary, or cannot exist at all.

Wherever the right is imperfect, the corresponding obligation is so too. I am obliged to prefer the best candidate, to relieve the poor, be grateful to my benefactors, take care of my children, and reverence my parents; but in all these cases, my obligation, like their right, is imperfect.

I call these obligations "imperfect," in conformity to the established language of writers upon the subject. The term, however, seems ill chosen on this account, that it leads many to imagine, that there is less guilt in the violation of an imperfect obligation, than of a perfect one: which is a groundless notion. For an obligation being perfect or imperfect, determines only whether violence may or may not be employed to enforce it; and determines nothing else. The degree of guilt incurred by violating the obligation is a different thing, and is determined by circumstances altogether independent of this distinction. A man who by a partial, prejudiced, or corrupt vote, disappoints a worthy candidate of a station in life, upon which his hopes, possibly, or livelihood, depended, and who thereby grievously discourages merit and emulation in others, commits, I am persuaded, a much greater crime, than if he filched a book out of a library, or picked a pocket of a handkerchief; though in the one case he violates only an imperfect right, in the other a perfect one.

As positive precepts are often indeterminate in their extent, and as the indeterminateness of an obligation is that which makes it imperfect; it comes to pass, that positive precepts commonly produce an imperfect obligation.

Negative precepts or prohibitions, being generally precise, constitute accordingly perfect obligations.

The fifth commandment is positive, and the duty which results from it is imperfect.

The sixth commandment is negative, and imposes a perfect obligation.

Religion and virtue find their principal exercise among the imperfect obligations; the laws of civil society taking pretty good care of the rest.

Chapter 11
THE GENERAL RIGHTS OF MANKIND

By the General Rights of Mankind, I mean the rights which belong to the species collectively; the original stock, as I may say, which they have since distributed among themselves.

These are,

1. A right to the fruits or vegetable produce of the earth.

The insensible parts of the creation are incapable of injury; and it is nugatory to inquire into the right, where the use can be attended with no injury. But it may be worth observing, for the sake of an inference which will appear below, that, as God had created us with a want and desire of food, and provided things suited by their nature to sustain and satisfy us, we may fairly presume, that he intended we should apply these things to that purpose.

2. A right to the flesh of animals.

This is a very different claim from the former. Some excuse seems necessary for the pain and loss which we occasion to brutes, by restraining them of their liberty, mutilating their bodies, and, at last, putting an end to their lives (which we suppose to be the whole of their existence), for our pleasure or conveniency.

The reasons alleged in vindication of this practice, are the following: that the several species of brutes being created to prey upon one another, affords a kind of analogy to prove that the human species were intended to feed upon them; that, if let alone, they would overrun the earth, and exclude mankind from the occupation of it; that they are requited for what they suffer at our hands, by our care and protection.

Upon which reasons I would observe, that *the analogy* contended for is extremely lame; since brutes have no power to support life by any other means, and since we have; for the whole human species might subsist entirely upon fruit, pulse, herbs, and roots, as many tribes of Hindoos actually do. The two other reasons may be valid reasons, as far as they go; for, no doubt, if man had been supported entirely by vegetable food, a great part of those animals which die to furnish his table would never have lived: but they by no means justify our right over the lives of brutes to the extent in which we exercise it. What danger is there, for instance, of fish interfering with us, in the occupation of their element? or what do *we* contribute to their support or preservation?

It seems to me, that it would be difficult to defend this right by any arguments which the light and order of nature afford; and that we are beholden for it to the permission recorded in Scripture, Gen. ix. 1,2,3: "And God blessed Noah and his sons, and said unto them, Be fruitful, and multiply, and replenish the earth: and the fear of you, and the dread of you, shall be upon every beast of the earth, and upon every fowl of the air, and upon all that moveth upon the earth, and upon all the fishes of the sea; into your hand are they delivered; every moving thing shall be meat for you; even as the green herb, have I given you all things." To Adam and his posterity had been granted, at the creation, "every green herb for meat," and nothing more. In the last clause of the passage now produced, the old grant is recited, and extended to the flesh of animals; "even as the green herb, have I given you all things." But this was not till after the flood; the inhabitants of the antediluvian world had therefore no such permission, that we know of. Whether they actually refrained from the flesh of animals, is another question. Abel, we read, was a keeper of

sheep; and for what purpose he kept them, except for food, is difficult to say (unless it were sacrifices): might not, however, some of the
stricter sects among the antediluvians be scrupulous as to this point?
and might not Noah and his family be of this description? for it is
not probable that God would publish a permission, to authorise a
practice which had never been disputed.

Wanton, and, what is worse, studied cruelty to brutes, is certainly wrong, as coming within one of these reasons.

———

From reason then, or revelation, or from both together, it
appears to be God Almighty's intention, that the productions of
the earth should be applied to the sustentation of human life. Consequently all waste and misapplication of these productions, is contrary to the Divine intention and will; and therefore wrong, for the
same reason that any other crime is so. Such as, what is related of
William the Conqueror, the converting of twenty manors into a
forest for hunting; or, which is not much better, suffering them to
continue in that state; or the letting of large tracts of land lie barren, because the owner cannot cultivate them, nor will part with
them to those who can; or destroying, or suffering to perish, great
part of an article of human provision, in order to enhance the price
of the remainder, (which is said to have been, till lately, the case
with fish caught upon the English coast); or diminishing the breed
of animals, by a wanton, or improvident, consumption of the
young, as of the spawn of shell-fish, or the fry of salmon, by the use
of unlawful nets, or at improper seasons: to this head may also be
referred, what is the same evil in a smaller way, the expending
of human food on superfluous dogs or horses; and lastly, the
reducing of the quantity, in order to alter the quality, and to alter

it generally for the worse; as the distillation of spirits from bread-corn, the boiling down of solid meat for sauces, essences, &c.

This seems to be the lesson which our Saviour, after his manner, inculcates, when he bids his disciples "gather up the fragments, that nothing be lost." And it opens indeed a new field of duty. Schemes of wealth or profit, prompt the active part of mankind to cast about, how they may convert their property to the most advantage; and their own advantage, and that of the public, commonly concur. But it has not as yet entered into the minds of mankind, to reflect that it is a *duty*, to add what we can to the common stock of provision, by extracting out of our estates the most they will yield; or that it is any sin to neglect this.

From the same intention of God Almighty, we also deduce another conclusion, namely, "that nothing ought to be made exclusive property, which can be conveniently enjoyed in common."

It is the general intention of God Almighty, that the produce of the earth be applied to the use of man. This appears from the constitution of nature, or, if you will, from his express declaration; and this is all that appears at first. Under this general donation, one man has the same right as another. You pluck an apple from a tree, or take a lamb from a flock, for your immediate use and nourishment, and I do the same; and we both plead for what we do, the general intention of the Supreme Proprietor. So far all is right: but you cannot claim the whole tree, or the whole flock, and exclude me from any share of them, and plead this general intention for what you do. The plea will not serve you; you must show something more. You must show, by probable arguments at least, that it is God's intention, that these things should be parcelled out to individuals; and that the established distribution, under which you claim, should be upholden. Show me this, and I am satisfied. But until this be shown, the general intention, which has been made appear, and which is all that does appear, must prevail; and, under that, my title is as good as yours. Now there is no argument to induce such a presumption, but one; that the thing cannot be enjoyed at all, or enjoyed with the same, or with nearly the same advantage, while it continues in common, as when appropriated. This is true, where there is not enough for all, or where the article in question requires care or labour in the production or preservation: but where no such reason obtains, and the thing is in its nature capable of being enjoyed by as many as will, it seems an arbitrary usurpation upon the rights of mankind, to confine the use of it to any.

If a medicinal spring were discovered in a piece of ground which was private property, copious enough for every purpose to which it could be applied, I would award a compensation to the owner of the field, and a liberal profit to the author of the discovery, especially if he had bestowed pains or expense upon the search: but I question whether any human laws would be justified, or would justify the owner, in prohibiting mankind from the use of the water, or setting such a price upon it as would almost amount to a prohibition.

If there be fisheries, which are inexhaustible, as the cod-fishery upon the Banks of Newfoundland, and the herring-fishery in the British seas, are said to be; then all those conventions, by which one or two nations claim to themselves, and guaranty to each other, the exclusive enjoyment of these fisheries, are so many encroachments upon the general rights of mankind.

Upon the same principle may be determined a question, which makes a great figure in books of natural law, *utrum mare sit liberum?* that is, as I understand it, whether the exclusive right of navigating particular seas, or a control over the navigation of these seas, can be claimed, consistently with the law of nature, by any nation? What is necessary for each nation's safety, we allow; as their own bays, creeks, and harbours, the sea contiguous to, that is, within cannon-shot, or three leagues of their coast: and upon this principle of safety (if upon any principle) must be defended the claim of the Venetian State to the Adriatic, of Denmark to the Baltic Sea, and of Great Britain to the seas which invest the island. But, when Spain asserts a right to the Pacific Ocean, or Portugal to the Indian Seas, or when any nation extends its pretensions much beyond the limits of its own territories, they erect a claim which interferes with the benevolent designs of Providence, and which no human authority can justify.

3. Another right, which may be called a general right, as it is incidental to every man who is in a situation to claim it, is the right of extreme necessity; by which is meant, a right to use or destroy another's property, when it is necessary for our own preservation to do so; as a right to take, without or against the owner's leave, the first food, clothes, or shelter, we meet with, when we are in danger of perishing through want of them; a right to throw goods overboard to save the ship; or to pull down a house, in order to stop the progress of a fire; and a few other instances of the same kind. Of which right the foundation seems to be this: that when property was first instituted, the institution was not intended to operate to the destruction of any; therefore when such consequences would follow, all regard to it is superseded. Or rather, perhaps, these are the few cases, where the particular consequence exceeds the general consequence; where the remote mischief resulting from the violation of the general rule, is overbalanced by the immediate advantage.

Restitution however is due, when in our power: because the laws of property are to be adhered to, so far as consists with safety; and because restitution, which is one of those laws, supposes the danger to be over. But what is to be restored? Not the full value of the property destroyed, but what it was worth at the time of destroying it; which, considering the danger it was in of perishing, might be very little.

Book III
Relative Duties

Chapter 1
OF PROPERTY

If you should see a flock of pigeons in a field of corn; and if (instead of each picking where and what it liked, taking just as much as it wanted, and no more) you should see ninety-nine of them gathering all they got, into a heap; reserving nothing for themselves, but the chaff and the refuse; keeping this heap for one, and that the weakest, perhaps worst, pigeon of the flock; sitting round, and looking on, all the winter, whilst this one was devouring, throwing about, and wasting it; and if a pigeon more hardy or hungry than the rest, touched a grain of the hoard, all the others instantly flying upon it, and tearing it to pieces; if you should see this, you would see nothing more than what is every day practised and established among men. Among men, you see the ninety-and-nine toiling and scraping together a heap of superfluities for one (and this one too, oftentimes the feeblest and worst of the whole set, a child, a woman, a madman, or a fool); getting nothing for themselves all the while, but a little of the coarsest of the provision, which their own industry produces; looking quietly on, while they see the fruits of all their labour spent or spoiled; and if one of the number take or touch a particle of the hoard, the others joining against him, and hanging him for the theft.

Chapter 2
THE USE OF THE INSTITUTION OF PROPERTY

There must be some very important advantages to account for an institution, which, in the view of it above given, is so paradoxical and unnatural.

The principal of these advantages are the following:

I. It increases the produce of the earth.

The earth, in climates like ours, produces little without cultivation: and none would be found willing to cultivate the ground, if others were to be admitted to an equal share of the produce. The same is true of the care of flocks and herds of tame animals.

Crabs and acorns, red deer, rabbits, game, and fish, are all which we should have to subsist upon in this country, if we trusted to the spontaneous productions of the soil; and it fares not much better with other countries. A nation of North-American savages, consisting of two or three hundred, will take up, and be half-starved upon, a tract of land, which in Europe, and with European management, would be sufficient for the maintenance of as many thousands.

In some fertile soils, together with great abundance of fish upon their coasts, and in regions where clothes are unnecessary, a considerable degree of population may subsist without property in land; which is the case in the islands of Otaheite: but in less favoured situations, as in the country of New Zealand, though this sort of property obtain in a small degree, the inhabitants, for want of a more secure and regular establishment of it, are driven oftentimes by the scarcity of provision to devour one another.

II. It preserves the produce of the earth to maturity.

We may judge what would be the effects of a community of right to the productions of the earth, from the trifling specimens which we see of it at present. A cherry-tree in a hedge-row, nuts in a wood, the grass of an unstinted pasture, are seldom of much advantage to any body, because people do not wait for the proper season of reaping them. Corn, if any were sown, would never ripen; lambs and calves would never grow up to sheep and cows, because the first person that met them would reflect, that he had better take them as they are, than leave them for another.

III. It prevents contests.

War and waste, tumult and confusion, must be unavoidable and eternal, where there is not enough for all, and where there are no rules to adjust the division.

IV. It improves the conveniency of living.

This it does two ways. It enables mankind to divide themselves into distinct professions; which is impossible, unless a man can exchange the productions of his own art for what he wants from others; and exchange implies property. Much of the advantage of civilised over savage life, depends upon this. When a man is from necessity his own tailor, tent-maker, carpenter, cook, huntsman, and fisherman, it is not probable that he will be expert at any of his callings. Hence the rude habitations, furniture, clothing, and implements, of savages; and the tedious length of time which all their operations require.

It likewise encourages those arts, by which the accommodations of human life are supplied, by appropriating to the artist the benefit of his discoveries and improvements; without which appropriation, ingenuity will never be exerted with effect.

Upon these several accounts we may venture, with a few exceptions, to pronounce, that even the poorest and the worst provided, in countries where property and the consequences of property prevail, are in a better situation, with respect to food, raiment, houses, and what are called the necessaries of life, than *any* are in places where most things remain in common.

The balance, therefore, upon the whole, must preponderate in favour of property with a manifest and great excess.

Inequality of property, in the degree in which it exists in most countries of Europe, abstractedly considered, is an evil: but it is an evil which flows from those rules concerning the acquisition and disposal of property, by which men are incited to industry, and by which the object of their industry is rendered secure and valuable. If there be any great inequality unconnected with this origin, it ought to be corrected.

Chapter 3
THE HISTORY OF PROPERTY

The first objects of property were the fruits which a man gathered, and the wild animals he caught; next to these, the tents or houses which he built, the tools he made use of to catch or prepare his food; and afterwards weapons of war and offence. Many of the savage tribes in North America have advanced no further than this yet; for they are said to reap their harvest, and return the produce of their market with foreigners, into the common hoard or treasury of the tribe. Flocks and herds of tame animals soon became property; Abel, the second from Adam, was a keeper of sheep; sheep and oxen, camels and asses, composed the wealth of the Jewish patriarchs, as they do still of the modern Arabs. As the world was first peopled in the East, where there existed a great scarcity of water, wells probably were next made property; as we learn from the frequent and serious mention of them in the Old Testament; the contentions and treaties about them;* and from its being recorded, among the most memorable achievements of very eminent men, that they dug or discovered a well. Land, which is now so important a part of property, which alone our laws call real property, and regard upon all occasions with such peculiar attention, was probably not made property in any country, till long after the institution of many other species of property, that is, till the country became populous, and tillage began to be thought of. The first partition of an estate which we read of, was that which took place between Abram and Lot, and was one of the simplest imaginable: "If thou wilt take the left hand, then I will go to the right; or if thou depart to the right hand, then I will go to the left." There are no traces of property in land in Caesar's account of Britain; little of it in the history of the Jewish patriarchs; none of it found amongst the nations of North America; the Scythians are expressly said to have appropriated their cattle and houses, but to have left their land in common.

Property in immoveables continued at first no longer than the occupation: that is, so long as a man's family continued in possession of a cave, or whilst his flocks depastured upon a neighbouring hill, no one attempted, or thought he had a right, to disturb or drive them out: but when the man quitted his cave, or changed his pasture, the first who found them unoccupied, entered upon them, by the same title as his predecessor's; and made way in his turn for any one that happened to succeed him. All more permanent property in land was probably posterior to civil government and to laws; and therefore settled by these, or according to the will of the reigning chief.

*Genesis xxi. 25; xxvi. 18.

Chapter 4
In What the Right of Property Is
Founded

We now speak of Property in Land: and there is a difficulty in explaining the origin of this property, consistently with the law of nature; for the land was once, no doubt, common; and the question is, how any particular part of it could justly be taken out of the common, and so appropriated to the first owner, as to give him a better right to it than others; and, what is more, a right to exclude all others from it.

Moralists have given many different accounts of this matter; which diversity alone, perhaps, is a proof that none of them are satisfactory.

One tells us that mankind, when they suffered a particular person to occupy a piece of ground, by tacit consent relinquished their right to it; and as the piece of ground, they say, belonged to mankind collectively, and mankind thus gave up their right to the first peaceable occupier, it thenceforward became his property, and no one afterwards had a right to molest him in it.

The objection to this account is, that consent can never be presumed from silence, where the person whose consent is required knows nothing about the matter; which must have been the case with all mankind, except the neighbourhood of the place where the appropriation was made. And to suppose that the piece of ground previously belonged to the neighbourhood, and that they had a just power of conferring a right to it upon whom they pleased, is to suppose the question resolved, and a partition of land to have already taken place.

Another says, that each man's limbs and labour are his own exclusively; that, by occupying a piece of ground, a man inseparably mixes his labour with it; by which means the piece of ground becomes thenceforward his own, as you cannot take it from him without depriving him at the same time of something which is indisputably *his*.

This is Mr. Locke's solution; and seems indeed a fair reason, where the value of the labour bears a considerable proportion to the value of the thing; or where the thing derives its chief use and value from the labour. Thus game and fish, though they be common whilst at large in the woods or water, instantly become the property of the person that catches them; because an animal, when caught, is much more valuable than when at liberty; and this increase of value, which is inseparable from, and makes a great part of, the whole value, is strictly the property of the fowler or fisherman, being the produce of his personal labour. For the same reason, wood or iron, manufactured into utensils, becomes the property of the manufacturer; because the value of the workmanship far exceeds that of the materials. And upon a similar principle, a parcel of unappropriated ground, which a man should pare, burn, plough, harrow, and sow, for the production of corn, would justly enough be thereby made his own. But this will hardly hold, in the manner it has been applied, of taking a ceremonious possession of a tract of land, as navigators do of new-discovered islands, by erecting a standard, engraving an inscription, or publishing a proclamation to the birds and beasts; or of turning your cattle into a piece of ground, setting up a landmark, digging a ditch, or planting a hedge round it. Nor will even the clearing, manuring, and ploughing of a field, give the first occupier a right to it in perpetuity, and after this cultivation and all effects of it are ceased.

Another, and in my opinion a better, account of the first right of ownership, is the following: that, as God has provided these things for the use of all, he has of consequence given each leave to take of them what he wants: by virtue therefore of this leave, a man may appropriate what he stands in need of to his own use, without asking, or waiting for, the consent of others; in like manner as, when an entertainment is provided for the freeholders of a county, each freeholder goes, and eats and drinks what he wants or chooses, without having or waiting for the consent of the other guests.

But then this reason justifies property, as far as necessaries alone, or, at the most, as far as a competent provision for our natural exigencies. For, in the entertainment we speak of (allowing the comparison to hold in all points), although every particular freeholder may sit down and eat till he be satisfied, without any other leave than that of the master of the feast, or any other proof of that leave than the general invitation, or the manifest design with which the entertainment is provided; yet you would hardly permit any one to fill his pockets or his wallet, or to carry away with him a quantity of provision to be hoarded up, or wasted, or given to his dogs, or stewed down into sauces, or converted into articles of superfluous luxury; especially if, by so doing, he pinched the guests at the lower end of the table.

These are the accounts that have been given of the matter by the best writers upon the subject, but, were these accounts perfectly unexceptionable, they would none of them, I fear, avail us in vindicating our present claims of property in land, unless it were more probable than it is, that our estates were actually acquired at first, in some of the ways which these accounts suppose; and that a regular regard had been paid to justice, in every successive transmission of them since; for, if one link in the chain fail, every title posterior to it falls to the ground.

The real foundation of our right is, THE LAW OF THE LAND.

It is the intention of God, that the produce of the earth be applied to the use of man: this intention cannot be fulfilled without establishing property; it is consistent, therefore, with his will, that property be established. The land cannot be divided into separate property, without leaving it to the law of the country to regulate that division: it is consistent therefore with the same will, that the law should regulate the division; and, consequently, "consistent with the will of God," or "right," that I should possess that share which these regulations assign me.

By whatever circuitous train of reasoning you attempt to derive this right, it must terminate at last in the will of God; the straightest, therefore, and shortest way of arriving at this will, is the best.

Hence it appears, that my right to an estate does not at all depend upon the manner or justice of the original acquisition; nor upon the justice of each subsequent change of possession. It is not, for instance, the less, nor ought it to be impeached, because the estate was taken possession of at first by a family of aboriginal Britons, who happened to be stronger than their neighbours; nor because the British possessor was turned out by a Roman, or the Roman by a Saxon invader; nor because it was seized, without colour of right or reason, by a follower of the Norman adventurer; from whom, after many interruptions of fraud and violence, it has at length devolved to me.

Nor does the owner's right depend upon the *expediency* of the law which gives it to him. On one side of a brook, an estate descends to the eldest son; on the other side, to all the children alike. The right of the claimants under both laws of inheritance is equal; though the expediency of such opposite rules must necessarily be different.

The principles we have laid down upon this subject, apparently tend to a conclusion of which a bad use is apt to be made. As the right of property depends upon the law of the land, it seems to follow, that a man has a right to keep and take every thing which the law will allow him to keep and take; which in many cases will authorize the most flagitious chicanery. If a creditor upon a simple contract neglect to demand his debt for six years, the debtor may refuse to pay it: would it be *right* therefore to do so, where he is conscious of the justice of the debt? If a person, who is under twenty-one years of age,

contract a bargain (other than for necessaries), he may avoid it by
pleading his minority: but would this be a fair plea, where the bargain
was originally just? The distinction to be taken in such cases is this:
With the law, we acknowledge, resides the disposal of property: so
long, therefore, as we keep within the design and intention of a law,
that law will justify us, as well *in foro conscientiae*, as *in foro humano*,
whatever be the equity or expediency of the law itself. But when we
convert to one purpose, a rule or expression of law, which is intended
for another purpose, then we plead in our justification, not the intention of the law, but the words: that is, we plead a dead letter, which
can signify nothing; for words *without* meaning or intention, have no
force or effect in justice; much less, words taken *contrary* to the meaning and intention of the speaker or writer. To apply this distinction
to the examples just now proposed: in order to protect men against
antiquated demands, from which it is not probable they should have
preserved the evidence of their discharge, the law prescribes a limited
time to certain species of private securities, beyond which it will not
enforce them, or lend its assistance to the recovery of the debt. If a
man be ignorant or dubious of the justice of the demand made upon
him, he may conscientiously plead this limitation: because *he applies*
the rule of law to the purpose for which it was intended. But when he
refuses to pay a debt, of the reality of which he is conscious, he cannot, as before, plead the intention of the statute, and the supreme
authority of law, unless he could show, that the law *intended* to interpose its supreme authority, to acquit men of debts, of the existence
and justice of which they were themselves sensible. Again, to preserve
youth from the practices and impositions to which their inexperience
exposes them, the law compels the payment of no debts incurred
within a certain age, nor the performance of any engagements, except
for such necessaries as are suited to their condition and fortunes. If a
young person therefore perceive that he has been practised or
imposed upon, he may honestly avail himself of the privilege of his
nonage, to defeat the circumvention. But, if he shelter himself under

this privilege, to avoid a fair obligation, or an equitable contract, he extends the privilege to a case, in which it is not allowed by intention of law, and in which consequently it does not, in natural justice, exist.

———————

As property is the principal subject of justice, or of "the determinate relative duties," we have put down what we had to say upon *it* in the first place: we now proceed to state these duties in the best order we can.

Chapter 5
PROMISES

   I. From whence the obligation to perform promises arises.
  II. In what sense promises are to be interpreted.
 III. In what cases promises are not binding.

I. *From whence the obligation to perform promises arises.*

They who argue from innate moral principles, suppose a sense of the obligation of promises to be one of them; but without assuming this, or any thing else, without proof, the obligation to perform promises may be deduced from the necessity of such a conduct to the well-being, or the existence indeed, of human society.

Men act from expectation. Expectation is in most cases determined by the assurances and engagements which we receive from others. If no dependence could be placed upon these assurances, it would be impossible to know what judgement to form of many future events, or how to regulate our conduct with respect to them. Confidence therefore in promises, is essential to the intercourse of human life; because, without it, the greatest part of our conduct would proceed upon chance. But there could be no confidence in promises, if men were not obliged to perform them; the obligation therefore to perform promises, is essential to the same ends, and in the same degree.

Some may imagine, that if this obligation were suspended, a general caution and mutual distrust would ensue, which might do as well: but this is imagined, without considering how, every hour of our lives, we trust to, and depend upon, others; and how impossible it is, to stir a step, or, what is worse, to sit still a moment, without such trust and dependence. I am now writing at my ease, not doubting (or rather never distrusting, and therefore never thinking about it) that the butcher will send in the joint of meat which I ordered; that his servant will bring it; that my cook will dress it; that my footman will serve it up; and that I shall find it upon table at one o'clock. Yet have I nothing for all this, but the promise of the butcher, and the implied promise of his servant and mine. And the same holds of the most important as well as the most familiar occurrences of social life. In the one, the intervention of promises is formal, and is seen and acknowledged; our instance, therefore, is intended to show it in the other, where it is not so distinctly observed.

II. *In what sense promises are to be interpreted.*

Where the terms of promise admit of more senses than one, the promise is to be performed "in that sense in which the promiser apprehended, at the time, that the promisee received it."

It is not the sense in which the promiser actually intended it, that always governs the interpretation of an equivocal promise; because, at that rate, you might excite expectations, which you never meant, nor would be obliged to satisfy. Much less is it the sense, in which the promisee actually received the promise; for, according to that rule, you might be drawn into engagements which you never designed to undertake. It must therefore be the sense (for there is no other remaining) in which the promiser believed that the promisee accepted his promise.

This will not differ from the actual intention of the promiser, where the promise is given without collusion or reserve: but we put the rule in the above form, to exclude evasion in cases in which the popular meaning of a phrase, and the strict grammatical signification of the words, differ; or, in general, wherever the promiser attempts to make his escape through some ambiguity in the expressions which he used.

Temures promised the garrison of Sebastia, that, if they would surrender, *no blood should be shed.* The garrison surrendered: and Temures buried them all alive. Now Temures fulfilled the promise in one sense, and in the sense too in which he intended it at the time; but not in the sense in which the garrison of Sebastia actually received it, nor in the sense in which Temures himself knew that the garrison received it: which last sense, according to our rule, was the sense in which he was in conscience bound to have performed it.

From the account we have given of the obligation of promises, it is evident, that this obligation depends upon the *expectations* which we knowingly and voluntarily excite. Consequently, any action or conduct towards another, which we are sensible excites expectations in that other, is as much a promise, and creates as strict an obligation, as the most express assurances. Taking, for instance, a kinsman's child, and educating him for a liberal profession, or in a manner suitable only for the heir of a large fortune, as much obliges us to place him in that profession, or to leave him such a fortune, as if we had given him a promise to do so under our hands and seals. In like manner, a great man, who encourages an indigent retainer; or a minister of state, who distinguishes and caresses at his levee one who is in a situation to be obliged by his patronage; engages, by such behaviour, to provide for him. This is the foundation of *tacit promises.*

You may either simply declare your present intention, or you may accompany your declaration with an engagement to abide by it, which constitutes a complete promise. In the first case, the duty is satisfied, if you were *sincere* at the time, that is, if you entertained at the time the intention you expressed, however soon, or for whatever reason, you afterwards change it. In the latter case, you have parted with the liberty of changing. All this is plain: but it must be observed, that most of those forms of speech, which, strictly taken, amount to no more than declarations of present intention, do yet, in the usual way of understanding them, excite the expectation, and therefore carry with them the force of absolute promises. Such as, "I intend you this place"—"I design to leave you this estate"—"I purpose giving you my vote"—"I mean to serve you." In which, although the "intention," the "design," the "purpose," the "meaning," be expressed in words of the present time, yet you cannot afterwards recede from them without a breach of good faith. If you choose therefore to make known your present intention, and yet to reserve to yourself the liberty of changing it, you must guard your expressions by an additional clause, as, "I intend *at present*," "*if I do not alter*," or the like. And after all, as there can be no reason for communicating your intention, but to excite some degree of expectation or other, a wanton change of an intention which is once disclosed, always disappoints somebody; and is always, for that reason, wrong.

There is, in some men, an infirmity with regard to promises, which often betrays them into great distress. From the confusion, or hesitation, or obscurity, with which they express themselves, especially when overawed or taken by surprise, they sometimes encourage expectations, and bring upon themselves demands, which, possibly, they never dreamed of. This is a want, not so much of integrity, as of presence of mind.

III. *In what cases promises are not binding.*

1. Promises are not binding, where the performance is *impossible*.

But observe, that the promiser is guilty of a fraud, if he be secretly aware of the impossibility, at the time of making the promise. For, when any one promises a thing, he asserts his belief, at least, of the possibility of performing it; as no one can accept or understand a promise under any other supposition. Instances of this sort are the following: The minister promises a place, which he knows to be engaged, or not at his disposal: A father, in settling marriage-articles, promises to leave his daughter an estate, which he knows to be entailed upon the heir male of his family: A merchant promises a ship, or share of a ship, which he is privately advised is lost at sea: An incumbent promises to resign a living, being previously assured that his resignation will not be accepted by the bishop. The promiser, as in these cases, with knowledge of the impossibility, is justly answerable in an equivalent; but otherwise not.

When the promiser himself occasions the impossibility, it is neither more nor less than a direct breach of the promise; as when a soldier maims, or a servant disables himself, to get rid of his engagements.

2. Promises are not binding, where the performance is *unlawful*.

There are two cases of this: one, where the unlawfulness is known to the parties, at the time of making the promise; as where an assassin promises his employer to despatch his rival or his enemy; a servant to betray his master; a pimp to procure a mistress; or a *friend* to give his assistance in a scheme of seduction. The parties in these cases are not obliged to perform what the promise requires, *because they were under a prior obligation to the contrary*. From which prior obligation what is there to discharge them? Their promise— their own act and deed. But an obligation, from which a man can discharge himself by his own act, is no obligation at all. The guilt therefore of such promises lies in the making, not in the breaking of them; and if, in the interval betwixt the promise and the performance, a man so far recover his reflection, as to repent of his engagements, he ought certainly to break through them.

The other case is, where the unlawfulness did not exist, or was not known, at the time of making the promise; as where a merchant promises his correspondent abroad, to send him a ship-load of corn at a time appointed, and before the time arrive, an embargo is laid upon the exportation of corn—A woman gives a promise of marriage; before the marriage, she discovers that her intended husband is too nearly related to her, or that he has a wife yet living. In all such cases, where the contrary does not appear, it must be presumed that the parties supposed what they promised to be lawful, and that the promise proceeded entirely upon this supposition. The lawfulness therefore becomes a condition of the promise; which condition failing, the obligation ceases. Of the same nature was Herod's promise to his daughter-in-law, "that he would give her whatever she asked, even to the half of his kingdom." The promise was not unlawful in the terms in which Herod delivered it; and when it became so by the daughter's choice, by her demanding "John the Baptist's head," Herod was discharged from the obligation of it, for the reason now laid down, as well as for that given in the last paragraph.

This rule, "that promises are void, where the performance is unlawful," extends also to imperfect obligations: for, the reason of the rule holds of all obligations. Thus, if you promise a man a place, or your vote, and he afterwards render himself unfit to receive either, you are absolved from the obligation of your promise; or, if a better candidate appear, and it be a case in which you are bound by oath, or otherwise, to govern yourself by the qualification, the promise must be broken through.

And here I would recommend, to young persons especially, a caution, from the neglect of which many involve themselves in embarrassment and disgrace; and that is, "never to give a promise, which may interfere in the event with their duty"; for, if it do so interfere, their duty must be discharged, though at the expense of their promise, and not unusually of their good name.

The specific performance of promises is reckoned a perfect obligation. And many casuists have laid down, in opposition to what has been here asserted, that, where a perfect and an imperfect obligation clash, the perfect obligation is to be preferred. For which opinion, however, there seems to be no reason, but what arises from the terms "perfect" and "imperfect," the impropriety of which has been remarked above. The truth is, of two contradictory obligations, that ought to prevail which is prior in point of time.

It is the *performance* being unlawful, and not unlawfulness in the subject or motive of the promise, which destroys its validity: therefore a bribe, after the vote is given; the wages of prostitution; the reward of any crime, after the crime is committed; ought, if promised, to be paid. For the sin and mischief, by this supposition, are over; and will be neither more nor less for the performance of the promise.

In like manner, a promise does not lose its obligation merely because it proceeded from an *unlawful motive*. A certain person, in the life-time of his wife, who was then sick, had paid his addresses, and promised marriage, to another woman; the wife died; and the woman demanded performance of the promise. The man, who, it seems, had changed his mind, either felt or pretended doubts concerning the obligation of such a promise, and referred his case to Bishop Sanderson, the most eminent, in this kind of knowledge, of his time. Bishop Sanderson, after writing a dissertation upon the question, adjudged the promise to be void. In which, however, upon our principles, he was wrong: for, however criminal the affection might be, which induced the promise, the performance, when it was demanded, was lawful; which is the only lawfulness required.

A promise cannot be deemed unlawful, where it produces, when performed, no effect, beyond what would have taken place had the promise never been made. And this is the single case, in which the obligation of a promise will justify a conduct, which, unless it had been promised, would be unjust. A captive may lawfully recover his liberty, by a promise of neutrality; for his conqueror takes nothing by the promise, which he might not have secured by his death or confinement; and neutrality would be innocent in him, although criminal in another. It is manifest, however, that promises which come into the place of coercion, can extend no further than to passive compliances; for coercion itself could compel no more. Upon the same principle, promises of secrecy ought not to be violated, although the public would derive advantage from the discovery. Such promises contain no unlawfulness in them, to destroy their obligation: for, as the information would not have been imparted upon any other condition, the public lose nothing by the promise, which they would have gained without it.

3. Promises are not binding, where they *contradict a former promise.*

Because the performance is then unlawful; which resolves this case into the last.

4. Promises are not binding *before acceptance;* that is, before notice given to the promisee; for, where the promise is beneficial, if notice be given, acceptance may be presumed. Until the promise be communicated to the promisee, it is the same only as a resolution in the mind of the promiser, which may be altered at pleasure. For no expectation has been excited, therefore none can be disappointed.

But suppose I declare my intention to a third person, who, without any authority from me, conveys my declaration to the promisee; is that such a notice as will be binding upon me? It certainly is not: for I have not done that which constitutes the essence of a promise—I have not *voluntarily* excited expectation.

5. Promises are not binding which are *released by the promisee.*

This is evident: but it may be sometimes doubted who the promisee is. If I give a promise *to* A, of a place or vote for B; as to a father for his son; to an uncle for his nephew; to a friend of mine, for a relation or friend of his; then A is the promisee, whose consent I must obtain, to be released from the engagement.

If I promise a place or vote to B *by* A, that is, if A be a messenger to convey the promise, as if I should say, "You may tell B that he shall have this place, or may depend upon my vote"; or if A be employed to introduce B's request, and I answer in any terms which amount to a compliance with it: then B is the promisee.

Promises to one person, for the benefit of another, are not released by the death of the promisee: for his death neither makes the performance impracticable, nor implies any consent to release the promiser from it.

6. *Erroneous* promises are not binding in certain cases; as,

1. Where the error proceeds from the mistake or misrepresentation of the promisee.

Because a promise evidently supposes the truth of the account, which the promisee relates in order to obtain it. A beggar solicits your charity, by a story of the most pitiable distress; you promise to relieve him, if he will call again: In the interval you discover his story to be made up of lies; this discovery, no doubt, releases you from your promise. One who wants your service, describes the business or office for which he would engage you; you promise to undertake it; when you come to enter upon it, you find the profits less, the labour more, or some material circumstance different from the account he gave you: In such case, you are not bound by your promise.

2. When the promise is understood by the promisee to proceed upon a certain supposition, or when the promiser apprehended it to be so understood, and that supposition turns out to be false; then the promise is not binding.

This intricate rule will be best explained by an example. A father receives an account from abroad, of the death of his only son; soon after which, he promises his fortune to his nephew. The account turns out to be false. The father, we say, is released from his promise; not merely because he never would have made it, had he known the truth of the case, for that alone will not do; but because the nephew also himself understood the promise to proceed upon the supposition of his cousin's death: or, at least, his uncle thought he so understood it; and could not think otherwise. The promise proceeded upon this supposition in the promiser's own apprehension, and as he believed, in the apprehension of both parties; and this belief of his, is the precise circumstance which sets him free. The foundation of the rule is plainly this: a man is bound only to satisfy the expectation which he intended to excite; whatever condition therefore he intended to subject that expectation to, becomes an essential condition of the promise.

Errors, which come not within this description, do not annul the obligation of a promise. I promise a candidate my vote; presently another candidate appears, for whom I certainly would have reserved it, had I been acquainted with his design. Here therefore, as before, my promise proceeded from an error; and I never should have given such a promise, had I been aware of the truth of the case, as it has turned out. But the *promisee* did not know this; *he* did not receive the promise, subject to any such condition, or as proceeding from any such supposition; nor did I at the time imagine he so received it. This error, therefore, of mine, must fall upon my own head, and the promise be observed notwithstanding. A father promises a certain fortune with his daughter, supposing himself to be worth so much—his circumstances turn out, upon examination, worse than he was aware of. Here again the promise was erroneous, but, for the reason assigned in the last case, will nevertheless be obligatory.

The case of erroneous promises, is attended with some difficulty: for, to allow every mistake, or change of circumstances, to dissolve the obligation of a promise, would be to allow a latitude, which might evacuate the force of almost all promises: and, on the other hand, to gird the obligation so tight, as to make no allowances for manifest and fundamental errors, would, in many instances, be productive of great hardship and absurdity.

It has long been controverted amongst moralists, whether promises be binding, which are extorted by violence or fear. The obligation of all promises results, we have seen, from the necessity or the use of that confidence which mankind repose in them. The question, therefore, whether these promises are binding, will depend upon this; whether mankind, upon the whole, are bene-fited by the confidence placed on such promises? A highwayman attacks you—and being disappointed of his booty, threatens or prepares to murder you; you promise, with many solemn assever-ations, that if he will spare your life, he shall find a purse of money left for him, at a place appointed; upon the faith of this promise, he forbears from further violence. Now, your life was saved by the confidence reposed in a promise extorted by fear; and the lives of many others may be saved by the same. This is a good conse-quence. On the other hand, confidence in promises like these, greatly facilitates the perpetration of robberies: they may be made the instruments of almost unlimited extortion. This is a bad con-sequence: and in the question between the importance of these opposite consequences, resides the doubt concerning the obliga-tions of such promises.

There are other cases which are plainer; as where a magistrate confines a disturber of the public peace in gaol, till he promise to behave better; or a prisoner of war promises, if set at liberty, to return within a certain time. These promises, say moralists, are binding, because the violence or duress is just; but, the truth is, because there is the same use of confidence in these promises, as of confidence in the promises of a person at perfect liberty.

———

Vows are promises to God. The obligation cannot be made out upon the same principle as that of other promises. The violation of them, nevertheless, implies a want of reverence to the Supreme Being; which is enough to make it sinful.

There appears no command or encouragement in the Christian Scriptures to make vows; much less any authority to break through them when they are made. The few instances* of vows which we read of in the New Testament, were religiously observed.

The rules we have laid down concerning promises, are applicable to vows. Thus Jephtha's vow, taken in the sense in which that transaction is commonly understood, was not binding; because the performance, in that contingency, became unlawful.

Chapter 6
CONTRACTS

A contract is a mutual promise. The obligation therefore of contracts, the sense in which they are to be interpreted, and the cases where they are not binding, will be the same as of promises.

From the principle established in the last chapter, "that the obligation of promises is to be measured by the expectation which the promiser any how voluntarily and knowingly excites," results a rule, which governs the construction of all contracts, and is capable, from its simplicity, of being applied with great ease and certainty, *viz.* That

*Acts xviii. 18; xxi. 23.

Whatever is expected by one side, and known to be so expected by the other, is to be deemed a part or condition of the contract.

The several kinds of contracts, and the order in which we propose to consider them, may be exhibited at one view, thus:

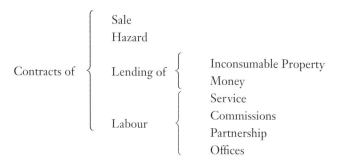

Contracts of {
  Sale
  Hazard
  Lending of { Inconsumable Property
               Money
  Labour { Service
           Commissions
           Partnership
           Offices

Chapter 7
CONTRACTS OF SALE

The rule of justice, which wants with most anxiety to be inculcated in the making of bargains, is, that the seller is bound in conscience to disclose the faults of what he offers to sale. Amongst other methods of proving this, one may be the following:

I suppose it will be allowed, that to advance a direct falsehood, in recommendation of our wares, by ascribing to them some quality which we know that they have not, is dishonest. Now compare with this the designed concealment of some fault, which we know that they have. The motives and the effects of actions are the only points of comparison, in which their moral quality can differ: but the motive in these two cases is the same, *viz.* to procure a higher price than we expect otherwise to obtain: the effect, that is, the prejudice to the buyer, is also the same; for he finds himself equally out of pocket by his bargain, whether the commodity, when he gets home with it, turn out worse than he had supposed, by the want of some quality which he expected, or the discovery of some fault which he did not expect. If therefore actions be the same, as to all moral purposes, which proceed from the same motives, and produce the same effects; it is making a distinction without a difference, to esteem it a *cheat* to magnify beyond the truth the virtues of what we have to sell, but none to conceal its faults.

It adds to the value of this kind of honesty, that the faults of many things are of a nature not to be known by any, but by the persons who have used them; so that the buyer has no security from imposition, but in the ingenuousness and integrity of the seller.

There is one exception however to this rule; namely, where the silence of the seller implies some fault in the thing to be sold, and where the buyer has a compensation in the price for the risk which he runs: as where a horse, in a London repository, is sold by public auction, without warranty; the want of warranty is notice of some unsoundness, and produces a proportionable abatement in the price.

To this of concealing the faults of what we want to put off, may be referred the practice of passing bad money. This practice we sometimes hear defended by a vulgar excuse, that we have taken the money for good, and must therefore get rid of it. Which excuse is much the same as if one, who had been robbed upon the highway, should allege that he had a right to reimburse himself out of the pocket of the first traveller he met; the justice of which reasoning, the traveller possibly may not comprehend.

Where there exists no monopoly or combination, the market-price is always a fair price; because it will always be proportionable to the use and scarcity of the article. Hence, there need be no scruple about demanding or taking the market-price; and all those expressions, "provisions are extravagantly dear," "corn bears an unreasonable price," and the like, import no unfairness or unreasonableness in the seller.

If your tailor or your draper charge, or even ask of you, more for a suit of clothes, than the market-price, you complain that you are imposed upon; you pronounce the tradesman who makes such a charge, dishonest: although, as the man's goods were his own, and he had a right to prescribe the terms upon which he would consent to part with them, it may be questioned what dishonesty there can be in the case, or wherein the imposition consists. Whoever opens a shop, or in any manner exposes goods to public sale, virtually engages to deal with his customers at a market-price; because it is upon the faith and opinion of such an engagement, that any one comes within his shop-doors, or offers to treat with him. This is expected by the buyer; is known to be so expected by the seller; which is enough, according to the rule delivered above, to make it a part of the contract between them, though not a syllable be said about it. The breach of this implied contract constitutes the fraud inquired after.

Hence, if you disclaim any such engagement, you may set what value you please upon your property. If, upon being asked to sell a house, you answer that the house suits your fancy or conveniency, and that you will not turn yourself out of it, under such a price; the price fixed may be double of what the house cost, or would fetch at a public sale, without any imputation of injustice or extortion upon you.

If the thing sold, be damaged, or perish, between the sale and the delivery, ought the buyer to bear the loss, or the seller? This will depend upon the particular construction of the contract. If the seller, either expressly, or by implication, or by custom, engage to *deliver* the goods; as if I buy a set of china, and the china-man ask me to what place he shall bring or send them, and they be broken in the conveyance, the seller must abide by the loss. If the thing sold, remain with the seller, at the instance, or for the conveniency of the buyer, then the buyer undertakes the risk; as if I buy a horse, and mention, that I will send for it on such a day (which is in effect desiring that it may continue with the seller till I do send for it), then, whatever misfortune befalls the horse in the mean time, must be at my cost.

And here, once for all, I would observe, that innumerable questions of this sort are determined solely by *custom;* not that custom possesses any proper authority to alter or ascertain the nature of right and wrong; but because the contracting parties are presumed to include in their stipulation, all the conditions which custom has annexed to contracts of the same sort: and when the usage is notorious, and no exception made to it, this presumption is generally agreeable to the fact.*

If I order a pipe of port from a wine-merchant abroad; at what period the property passes from the merchant to me; whether upon delivery of the wine at the merchant's warehouse; upon its being put on shipboard at Oporto; upon the arrival of the ship in England; at its destined port; or not till the wine be committed to my servants, or deposited in my cellar; are all questions which admit of no decision, but what custom points out. Whence, in justice, as well as law, what is called the *custom of merchants*, regulates the construction of mercantile concerns.

Chapter 8
CONTRACTS OF HAZARD

By Contracts of Hazard, I mean gaming and insurance.

What some say of this kind of contracts, "that one side ought not to have any advantage over the other," is neither practicable

---

* It happens here, as in many cases, that what the parties ought to do, and what a judge or arbitrator would award to be done, may be very different. What the parties ought to do by virtue of their contract, depends upon their consciousness at the time of making it; whereas a third person finds it necessary to found his judgement upon presumptions, which presumptions may be false, although the most probable that he could proceed by.

nor true. It is not practicable; for that perfect equality of skill and judgement, which this rule requires, is seldom to be met with. I might not have it in my power to play with fairness a game at cards, billiards, or tennis; lay a wager at a horse-race; or underwrite a policy of insurance, once in a twelve-month, if I must wait till I meet with a person, whose art, skill, and judgement, in these matters, is neither greater nor less than my own. Nor is this equality requisite to the justice of the contract. One party may give to the other the whole of the stake, if he please, and the other party may justly accept it, if it be given him; much more therefore may one give to the other a part of the stake; or, what is exactly the same thing, an advantage in the chance of winning the whole.

The proper restriction is, that neither side have an advantage by means of which the other is not aware; for this is an advantage taken, without being *given*. Although the event be still an uncertainty, your advantage in the chance has a certain value; and so much of the stake, as that value amounts to, is taken from your adversary without his knowledge, and therefore without his consent. If I sit down to a game at whist, and have an advantage over the adversary, by means of a better memory, closer attention, or a superior knowledge of the rules and chances of the game, the advantage is fair; because it is obtained by means of which the adversary is aware: for he is aware, when he sits down with me, that I shall exert the skill that I possess to the utmost. But if I gain an advantage by packing the cards, glancing my eye into the adversaries' hands, or by concerted signals with my partner, it is a dishonest advantage; because it depends upon means which the adversary never suspects that I make use of.

The same distinction holds of all contracts into which chance enters. If I lay a wager at a horse-race, founded upon the conjecture I form from the appearance, and character, and breed, of the horses, I am justly entitled to any advantage which my judgment gives me: but, if I carry on a clandestine correspondence with the jockeys, and find out from them, that a trial has been actually made, or that it is

settled beforehand which horse shall win the race; all such information is so much fraud, because derived from sources which the other
did not suspect, when he proposed or accepted the wager.

In speculations in trade, or in the stocks, if I exercise my judgement upon the general aspect and prospect of public affairs, and
deal with a person who conducts himself by the same sort of
judgement; the contract has all the equality in it which is necessary: but if I have access to secrets of state at home, or private
advice of some decisive measure or event abroad, I cannot avail
myself of these advantages with justice, because they are excluded
by the contract, which proceeded upon the supposition that I had
no such advantage.

In insurances, in which the underwriter computes his risk
entirely from the account given by the person insured, it is absolutely necessary to the justice and validity of the contract, that this
account be exact and complete.

Chapter 9
CONTRACTS OF LENDING OF
INCONSUMABLE PROPERTY

When the identical loan is to be returned, as a book, a horse, a
harpsichord, it is called *inconsumable;* in opposition to corn, wine,
money, and those things which perish, or are parted with, in the
use, and can therefore only be restored in kind.

The questions under this head are few and simple. The first is, if
the thing lent be lost or damaged, who ought to bear the loss or damage? If it be damaged by the use, or by accident in the use, for which
it was lent, the lender ought to bear it; as if I hire a job-coach, the
wear, tear, and soiling of the coach, must belong to the lender; or a

horse, to go a particular journey, and in going the proposed journey, the horse die, or be lamed, the loss must be the lender's: on the contrary, if the damage be occasioned by the fault of the borrower, or by accident in some use for which it was not lent, then the borrower must make it good; as if the coach be overturned or broken to pieces by the carelessness of your coachman; or the horse be hired to take a morning's ride upon, and you go a hunting with him, or leap him over hedges, or put him into your cart or carriage, and he be strained, or staked, or galled, or accidentally hurt, or drop down dead, whilst you are thus using him; you must make satisfaction to the owner.

The two cases are distinguished by this circumstance: that in one case, the owner foresees the damage or risk, and therefore consents to undertake it; in the other case he does not.

It is possible that an estate or a house may, during the term of a lease, be so increased or diminished in its value, as to become worth much more, or much less, than the rent agreed to be paid for it. In some of which cases it may be doubted, to whom, of natural right, the advantage or disadvantage belongs. The rule of justice seems to be this: If the alteration might be *expected* by the parties, the hirer must take the consequence; if it could not, the owner. An orchard, or a vineyard, or a mine, or a fishery, or a decoy, may this yield nothing, or next to nothing, yet the tenant shall pay his rent; and if they next year produce tenfold the usual profit, no more shall be demanded; because the produce is in its nature precarious, and this variation might be expected. If an estate in the fens of Lincolnshire, or the isle of Ely, be overflowed with water, so as to be incapable of occupation, the tenant, notwithstanding, is bound by his lease; because he entered into it with a knowledge and foresight of the danger. On the other hand, if, by the irruption of the sea into a country where it was never known to have come before, by the change of the course of a river, the fall of a rock, the breaking out of a volcano, the bursting of a moss, the incursions of an enemy, or by a mortal contagion amongst the cattle; if, by means like these, an estate change or lose its value, the loss shall fall upon the owner; that is, the tenant shall either be discharged from his agreement, or be entitled to an abatement of rent. A house in London, by the building of a bridge, the opening of a new road or street, may become of ten times its former value; and, by contrary causes, may be as much reduced in value: here also, as before, the owner, not the hirer, shall be affected by the alteration. The reason upon which our determination proceeds is this; that changes such as these, being neither foreseen, nor provided for, by the contracting parties, form no part or condition of the contract; and therefore ought to have the same effect as if no contract at all had been made (for none was made with respect to *them*), that is, ought to fall upon the owner.

Chapter 10
CONTRACTS CONCERNING THE LENDING OF MONEY

There exists no reason in the law of nature, why a man should not be paid for the lending of his money, as well as of any other property into which the money might be converted.

The scruples that have been entertained upon this head, and upon the foundation of which, the receiving of interest or usury (for they formerly meant the same thing) was once prohibited in almost all Christian countries,* arose from a passage in the law of

---

* By a statute of JAMES the First, interest above eight pounds per cent. was prohibited (and consequently under that rate allowed), with this sage provision: *That this statute shall not be construed or expounded to allow the practice of usury in point of religion or conscience.*

Moses, Deuteronomy, xxiii. 19, 20: "Thou shalt not lend upon usury to thy brother; usury of money, usury of victuals, usury of any thing that is lent upon usury: unto a stranger thou mayest lend upon usury; but unto thy brother thou shalt not lend upon usury."

This prohibition is now generally understood to have been intended for the Jews alone, as part of the civil or political law of that nation, and calculated to preserve amongst themselves that distribution of property, to which many of their institutions were subservient; as the marriage of an heiress within her own tribe; of a widow who was left childless, to her husband's brother; the year of jubilee, when alienated estates reverted to the family of the original proprietor—regulations which were never thought to be binding upon any but the commonwealth of Israel.

This interpretation is confirmed, I think, beyond all controversy, by the distinction made in the law, between a Jew and a foreigner: "unto a stranger thou mayest lend upon usury, but unto thy brother thou mayest not lend upon usury"; a distinction which could hardly have been admitted into a law, which the Divine Author intended to be of moral and of universal obligation.

The rate of interest has in most countries been regulated by law. The Roman law allowed of twelve pounds per cent., which Justinian reduced at one stroke to four pounds. A statute of the thirteenth year of Queen Elizabeth, which was the first that tolerated the receiving of interest in England at all, restrained it to ten pounds per cent.; a statute of James the First, to eight pounds; of Charles the Second, to six pounds; of Queen Anne, to five pounds, on pain of forfeiture of treble the value of the money lent: at which rate and penalty the matter now stands. The policy of these regulations is, to check the power of accumulating wealth without industry; to give encouragement to trade, by enabling adventurers in it to borrow money at a moderate price; and of late years, to enable the state to borrow the subject's money itself.

Compound interest, though forbidden by the law of England, is agreeable enough to natural equity; for interest detained after it is due, becomes, to all intents and purposes, part of the sum lent.

It is a question which sometimes occurs, how money borrowed in one country ought to be paid in another, where the relative value of the precious metals is not the same. For example, suppose I borrow a hundred guineas in London, where each guinea is worth one-and-twenty shillings, and meet my creditor in the East Indies, where a guinea is worth no more perhaps than nineteen; is it a satisfaction of the debt to return a hundred guineas, or must I make up so many times one-and-twenty shillings? I should think the latter; for it must be presumed, that my creditor, had he not lent me his guineas, would have disposed of them in such a manner, as to have now had, in the place of them, so many one-and-twenty shillings; and the question supposes that he neither intended, nor ought to be a sufferer, by parting with the possession of his money to me.

When the relative value of coin is altered by an act of the state, if the alteration would have extended to the identical pieces which were lent, it is enough to return an equal number of pieces of the same denomination, or their present value in any other. As, if guineas were reduced by act of parliament to twenty shillings, so many twenty shillings, as I borrowed guineas, would be a just repayment. It would be otherwise, if the reduction was owing to a debasement of the coin; for then respect ought to be had to the comparative value of the old guinea and the new.

Whoever borrows money is bound in conscience to repay it. This, every man can see; but every man cannot see, or does not however reflect, that he is, in consequence, also bound to use the means necessary to enable himself to repay it. "If he pay the money when he has it, or has it to spare, he does all that an honest man can do," and all, he imagines, that is required of him; whilst the previous measures, which are necessary to furnish him with that money, he makes no part of his care, nor observes to be as much his duty as the other; such as selling a family-seat or a family estate, contracting his plan of expense, laying down his equipage, reducing the number of his servants, or any of those humiliating sacrifices, which justice requires of a man in debt, the moment he perceives that he has no reasonable prospect of paying his debts without them. An expectation which depends upon the continuance of his own life, will not satisfy an honest man, if a better provision be in his power; for it is a breach of faith to subject a creditor, when we can help it, to the risk of our life, be the event what it will; that not being the security to which credit was given.

I know few subjects which have been more misunderstood, than the law which authorises the imprisonment of insolvent debtors. It has been represented as a gratuitous cruelty, which contributed nothing to the reparation of the creditor's loss, or to the advantage of the community. This prejudice arises principally from considering the sending of a debtor to gaol, as an act of private satisfaction to the creditor, instead of a public punishment. As an act of satisfaction or revenge, it is always wrong in the motive, and often intemperate and undistinguishing in the exercise. Consider it as a public punishment; founded upon the same reason, and subject to the same rules, as other punishments; and the justice of it, together with the degree to which it should be extended, and the objects upon whom it may be inflicted, will be apparent. There are frauds relating to insolvency, against which it is as necessary to provide punishment, as for any public crimes whatever: as where a man gets your money into his possession, and forthwith runs away with it; or, what is little better, squanders it in vicious expenses; or stakes it at the gaming-table; in the Alley; or upon wild adventures in trade; or is conscious at the time he borrows it, that he can never repay it; or wilfully puts it out of his power, by profuse living; or conceals his effects, or transfers them by collusion to another: not to mention the obstinacy of some debtors, who had rather rot in a gaol, than deliver up their estates; for, to say the truth, the first absurdity is in the law itself, which leaves it in a debtor's power to withhold any part of his property from the claim of his creditors. The only question is, whether the punishment be properly placed in the hands of an exasperated creditor: for which it may be said, that these frauds are so subtile and versatile, that nothing but a discretionary power can overtake them; and that no discretion is likely to be so well informed, so vigilant, or so active, as that of the creditor.

It must be remembered, however, that the confinement of a debtor in gaol is a *punishment;* and that every punishment supposes a crime. To pursue, therefore, with the extremity of legal rigour, a sufferer, whom the fraud or failure of others, his own want of capacity, or the disappointments and miscarriages to which all human affairs are subject, have reduced to ruin, merely because we are provoked by our loss, and seek to relieve the pain we feel by that which we inflict, is repugnant not only to humanity, but to justice: for it is to pervert a provision of law, designed for a different and a salutary purpose, to the gratification of private spleen and resentment. Any alteration in these laws, which could distinguish the degrees of guilt, or convert the service of the insolvent debtor to some public profit, might be an improvement; but any considerable mitigation of their rigour, under colour of relieving the poor, would increase their hardships. For whatever deprives the creditor of his power of coercion, deprives him of his security; and as this must add greatly to the difficulty of obtaining credit, the poor, especially the lower sort of tradesmen, are the first who would suffer by such a regulation. As tradesmen must buy *before* they sell, you would exclude from trade two thirds of those who now carry it on, if none were enabled to enter into it without a capital sufficient for prompt payments. An advocate, therefore, for the interests of this important class of the community, will deem it more eligible, that one out of a thousand should be sent to gaol by his creditors, than that the nine hundred and ninety-nine should be straitened and embarrassed, and many of them lie idle, by the want of credit.

Chapter 11
CONTRACTS OF LABOUR

Service

Service in this country is, as it ought to be, voluntary, and by contract; and the master's authority extends no further than the terms or equitable construction of the contract will justify.

The treatment of servants, as to diet, discipline, and accommodation, the kind and quantity of work to be required of them, the intermission, liberty, and indulgence to be allowed them, must be determined in a great measure by custom; for where the contract involves so many particulars, the contracting parties express a few perhaps of the principal, and, by mutual understanding, refer the rest to the known custom of the country in like cases.

A servant is not bound to obey the unlawful commands of his master; to minister, for instance, to his unlawful pleasures; or to assist him by unlawful practices in his profession; as in smuggling or adulterating the articles in which he deals. For the servant is bound by nothing but his own promise; and the obligation of a promise extends not to things unlawful.

For the same reason, the master's authority is no *justification* of the servant in doing wrong; for the servant's own promise, upon which that authority is founded, would be none.

Clerks and apprentices ought to be employed entirely in the profession or trade which they are intended to learn. Instruction is their hire; and to deprive them of the opportunities of instruction, by taking up their time with occupations foreign to their business, is to defraud them of their wages.

The master is responsible for what a servant does in the ordinary course of his employment; for it is done under a general authority committed to him, which is in justice equivalent to a specific direction. Thus, if I pay money to a banker's clerk, the banker is accountable; but not if I had paid it to his butler or his footman, whose business it is not to receive money. Upon the same principle, if I once send a servant to take up goods upon credit, whatever goods he afterwards takes up at the same shop, so long as he continues in my service, are justly chargeable to my account.

The law of this country goes great lengths in intending a kind of concurrence in the master, so as to charge him with the consequences of his servant's conduct. If an inn-keeper's servant rob his guests, the inn-keeper must make restitution; if a farrier's servant lame a horse, the farrier must answer for the damage; and still further, if your coachman or carter drive over a passenger in the road, the passenger may recover from you a satisfaction for the hurt he suffers. But these determinations stand, I think, rather upon the authority of the law, than any principle of natural justice.

There is a carelessness and facility in "giving characters," as it is called, of servants, especially when given in writing, or according to some established form, which, to speak plainly of it, is a cheat upon those who accept them. They are given with so little reserve and veracity, "that I should as soon depend," says the author of the Rambler, "upon an acquittal at the Old Bailey, by way of recommendation of a servant's honesty, as upon one of these characters." It is sometimes carelessness; and sometimes also to get rid of a bad servant without the uneasiness of a dispute; for which nothing can be pleaded but the most ungenerous of all excuses, that the person whom we deceive is a stranger.

There is a conduct the reverse of this, but more injurious, because the injury falls where there is no remedy; I mean the obstructing of a servant's advancement, because you are unwilling to spare his service. To stand in the way of your servant's interest, is a poor return for his fidelity; and affords slender encouragement for good behaviour, in this numerous and therefore important part of the community. It is a piece of injustice which, if practised towards an equal, the law of honour would lay hold of; as it is, it is neither uncommon nor disreputable.

A master of a family is culpable, if he permit any vices among his domestics, which he might restrain by due discipline, and a proper interference. This results from the general obligation to prevent misery when in our power; and the assurance which we have, that vice and misery at the long run go together. Care to maintain in his family a sense of virtue and religion, received the Divine approbation in the person of ABRAHAM, Gen. xviii. 19: "I know him, that he will command his children, and *his household* after him; and they shall keep the way of the LORD, to do justice and judgement." And indeed no authority seems so well adapted to this purpose, as that of masters of families; because none operates upon the subjects of it with an influence so immediate and constant.

What the Christian Scriptures have delivered concerning the relation and reciprocal duties of masters and servants, breathes a spirit of liberality, very little known in ages when servitude was slavery; and which flowed from a habit of contemplating mankind under the common relation in which they stand to their Creator, and with respect to their interest in another existence:* "Servants, be obedient to them that are your masters, according to the flesh, with fear and trembling; in singleness of your heart, as unto

---

*Eph. vi. 5–9.

Christ; not with eye-service, as men-pleasers, but as the servants of Christ, doing the will of God from the heart; *with good will, doing service as to the Lord, and not to men;* knowing that whatsoever good thing any man doeth, the same shall he receive of the LORD, whether he be bond or free. And ye masters, do the same thing unto them, forbearing threatening; *knowing that your Master also is in heaven;* neither is there respect of persons with him." The idea of referring their service to God, of considering *him* as having appointed them their task, that they were doing *his* will, and were to look to *him* for their reward, was new; and affords a greater security to the master than any inferior principle, because it tends to produce a steady and cordial obedience, in the place of that constrained service, which can never be trusted out of sight, and which is justly enough called eye-service. The exhortation to masters, to keep in view their own subjection and accountableness, was no less seasonable.

Chapter 12
CONTRACTS OF LABOUR

Commissions

Whoever undertakes another man's business, makes it his own, that is, promises to employ upon it the same care, attention, and diligence, that he would do if it were actually his own: for he knows that the business was committed to him with that expectation. And he promises nothing more than this. Therefore an agent is not obliged to wait, inquire, solicit, ride about the country, toil, or study, whilst there remains a possibility of benefiting his employer. If he exert so much of his activity, and use such caution, as the value of the business, in his judgement, deserves; that is, as he would have thought sufficient if the same interest of his own had been at stake, he has discharged his duty, although it should afterwards turn out, that by more activity, and longer perseverance, he might have concluded the business with greater advantage.

This rule defines the duty of factors, stewards, attorneys, and advocates.

One of the chief difficulties of an agent's situation is, to know how far he may depart from his instructions, when, from some change or discovery in the circumstances of his commission, he sees reason to believe that his employer, if he were present, would alter his intention. The latitude allowed to agents in this respect will be different, according as the commission was confidential or ministerial; and according as the general rule and nature of the service require a prompt and precise obedience to orders, or not. An attorney, sent to treat for an estate, if he found out a flaw in the title, would desist from proposing the price he was directed to propose; and very properly. On the other hand, if the commander-in-chief of an army detach an officer under him upon a particular service, which service turns out more difficult, or less expedient, than was supposed; insomuch that the officer is convinced, that his commander, if he were acquainted with the true state in which the affair is found, would recall his orders; yet must this officer, if he cannot wait for fresh directions without prejudice to the expedition he is sent upon, pursue, at all hazards, those which he brought out with him.

What is trusted to an agent, may be lost or damaged in his hands by *misfortune*. An agent who acts without pay, is clearly not answerable for the loss; for, if he give his labour for nothing, it cannot be presumed that he gave also security for the success of it. If the agent be hired to the business, the question will depend upon the apprehension of the parties at the time of making the contract; which apprehension of theirs must be collected chiefly from custom, by which probably it was guided. Whether a public carrier ought to account for goods sent by him; the owner or master of a ship for the cargo; the post-office for letters, or bills enclosed in letters, where the loss is not imputed to any fault or neglect of theirs; are questions of this sort. Any expression which by implication amounts to a promise, will be binding upon the agent, without custom; as where the proprietors of a stage-coach advertise that they will *not* be accountable for money, plate, or jewels, this makes them accountable for every thing else; or where the price is too much for the labour, part of it may be considered as a premium for insurance. On the other hand, any caution on the part of the owner to guard against danger, is evidence that he considers the risk to be his: as cutting a bank-bill in two, to send by the post at different times.

Universally, unless a *promise*, either express or tacit, can be proved against the agent, the loss must fall upon the owner.

The agent may be a sufferer in his own person or property by the business which he undertakes; as where one goes a journey for another, and lames his horse, or is hurt himself by a fall upon the road; can the agent in such a case claim a compensation for the misfortune? Unless the same be provided for by express stipulation, the agent is not entitled to any compensation from his employer on that account: for where the danger is not foreseen, there can be no reason to believe that the employer engaged to indemnify the agent against it: still less where it is foreseen: for whoever knowingly undertakes a dangerous employment, in common construction, takes upon himself the danger and the consequences; as where a fireman undertakes for a reward to rescue a box of writings from the flames; or a sailor to bring off a passenger from a ship in a storm.

Chapter 13
CONTRACTS OF LABOUR

Partnership

I know nothing upon the subject of partnership that requires explanation, but in what manner the profits are to be divided, where one partner contributes money, and the other labour; which is a common case.

Rule. From the stock of the partnership deduct the sum advanced, and divide the remainder between the moneyed partner and the labouring partner, in the proportion of the interest of the money to the wages of the labourer, allowing such a rate of interest as money might be borrowed for upon the same security, and such wages as a journeyman would require for the same labour and trust.

Example. A advances a thousand pounds, but knows nothing of the business; B produces no money, but has been brought up to the business, and undertakes to conduct it. At the end of the year, the stock and the effects of the partnership amount to twelve hundred pounds; consequently there are two hundred pounds to be divided. Now, nobody would lend money upon the event of the business succeeding, which is A's security, under six per cent.; therefore A must be allowed sixty pounds for the interest of his money. B, before he engaged in the partnership, earned thirty pounds a year, in the same employment; his labour therefore ought to be valued at thirty pounds: and the two hundred pounds must be divided between the parties in the proportion of sixty to thirty: that is, A must receive one hundred and thirty-three pounds six shillings and eight pence, and B sixty-six pounds thirteen shillings and four pence.

If there be nothing gained, A loses his interest, and B his labour; which is right. If the original stock be diminished, by this rule B loses only his labour, as before; whereas A loses his interest, and part of the principal; for which eventual disadvantage A is compensated, by having the interest of his money computed at six per cent. in the division of the profits, when there are any.

It is true that the division of the profit is seldom forgotten in the constitution of the partnership, and is therefore commonly settled by express agrecments: but these agreements, to be equitable, should pursue the principle of the rule here laid down.

All the partners are bound to what any one of them does in the course of the business; for, *quoad hoc*, each partner is considered as an authorised agent for the rest.

Chapter 14
CONTRACTS OF LABOUR

Offices

In many offices, as schools, fellowships of colleges, professorships of the universities, and the like, there is a two-fold contract; one with the founder, the other with the electors.

The contract with the founder obliges the incumbent of the office to discharge every duty appointed by the charter, statutes, deed of gift, or will of the founder; because the endowment was given, and consequently accepted, for that purpose, and upon those conditions.

The contract with the electors extends this obligation to all duties that have been *customarily* connected with and reckoned a part of the office, though not prescribed by the founder; for the electors expect from the person they choose, all the duties which his predecessors have discharged; and as the person elected cannot be ignorant of their expectation, if he meant to have refused this condition, he ought to have apprised them of his objection.

And here let it be observed, that the electors can excuse the conscience of the person elected, from this last class of duties alone; because this class results from a contract to which the electors and the person elected are the only parties. The other class of duties results from a different contract.

It is a question of some magnitude and difficulty, what offices may be conscientiously supplied by a deputy.

We will state the several objections to the substitution of a deputy; and then it will be understood, that a deputy may be allowed in all cases to which these objections do not apply.

An office may not be discharged by deputy,

1. Where a particular confidence is reposed in the judgement and conduct of the person appointed to it; as the office of a steward, guardian, judge, commander-in-chief by land or sea.

2. Where the custom hinders; as in the case of schoolmasters, tutors, and of commissions in the army or navy.

3. Where the duty cannot, from its nature, be so well performed by a deputy; as the deputy-governor of a province may not possess the legal authority, or the actual influence, of his principal.

4. When some inconveniency would result to the service in general from the permission of deputies in such cases: for example, it is probable that military merit would be much discouraged, if the duties belonging to commissions in the army were generally allowed to be executed by substitutes.

The non-residence of the parochial clergy, who supply the duty of their benefices by curates, is worthy of a more distinct consideration. And in order to draw the question upon this case to a point, we will suppose the officiating curate to discharge every duty which his principal, were he present, would be bound to discharge, and in a manner equally beneficial to the parish: under which circumstances, the only objection to the absence of the principal, at least the only one of the foregoing objections, is the last.

And, in my judgement, the force of this objection will be much diminished, if the absent rector or vicar be, in the mean time, engaged in any function or employment of equal, or of greater, importance to the general interest of religion. For the whole revenue of the national church may properly enough be considered as a common fund for the support of the national religion; and if a clergyman be serving the cause of Christianity and protestantism, it can make little difference, out of what particular portion of this fund, that is, by the tithes and glebe of what particular parish, his service be requited; any more than it can prejudice the king's service that an officer who has signalised his merit in America, should be rewarded with the government of a fort or castle in Ireland, which he never saw; but for the custody of which, proper provision is made, and care taken.

Upon the principle thus explained, this indulgence is due to none more than to those who are occupied in cultivating or communicating religious knowledge, or the sciences subsidiary to religion.

This way of considering the revenues of the church as a common fund for the same purpose, is the more equitable, as the value of particular preferments bears no proportion to the particular charge or labour.

But when a man draws upon this fund, whose studies and employments bear no relation to the object of it, and who is no further a minister of the Christian religion than as a cockade makes a soldier, it seems a misapplication little better than a robbery.

And to those who have the management of such matters I submit this question, whether the impoverishment of the fund, by converting the best share of it into *annuities* for the gay and illiterate youth of great families, threatens not to starve and stifle the little clerical merit that is left amongst us?

All legal dispensations from residence proceed upon the supposition, that the absentee is detained from his living by some engagement of equal or of greater public importance. Therefore, if, in a case where no such reason can with truth be pleaded, it be said that this question regards a right of property, and that all right of property awaits the disposition of law; that, therefore, if the law, which gives a man the emoluments of a living, excuse him from residing upon it, he is excused in conscience; we answer that the law does not excuse him *by intention*, and that all other excuses are fraudulent.

Chapter 15
LIES

A lie is a breach of promise: for whoever seriously addresses his discourse to another, tacitly promises to speak the truth, because he knows that the truth is expected.

Or the obligation of veracity may be made out from the direct ill consequences of lying to social happiness. Which consequences consist, either in some specific injury to particular individuals, or in the destruction of that confidence which is essential to the intercourse of human life; for which latter reason, a lie may be pernicious in its general tendency, and therefore criminal, though it produce no particular or visible mischief to any one.

There are falsehoods which are not lies; that is, which are not criminal: as,

1. Where no one is deceived; which is the case in parables, fables, novels, jests, tales to create mirth, ludicrous embellishments of a story, where the declared design of the speaker is not to inform, but to divert; compliments in the subscription of a letter, a servant's *denying* his master, a prisoner's pleading not guilty, an advocate asserting the justice, or his belief of the justice, of his client's cause. In such instances, no confidence is destroyed, because none

was reposed; no promise to speak the truth is violated, because none was given, or understood to be given.

2. Where the person to whom you speak has no right to know the truth, or, more properly, where little or no inconveniency results from the want of confidence in such cases; as where you tell a falsehood to a madman, for his own advantage; to a robber, to conceal your property; to an assassin, to defeat or divert him from his purpose. The particular consequence is by the supposition beneficial; and, as to the general consequence, the worst that can happen is, that the madman, the robber, the assassin, will not trust you again; which (beside that the first is incapable of deducing regular conclusions from having been once deceived, and the last two not likely to come a second time in your way) is sufficiently compensated by the immediate benefit which you propose by the falsehood.

It is upon this principle, that, by the laws of war, it is allowed to deceive an enemy by feints, false colours,* spies, false intelligence, and the like; but by no means in treaties, truces, signals of capitulation or surrender: and the difference is, that the former suppose hostilities to continue, the latter are calculated to terminate or suspend them. In the *conduct* of war, and whilst the war continues, there is no use, or rather no place, for confidence betwixt the contending parties; but in whatever relates to the *termination* of war, the most religious fidelity is expected, because without it wars could not cease, nor the victors be secure, but by the entire destruction of the vanquished.

Many people indulge, in serious discourse, a habit of fiction and exaggeration, in the accounts they give of themselves, of their acquaintance, or of the extraordinary things which they have seen

---

*There have been two or three instances of late, of English ships decoying an enemy into their power, by counterfeiting signals of distress; an artifice which ought to be reprobated by the common indignation of mankind! for, a few examples of captures effected by this stratagem, would put an end to that promptitude in affording assistance to ships in distress, which is the best virtue in a seafaring character, and by which the perils of navigation are diminished to all.—A.D. 1775.

or heard: and so long as the facts they relate are indifferent, and their narratives, though false, are inoffensive, it may seem a superstitious regard to truth to censure them merely for truth's sake.

In the first place, it is almost impossible to pronounce beforehand, with certainty, concerning any lie, that it is inoffensive. *Volat irrevocabile;* and collects sometimes accretions in its flight, which entirely change its nature. It may owe possibly its mischief to the officiousness or misrepresentation of those who circulate it; but the mischief is, nevertheless, in some degree chargeable upon the original editor.

In the next place, this liberty in conversation defeats its own end. Much of the pleasure, and all the benefit, of conversation, depends upon our opinion of the speaker's veracity; for which this rule leaves no foundation. The faith indeed of a hearer must be extremely perplexed, who considers the speaker, or believes that the speaker considers himself, as under no obligation to adhere to truth, but according to the particular importance of what he relates.

But beside and above both these reasons, *white* lies always introduce others of a darker complexion. I have seldom known any one who deserted truth in trifles, that could be trusted in matters of importance. Nice distinctions are out of the question, upon occasions which, like those of speech, return every hour. The habit, therefore, of lying, when once formed, is easily extended, to serve the designs of malice or interest—like all habits, it spreads indeed of itself.

Pious frauds, as they are improperly enough called, pretended inspirations, forged books, counterfeit miracles, are impositions of a more serious nature. It is possible that they may sometimes, though seldom, have been set up and encouraged, with a design to do good: but the good they aim at requires that the belief of them should be perpetual, which is hardly possible; and the detection of the fraud is sure to disparage the credit of all pretensions of the same nature. Christianity has suffered more injury from this cause, than from all other causes put together.

As there may be falsehoods which are not lies, so there may be lies without literal or direct falsehood. An opening is always left for this species of prevarication, when the literal and grammatical signification of a sentence is different from the popular and customary meaning. It is the wilful deceit that makes the lie; and we wilfully deceive, when our expressions are not true in the sense in which we believe the hearer to apprehend them: besides that it is absurd to contend for any sense of words, in opposition to usage; for all senses of all words are founded upon usage, and upon nothing else.

Or a man may *act* a lie; as by pointing his finger in a wrong direction, when a traveller inquires of him his road; or when a tradesman shuts up his windows, to induce his creditors to believe that he is abroad: for, to all moral purposes, and therefore as to veracity, speech and action are the same; speech being only a mode of action.

Or, lastly, there may be lies of *omission*. A writer of English history, who, in his account of the reign of Charles the First, should wilfully suppress any evidence of that prince's despotic measures and designs, might be said to lie; for, by entitling his book a *History of England*, he engages to relate the whole truth of the history, or, at least, all that he knows of it.

Chapter 16
OATHS

   I. Forms of Oaths.
  II. Signification.
 III. Lawfulness.
 IV. Obligation.
  V. What Oaths do not bind.
 VI. In what Sense Oaths are to be interpreted.

I. The forms of oaths, like other religious ceremonies, have in all ages been various; consisting, however, for the most part, of some bodily action,* and of a prescribed form of words. Amongst the Jews, the juror held up his right hand towards heaven, which explains a passage in the 144th Psalm; "Whose mouth speaketh vanity, and *their right hand is a right hand of falsehood.*" The same form is retained in Scotland still. Amongst the same Jews, an oath of fidelity was taken, by the servant's putting his hand under the thigh of his lord, as Eliezer did to Abraham, Gen. xxiv. 2; from whence, with no great variation, is derived perhaps the form of doing homage at this day, by putting the hands between the knees, and within the hands, of the liege.

Amongst the Greeks and Romans, the form varied with the subject and occasion of the oath. In private contracts, the parties took hold of each other's hand, whilst they swore to the performance; or they touched the altar of the god by whose divinity they swore. Upon more solemn occasions, it was the custom to slay a victim; and the beast being *struck down* with certain ceremonies and invocations, gave birth to the expressions τεμνειν ορκον, *ferire pactum;* and to our English phrase, translated from these, of "striking a bargain."

The forms of oaths in Christian countries are also very different; but in no country in the world, I believe, worse contrived, either to convey the meaning, or impress the obligation of an oath, than in our own. The juror with us, after repeating the promise or affirmation which the oath is intended to confirm, adds, "So help me God": or more frequently the substance of the oath is repeated to the juror by the officer or magistrate who administers it, adding

---

*It is commonly thought that oaths are denominated *corporal* oaths from the bodily action which accompanies them, of laying the right hand upon a book containing the four Gospels. This opinion, however, appears to be a mistake; for the term is borrowed from the ancient usage of touching, on these occasions, the *corporale,* or cloth which covered the consecrated elements.

in the conclusion, "So help you God." The energy of the sentence resides in the particle *so; so*, that is, *hâc lege*, upon condition of my speaking the truth, or performing this promise, and not otherwise, may God help me. The juror, whilst he hears or repeats the words of the oath, holds his right hand upon a Bible, or other book containing the four Gospels. The conclusion of the oath sometimes runs, "Ita me Deus adjuvet, et haec sancta evangelia," or "So help me God, and the contents of this book": which last clause forms a connexion between the words and action of the juror, that before was wanting. The juror then kisses the book: the kiss, however, seems rather an act of reverence to the contents of the book (as, in the popish ritual, the priest kisses the Gospel before he reads it), than any part of the oath.

This obscure and elliptical form, together with the levity and frequency with which it is administered, has brought about a general inadvertency to the obligation of oaths; which, both in a religious and political view, is much to be lamented: and it merits public consideration, whether the requiring of oaths on so many frivolous occasions, especially in the Customs, and in the qualification for petty offices, has any other effect, than to make them cheap in the minds of the people. A pound of tea cannot travel regularly from the ship to the consumer, without costing half a dozen oaths at the least; and the same security for the due discharge of their office, namely, that of an oath, is required from a churchwarden and an archbishop, from a petty constable and the chief justice of England. Let the law continue its own sanctions, if they be thought requisite; but let it spare the solemnity of an oath. And where, from the want of something better to depend upon, it is necessary to accept men's own word or own account, let it annex to prevarication penalties proportioned to the public mischief of the offence.

II. But whatever be the form of an oath, the *signification* is the same. It is "the calling upon God to witness, *i.e.* to take notice of, what we say," and it is "invoking his vengeance, or renouncing his favour, if what we say be false, or what we promise be not performed."

III. Quakers and Moravians refuse to swear upon any occasion; founding their scruples concerning the *lawfulness* of oaths upon our Saviour's prohibition, Matt. v. 34. "I say unto you, Swear not at all."

The answer which we give to this objection cannot be understood without first stating the whole passage: "Ye have heard that it hath been said by them of old time, Thou shalt not forswear thyself, but shalt perform unto the Lord thine oaths. But I say unto you, Swear not at all; neither by heaven, for it is God's throne; nor by the earth, for it is his footstool; neither by Jerusalem, for it is the city of the great King. Neither shalt thou swear by thy head, because thou canst not make one hair white or black. But let your communication be, Yea, yea; Nay, nay: for whatsoever is more than these, cometh of evil."

To reconcile with this passage of Scripture the practice of swearing, or of taking oaths, when required by law, the following observations must be attended to:

1. It does not appear that swearing "by heaven," "by the earth," "by Jerusalem," or "by their own head," was a form of swearing ever made use of amongst the Jews in judicial oaths: and consequently, it is not probable that they were judicial oaths, which Christ had in his mind when he mentioned those instances.

2. As to the seeming universality of the prohibition, "Swear not at all," the emphatic clause "not at all" is to be read in connexion with what follows; "not at all," *h.e.* neither "by the heaven," nor by "the earth," nor "by Jerusalem," nor "by thy head"; "*not at all,*" does not mean upon no occasion, but by none of these forms. Our Saviour's argument seems to suppose, that the people to whom he spake made a distinction between swearing directly by the "name of God," and swearing by those inferior objects of veneration, "the

heavens," "the earth," "Jerusalem," or "their own head." In oppo-sition to which distinction, he tells them, that on account of the relation which these things bore to the Supreme Being, to swear by any of them, was in effect and substance to swear by *him*; "by heaven, for it is his throne; by the earth, for it is his footstool; by Jerusalem, for it is the city of the great King; by thy head, for it is *his* workmanship, not *thine*—thou canst not make one hair white or black": for which reason he says, "Swear *not at all*," that is, nei-ther directly by God, nor indirectly by any thing related to him. This interpretation is greatly confirmed by a passage in the twenty-third chapter of the same Gospel, where a similar distinction, made by the Scribes and Pharisees, is replied to in the same manner.

3. Our Saviour himself being "adjured by the living God," to declare whether he was the Christ, the Son of God, or not, conde-scended to answer the high-priest, without making any objection to the oath (for such it was) upon which he examined him. "*God is my witness*," says St. Paul to the Romans, "that without ceasing I make mention of you in my prayers": and to the Corinthians still more strongly, "*I call God for a record upon my soul*, that to spare you, I came not as yet to Corinth." Both these expressions contain the nature of oaths. The Epistle to the Hebrews speaks of the custom of swearing judicially, without any mark of censure or disapproba-tion: "Men verily swear by the greater; and an oath, for confirma-tion, is to them an end of all strife."

Upon the strength of these reasons, we explain our Saviour's words to relate, not to judicial oaths, but to the practice of vain, wanton, and unauthorised swearing, in common discourse. Saint James's words, chap. v. 12, are not so strong as our Saviour's, and therefore admit the same explanation with more ease.

IV. Oaths are nugatory, that is, carry with them no *proper* force or obligation, unless we believe that God will punish false swearing with more severity than a simple lie, or breach of promise; for which belief there are the following reasons:

1. Perjury is a sin of greater deliberation. The juror has the thought of God and of religion upon his mind at the time; at least, there are very few who can shake them off entirely. He offends, therefore, if he do offend, with a high hand; in the face, that is, and in defiance of the sanctions of religion. His offence implies a disbelief or contempt of God's knowledge, power, and justice; which cannot be said of a lie, where there is nothing to carry the mind to any reflection upon the Deity, or the Divine Attributes at all.

2. Perjury violates a superior confidence. Mankind must trust to one another; and they have nothing better to trust to than one another's oath. Hence legal adjudications, which govern and affect every right and interest on this side of the grave, of necessity proceed and depend upon oaths. Perjury, therefore, in its general consequence, strikes at the security of reputation, property, and even of life itself. A lie cannot do the same mischief, because the same credit is not given to it.*

3. God directed the Israelites to swear by his name;[†] and was pleased, "in order to show the immutability of his own counsel,[‡] to confirm his covenant with that people by an oath: neither of which it is probable he would have done, had he not intended to represent oaths as having some meaning and effect beyond the obligation of a bare promise; which effect must be owing to the severer punishment with which he will vindicate the authority of oaths.

---

*Except, indeed, where a Quaker's or Moravian's affirmation is accepted in the place of an oath; in which case, a lie partakes, so far as this reason extends, of the nature and guilt of perjury.

[†] Deut. vi. 13. x. 20.

[‡] Heb. vi. 17.

V. Promissory oaths are *not binding* where the promise itself would not be so: for the several cases of which, see the Chapter of Promises.

VI. As oaths are designed for the security of the imposer, it is manifest that they must be *interpreted* and performed in the sense in which the imposer intends them; otherwise, they afford no security to *him*. And this is the meaning and reason of the rule, "jurare in animum imponentis"; which rule the reader is desired to carry along with him, whilst we proceed to consider certain particular oaths, which are either of greater importance, or more likely to fall in our way, than others.

Chapter 17

OATH IN EVIDENCE

The witness swears "to speak the truth, the whole truth, and nothing but the truth, touching the matter in question."

Upon which it may be observed, that the designed concealment of any truth, which relates to the matter in agitation, is as much a violation of the oath, as to testify a positive falsehood; and this, whether the witness be interrogated as to that particular point or not. For when the person to be examined is sworn upon a *voir dire*, that is, in order to inquire whether he ought to be admitted to give evidence in the cause at all, the form runs thus: "You shall true answer make to all such questions as shall be asked you": but when he comes to be sworn *in chief*, he swears "to speak the whole truth," without restraining it, as before, to the questions that shall be asked: which difference shows, that the law intends, in this latter case, to require of the witness, that he give a complete and unreserved account of what he knows of the subject of the trial, whether the questions proposed to him reach the extent of his knowledge or not. So that if it be inquired of the witness afterwards, why he did not inform the court so and so, it is not a sufficient, though a very common answer, to say, "because it was never asked me."

I know but one exception to this rule; which is, when a full discovery of the truth tends to accuse the witness himself of some legal crime. The law of England constrains no man to become his own accuser; consequently imposes the oath of testimony with this tacit reservation. But the exception must be confined to *legal* crimes. A point of honour, of delicacy, or of reputation, may make a witness backward to disclose some circumstance with which he is acquainted; but will in no wise justify his concealment of the truth, unless it could be shown, that the law which imposes the oath, intended to allow this indulgence to such motives. The exception of which we are speaking is also withdrawn by a compact between the magistrate and the witness, when an accomplice is admitted to give evidence against the partners of his crime.

Tenderness to the prisoner, although a specious apology for concealment, is no just excuse: for if this plea be thought sufficient, it takes the administration of penal justice out of the hands of judges and juries, and makes it depend upon the temper of prosecutors and witnesses.

Questions may be asked, which are irrelative to the cause, which affect the witness himself, or some third person; in which, and in all cases where the witness doubts of the pertinency and propriety of the question, he ought to refer his doubts to the court. The answer of the court, in relaxation of the oath, is authority enough to the witness; for the law which imposes the oath, may remit what it will of the obligation: and it belongs to the court to declare what the mind of the law is. Nevertheless, it cannot be said universally, that the answer of the court is conclusive upon the conscience of the witness; for his obligation depends upon what he apprehended, at the time of taking the oath, to be the design of the law in imposing it, and no after-requisition or explanation by the court can carry the obligation beyond that.

Chapter 18
OATH OF ALLEGIANCE

"I do sincerely promise and swear, that I will be faithful and bear true *allegiance* to his Majesty King GEORGE." Formerly the oath of allegiance ran thus: "I do promise to be true and faithful to the king and his heirs, and truth and faith to bear, of life, and limb, and ter-rene honour; and not to know or hear of any ill or damage intended him, without defending him therefrom": and was altered at the Revolution to the present form. So that the present oath is a relaxation of the old one. And as the oath was intended to ascertain, not so much the extent of the subject's obedience, as the person to whom it was due, the legislature seems to have wrapped up its meaning upon the former point, in a word purposely made choice of for its general and indeterminate signification.

It will be most convenient to consider, first, what the oath excludes as inconsistent with it; secondly, what it permits.

1. The oath excludes all intention to support the claim or pretensions of any other person or persons to the crown and government, than the reigning sovereign. A Jacobite, who is persuaded of the Pretender's right to the crown, and who moreover designs to join with the adherents to that cause to assert this right, whenever a proper opportunity, with a reasonable prospect of success, presents itself, cannot take the oath of allegiance; or, if he could, the oath of abjuration follows, which contains an express renunciation of all opinions in favour of the claim of the exiled family.

2. The oath excludes all design, at the time, of attempting to depose the reigning prince, for any reason whatever. Let the

justice of the Revolution be what it would, no honest man could have taken even the present oath of allegiance to James the Second, who entertained, at the time of taking it, a design of joining in the measures which were entered into to dethrone him.

3. The oath forbids the taking up of arms against the reigning prince, with views of private advancement, or from motives of personal resentment or dislike. It is possible to happen in this, what frequently happens in despotic governments, that an ambitious general, at the head of the military force of the nation, might, by a conjuncture of fortunate circumstances, and a great ascendency over the minds of the soldiery, depose the prince upon the throne, and make way to it for himself, or for some creature of his own. A person in this situation would be withholden from such an attempt by the oath of allegiance, if he paid regard to it. If there were any who engaged in the rebellion of the year forty-five, with the expectation of titles, estates, or preferment; or because they were disappointed, and thought themselves neglected and ill-used at court; or because they entertained a family animosity, or personal resentment, against the king, the favourite, or the minister—if any were induced to take up arms by these motives, they added to the many crimes of an unprovoked rebellion, that of wilful and corrupt perjury. If, in the late American war, the same motives determined others to connect themselves with that opposition, their part in it was chargeable with perfidy and falsehood to their oath, whatever was the justice of the opposition itself, or however well-founded their own complaints might be of private injury.

We are next to consider what the oath of allegiance permits, or does not require.

1. It permits resistance to the king, when his ill behaviour or imbecility is such, as to make resistance beneficial to the community. It may fairly be presumed that the Convention Parliament, which introduced the oath in its present form, did not

intend, by imposing it, to exclude all resistance, since the members of that legislature had many of them recently taken up arms against James the Second, and the very authority by which they sat together was itself the effect of a successful opposition to an acknowledged sovereign. Some resistance, therefore, was meant to be allowed; and, if any, it must be that which has the public interest for its object.

2. The oath does not require obedience to such commands of the king as are unauthorised by law. No such obedience is implied by the terms of the oath; the *fidelity* there promised, is intended of fidelity in opposition to his enemies, and not in opposition to law; and *allegiance*, at the utmost, can only signify obedience to lawful commands. Therefore, if the king should issue a proclamation, levying money, or imposing any service or restraint upon the subject beyond what the crown is empowered by law to enjoin, there would exist no sort of obligation to obey such a proclamation, in consequence of having taken the oath of allegiance.

3. The oath does not require that we should continue our allegiance to the king, after he is actually and absolutely deposed, driven into exile, carried away captive, or otherwise rendered incapable of exercising the regal office, whether by his fault or without it. The promise of allegiance implies, and is understood by all parties to suppose, that the person to whom the promise is made continues king; continues, that is, to exercise the power, and afford the protection, which belongs to the office of king: for, it is the possession of this power, which makes such a particular person the object of the oath; without it, why should I swear allegiance to this man, rather than to any man in the kingdom? Beside which, the contrary doctrine is burthened with this consequence, that every conquest, revolution of government, or disaster which befalls the person of the prince, must be followed by perpetual and irremediable anarchy.

Chapter 19
OATH AGAINST BRIBERY IN THE ELECTION
OF MEMBERS OF PARLIAMENT

"I do swear, I have not received, or had, by myself, or any person whatsoever, in trust for me, or for my use and benefit, directly or indirectly, any sum or sums of money, office, place, or employment, gift, or reward, or any promise or security, for any money, office, employment, or gift, in order to give my vote at this election."

The several contrivances to evade this oath, such as the electors accepting money under colour of borrowing it, and giving a promissory note, or other security, for it, which is cancelled after the election; receiving money from a stranger, or a person in disguise, or out of a drawer, or purse, left open for the purpose; or promises of money to be paid after the election; or stipulating for a place, living, or other private advantage of any kind; if they escape the legal penalties of perjury, incur the moral guilt; for they are manifestly within the mischief and design of the statute which imposes the oath, and within the terms indeed of the oath itself; for the word "indirectly" is inserted on purpose to comprehend such cases as these.

Chapter 20
OATH AGAINST SIMONY

From an imaginary resemblance between the purchase of a benefice, and Simon Magus's attempt to purchase the gift of the Holy Ghost (Acts viii. 19), the obtaining of ecclesiastical preferment by pecuniary considerations has been termed *Simony*.

The sale of advowsons is inseparable from the allowance of private patronage; as patronage would otherwise devolve to the most indigent, and for that reason the most improper hands it could be placed in. Nor did the law ever intend to prohibit the passing of advowsons from one patron to another; but to restrain the patron, who possesses the right of presenting at the vacancy, from being influenced, in the choice of his presentee, by a bribe, or benefit to himself. It is the same distinction with that which obtains in a free-holder's vote for his representative in parliament. The right of voting, that is, the freehold to which the right pertains, may be bought and sold as freely as any other property; but the exercise of that right, the vote itself, may not be purchased, or influenced by money.

For this purpose, the law imposes upon the presentee, who is generally concerned in the simony, if there be any, the following oath: "I do swear that I have made no *simoniacal* payment, contract, or promise, directly or indirectly, by myself, or by any other to my knowledge, or with my consent, to any person or persons whatso-ever, for or concerning the procuring and obtaining of this eccle-siastical place, &c.; nor will, at any time hereafter, perform, or satisfy, any such kind of payment, contract, or promise, made by any other without my knowledge or consent: So help me God, through Jesus Christ!"

It is extraordinary that Bishop Gibson should have thought this oath to be against all promises whatsoever, when the terms of the oath expressly restrain it to *simoniacal* promises; and the law alone must pronounce what promises, as well as what payments and con-tracts, are simoniacal, and consequently come within the oath; and what do not so.

Now the law adjudges to be simony,

1. All payments, contracts, or promises, made by any person for a benefice *already vacant*. The advowson of a void turn, by law, cannot be transferred from one patron to another; therefore, if the void turn be procured by money, it must be by a pecuniary

influence upon the then subsisting patron in the choice of his presentee, which is the very practice the law condemns.

2. A clergyman's purchasing of the *next turn* of a benefice *for himself*, "directly or indirectly," that is, by himself, or by another person with his money. It does not appear that the law prohibits a clergyman from purchasing the perpetuity of a patronage, more than any other person: but purchasing the perpetuity, and forthwith selling it again with a reservation of the next turn, and with no other design than to possess himself of the next turn, is *in fraudem legis*, and inconsistent with the oath.

3. The procuring of a piece of preferment, by ceding to the patron any rights, or probable rights, belonging to it. This is simony of the worst kind; for it is not only buying preferment, but robbing the succession to pay for it.

4. Promises to the patron of a portion of the profit, of a remission of tithes and dues, or other advantage out of the produce of the benefice; which kind of compact is a pernicious condescension in the clergy, independent of the oath; for it tends to introduce a practice, which may very soon become general, of giving the revenue of churches to the lay patrons, and supplying the duty by indigent stipendiaries.

5. General bonds of resignation, that is, bonds to resign upon demand.

I doubt not but that the oath against simony is binding upon the consciences of those who take it, though I question much the expediency of requiring it. It is very fit to debar public patrons, such as the king, the lord chancellor, bishops, ecclesiastical corporations, and the like, from this kind of traffic: because from them may be expected some regard to the qualifications of the persons whom they promote. But the oath lays a snare for the integrity of the clergy; and I do not perceive, that the requiring of it in cases of private patronage produces any good effect, sufficient to compensate for this danger.

Where advowsons are holden along with manors, or other principal estates, it would be an easy regulation to forbid that they should ever hereafter be separated; and would, at least, keep church preferment out of the hands of brokers.

Chapter 21
Oaths to Observe Local Statutes

Members of colleges in the Universities, and of other ancient foundations, are required to swear to the observance of their respective statutes; which observance is become in some cases unlawful, in others impracticable, in others useless, in others inconvenient.

Unlawful directions are countermanded by the authority which made them unlawful.

Impracticable directions are dispensed with by the necessity of the case.

The only question is, how far the members of these societies may take upon themselves to judge of the *inconveniency* of any particular direction, and make that a reason for laying aside the observation of it.

The *animus imponentis*, which is the measure of the juror's duty, seems to be satisfied, when nothing is omitted, but what, from some change in the circumstances under which it was prescribed, it may fairly be presumed that the founder himself would have dispensed with.

To bring a case within this rule, the *inconveniency* must—

1. Be manifest; concerning which there is no doubt.

2. It must arise from some change in the circumstances of the institution: for, let the inconveniency be what it will, if it existed at the time of the foundation, it must be presumed that the founder did not deem the avoiding of it of sufficient importance to alter his plan.

3. The direction of the statute must not only be inconvenient in the general (for so may the institution itself be), but prejudicial to the particular end proposed by the institution: for, it is this last circumstance which proves that the founder would have dispensed with it in pursuance of his own purpose.

The statutes of some colleges forbid the speaking of any language but Latin, within the walls of the college; direct that a certain number, and not fewer than that number, be allowed the use of an apartment amongst them; that so many hours of each day be employed in public exercises, lectures, or disputations; and some other articles of discipline adapted to the tender years of the students who in former times resorted to universities. Were colleges to retain such rules, nobody now-a-days would come near them. They are laid aside therefore, though parts of the statutes, and as such included within the oath, not merely because they are inconvenient, but because there is sufficient reason to believe, that the founders themselves would have dispensed with them, as subversive of their own designs.

Chapter 22
Subscription to Articles of Religion

Subscription to articles of religion, though no more than a *declaration* of the subscriber's assent, may properly enough be considered in connexion with the subject of oaths, because it is governed by the same rule of interpretation:

Which rule is the *animus imponentis.*

The inquiry, therefore, concerning subscription will be, *quis imposuit, et quo animo?*

The bishop who receives the subscription, is not the imposer, any more than the crier of a court, who administers the oath to the jury and witnesses, is the person that imposes it; nor, consequently, is the private opinion or interpretation of the bishop of any signification to the subscriber, one way or other.

The compilers of the Thirty-nine Articles are not to be considered as the imposers of subscription, any more than the framer or drawer up of a law is the person that enacts it.

The legislature of the 13th Eliz. is the imposer, whose intention the subscriber is bound to satisfy.

They who contend, that nothing less can justify subscription to the Thirty-nine Articles, than the actual belief of each and every separate proposition contained in them, must suppose, that the legislature expected the consent of ten thousand men, and that in perpetual succession, not to one controverted proposition, but to many hundreds. It is difficult to conceive how this could be expected by any, who observed the incurable diversity of human opinion upon all subjects short of demonstration.

If the authors of the law did not intend this, what did they intend?

They intended to exclude from offices in the church,

1. All abettors of popery.

2. Anabaptists; who were at that time a powerful party on the Continent.

3. The Puritans; who were hostile to an episcopal constitution: and in general the members of such leading sects or foreign establishments as threatened to overthrow our own.

Whoever finds himself comprehended within these descriptions, ought not to subscribe. Nor can a subscriber to the Articles take advantage of any latitude which our rule may seem to allow, who is not first convinced that he is truly and substantially satisfying the intention of the legislature.

During the present state of ecclesiastical patronage, in which private individuals are permitted to impose teachers upon parishes with which they are often little or not at all connected, some limitation of the patron's choice may be necessary to prevent unedifying contentions between neighbouring teachers, or between the teachers and their respective congregations. But this danger, if it exist, may be provided against with equal effect, by converting the articles of faith into articles of peace.

Chapter 23
WILLS

The fundamental question upon this subject is, whether Wills are of natural or of adventitious right? that is, whether the right of directing the disposition of property after his death belongs to a man in a state of nature, and by the law of nature, or whether it be given him entirely by the positive regulations of the country he lives in?

The immediate produce of each man's personal labour, as the tools, weapons, and utensils, which he manufactures, the tent or hut that he builds, and perhaps the flocks and herds which he breeds and rears, are as much his own as the labour was which he employed upon them, that is, are his property naturally and absolutely; and consequently he may give or leave them to whom he pleases, there being nothing to limit the continuance of his right, or to restrain the alienation of it.

But every other species of property, especially property in land, stands upon a different foundation.

We have seen, in the Chapter upon Property, that, in a state of nature, a man's right to a particular spot of ground arises from his using it, and his wanting it; consequently ceases with the use and want: so that at his death the estate reverts to the community, without any regard to the last owner's will, or even any preference of his family, further than as they become the first occupiers after him, and succeed to the same want and use.

Moreover, as natural rights cannot, like rights created by act of parliament, expire at the end of a certain number of years; if the testator have a right, by the law of nature, to dispose of his property one moment after his death, he has the same right to direct the disposition of it for a million of ages after him; which is absurd.

The ancient apprehensions of mankind upon the subject were conformable to this account of it: for, wills have been introduced into most countries by a positive act of the state; as by the Laws of Solon into Greece; by the Twelve Tables into Rome; and that not till after a considerable progress had been made in legislation, and in the oeconomy of civil life. Tacitus relates, that amongst the Germans they were disallowed; and what is more remarkable, in this country, since the Conquest, lands could not be devised by will, till within little more than two hundred years ago, when this privilege was restored to the subject, by an act of parliament, in the latter end of the reign of Henry the Eighth.

No doubt, many beneficial purposes are attained by extending the owner's power over his property beyond his life, and beyond his natural right. It invites to industry; it encourages marriage; it secures the dutifulness and dependency of children: but a limit must be assigned to the duration of this power. The utmost extent to which, in any case, entails are allowed by the laws of England to operate, is during the lives in existence at the death of the testator, and one-and-twenty years beyond these; after which, there are ways and means of setting them aside.

From the consideration that wills are the creatures of the municipal law which gives them their efficacy, may be deduced a determination of the question, whether the intention of the testator in an *informal* will be binding upon the conscience of those, who, by operation of law, succeed to his estate. By an *informal* will, I mean a

will void in law for want of some requisite formality, though no doubt
be entertained of its meaning or authenticity: as, suppose a man make
his will, devising his freehold estate to his sister's son, and the will be
attested by two only, instead of three, subscribing witnesses; would
the brother's son, who is heir at law to the testator, be bound in conscience to resign his claim to the estate, out of deference to his uncle's
intention? or, on the contrary, would not the devisee under the will
be bound, upon discovery of this flaw in it, to surrender the estate,
suppose he had gained possession of it, to the heir at law?

Generally speaking, the heir at law is not bound by the intention
of the testator: for the intention can signify nothing, unless the person intending have a right to govern the descent of the estate. That
is the first question. Now this right the testator can only derive
from the law of the land: but the law confers the right upon certain
conditions, with which conditions he has not complied; therefore,
the testator can lay no claim to the power which he pretends to
exercise, as he hath not entitled himself to the benefit of that law, by
virtue of which alone the estate ought to attend his disposal. Consequently, the devisee under the will, who, by concealing this flaw
in it, keeps possession of the estate, is in the situation of any other
person who avails himself of his neighbour's ignorance to detain
from him his property. The will is so much waste paper, from the
defect of right in the person who made it. Nor is this catching at an
expression of law to pervert the substantial design of it: for I apprehend it to be the deliberate mind of the legislature, that no will
should take effect upon real estates, unless authenticated in the precise manner which the statute describes. Had testamentary dispositions been founded in any natural right, independent of positive
constitutions, I should have thought differently of this question: for
then I should have considered the law rather as refusing its assistance to enforce the right of the devisee, than as extinguishing or
working any alteration in the right itself.

And after all, I should choose to propose a case, where no consideration of pity to distress, of duty to a parent, or of gratitude to a benefactor, interfered with the general rule of justice.

The regard due to kindred in the disposal of our fortune (except the case of lineal kindred, which is different) arises either from the respect we owe to the presumed intention of the ancestor from whom we received our fortunes, or from the expectations which we have encouraged. The intention of the ancestor is presumed with greater certainty, as well as entitled to more respect, the fewer degrees he is removed from us; which makes the difference in the different degrees of kindred. For instance, it may be presumed to be a father's intention and desire, that the inheritance which he leaves, after it has served the turn and generation of one son, should remain a provision for the families of his other children, equally related and dear to him as the oldest. Whoever, therefore, without cause, gives away his patrimony from his brother's or sister's family, is guilty not so much of an injury to them, as of ingratitude to his parent. The deference due from the possessor of a fortune to the presumed desire of his ancestor, will also vary with this circumstance: whether the ancestor earned the fortune by his personal industry, acquired it by accidental successes, or only transmitted the inheritance which he received.

Where a man's fortune is acquired by himself, and he has done nothing to excite expectation, but rather has refrained from those particular attentions which tend to cherish expectation, he is perfectly disengaged from the force of the above reasons, and at liberty to leave his fortune to his friends, to charitable or public purposes, or to whom he will: the same blood, proximity of blood, and the like, are merely modes of speech, implying nothing real, nor any obligation of themselves.

There is always, however, a reason for providing for our poor relations, in preference to others who may be equally necessitous, which is, that if we do not, no one else will; mankind, by an established consent, leaving the reduced branches of good families to the bounty of their wealthy alliances.

The not making a will is a very culpable omission, where it is attended with the following effects: where it leaves daughters, or younger children, at the mercy of the oldest son; where it distributes a personal fortune equally amongst the children, although there be no equality in their exigencies or situations; where it leaves an opening for litigation; or lastly, and principally, where it defrauds creditors; for, by a defect in our laws, which has been long and strangely overlooked, real estates are not subject to the payment of debts by simple contract, unless made so by will; although credit is, in fact, generally given to the possession of such estates: he, therefore, who neglects to make the necessary appointments for the payment of his debts, as far as his effects extend, sins, as it has been justly said, in his grave; and if he omits this on purpose to defeat the demands of his creditors, he dies with a deliberate fraud in his heart.

Anciently, when any one died without a will, the bishop of the diocese took possession of his personal fortune, in order to dispose of it for the benefit of his soul, that is, to pious or charitable uses. It became necessary, therefore, that the bishop should be satisfied of the authenticity of the will, when there was any, before he resigned the right which he had to take possession of the dead man's fortune in case of intestacy. In this way wills, and controversies relating to wills, came within the cognisance of ecclesiastical courts; under the jurisdiction of which, wills of personals (the only wills that were made formerly) still continue, though in truth, no more now-a-days connected with religion, than any other instruments of conveyance. This is a peculiarity in the English laws.

Succession to *intestates* must be regulated by positive rules of law, there being no principle of natural justice whereby to ascertain the proportion of the different claimants: not to mention that the claim itself, especially of collateral kindred, seems to have little foundation in the law of nature.

These regulations should be guided by the duty and presumed inclination of the deceased, so far as these considerations can be consulted by general rules. The statutes of Charles the Second, commonly called the Statutes of Distribution, which adopt the rule of the Roman law in the distribution of personals, are sufficiently equitable. They assign one-third to the widow, and two-thirds to the children; in case of no children, one half to the widow, and the other half to the next of kin; where neither widow nor lineal descendants survive, the whole to the next of kin, and to be equally divided amongst kindred of equal degree, without distinction of whole blood and half blood, or of consanguinity by the father's or mother's side.

The descent of real estates, of houses, that is, and land, having been settled in more remote and in ruder times, is less reasonable. There never can be much to complain of in a rule which every person may avoid, by so easy a provision as that of making his will: otherwise, our law in this respect is chargeable with some flagrant absurdities; such as, that an estate shall in no wise go to the brother or sister of the half blood, though it came to the deceased from the common parent; that it shall go to the remotest relation the intestate has in the world, rather than to his own father or mother; or even be forfeited for want of an heir, though both parents survive; that the most distant paternal relation shall be preferred to an uncle, or own cousin, by the mother's side, notwithstanding the estate was purchased and acquired by the intestate himself.

Land not being so divisible as money, may be a reason for making a difference in the course of inheritance: but there ought to be no difference but what is founded upon that reason. The Roman law made none.

Book III

PART II
OF RELATIVE DUTIES WHICH ARE INDETERMINATE

Chapter 1
CHARITY

I use the term Charity neither in the common sense of bounty to the poor, nor in St. Paul's sense of benevolence to all mankind: but I apply it at present, in a sense more commodious to my purpose, to signify *the promoting the happiness of our inferiors*.

Charity, in this sense, I take to be the principal province of virtue and religion: for, whilst worldly prudence will direct our behaviour towards our superiors, and politeness towards our equals, there is little beside the consideration of duty, or an habitual humanity which comes into the place of consideration, to produce a proper conduct towards those who are beneath us, and dependant upon us.

There are three principal methods of promoting the happiness of our inferiors.

1. By the treatment of our domestics and dependants.
2. By professional assistance.
3. By pecuniary bounty.

Chapter 2
CHARITY

———

The Treatment of Our Domestics and Dependants

A party of friends setting out together upon a journey, soon find it to be the best for all sides, that while they are upon the road, one of the company should wait upon the rest; another ride forward to seek out lodging and entertainment; a third carry the portmanteau; a fourth take charge of the horses; a fifth bear the purse, conduct and direct the route; not forgetting, however, that, as they were equal and independent when they set out, so they are all to return to a level again at their journey's end. The same regard and respect; the same forbearance, lenity, and reserve in using their service; the same mildness in delivering commands; the same study to make their journey comfortable and pleasant, which he whose lot it was to direct the rest, would in common decency think himself bound to observe towards them; ought we to show to those who, in the casting of the parts of human society, happen to be placed within our power, or to depend upon us.

Another reflection of a like tendency with the former is, that our obligation to them is much greater than theirs to us. It is a mistake to suppose, that the rich man maintains his servants, tradesmen, tenants, and labourers: the truth is, they maintain him. It is their industry which supplies his table, furnishes his wardrobe, builds his houses, adorns his equipage, provides his amusements. It is not the estate, but the labour employed upon it, that pays his rent. All that he does, is to distribute what others produce; which is the least part of the business.

Nor do I perceive any foundation for an opinion, which is often handed round in genteel company, that good usage is thrown away upon low and ordinary minds; that they are insensible of kindness, and incapable of gratitude. If by "low and ordinary minds" are meant the minds of men in low and ordinary stations, they seem to be affected by benefits in the same way that all others are, and to be no less ready to requite them: and it would be a very unaccountable law of nature if it were otherwise.

Whatever uneasiness we occasion to our domestics, which neither promotes our service, nor answers the just ends of punishment, is manifestly wrong; were it only upon the general principle of diminishing the sum of human happiness.

By which rule we are forbidden,

1. To enjoin unnecessary labour or confinement from the mere love and wantonness of domination.

2. To insult our servants by harsh, scornful, or opprobrious language.

3. To refuse them any harmless pleasures:

And, by the same principle, are also forbidden causeless or immoderate anger, habitual peevishness, and groundless suspicion.

Chapter 3
SLAVERY

The prohibitions of the last chapter extend to the treatment of slaves, being founded upon a principle independent of the contract between masters and servants.

I define slavery to be "an obligation to labour for the benefit of the master, without the contract or consent of the servant."

This obligation may arise, consistently with the law of nature, from three causes:

1. From crimes.
2. From captivity.
3. From debt.

In the first case, the continuance of the slavery, as of any other punishment, ought to be proportioned to the crime; in the second and third cases, it ought to cease, as soon as the demand of the injured nation, or private creditor, is satisfied.

The slave-trade upon the coast of Africa is not excused by these principles. When slaves in that country are brought to market, no questions, I believe, are asked about the origin or justice of the vendor's title. It may be presumed, therefore, that this title is not always, if it be ever, founded in any of the causes above assigned.

But defect of right in the first purchase is the least crime with which this traffic is chargeable. The natives are excited to war and mutual depredation, for the sake of supplying their contracts, or furnishing the market with slaves. With this the wickedness begins. The slaves, torn away from parents, wives, children, from their friends and companions, their fields and flocks, their home and country, are transported to the European settlements in America, with no other accommodation on ship-board than what is provided for brutes. This is the second stage of cruelty; from which the miserable exiles are delivered, only to be placed, and that for life, in subjection to a dominion and system of laws, the most merciless and tyrannical that ever were tolerated upon the face of the earth; and from all that can be learned by the accounts of the people upon the spot, the inordinate authority which the plantation-laws confer upon the slave-holder is exercised, by the *English* slave-holder especially, with rigour and brutality.

But *necessity* is pretended; the name under which every enormity is attempted to be justified. And, after all, what is the necessity? It has never been proved that the land could not be cultivated there, as it is here, by hired servants. It is said that it could not be cultivated with quite the same conveniency and cheapness, as by the labour of slaves: by which means, a pound of sugar, which

the planter now sells for sixpence, could not be afforded under
sixpence-halfpenny—and this is the *necessity*.

The great revolution which has taken place in the Western world
may probably conduce (and who knows but that it was designed?) to
accelerate the fall of this abominable tyranny: and now that this contest, and the passions which attend it, are no more, there may succeed perhaps a season for reflecting, whether a legislature which had
so long lent its assistance to the support of an institution replete with
human misery, was fit to be trusted with an empire the most extensive that ever obtained in any age or quarter of the world.

Slavery was a part of the civil constitution of most countries,
when Christianity appeared; yet no passage is to be found in the
Christian Scriptures, by which it is condemned or prohibited. This
is true; for Christianity, soliciting admission into all nations of the
world, abstained, as behoved it, from intermeddling with the civil
institutions of any. But does it follow, from the silence of Scripture
concerning them, that all the civil institutions which then prevailed
were right? or that the bad should not be exchanged for better?

Besides this, the discharging of slaves from all obligation to
obey their masters, which is the consequence of pronouncing slavery to be unlawful, would have had no better effect than to let loose
one half of mankind upon the other. Slaves would have been
tempted to embrace a religion, which asserted their right to freedom; masters would hardly have been persuaded to consent to
claims founded upon such authority; the most calamitous of all
contests, a *bellum servile*, might probably have ensued, to the
reproach, if not the extinction, of the Christian name.

The truth is, the emancipation of slaves should be gradual, and
be carried on by provisions of law, and under the protection of civil
government. Christianity can only operate as an alterative. By the
mild diffusion of its light and influence, the minds of men are
insensibly prepared to perceive and correct the enormities, which

folly, or wickedness, or accident, have introduced into their public establishments. In this way the Greek and Roman slavery, and since these, the feudal tyranny, has declined before it. And we trust that, as the knowledge and authority of the same religion advance in the world, they will banish what remains of this odious institution.

Chapter 4
CHARITY

Professional Assistance

This kind of beneficence is chiefly to be expected from members of the legislature, magistrates, medical, legal, and sacerdotal professions.

1. The care of the poor ought to be the principal object of all laws; for this plain reason, that the rich are able to take care of themselves.

Much has been, and more might be, done by the laws of this country, towards the relief of the impotent, and the protection and encouragement of the industrious poor. Whoever applies himself to collect observations upon the state and operation of the poor-laws, and to contrive remedies for the imperfections and abuses which he observes, and digests these remedies into acts of parliament; and conducts them, by argument or influence, through the two branches of the legislature, or communicates his ideas to those who are more likely to carry them into effect; deserves well of a class of the community so numerous, that their happiness forms a principal part of the whole. The study and activity thus employed, is charity, in the most meritorious sense of the word.

2. The application of parochial relief is intrusted, in the first instance, to overseers and contractors, who have an interest in opposition to that of the poor, inasmuch as whatever they allow them

comes in part out of their own pocket. For this reason, the law has deposited with justices of the peace a power of superintendence and control; and the judicious interposition of this power is a most useful exertion of charity, and oft-times within the ability of those who have no other way of serving their generation. A country gentleman of very moderate education, and who has little to spare from his fortune, by learning so much of the poor-law as is to be found in Dr. Burn's Justice, and by furnishing himself with a knowledge of the prices of labour and provision, so as to be able to estimate the exigencies of a family, and what is to be expected from their industry, may, in this way, place out the one talent committed to him, to great account.

3. Of all private professions, that of medicine puts it in a man's power to do the most good at the least expense. Health, which is precious to all, is to the poor invaluable: and their complaints, as agues, rheumatisms, &c. are often such as yield to medicine. And, with respect to the expense, drugs at first hand cost little, and advice costs nothing, where it is only bestowed upon those who could not afford to pay for it.

4. The rights of the poor are not so important or intricate, as their contentions are violent and ruinous. A lawyer or attorney, of tolerable knowledge in his profession, has commonly judgement enough to adjust these disputes, with all the effect, and without the expense, of a law-suit; and he may be said to *give* a poor man twenty pounds, who prevents his throwing it away upon law. A *legal* man, whether of the profession or not, who, together with a spirit of conciliation, possesses the confidence of his neighbourhood, will be much resorted to for this purpose, especially since the great increase of costs has produced a general dread of going to law.

Nor is this line of beneficence confined to *arbitration*. Seasonable counsel, coming with the weight which the reputation of the adviser gives it, will often keep or extricate the rash and uninformed out of great difficulties.

Lastly, I know not a more exalted charity than that which presents a shield against the rapacity or persecution of a tyrant.

5. Betwixt argument and authority (I mean that authority which flows from voluntary respect, and attends upon sanctity and disinterestedness of character) something may be done, amongst the lower orders of mankind, towards the regulation of their conduct, and the satisfaction of their thoughts. This office belongs to the ministers of religion; or rather, whoever undertakes it, becomes a minister of religion. The inferior clergy, who are nearly upon a level with the common sort of their parishioners, and who on that account gain an easier admission to their society and confidence, have in this respect more in their power than their superiors: the discreet use of this power constitutes one of the most respectable functions of human nature.

Chapter 5
CHARITY

Pecuniary Bounty

I. *The obligation to bestow relief upon the poor.*
II. *The manner of bestowing it.*
III. *The pretences by which men excuse themselves from it.*

I. *The obligation to bestow relief upon the poor.*

They who rank pity amongst the original impulses of our nature rightly contend, that, when this principle prompts us to the relief of human misery, it indicates the Divine intention, and our duty. Indeed, the same conclusion is deducible from the existence of the passion, whatever account be given of its origin. Whether it be an instinct or a habit, it is in fact a property of our nature, which God appointed; and the final cause for which it was appointed, is to afford to the miserable, in the compassion of their fellow-creatures, a remedy for those inequalities and distresses which God foresaw that many must be exposed to, under every general rule for the distribution of property.

Beside this, the poor have a claim founded in the law of nature, which may be thus explained: All things were originally common. No one being able to produce a charter from Heaven, had any better title to a particular possession than his next neighbour. There were reasons for mankind's agreeing upon a separation of this common fund; and God for these reasons is presumed to have ratified it. But this separation was made and consented to, upon the expectation and condition that every one should have left a sufficiency for his subsistence, or the means of procuring it: and as no fixed laws for the regulation of property can be so contrived, as to provide for the relief of every case and distress which may arise, these cases and distresses, when their right and share in the common stock were given up or taken from them, were supposed to be left to the voluntary bounty of those who might be acquainted with the exigencies of their situation, and in the way of affording assistance. And, therefore, when the partition of property is rigidly maintained against the claims of indigence and distress, it is maintained in opposition to the intention of those who made it, and to *his*, who is the Supreme Proprietor of every thing, and who has filled the world with plenteousness, for the sustentation and comfort of all whom he sends into it.

The Christian Scriptures are more copious and explicit upon this duty than upon almost any other. The description which Christ hath left us of the proceedings of the last day, establishes the obligation of bounty beyond controversy: "When the Son of man shall come in his glory, and all the holy angels with him, then shall he sit upon the throne of his glory, and before him shall be gathered all nations; and he shall separate them one from another. Then shall the King say unto them on his right hand, Come, ye blessed of my Father, inherit the kingdom prepared for you from the foundation of the world: For I was an hungered, and ye gave me meat: I was thirsty, and ye gave me drink: I was a stranger, and ye took me in: naked, and ye clothed me: I was sick, and ye visited me: I was in prison, and ye came unto me. And inasmuch as ye have done it to one of the least of these my brethren, ye have done it unto me."* It is not necessary to understand this passage as a literal account of what will actually pass on that day. Supposing it only a scenical description of the rules and principles, by which the Supreme Arbiter of our destiny will regulate his decisions, it conveys the same lesson to us; it equally demonstrates of how great value and importance these duties in the sight of God are, and what stress will be laid upon them. The apostles also describe this virtue as propitiating the Divine favour in an eminent degree. And these recommendations have produced their effect. It does not appear that, before the times of Christianity, an infirmary, hospital, or public charity of any kind, existed in the world; whereas most countries in Christendom have long abounded with these institutions. To which may be added, that a spirit of private liberality seems to flourish amidst the decay of many other virtues; not to mention the legal provision for the poor, which obtains in this country, and which was unknown and unthought of by the most humanised nations of antiquity.

St. Paul adds upon the subject an excellent direction, and which is practicable by all who have any thing to give: "Upon the first day of the week (or any other stated time) let every one of you lay by in

*Matthew, xxv. 31.

store, as God hath prospered him." By which I understand St. Paul to recommend what is the very thing wanting with most men, *the being charitable upon a plan*; that is, upon a deliberate comparison of our fortunes with the reasonable expenses and expectation of our families, to compute what we can spare, and to lay by so much for charitable purposes in some mode or other. The *mode* will be a consideration afterwards.

The effect which Christianity produced upon some of its first converts, was such as might be looked for from a divine religion, coming with full force and miraculous evidence upon the consciences of mankind. It overwhelmed all worldly considerations in the expectation of a more important existence: "And the multitude of them that believed, were of one heart and of one soul; neither said any of them that aught of the things which he possessed was his own; but they had all things in common. Neither was there any among them that lacked; for as many as were possessors of lands or houses, sold them, and brought the prices of the things that were sold, and laid them down at the apostles' feet; and distribution was made unto every man according as he had need." Acts, iv. 32.

Nevertheless, this community of goods, however it manifested the sincere zeal of the primitive Christians, is no precedent for our imitation. It was confined to the Church at Jerusalem; continued not long there; was never enjoined upon any (Acts, v. 4); and, although it might suit with the particular circumstances of a small and select society, is altogether impracticable in a large and mixed community.

The conduct of the apostles upon the occasion deserves to be noticed. Their followers laid down their fortunes at their feet: but so far were they from taking advantage of this unlimited confidence, to enrich themselves, or to establish their own authority, that they soon after got rid of this business, as inconsistent with the main object of their mission, and transferred the custody and management of the public fund to deacons elected to that office by the people at large. (Acts, vi.)

II. *The manner of bestowing bounty; or the different kinds of charity.*

Every question between the different kinds of charity, supposes the sum bestowed to be the same.

There are three kinds of charity which prefer a claim to attention.

The first, and in my judgement one of the best, is to give stated and considerable sums, by way of pension or annuity, to individuals or families, with whose behaviour and distress we ourselves are acquainted. When I speak of *considerable* sums, I mean only that five pounds, or any other sum, given at once, or divided amongst five or fewer families, will do more good than the same sum distributed amongst a greater number in shillings or half-crowns; and that, because it is more likely to be properly applied by the persons who receive it. A poor fellow, who can find no better use for a shilling than to drink his benefactor's health, and purchase half an hour's recreation for himself, would hardly break into a guinea for any such purpose, or be so improvident as not to lay it by for an occasion of importance, *e.g.* for his rent, his clothing, fuel, or stock of winter's provision. It is a still greater recommendation of this kind of charity, that pensions and annuities, which are paid regularly, and can be expected at the time, are the only way by which we can prevent one part of a poor man's sufferings—the *dread* of want.

2. But as this kind of charity supposes that proper objects of such expensive benefactions fall within our private knowledge and observation, which does not happen to all, a second method of doing good, which is in every one's power who has the money to spare, is by subscription to public charities. Public charities admit of this argument in their favour, that your money goes farther towards attaining the end for which it is given, than it can do by any private and separate beneficence. A guinea, for example, contributed to an infirmary, becomes the means of providing one

patient at least with a physician, surgeon, apothecary, with medicine, diet, lodging, and suitable attendance; which is not the tenth
part of what the same assistance, if it could be procured at all,
would cost to a sick person or family in any other situation.

3. The last, and, compared with the former, the lowest exertion of benevolence, is in the relief of beggars. Nevertheless, I by
no means approve the indiscriminate rejection of all who implore
our alms in this way. Some may perish by such a conduct. Men are
sometimes overtaken by distress, for which all other relief would
come too late. Beside which, resolutions of this kind compel us to
offer such violence to our humanity, as may go near, in a little
while, to suffocate the principle itself; which is a very serious consideration. A good man, if he do not surrender himself to his feelings without reserve, will at least lend an ear to importunities
which come accompanied with outward attestations of distress; and
after a patient audience of the complaint, will direct himself, not so
much by any previous resolution which he may have formed upon
the subject, as by the circumstances and credibility of the account
that he receives.

There are other species of charity well contrived to make the
money expended *go far*: such as keeping down the price of fuel or
provision, in case of monopoly or temporary scarcity, by purchasing the articles at the best market, and retailing them at prime cost,
or at a small loss; or the adding of a bounty to particular species of
labour, when the price is accidentally depressed.

The proprietors of large estates have it in their power to facilitate the maintenance, and thereby to encourage the establishment,
of families (which is one of the noblest purposes to which the rich
and great can convert their endeavours), by building cottages, split-
ting farms, erecting manufactories, cultivating wastes, embanking
the sea, draining marshes, and other expedients, which the situation of each estate points out. If the profits of these undertakings

do not repay the expense, let the authors of them place the difference to the account of charity. It is true of almost all such projects, that the public is a gainer by them, whatever the owner be. And where the loss can be spared, this consideration is sufficient.

It is become a question of some importance, under what circumstances works of charity ought to be done in private, and when they may be made public without detracting from the merit of the action, if indeed they ever may; the Author of our religion having delivered a rule upon this subject which seems to enjoin universal secrecy: "When thou doest alms, let not thy left hand know what thy right hand doeth; that thy alms may be in secret, and thy Father, which seeth in secret, himself shall reward thee openly." (Matt. vi. 3, 4). From the preamble to this prohibition I think it, however, plain, that our Saviour's sole design was to forbid *ostentation*, and all publishing of good works which proceeds from that motive. "Take heed that ye do not your alms before men, *to be seen of them;* otherwise ye have no reward of your Father which is in heaven; therefore, when thou doest thine alms, do not sound a trumpet before thee, as the hypocrites do, in the synagogues and in the streets, *that they may have glory of men.* Verily I say unto you, they have their reward." ver. 2. There are motives for the doing our alms in public, beside those of *ostentation*, with which therefore our Saviour's rule has no concern: such as to testify our approbation of some particular species of charity, and to recommend it to others; to take off the prejudice which the want, or, which is the same thing, the suppression, of our name in the list of contributors might excite against the charity, or against ourselves. And, so long as these motives are free from any mixture of vanity, they are in no danger of invading our Saviour's prohibition; they rather seem to comply with another direction which he has left us: "Let your light so shine before men, that they may see your good works, and glorify your Father which is in heaven." If it be necessary to propose a precise distinction upon the subject, I can think of none better than the following: When our bounty is *beyond* our fortune and station, that is, when it is more than could be expected from us, our charity should be private, if privacy be practicable: when it is not more than might be expected, it may be public: for we cannot hope to influence others to the imitation of *extraordinary* generosity, and therefore want, in the former case, the only justifiable reason for making it public.

Having thus described several different exertions of charity, it may not be improper to take notice of a species of liberality, which is not *charity*, in any sense of the word: I mean the giving of entertainments or liquor, for the sake of popularity; or the rewarding, treating, and maintaining, the companions of our diversions, as hunters, shooters, fishers, and the like. I do not say that this is criminal; I only say that it is not charity; and that we are not to suppose, because we *give*, and give to the *poor*, that it will stand in the place, or supersede the obligation, of more meritorious and disinterested bounty.

III. *The pretences by which men excuse themselves from giving to the poor.*

1. "That they have nothing to spare," *i.e.* nothing for which they have not provided some other use; nothing which their plan or expense, together with the savings they have resolved to lay by, will not exhaust: never reflecting whether it be in their *power*, or that it is their *duty*, to retrench their expenses, and contract their plan, "that they may have to give to them that need": or, rather, that this ought to have been part of their plan originally.

2. "That they have families of their own, and that charity begins at home." The extent of this plea will be considered, when we come to explain the duty of parents.

3. "That charity does not consist in giving money, but in benevolence, philanthropy, love to all mankind, goodness of heart," &c. Hear St. James: "If a brother or sister be naked, and destitute of

daily food, and one of you say unto them, Depart in peace; be ye warmed and filled; notwithstanding *ye give them not those things which are needful to the body;* what doth it profit?" (James, ii. 15, 16.)

4. "That giving to the poor is not mentioned in St. Paul's description of charity, in the thirteenth chapter of his First Epistle to the Corinthians." This is not a description of charity, but of good-nature; and it is not necessary that every duty be mentioned in every place.

5. "That they pay the poor-rates." They might as well allege that they pay their debts: for the poor have the same right to that portion of a man's property which the laws assign to them, that the man himself has to the remainder.

6. "That they employ many poor persons"—for their own sake, not the poor's—otherwise it is a good plea.

7. "That the poor do not suffer so much as we imagine; that education and habit have reconciled them to the evils of their condition, and make them easy under it." Habit can never reconcile human nature to the extremities of cold, hunger, and thirst, any more than it can reconcile the hand to the touch of a red-hot iron: besides, the question is not, how unhappy any one is, but how much more happy we can make him.

8. "That these people, give them what you will, will never thank you, or think of you for it." In the first place, this is not true: in the second place, it was not for the sake of their thanks that you relieved them.

9. "That we are liable to be imposed upon." If a due inquiry be made, our merit is the same: beside that the distress is generally real, although the cause be untruly stated.

10. "That they should apply to their parishes." This is not always practicable: to which we may add, that there are many requisites to a comfortable subsistence, which parish relief does not

supply; and that there are some, who would suffer almost as much from receiving parish relief as by the want of it; and, lastly, that there are many modes of charity to which this answer does not relate at all.

11. "That giving money, encourages idleness and vagrancy." This is true only of injudicious and indiscriminate generosity.

12. "That we have too many objects of charity at home, to bestow any thing upon strangers; or, that there are other charities, which are more useful, or stand in greater need." The value of this excuse depends entirely upon the *fact*, whether we actually relieve those neighbouring objects, and contribute to those other charities.

Beside all these excuses, pride, or prudery, or delicacy, or love of ease, keep one half of the world out of the way of observing what the other half suffer.

Chapter 6
RESENTMENT

Resentment may be distinguished into *anger* and *revenge*.

By *anger*, I mean the pain we suffer upon the receipt of an injury or affront, with the usual effects of that pain upon ourselves.

By *revenge*, the inflicting of pain upon the person who has injured or offended us, farther than the just ends of punishment or reparation require.

Anger prompts to revenge; but it is possible to suspend the effect, when we cannot altogether quell the principle. We are bound also to endeavour to qualify and correct the principle itself. So that our duty requires two different applications of the mind; and, for that reason, anger and revenge may be considered separately.

Chapter 7
ANGER

"Be ye angry, and sin not"; therefore all anger is not sinful; I suppose, because some degree of it, and upon some occasions, is inevitable.

It becomes sinful, or contradicts, however, the rule of Scripture, when it is conceived upon slight and inadequate provocations, and when it continues long.

1. When it is conceived upon slight provocations: for, "charity suffereth long, is not easily provoked." "Let every man be slow to anger." Peace, long-suffering, gentleness, meekness, are enumerated among the fruits of the Spirit, Gal. v. 22, and compose the true Christian temper, as to this article of duty.

2. When it continues long: for, "let not the sun go down upon your wrath."

These precepts, and all reasoning indeed on the subject, suppose the passion of anger to be within our power; and this power consists not so much in any faculty we possess of appeasing our wrath at the time (for we are passive under the smart which an injury or affront occasions, and all we can then do, is to prevent its breaking out into action), as in so mollifying our minds by habits of just reflection, as to be less irritated by impressions of injury, and to be sooner pacified.

Reflections proper for this purpose, and which may be called the *sedatives* of anger, are the following: the possibility of mistaking the motives from which the conduct that offends us proceeded; how often *our* offences have been the effect of inadvertency, when they were construed into indications of malice; the inducement which prompted our adversary to act as he did, and how powerfully the same inducement has, at one time or other, operated upon ourselves: that he is suffering perhaps under a contrition, which he is ashamed, or wants opportunity, to confess; and how ungenerous it is to triumph by coldness or insult over a spirit already humbled in secret; that the returns of kindness are sweet, and that there is neither honour, nor virtue, nor use, in resisting them—for, some persons think themselves bound to cherish and keep alive their indignation, when they find it dying away of itself. We may remember that others have their passions, their prejudices, their favourite aims, their fears, their cautions, their interests, their sudden impulses, their varieties of apprehension, as well as we: we may recollect what hath sometimes passed in our minds, when we have gotten on the wrong side of a quarrel, and imagine the same to be passing in our adversary's mind now; when we became sensible of our misbehaviour, what palliations we perceived in it, and expected others to perceive; how we were affected by the kindness, and felt the superiority, of a generous reception and ready forgiveness; how persecution revived our spirits with our enmity, and seemed to justify the conduct in ourselves which we before blamed. Add to this, the indecency of extravagant anger; how it renders us, whilst it lasts, the scorn and sport of all about us, of which it leaves us, when it ceases, sensible and ashamed; the inconveniences and irretrievable misconduct into which our irascibility has sometimes betrayed us; the friendships it has lost us; the distresses and embarrassments in which we have been involved by it; and the sore repentance which, on one account or other, it always cost us.

But the reflection calculated above all others to allay the haughtiness of temper which is ever finding out provocations, and which renders anger so impetuous, is that which the Gospel proposes; namely, that we ourselves are, or shortly shall be, suppliants for mercy and pardon at the judgement-seat of God. Imagine our secret sins disclosed and brought to light; imagine us thus humbled and exposed; trembling under the hand of God; casting ourselves on his compassion; crying out for mercy; imagine such a creature to talk of satisfaction and revenge; refusing to be entreated, disdaining to forgive; extreme to mark and to resent what is done amiss—imagine, I say, this, and you can hardly frame to yourself an instance of more impious and unnatural arrogance.

The point is, to habituate ourselves to these reflections, till they rise up of their own accord when they are wanted, that is, instantly upon the receipt of an injury or affront, and with such force and colouring, as both to mitigate the paroxysms of our anger at the time, and at length to produce an alteration in the temper and disposition itself.

Chapter 8
REVENGE

All pain occasioned to another in consequence of an offence or injury received from him, further than what is calculated to procure reparation, or promote the just ends of punishment, is so much revenge.

There can be no difficulty in knowing when we occasion pain to another; nor much in distinguishing whether we do so, with a view only to the ends of punishment, or from revenge; for, in the one case we proceed with reluctance, in the other with pleasure.

It is highly *probable* from the light of nature, that a passion, which seeks its gratification immediately and expressly in giving pain, is disagreeable to the benevolent will and counsels of the Creator. Other passions and pleasures may, and often do, produce pain to some one: but then pain is not, as it is here, the object of the passion, and the direct cause of the pleasure. This *probability* is converted into certainty, if we give credit to the authority which dictated the several passages of the Christian Scriptures that condemn revenge, or, what is the same thing, which enjoin forgiveness.

We will set down the principal of these passages; and endeavour to collect from them, what conduct upon the whole is allowed towards an enemy, and what is forbidden.

"If ye forgive men their trespasses, your heavenly Father will also forgive you; but if ye forgive not men their trespasses, neither will your Father forgive your trespasses."—"And his lord was wroth, and delivered him to the tormentors, till he should pay all that was due unto him: so likewise shall my heavenly Father do also unto you, if ye from your hearts forgive not every one his brother their trespasses."—"Put on bowels of mercy, kindness, humbleness of mind, meekness, long-suffering; forbearing one another, forgiving one another, if any man have a quarrel against any, even as Christ forgave you, so also do ye."—"Be patient towards all men; see that none render evil for evil to any man."—"Avenge not yourselves, but rather give place unto wrath: for it is written, Vengeance is mine; I will repay, saith the Lord. Therefore, if thine enemy hunger, feed him; if he thirst, give him drink: for, in so doing, thou shalt heap coals of fire on his head. Be not overcome of evil, but overcome evil with good."*

I think it evident, from some of these passages taken separately, and still more so from all of them together, that *revenge*, as described in the beginning of this chapter, is forbidden in every degree, under all forms, and upon every occasion. We are likewise forbidden to refuse to an enemy even the most imperfect right: "if he hunger, feed him; if he thirst, give him drink";† which are examples of imperfect rights. If one who has offended us solicit

---

*Matt. vi. 14, 15: xviii. 34, 35. Col. iii. 12, 13. 1 Thess. v. 14, 15. Rom. xii. 19, 20, 21.

†See also Exodus, xxiii. 4. "If thou meet thine enemy's ox, or his ass, going astray, thou shalt surely bring it back to him again; if thou see the ass of him that hateth thee, lying under his burden, and wouldest forbear to help him, thou shalt surely help with him."

from us a vote to which his qualifications entitle him, we may not refuse it from motives of resentment, or the remembrance of what we have suffered at his hands. His right, and our obligation which follows the right, are not altered by his enmity to us, or by ours to him.

On the other hand, I do not conceive that these prohibitions were intended to interfere with the punishment or prosecution of public offenders. In the eighteenth chapter of St. Matthew, our Saviour tells his disciples; "If thy brother who has trespassed against thee neglect to hear the church, let him be unto thee as an heathen man, and a publican." Immediately after this, when St. Peter asked him, "How oft shall my brother sin against me, and I forgive him? till seven times?" Christ replied, "I say not unto thee until seven times, but until seventy times seven"; that is, as often as he repeats the offence. From these two adjoining passages compared together, we are authorised to conclude that the forgiveness of an enemy is not inconsistent with the proceeding against him as a public offender; and that the discipline established in religious or civil societies, for the restraint or punishment of criminals, ought to be upholden.

If the magistrate be not tied down with these prohibitions from the execution of his office, neither is the prosecutor; for the office of the prosecutor is as necessary as that of the magistrate.

Nor, by parity of reason, are private persons withholden from the correction of vice, when it is in their power to exercise it; provided they be assured that it is the guilt which provokes them, and not the injury; and that their motives are pure from all mixture and every particle of that spirit which delights and triumphs in the humiliation of an adversary.

Thus it is no breach of Christian charity, to withdraw our company or civility when the same tends to discountenance any vicious practice. This is one branch of that extrajudicial discipline, which supplies the defects and the remissness of law; and is expressly authorised by St. Paul (1 Cor. v. 11.); "But now I have written unto you not to keep company, if any man that is called a brother be a fornicator, or covetous, or an idolater, or a railer, or a drunkard, or an extortioner; with such an one, no not to eat." The use of this association against vice continues to be experienced in one remarkable instance, and might be extended with good effect to others. The confederacy amongst women of character, to exclude from their society kept-mistresses and prostitutes, contributes more perhaps to discourage that condition of life, and prevents greater numbers from entering into it, than all the considerations of prudence and religion put together.

We are likewise allowed to practise so much caution as not to put ourselves in the way of injury, or invite the repetition of it. If a servant or tradesman has cheated us, we are not bound to trust him again; for this is to encourage him in his dishonest practices, which is doing him much harm.

Where a benefit can be conferred only upon one or few, and the choice of the person upon whom it is conferred is a proper object of favour, we are at liberty to prefer those who have not offended us to those who have; the contrary being nowhere required.

Christ, who, as hath been well demonstrated,* estimated virtues by their solid utility, and not by their fashion or popularity, prefers this of the forgiveness of injuries to every other. He enjoins it oftener; with more earnestness; under a greater variety of forms; and with this weighty and peculiar circumstance, that the forgiveness of others is the condition upon which alone we are to expect, or even ask, from God, forgiveness for ourselves. And this preference is justified by the superior importance of the virtue itself. The feuds and animosities in families and between neighbours, which disturb the intercourse of

---

*See a View of the Internal Evidence of the Christian Religion.

human life, and collectively compose half the misery of it, have their foundation in the want of a forgiving temper; and can never cease, but by the exercise of this virtue, on one side, or on both.

Chapter 9
DUELLING

Duelling as a punishment is absurd; because it is an equal chance, whether the punishment fall upon the offender, or the person offended. Nor is it much better as a reparation: it being difficult to explain in what the *satisfaction* consists, or how it tends to undo the injury, or to afford a compensation for the damage already sustained.

The truth is, it is not considered as either. A law of honour having annexed the imputation of cowardice to patience under an affront, challenges are given and accepted with no other design than to prevent or wipe off this suspicion; without malice against the adversary, generally without a wish to destroy him, or any other concern than to preserve the duellist's own reputation and reception in the world.

The unreasonableness of this rule of manners is one consideration; the duty and conduct of individuals, while such a rule exists, is another.

As to which, the proper and single question is this, whether a regard for our own reputation is, or is not, sufficient to justify the taking away the life of another?

Murder is forbidden; and wherever human life is deliberately taken away, otherwise than by public authority, there is murder. The value and security of human life make this rule necessary; for I do not see what other idea or definition of murder can be admitted, which will not let in so much private violence, as to render society a scene of peril and bloodshed.

If unauthorised laws of honour be allowed to create exceptions to divine prohibitions, there is an end of all morality, as founded in the will of the Deity: and the obligation of every duty may, at one time or other, be discharged by the caprice and fluctuations of fashion.

"But a sense of shame is so much torture; and no relief presents itself otherwise than by an attempt upon the life of our adversary." What then? The distress which men suffer by the want of money is oftentimes extreme, and no resource can be discovered but that of removing a life which stands between the distressed person and his inheritance. The motive in this case is as urgent, and the means much the same, as in the former: yet this case finds no advocate.

Take away the circumstance of the duellist's exposing his own life, and it becomes assassination; add this circumstance, and what difference does it make? None but this, that fewer perhaps will imitate the example, and human life will be somewhat more safe, when it cannot be attacked without equal danger to the aggressor's own. Experience, however, proves that there is fortitude enough in most men to undertake this hazard; and were it otherwise, the defence, at best, would be only that which a highwayman or house-breaker might plead, whose attempt had been so daring and desperate, that few were likely to repeat the same.

In expostulating with the duellist, I all along suppose his adversary to fall. Which supposition I am at liberty to make, because, if he have no right to kill his adversary, he has none to attempt it.

In return, I forbear from applying to the case of duelling the Christian principle of the forgiveness of injuries; because it is possible to suppose the injury to be forgiven, and the duellist to act entirely from a concern for his own reputation: where this is not the case, the guilt of duelling is manifest, and is greater.

In this view it seems unnecessary to distinguish between him who gives, and him who accepts, a challenge: for, on the one hand, they incur an equal hazard of destroying life; and on the other, both act upon the same persuasion, that what they do is necessary, in order to recover or preserve the good opinion of the world.

Public opinion is not easily controlled by civil institutions: for which reason I question whether any regulations can be contrived, of sufficient force to suppress or change the rule of honour, which stigmatises all scruples about duelling with the reproach of cowardice.

The insufficiency of the redress which the law of the land affords, for those injuries which chiefly affect a man in his sensibility and reputation, tempts many to redress themselves. Prosecutions for such offences, by the trifling damages that are recovered, serve only to make the sufferer more ridiculous. This ought to be remedied.

For the army, where the point of honour is cultivated with exquisite attention and refinement, I would establish *a Court of Honour*, with a power of awarding those submissions and acknowledgements, which it is generally the purpose of a challenge to obtain; and it might grow into a fashion, with persons of rank of all professions, to refer their quarrels to this tribunal.

Duelling, as the law now stands, can seldom be overtaken by legal punishment. The challenge, appointment, and other previous circumstances, which indicate the intention with which the combatants met, being suppressed, nothing appears to a court of justice, but the actual rencounter; and if a person be slain when actually fighting with his adversary, the law deems his death nothing more than manslaughter.

Chapter 10
LITIGATION

"If it be *possible*, live peaceably with all men"; which precept contains an indirect confession that this is not always *possible*.

The instances* in the fifth chapter of Saint Matthew are rather to be understood as proverbial methods of describing the general duties of forgiveness and benevolence, and the temper which we ought to aim at acquiring, than as directions to be specifically observed; or of themselves of any great importance to be observed. The first of these is, "If thine enemy smite thee on thy right cheek, turn to him the other also"; yet, when one of the officers struck Jesus with the palm of his hand, we find Jesus rebuking him for the outrage with becoming indignation; "If I have spoken evil, bear witness of the evil; but if well, why smitest thou me?" (John xviii. 43.) It may be observed, likewise, that the several examples are drawn from instances of small and tolerable injuries. A rule which forbade all opposition to injury, or defence against it, could have no other effect, than to put the good in subjection to the bad, and deliver one half of mankind to the depredation of the other half; which must be the case, so long as some considered themselves as bound by such a rule, whilst others despised it. Saint Paul, though no one inculcated forgiveness and forbearance with a deeper sense of the value and obligation of these virtues, did not interpret either of them to require an unresisting submission to every contumely, or a neglect of the means of safety and self-defence. He took refuge in the laws of his country, and in the privileges of a Roman citizen, from the conspiracy of the Jews (Acts xxv. 11.); and from the clandestine violence of the chief captain (Acts xxii. 25.). And yet this is the same apostle who reproved the litigiousness of his Corinthian converts with so much severity. "Now, therefore, there is utterly a fault among you, because ye go to law one with

*"Whoever shall smite thee on thy right cheek, turn to him the other also: and if any man will sue thee at the law, and take away thy coat, let him have thy cloak also; and whosoever shall compel thee to go a mile, go with him twain."

another. Why do ye not rather take wrong? why do ye not rather suffer yourselves to be defrauded?"

On the one hand, therefore, Christianity excludes all vindictive motives, and all frivolous causes of prosecution; so that where the injury is small, where no good purpose of public example is answered, where forbearance is not likely to invite a repetition of the injury, or where the expense of an action becomes a punishment too severe for the offence; there the Christian is withholden by the authority of his religion from going to law.

On the other hand, a law-suit is inconsistent with no rule of the Gospel, when it is instituted,

1. For the establishing of some important right.

2. For the procuring a compensation for some considerable damage.

3. For the preventing of future injury.

But since it is supposed to be undertaken simply with a view to the ends of justice and safety, the prosecutor of the action is bound to confine himself to the cheapest process which will accomplish these ends, as well as to consent to any peaceable expedient for the same purpose; as to *a reference*, in which the arbitrators can do, what the law cannot, divide the damage, when the fault is mutual; or to *a compounding of the dispute*, by accepting a compensation in the gross, without entering into articles and items, which it is often very difficult to adjust separately.

As to the rest, the duty of the contending parties may be expressed in the following directions:

Not by appeals to prolong a suit against your own conviction.

Not to undertake or defend a suit against a poor adversary, or render it more dilatory or expensive than necessary, with the hope of intimidating or wearing him out by the expense.

Not to influence *evidence* by authority or expectation;

Nor to stifle any in your possession, although it make against you.

Hitherto we have treated of civil actions. In criminal prosecutions, the private injury should be forgotten, and the prosecutor proceed with the same temper, and upon the same motives, as the magistrate; the one being a necessary minister of justice as well as the other, and both bound to direct their conduct by a dispassionate care of the public welfare.

In whatever degree the punishment of an offender is conducive, or his escape dangerous, to the interest of the community, in the same degree is the party against whom the crime was committed bound to prosecute, because such prosecutions must in their nature originate from the sufferer.

Therefore great public crimes, as robberies, forgeries, and the like, ought not to be spared, from an apprehension of trouble or expense in carrying on the prosecution, from false shame, or misplaced compassion.

There are many offences, such as nuisances, neglect of public roads, forestalling, engrossing, smuggling, sabbath-breaking, profaneness, drunkenness, prostitution, the keeping of lewd or disorderly houses, the writing, publishing, or exposing to sale, lascivious books or pictures, with some others, the prosecution of which, being of equal concern to the whole neighbourhood, cannot be charged as a peculiar obligation upon any.

Nevertheless, there is great merit in the person who undertakes such prosecutions upon proper motives; which amounts to the same thing.

The character of an *informer* is in this country undeservedly odious. But where any public advantage is likely to be attained by information, or other activity in promoting the execution of the laws, a good man will despise a prejudice founded in no just reason, or will acquit himself of the imputation of interested designs by giving away his share of the penalty.

On the other hand, prosecutions for the sake of the reward, or for the gratification of private enmity, where the offence produces no public mischief, or where it arises from ignorance or inadvertency, are reprobated under the general description of *applying a rule of law to a purpose for which it was not intended.* Under which description may be ranked an officious revival of the laws against Popish priests, and dissenting teachers.

Chapter 11
GRATITUDE

Examples of ingratitude check and discourage voluntary beneficence; and in this, the mischief of ingratitude consists. Nor is the mischief small; for after all is done that can be done, towards providing for the public happiness, by prescribing rules of justice, and enforcing the observation of them by penalties or compulsion, much must be left to those offices of kindness, which men remain at liberty to exert or withhold. Now not only the choice of the objects, but the quantity and even the existence of this sort of kindness in the world, depends, in a great measure, upon the return which it receives: and this is a consideration of general importance.

A second reason for cultivating a grateful temper in ourselves, is the following: The same principle, which is touched with the kindness of a human benefactor, is capable of being affected by the divine goodness, and of becoming, under the influence of that affection, a source of the purest and most exalted virtue. The love of God is the sublimest gratitude. It is a mistake, therefore, to imagine, that this virtue is omitted in the Christian Scriptures; for every precept which commands us "to love God, because he first loved us," presupposes the principle of gratitude, and directs it to its proper object.

It is impossible to particularise the several expressions of gratitude, inasmuch as they vary with the character and situation of the benefactor, and with the opportunities of the person obliged; which variety admits of no bounds.

It may be observed, however, that gratitude can never oblige a man to do what is wrong, and what by consequence he is previously obliged not to do. It is no ingratitude to refuse to do, what we cannot reconcile to any apprehensions of our duty; but it is ingratitude and hypocrisy together, to pretend this reason, when it is not the real one: and the frequency of such pretences has brought this apology for non-compliance with the will of a benefactor into unmerited disgrace.

It has long been accounted a violation of delicacy and generosity to upbraid men with the favours they have received: but it argues a total destitution of both these qualities, as well as of moral probity, to take advantage of that ascendency which the conferring of benefits justly creates, to draw or drive those whom we have obliged into mean or dishonest compliances.

Chapter 12
Slander

Speaking is acting, both in philosophical strictness, and as to all moral purposes: for if the mischief and motive of our conduct be the same, the means which we use make no difference.

And this is in effect what our Saviour declares, Matt. xii. 37: "By thy words thou shalt be justified, and by thy words thou shalt be condemned": by thy words, as well, that is, as by thy actions; the one shall be taken into the account as well as the other, for they both possess the same property of voluntarily producing good or evil.

Slander may be distinguished into two kinds; *malicious* slander, and *inconsiderate* slander.

Malicious slander is the relating of either truth or falsehood, for the purpose of creating misery.

I acknowledge that the truth or falsehood of what is related varies the degree of guilt considerably; and that slander, in the ordinary acceptation of the term, signifies the circulation of mischievous *falsehoods*: but truth may be made instrumental to the success of malicious designs as well as falsehood; and if the end be bad, the means cannot be innocent.

I think the idea of slander ought to be confined to the production of *gratuitous* mischief. When we have an end or interest of our own to serve, if we attempt to compass it by falsehood, it is *fraud;* if by a publication of the truth, it is not without some additional circumstance of breach of promise, betraying of confidence, or the like, to be deemed criminal.

Sometimes the pain is intended for the person to whom we are speaking; at other times, an enmity is to be gratified by the prejudice or disquiet of a third person. To infuse suspicions, to kindle or continue disputes, to avert the favour and esteem of benefactors from their dependents, to render some one whom we dislike contemptible or obnoxious in the public opinion, are all offices of slander; of which the guilt must be measured by the intensity and extent of the misery produced.

The disguises under which slander is conveyed, whether in a whisper, with injunctions of secrecy, by way of caution, or with affected reluctance, are all so many aggravations of the offence, as they indicate more deliberation and design.

Inconsiderate slander is a different offence, although the same mischief actually follow, and although the mischief might have been foreseen. The not being conscious of that design which we have hitherto attributed to the slanderer, makes the difference.

The guilt here consists in the want of that regard to the consequences of our conduct, which a just affection for human happiness, and concern for our duty, would not have failed to have produced in us. And it is no answer to this crimination to say, that we entertained no evil *design*. A servant may be a very bad servant, and yet seldom or never *design* to act in opposition to his master's interest or will: and his master may justly punish such servant for a thoughtlessness and neglect nearly as prejudicial as deliberate disobedience. I accuse you not, he may say, of any express intention to hurt me; but had not the fear of my displeasure, the care of my interest, and indeed all the qualities which constitute the merit of a good servant, been wanting in you, they would not only have excluded every direct purpose of giving me uneasiness, but have been so far present to your thoughts, as to have checked that unguarded licentiousness by which I have suffered so much, and inspired you in its place with an habitual solicitude about the effects and tendency of what you did or said. This very much resembles the case of all sins of inconsideration; and, amongst the foremost of these, that of inconsiderate slander.

Information communicated for the real purpose of warning, or cautioning, is not slander.

Indiscriminate praise is the opposite of slander, but it is the opposite extreme; and, however it may affect to be thought to be excess of candour, is commonly the effusion of a frivolous understanding, or proceeds from a settled contempt of all moral distinctions.

BOOK III

PART III

OF RELATIVE DUTIES WHICH RESULT
FROM THE CONSTITUTION
OF THE SEXES

The constitution of the sexes is the foundation of *marriage*.

Collateral to the subject of marriage, are fornication, seduction, adultery, incest, polygamy, divorce.

Consequential to marriage, is the relation and reciprocal duty of parent and child.

We will treat of these subjects in the following order: first, of the public use of marriage institutions; secondly, of the subjects collateral to marriage, in the order in which we have here proposed them; thirdly, of marriage itself; and, lastly, of the relation and reciprocal duties of parents and children.

Chapter 1
OF THE PUBLIC USE OF
MARRIAGE INSTITUTIONS

The public use of marriage institutions consists in their promoting the following beneficial effects.

1. The private comfort of individuals, especially of the female sex. It may be true, that all are not interested in this reason; nevertheless, it is a reason to all for abstaining from any conduct which

tends in its general consequence to obstruct marriage; for whatever promotes the happiness of the majority, is binding upon the whole.

2. The production of the greatest number of healthy children, their better education, and the making of due provision for their settlement in life.

3. The peace of human society, in cutting off a principal source of contention, by assigning one or more women to one man, and protecting his exclusive right by sanctions of morality and law.

4. The better government of society, by distributing the community into separate families, and appointing over each the authority of a master of a family, which has more actual influence than all civil authority put together.

5. The same end, in the additional security which the state receives for the good behaviour of its citizens, from the solicitude they feel for the welfare of their children, and from their being confined to permanent habitations.

6. The encouragement of industry.

Some ancient nations appear to have been more sensible of the importance of marriage institutions than we are. The Spartans obliged their citizens to marry by penalties, and the Romans encouraged theirs by the *jus trium liberorum*. A man who had no child, was entitled by the Roman law only to one half of any legacy that should be left him, that is, at the most, could only receive one half of the testator's fortune.

Chapter 2
FORNICATION

The first and great mischief, and by consequence the guilt, of promiscuous concubinage, consists in its tendency to diminish marriages, and thereby to defeat the several beneficial purposes enumerated in the preceding chapter.

Promiscuous concubinage discourages marriage, by abating the chief temptation to it. The male part of the species will not undertake the encumbrance, expense, and restraint of married life, if they can gratify their passions at a cheaper price; and they will undertake any thing, rather than not gratify them.

The reader will learn to comprehend the magnitude of this mischief, by attending to the importance and variety of the uses to which marriage is subservient; and by recollecting withal, that the malignity and moral quality of each crime is not to be estimated by the particular effect of one offence, or of one person's offending, but by the general tendency and consequence of crimes of the same nature. The libertine may not be conscious that these irregularities hinder his own marriage, from which he is deterred, he may allege, by different considerations; much less does he perceive how *his* indulgences can hinder other men from marrying; but what will he say would be the consequence, if the same licentiousness were universal? or what should hinder its becoming universal, if it be innocent or allowable in him?

2. Fornication supposes prostitution; and prostitution brings and leaves the victims of it to almost certain misery. It is no small quantity of misery in the aggregate, which, between want, disease, and insult, is suffered by those outcasts of human society, who infest populous cities; the whole of which is a *general consequence* of fornication, and to the increase and continuance of which, every act and instance of fornication contributes.

3. Fornication* produces habits of ungovernable lewdness, which introduce the more aggravated crimes of seduction, adultery, violation, &c. Likewise, however it be accounted for, the criminal commerce of the sexes corrupts and depraves the mind

---

*Of this passion it has been truly said, that "irregularity has no limits; that one excess draws on another; that the most easy, therefore, as well as the most excellent way of being virtuous, is to be so entirely." Ogden, Serm. xvi.

and moral character more than any single species of vice whatsoever. That ready perception of guilt, that prompt and decisive resolution against it, which constitutes a virtuous character, is seldom found in persons addicted to these indulgences. They prepare an easy admission for every sin that seeks it; are, in low life, usually the first stage in men's progress to the most desperate villanies; and, in high life, to that lamented dissoluteness of principle, which manifests itself in a profligacy of public conduct, and a contempt of the obligations of religion and of moral probity. Add to this, that habits of libertinism incapacitate and indispose the mind for all intellectual, moral, and religious pleasures; which is a great loss to any man's happiness.

4. Fornication perpetuates a disease, which may be accounted one of the sorest maladies of human nature; and the effects of which are said to visit the constitution of even distant generations.

The passion being natural, proves that it was intended to be gratified; but under what restrictions, or whether without any, must be collected from different considerations.

The Christian Scriptures condemn fornication absolutely and peremptorily. "Out of the heart," says our Saviour, "proceed evil thoughts, murders, adulteries, *fornication*, thefts, false witness, blasphemies; these are the things which defile a man." These are Christ's own words: and one word from him upon the subject is final. It may be observed with what society fornication is classed; with murders, thefts, false witness, blasphemies. I do not mean that these crimes are all equal, because they are all mentioned together; but it proves that they are all crimes. The apostles are more full upon this topic. One well-known passage in the Epistle to the Hebrews may stand in the place of all others; because, admitting the authority by which the apostles of Christ spake and wrote, it is decisive: "Marriage and the bed undefiled is honourable amongst all men: but whoremongers and adulterers God will judge"; which was a great deal to say, at a time when it was not agreed, even amongst philosophers themselves, that fornication was a crime.

The Scriptures give no sanction to those austerities, which have been since imposed upon the world under the name of Christ's religion; as the celibacy of the clergy, the praise of perpetual virginity, the *prohibitio concubitûs cum gravidâ uxore;* but with a just knowledge of, and regard to, the condition and interest of the human species, have provided, in the marriage of one man with one woman, an adequate gratification for the propensities of their nature, and have *restricted* them to that gratification.

The avowed toleration, and in some countries the licensing, taxing, and regulating of public brothels, has appeared to the people an authorising of fornication; and has contributed, with other causes, so far to vitiate the public opinion, that there is no practice of which the immorality is so little thought of or acknowledged, although there are few in which it can more plainly be made out. The legislators who have patronised receptacles of prostitution, ought to have foreseen this effect, as well as considered, that whatever facilitates fornication, diminishes marriages. And, as to the usual apology for this relaxed discipline, the danger of greater enormities, if access to prostitutes were too strictly watched and prohibited, it will be time enough to look to that, when the laws and the magistrates have done their utmost. The greatest vigilance of both will do no more, than oppose some bounds and some difficulties to this intercourse. And, after all, these pretended fears are without foundation in experience. The men are in all respects the most virtuous, in countries where the women are most chaste.

There is a species of cohabitation, distinguishable, no doubt, from vagrant concubinage, and which, by reason of its resemblance to marriage, may be thought to participate of the sanctity and innocence of that estate; I mean the case of *kept mistresses,* under the favourable circumstance of mutual fidelity. This case I have heard defended by some such apology as the following:

"That the marriage-rite being different in different countries, and in the same country amongst different sects, and with some scarce any thing; and, moreover, not being prescribed or even mentioned in Scripture, can be accounted for only as of a form and ceremony of human invention: that, consequently, if a man and woman betroth and confine themselves to each other, their inter-course must be the same, as to all moral purposes, as if they were legally married; for the addition or omission of that which is a mere form and ceremony, can make no difference in the sight of God, or in the actual nature of right and wrong."

To all which it may be replied,

1. If the situation of the parties be the same thing as marriage, why do they not marry?

2. If the man choose to have it in his power to dismiss the woman at his pleasure, or to retain her in a state of humiliation and dependence inconsistent with the rights which marriage would confer upon her, it is not the same thing.

It is not at any rate the same thing to the children.

Again, as to the marriage-rite being a mere form, and that also variable, the same may be said of signing and sealing of bonds, wills, deeds of conveyance, and the like, which yet make a great difference in the rights and obligations of the parties concerned in them.

And with respect to the rite not being appointed in Scripture—the Scriptures forbid fornication, that is, cohabitation without marriage, leaving it to the law of each country to pronounce what is, or what makes, a marriage; in like manner as they forbid thefts, that is, the taking away of another's property, leaving it to the municipal law to fix what makes the thing property, or whose it is; which also, as well as marriage, depend upon arbitrary and muta-ble forms.

Laying aside the injunctions of Scripture, the plain account of the question seems to be this: It is immoral, because it is pernicious, that men and women should cohabit, without undertaking certain irrevocable obligations, and mutually conferring certain civil rights; if, therefore, the law has annexed these rights and obligations to certain forms, so that they cannot be secured or undertaken by any other means, which is the case here (for, whatever the parties may promise to each other, nothing but the marriage-ceremony can make their promise irrevocable), it becomes in the same degree immoral, that men and women should cohabit without the interposition of these forms.

If fornication be criminal, all those incentives which lead to it are accessaries to the crime, as lascivious conversation, whether expressed in obscene, or disguised under modest phrases; also wanton songs, pictures, books; the writing, publishing, and circulating of which, whether out of frolic, or for some pitiful profit, is productive of so extensive a mischief from so mean a temptation, that few crimes, within the reach of private wickedness, have more to answer for, or less to plead in their excuse.

Indecent conversation, and by parity of reason all the rest, are forbidden by Saint Paul, Eph. iv. 29: "Let no corrupt communication proceed out of your mouth"; and again, Col. iii. 8: "Put off filthy communication out of your mouth."

The invitation, or voluntary admission, of impure thoughts, or the suffering them to get possession of the imagination, falls within the same description, and is condemned by Christ, Matt. v. 28: "Whosoever looketh on a woman to lust after her, hath

committed adultery with her already in his heart." Christ, by
thus enjoining a regulation of the thoughts, strikes at the root
of the evil.

Chapter 3
SEDUCTION

The *seducer* practises the same stratagems to draw a woman's person into his power, that a *swindler* does to get possession of your
goods, or money; yet the *law of honour*, which abhors deceit,
applauds the address of a successful intrigue; so much is this capricious rule guided by names, and with such facility does it accommodate itself to the pleasures and conveniency of higher life!

Seduction is seldom accomplished without fraud; and the fraud
is by so much more criminal than other frauds, as the injury effected
by it is greater, continues longer, and less admits reparation.

This injury is threefold: to the woman, to her family, and to the
public.

I. The injury to the woman is made up of the *pain* she suffers
from shame, or the *loss* she sustains in her reputation and prospects
of marriage, and of the *depravation of her moral principle*.

1. This *pain* must be extreme, if we may judge of it from those
barbarous endeavours to conceal their disgrace, to which women,
under such circumstances, sometimes have recourse; comparing
also this barbarity with their passionate fondness for their offspring
in other cases. Nothing but an agony of mind the most insupportable can induce a woman to forget her nature, and the pity which
even a stranger would show to a helpless and imploring infant. It is
true, that all are not urged to this extremity; but if any are, it affords
an indication of how much all suffer from the same cause. What
shall we say to the authors of such mischief?

2. The *loss* which a woman sustains by the ruin of her reputation almost exceeds computation. Every person's happiness depends in part upon the respect and reception which they meet with in the world; and it is no inconsiderable mortification, even to the firmest tempers, to be rejected from the society of their equals, or received there with neglect and disdain. But this is not all, nor the worst. By a rule of life, which it is not easy to blame, and which it is impossible to alter, a woman loses with her chastity the chance of marrying at all, or in any manner equal to the hopes she had been accustomed to entertain. Now marriage, whatever it be to a man, is that from which every woman expects her chief happiness. And this is still more true in low life, of which condition the women are who are most exposed to solicitations of this sort. Add to this, that where a woman's maintenance depends upon her character (as it does, in a great measure, with those who are to support themselves by service), little sometimes is left to the forsaken sufferer, but to starve for want of employment, or to have recourse to prostitution for food and raiment.

3. As a woman collects her virtue into this point, the loss of her chastity is generally the *destruction of her moral principle;* and this consequence is to be apprehended, whether the criminal intercourse be discovered or not.

II. The injury to the family may be understood, by the application of that infallible rule, "of doing to others, what *we would* that others should do unto us." Let a father or a brother say, for what consideration they would suffer this injury to a daughter or a sister; and whether any, or even a total, loss of fortune, could create equal affliction and distress. And when they reflect upon this, let them distinguish, if they can, between a robbery, committed upon their property by fraud or forgery, and the ruin of their happiness by the treachery of a seducer.

III. The public at large lose the benefit of the woman's service in her proper place and destination, as a wife and parent. This, to the whole community, may be little; but it is often more than all the good which the seducer does to the community can recompense. Moreover, prostitution is supplied by seduction; and in proportion to the danger there is of the woman's betaking herself, after her first sacrifice, to a life of public lewdness, the seducer is answerable for the multiplied evils to which his crime gives birth.

Upon the whole, if we pursue the effects of seduction through the complicated misery which it occasions, and if it be right to estimate crimes by the mischief they knowingly produce, it will appear something more than mere invective to assert, that not one half of the crimes, for which men suffer death by the laws of England, are so flagitious as this.*

Chapter 4
ADULTERY

A new sufferer is introduced, the injured husband, who receives a wound in his sensibility and affections, the most painful and incurable that human nature knows. In all other respects, adultery on the part of the man who solicits the chastity of a married woman, includes the crime of seduction, and is attended with the same mischief.

The infidelity of the woman is aggravated by cruelty to her children, who are generally involved in their parents' shame, and always made unhappy by their quarrel.

If it be said that these consequences are chargeable not so much upon the crime, as the discovery, we answer, first, that the crime

---

*Yet the law has provided no punishment for this offence beyond a pecuniary satisfaction to the injured family; and this can only be come at, by one of the quaintest fictions in the world; by the father's bringing his action against the seducer, for the loss of his daughter's service, during her pregnancy and nurturing.

could not be discovered unless it were committed, and that the commission is never secure from discovery; and secondly, that if we excuse adulterous connexions, whenever they can hope to escape detection, which is the conclusion to which this argument conducts us, we leave the husband no other security for his wife's chastity, than in her want of opportunity or temptation; which would probably either deter men from marrying, or render marriage a state of such jealousy and alarm to the husband, as must end in the slavery and confinement of the wife.

The vow, by which married persons mutually engage their fidelity, "is witnessed before God," and accompanied with circumstances of solemnity and religion, which approach to the nature of an oath. The married offender therefore incurs a crime little short of perjury, and the seduction of a married woman is little less than subornation of perjury—and this guilt is independent of the discovery.

All behaviour which is designed, or which knowingly tends, to captivate the affection of a married woman, is a barbarous intrusion upon the peace and virtue of a family, though it fall short of adultery.

The usual and only apology for adultery is, the prior transgression of the other party. There are degrees, no doubt, in this, as in other crimes: and so far as the bad effects of adultery are anticipated by the conduct of the husband or wife who offends first, the guilt of the second offender is less. But this falls very far short of a justification; unless it could be shown that the obligation of the marriage-vow depends upon the condition of reciprocal fidelity; for which construction there appears no foundation, either in expediency, or in the terms of the promise, or in the design of the legislature which prescribed the marriage-rite. Moreover, the rule contended for by this plea has a manifest tendency to multiply the offence, but none to reclaim the offender.

The way of considering the offence of one party as a *provocation* to the other, and the other as only *retaliating* the injury by repeating the crime, is a childish trifling with words.

"Thou shalt not commit adultery," was an interdict delivered by God himself. By the Jewish law, adultery was capital to both parties in the crime: "Even he that committeth adultery with his neighbour's wife, the adulterer and adulteress shall surely be put to death."—Levit. xx. 10. Which passages prove, that the Divine Legislator placed a great difference between adultery and fornication. And with this agree the Christian Scriptures: for, in almost all the catalogues they have left us of crimes and criminals, they enumerate "fornication, adultery, whoremongers, adulterers," (Matthew, xv. 19. 1 Cor. vi. 9. Gal. v. 9. Heb. viii. 4.) by which mention of both, they show that they did not consider them as the same: but that the crime of adultery was, in their apprehension, distinct from, and accumulated upon, that of fornication.

The history of the woman taken in adultery, recorded in the eighth chapter of St. John's Gospel, has been thought by some to give countenance to that crime. As Christ told the woman, "Neither do I *condemn* thee," we must believe, it is said, that he deemed her conduct either not criminal, or not a crime, however, of the heinous nature which we represent it to be. A more attentive examination of the case will, I think, convince us, that from *it* nothing can be concluded as to Christ's opinion concerning adultery, either one way or the other. The transaction is thus related: "Early in the morning Jesus came again into the temple, and all the people came unto him: and he sat down and taught them. And the Scribes and Pharisees brought unto him a woman taken in adultery: and when they had set her in the midst, they say unto him, Master, this woman was taken in adultery, in the very act: now Moses, in the law, commanded that such should be stoned; but what sayest thou?

This they said tempting him, that they might have to accuse him. But Jesus stooped down, and with his finger wrote on the ground, as though he heard them not. So when they continued asking him, he lift up himself, and said unto them, He that is without sin amongst you, let him first cast a stone at her; and again he stooped down and wrote on the ground: and they which heard it, being convicted by their own conscience, went out one by one, beginning at the eldest, even unto the last; and Jesus was left alone, and the woman standing in the midst. When Jesus had lift up himself, and saw none but the woman, he said unto her, Woman, where are those thine accusers? hath no man condemned thee? She said unto him, No man, Lord. And he said unto her, *Neither do I condemn thee;* go, and sin no more."

"This they said tempting him, that they might have to accuse him"; to draw him, that is, into an exercise of judicial authority, that they might have to accuse him before the Roman governor, of usurping or intermeddling with the civil government. This was their design; and Christ's behaviour throughout the whole affair proceeded from a knowledge of this design, and a determination to defeat it. He gives them at first a cold and sullen reception, well suited to the insidious intention with which they came: "He stooped down, and with his finger wrote on the ground, as though he heard them not." "When they *continued* asking him," when they teased him to speak, he dismissed them with a rebuke, which the impertinent malice of their errand, as well as the sacred character of many of them, deserved: "He that is without sin (that is, this sin) among you, let him first cast a stone at her." This had its effect. Stung with the reproof, and disappointed of their aim, they stole away one by one, and left Jesus and the woman alone. And then follows the conversation, which is the part of the narrative most material to our present subject. "Jesus said unto her, Woman, where are those thine accusers? hath no man condemned thee? She said, No man, Lord. And Jesus said unto her, Neither do I condemn thee; go, and sin no more." Now, when Christ asked the woman, "Hath no man *condemned* thee?" he certainly spoke, and was understood by the woman to speak, of a legal and judicial condemnation; otherwise, her answer, "No man, Lord," was not true. In every other sense of condemnation, as blame, censure, reproof, private judgement, and the like, many had condemned her; all those indeed who brought her to Jesus. If then a judicial sentence was what Christ meant by *condemning* in the question, the common use of language requires us to suppose that he meant the same in his reply, "Neither do I condemn thee," *i.e.* I pretend to no judicial character or authority over thee; it is no office or business of mine to pronounce or execute the sentence of the law.

When Christ adds, "Go, and sin no more," he in effect tells her, that she had sinned already: but as to the degree or quality of the sin, or Christ's opinion concerning it, nothing is declared, or can be inferred, either way.

Adultery, which was punished with death during the Usurpation, is now regarded by the law of England only as a civil injury; for which the imperfect satisfaction that money can afford, may be recovered by the husband.

Chapter 5
INCEST

In order to preserve chastity in families, and between persons of different sexes, brought up and living together in a state of unreserved intimacy, it is necessary by every method possible to inculcate an abhorrence of incestuous conjunctions; which abhorrence can only be upholden by the absolute reprobation of *all* commerce of the sexes between near relations. Upon this principle, the *marriage* as well as other cohabitations of brothers and sisters, of lineal kindred, and of all who usually live in the same family, may be said to be forbidden by the law of nature.

Restrictions which extend to remoter degrees of kindred than what this reason makes it necessary to prohibit from intermarriage, are founded in the authority of the positive law which ordains them, and can only be justified by their tendency to diffuse wealth, to connect families, or to promote some political advantage.

The Levitical law, which is received in this country, and from which the rule of the Roman law differs very little, prohibits* marriage between relations, within *three* degrees of kindred; computing the generations, not from, but through the common ancestor, and accounting affinity the same as consanguinity. The issue, however, of such marriages are not bastardised, unless the parents be divorced during their life-time.

The Egyptians are said to have allowed of the marriage of brothers and sisters. Amongst the Athenians, a very singular regulation prevailed; brothers and sisters of the half-blood, if related by the father's side, might marry; if by the mother's side, they were prohibited from marrying. The same custom also probably obtained in Chaldea so early as the age in which Abraham left it; for he and Sarah his wife stood in this relation to each other: "And yet, indeed, she is my sister; she is the daughter of my father, but not of my mother; and she became my wife." Gen. xx. 12.

---

*The Roman law continued the prohibition to the descendants of brothers and sisters without limits. In the Levitical and English law, there is nothing to hinder a man from marrying his *great*-niece.

Chapter 6
POLYGAMY

The equality* in the number of males and females born into the world, intimates the intention of God, that one woman should be assigned to one man: for if to one man be allowed an exclusive right to five or more women, four or more men must be deprived of the exclusive possession of any; which could never be the order intended.

It seems also a significant indication of the divine will, that he at first created only one woman to one man. Had God intended polygamy for the species, it is probable he would have begun with it; especially as, by giving to Adam more wives than one, the multiplication of the human race would have proceeded with a quicker progress.

Polygamy not only violates the constitution of nature, and the apparent design of the Deity, but produces to the parties themselves, and to the public, the following bad effects: contests and jealousies amongst the wives of the same husband; distracted affections, or the loss of all affection, in the husband himself; a voluptuousness in the rich, which dissolves the vigour of their intellectual as well as active faculties, producing that indolence and imbecility both of mind and body, which have long characterised the nations of the East; the abasement of one half of the human species, who, in countries where polygamy obtains, are

---

*This equality is not exact. The number of male infants exceeds that of females in the proportion of nineteen to eighteen, or thereabouts: which excess provides for the greater consumption of males by war, seafaring, and other dangerous or unhealthy occupations.

degraded into mere instruments of physical pleasure to the other half; neglect of children; and the manifold, and sometimes unnatural mischiefs, which arise from a scarcity of women. To compensate for these evils, polygamy does not offer a single advantage. In the article of population, which it has been thought to promote, the community gain nothing:* for the question is not, whether one man will have more children by five or more wives than by one; but whether these five wives would not bear the same or a greater number of children to five separate husbands. And as to the care of the children, when produced, and the sending of them into the world in situations in which they may be likely to form and bring up families of their own, upon which the increase and succession of the human species in a great degree depend; this is less provided for, and less practicable, where twenty or thirty children are to be supported by the attention and fortunes of one father, than if they were divided into five or six families, to each of which were assigned the industry and inheritance of two parents.

*Nothing, I mean, compared with a state in which marriage is nearly universal. Where marriages are less general, and many women unfruitful from the want of husbands, polygamy might at first add a little to population; and but a little: for, as a variety of wives would be sought chiefly from temptations of voluptuousness, it would rather increase the demand for female beauty, than for the sex at large. And this *little* would soon be made less by many deductions. For, first, as none but the opulent can maintain a plurality of wives, where polygamy obtains, the rich indulge in it, while the rest take up with a vague and barren incontinency. And, secondly, women would grow less jealous of their virtue, when they had nothing for which to reserve it, but a chamber in the *haram*; when their chastity was no longer to be rewarded with the rights and happiness of a wife, as enjoyed under the marriage of one woman to one man. These considerations may be added to what is mentioned in the text, concerning the easy and early settlement of children in the world.

Whether simultaneous polygamy was permitted by the law of Moses, seems doubtful:* but whether permitted or not, it was certainly practised by the Jewish patriarchs, both before that law, and under it. The permission, if there were any, might be like that of divorce, "for the hardness of their heart," in condescension to their established indulgences, rather than from the general rectitude or propriety of the thing itself. The state of manners in Judea had probably undergone a reformation in this respect before the time of Christ, for in the New Testament we meet with no trace or mention of any such practice being tolerated.

For which reason, and because it was likewise forbidden amongst the Greeks and Romans, we cannot expect to find any express law upon the subject in the Christian code. The words of Christ[†] (Matt. xix. 9.) may be construed by an easy implication to prohibit polygamy: for, if "whoever putteth away his wife, and *marrieth* another, committeth adultery," he who marrieth another *without* putting away the first, is no less guilty of adultery: because the adultery does not consist in the repudiation of the first wife (for, however unjust or cruel that may be, it is not adultery), but in entering into a second marriage during the legal existence and obligation of the first. The several passages in Saint Paul's writings, which speak of marriage, always suppose it to signify the union of one man with one woman. Upon this supposition he argues, Rom. vii. 1, 2, 3: "Know ye not, brethren (for I speak to them that know the law), how that the law hath dominion over a man, as long as he liveth? For the woman which hath an husband, is bound by the law to her husband so long as he liveth; but if the husband be dead, she is loosed from the law of her husband: so then, if while her husband

---

*See Deut. xvii. 17; xxi. 15.

[†]"I say unto you, Whosoever shall put away his wife, except it be for fornication, and shall marry another, committeth adultery."

liveth she be married to another man, she shall be called an adulteress." When the same apostle permits marriage to his Corinthian
converts (which, "for the present distress," he judges to be inconvenient), he restrains the permission to the marriage of one husband with one wife: "It is good for a man not to touch a woman;
nevertheless, to avoid fornication, let every man have his own wife,
and let every woman have her own husband."

The manners of different countries have varied in nothing more
than in their domestic constitutions. Less polished and more luxurious nations have either not perceived the bad effects of polygamy,
or, if they did perceive them, they who in such countries possessed
the power of reforming the laws have been unwilling to resign their
own gratifications. Polygamy is retained at this day among the
Turks, and throughout every part of Asia, in which Christianity is
not professed. In Christian countries, it is universally prohibited. In
Sweden, it is punished with death. In England, besides the nullity of
the second marriage, it subjects the offender to transportation, or
imprisonment and branding, for the first offence, and to capital
punishment for the second. And whatever may be said in behalf of
polygamy when it is authorised by the law of the land, the marriage
of a second wife during the life-time of the first, in countries where
such a second marriage is void, must be ranked with the most dangerous and cruel of those frauds, by which a woman is cheated out
of her fortune, her person, and her happiness.

The ancient Medes compelled their citizens, in one canton, to
take seven wives; in another, each woman to receive five husbands:
according as war had made, in one quarter of their country, an
extraordinary havoc among the men, or the women had been carried away by an enemy from another. This regulation, so far as it
was adapted to the proportion which subsisted between the number of males and females, was founded in the reason upon which
the most approved nations of Europe proceed at present.

Caesar found amongst the inhabitants of this island a species of polygamy, if it may be so called, which was perfectly singular. *Uxores*, says he, *habent deni duodenique inter se communes; et maxime fratres cum fratribus, parentesque cum liberis: sed si qui sint ex his nati, eorum habentur liberi, quo primum virgo quaeque deducta est.*

Chapter 7
OF DIVORCE

By *divorce*, I mean the dissolution of the marriage-contract, by the act, and at the will, of the husband.

This power was allowed to the husband, among the Jews, the Greeks, and latter Romans; and is at this day exercised by the Turks and Persians.

The congruity of such a right with the law of nature, is the question before us.

And, in the first place, it is manifestly inconsistent with the duty which the parents owe to their children; which duty can never be so well fulfilled as by their cohabitation and united care. It is also incompatible with the right which the mother possesses, as well as the father, to the gratitude of her children and the comfort of their society; of both which she is almost necessarily deprived, by her dismission from her husband's family.

Where this objection does not interfere, I know of no principle of the law of nature applicable to the question, beside that of general expediency.

For, if we say, that arbitrary divorces are excluded by the terms of the marriage-contract, it may be answered, that the contract might be so framed as to admit of this condition.

If we argue, with some moralists, that the obligation of a contract naturally continues, so long as the purpose, which the contracting parties had in view, requires its continuance; it will be difficult to show what purpose of the contract (the care of children excepted) should confine a man to a woman, from whom he seeks to be loose.

If we contend, with others, that a contract cannot, by the law of nature, be dissolved, unless the parties be replaced in the situation which each possessed before the contract was entered into; we shall be called upon to prove this to be a universal or indispensable property of contracts.

I confess myself unable to assign any circumstance in the marriage-contract, which essentially distinguishes it from other contracts, or which proves that it contains, what many have ascribed to it, a natural incapacity of being dissolved by the consent of the parties, at the option of one of them, or either of them. But if we trace the effects of such a rule upon the general happiness of married life, we shall perceive reasons of expediency, that abundantly justify the policy of those laws which refuse to the husband the power of divorce, or restrain it to a few extreme and specific provocations: and our principles teach us to pronounce that to be contrary to the law of nature, which can be proved to be detrimental to the common happiness of the human species.

A lawgiver, whose counsels are directed by views of general utility, and obstructed by no local impediment, would make the marriage-contract indissoluble during the joint lives of the parties, for the sake of the following advantages:

I. Because this tends to preserve peace and concord between married persons, by perpetuating their common interest, and by inducing a necessity of mutual compliance.

There is great weight and substance in both these considerations. An earlier termination of the union would produce a separate interest. The wife would naturally look forward to the dissolution of the partnership, and endeavour to draw to herself a fund against the time when she was no longer to have access to the same resources. This would beget peculation on one side, and mistrust on the other; evils which at present very little disturb the confidence of married life. The second effect of making the union determinable only by death, is not less beneficial. It necessarily happens that adverse tempers, habits, and tastes, oftentimes meet in marriage. In which case, each party must take pains to give up what offends, and practise what may gratify the other. A man and woman in love with each other do this insensibly; but love is neither general nor durable: and where that is wanting, no lessons of duty, no delicacy of sentiment, will go half so far with the generality of mankind and womankind as this one intelligible reflection, that they must each make the best of their bargain; and that, seeing they must either both be miserable, or both share in the same happiness, neither can find their own comfort, but in promoting the pleasure of the other. These compliances, though at first extorted by necessity, become in time easy and mutual; and, though less endearing than assiduities which take their rise from affection, generally procure to the married pair a repose and satisfaction sufficient for their happiness.

II. Because new objects of desire would be continually sought after, if men could, at will, be released from their subsisting engagements. Suppose the husband to have once preferred his wife to all other women, the duration of this preference cannot be trusted to. Possession makes a great difference: and there is no other security against the invitations of novelty, than the known impossibility of obtaining the object. Did the cause which brings the sexes together, hold them together by the same force with which it first attracted them to each other; or could the woman be restored to her personal integrity, and to all the advantages of her virgin estate; the power of divorce might be deposited in the hands of the husband, with less danger of abuse or inconveniency. But

constituted as mankind are, and injured as the repudiated wife generally must be, it is necessary to add a stability to the condition of
married women, more secure than the continuance of their husbands' affection; and to supply to both sides, by a sense of duty and
of obligation, what satiety has impaired of passion and of personal
attachment. Upon the whole, the power of divorce is evidently and
greatly to the disadvantage of the woman: and the only question
appears to be, whether the real and permanent happiness of one
half of the species should be surrendered to the caprice and voluptuousness of the other?

We have considered divorces as depending upon the will of the
husband, because that is the way in which they have actually
obtained in many parts of the world: but the same objections apply,
in a great degree, to divorces by mutual consent; especially when
we consider the indelicate situation and small prospect of happiness, which remains to the party who opposed his or her dissent to
the liberty and desire of the other.

The law of nature admits of an exception in favour of the injured
party, in cases of adultery, of obstinate desertion, of attempts upon
life, of outrageous cruelty, of incurable madness, and perhaps of
personal imbecility; but by no means indulges the same privilege to
mere dislike, to opposition of humours and inclinations, to contrariety of taste and temper, to complaints of coldness, neglect, severity, peevishness, jealousy: not that these reasons are trivial, but
because such objections may always be alleged, and are impossible
by testimony to be ascertained; so that to allow implicit credit to
them, and to dissolve marriages whenever either party thought fit
to pretend them, would lead in its effect to all the licentiousness of
arbitrary divorces.

Milton's story is well known. Upon a quarrel with his wife, he
paid his addresses to another woman, and set forth a public vindication of his conduct, by attempting to prove, that confirmed

dislike was as just a foundation for dissolving the marriage-contract, as adultery: to which position, and to all the arguments by which it can be supported, the above consideration affords a sufficient answer. And if a married pair, in actual and irreconcileable discord, complain that their happiness would be better consulted, by permitting them to determine a connexion which is become odious to both, it may be told them, that the same permission, as a general rule, would produce libertinism, dissension, and misery, amongst thousands, who are now virtuous, and quiet, and happy, in their condition: and it ought to satisfy them to reflect, that when their happiness is sacrificed to the operation of an unrelenting rule, it is sacrificed to the happiness of the community.

The Scriptures seem to have drawn the obligation tighter than the law of nature left it. "Whosoever," saith Christ, "shall put away his wife, except it be for fornication, and shall marry another, committeth adultery; and whoso marrieth her which is put away, doth commit adultery."—Matt. xix. 9. The law of Moses, for reasons of local expediency, permitted the Jewish husband to put away his wife: but whether for every cause, or for what causes, appears to have been controverted amongst the interpreters of those times. Christ, the precepts of whose religion were calculated for more general use and observation, revokes this permission (as given to the Jews "for the hardness of their hearts"), and promulges a law which was thenceforward to confine divorces to the single case of adultery in the wife. And I see no sufficient reason to depart from the plain and strict meaning of Christ's words. The rule was new. It both surprised and offended his disciples; yet Christ added nothing to relax or explain it.

Inferior causes may justify the separation of husband and wife, although they will not authorise such a dissolution of the marriage-contract as would leave either party at liberty to marry again: for it is that liberty, in which the danger and mischief of divorces principally consist. If the care of children does not require that

they should live together, and it is become, in the serious judgement of both, necessary for their mutual happiness that they
should separate, let them separate by consent. Nevertheless, this
necessity can hardly exist, without guilt and misconduct on one
side or on both. Moreover, cruelty, ill usage, extreme violence or
moroseness of temper, or other great and continued provocations,
make it lawful for the party aggrieved to withdraw from the society of the offender without his or her consent. The law which
imposes the marriage-vow, whereby the parties promise to "keep
to each other," or in other words, to live together, must be understood to impose it with a silent reservation of these cases; because
the same law has constituted a judicial relief from the tyranny of
the husband, by the divorce *à mensa et toro*, and by the provision
which it makes for the separate maintenance of the injured wife.
St. Paul likewise distinguishes between a wife's merely separating
herself from the family of her husband, and her marrying again:
"Let not the wife depart from her husband: but and if she do
depart, let her remain unmarried."

The law of this country, in conformity to our Saviour's injunc-
tion, confines the dissolution of the marriage-contract to the single
case of adultery in the wife; and a divorce even in that case can only
be brought about by the operation of an act of parliament, founded
upon a previous sentence in the ecclesiastical court, and a verdict
against the adulterer at common law: which proceedings taken
together, compose as complete an investigation of the complaint as
a cause can receive. It has lately been proposed to the legislature to
annex a clause to these acts, restraining the offending party from
marrying with the companion of her crime, who, by the course of
proceeding, is always known and convicted: for there is reason to
fear, that adulterous connexions are often formed with the prospect of bringing them to this conclusion; at least, when the seducer
has once captivated the affection of a married woman, he may avail

himself of this tempting argument to subdue her scruples, and complete his victory; and the legislature, as the business is managed at present, assists by its interposition the criminal design of the offenders, and confers a privilege where it ought to inflict a punishment. The proposal deserved an experiment: but something more penal will, I apprehend, be found necessary to check the progress of this alarming depravity. Whether a law might not be framed directing *the fortune of the adulteress to descend as in case of her natural death;* reserving, however, a certain proportion of the produce of it, by way of annuity, for her subsistence (such annuity, in no case, to exceed a fixed sum), and also so far suspending the estate in the hands of the heir as to preserve the inheritance to any children she might bear to a second marriage, in case there was none to succeed in the place of their mother by the first; whether, I say, such a law would not render female virtue in higher life less vincible, as well as the seducers of that virtue less urgent in their suit, we recommend to the deliberation of those who are willing to attempt the reformation of this important, but most incorrigible, class of the community. A passion for splendor, for expensive amusements and distinction, is commonly found, in that description of women who would become the objects of such a law, not less inordinate than their other appetites. A severity of the kind we propose, applies immediately to that passion. And there is no room for any complaint of injustice, since the provisions above stated, with others which might be contrived, confine the punishment, so far as it is possible, to the person of the offender; suffering the estate to remain to the heir, or within the family, of the ancestor from whom it came, or to attend the appointments of his will.

Sentences of the ecclesiastical courts, which release the parties *à vinculo matrimonii* by reason of impuberty, frigidity, consanguinity within the prohibited degrees, prior marriage, or want of the requisite consent of parents and guardians, are not dissolutions of the marriage-contract, but judicial declarations that there never was any marriage; such impediment subsisting at the time, as rendered the celebration of the marriage-rite a mere nullity. And the rite itself contains an exception of these impediments. The man and woman to be married are charged, "if they know any impediment why they may not be lawfully joined together, to confess it"; and assured "that so many as are coupled together, otherwise than God's word doth allow, are not joined together by God, neither is their matrimony lawful"; all which is intended by way of solemn notice to the parties, that the vow they are about to make will bind their consciences and authorise their cohabitation, only upon the supposition that no legal impediment exists.

Chapter 8
MARRIAGE

Whether it hath grown out of some tradition of the Divine appointment of marriage in the persons of our first parents, or merely from a design to impress the obligation of the marriage-contract with a solemnity suited to its importance, the marriage-rite, in almost all countries of the world, has been made a religious ceremony;* although marriage, in its own nature, and abstracted from the rules and declarations which the Jewish and Christian Scriptures deliver concerning it, be properly a civil contract, and nothing more.

With respect to one main article in matrimonial alliances, a total alteration has taken place in the fashion of the world; the wife

---

*It was not, however, in Christian countries required that marriages should be celebrated in churches, till the thirteenth century of the Christian aera. Marriages in *England* during the Usurpation, were solemnised before justices of the peace: but for what purpose this novelty was introduced, except to degrade the clergy, does not appear.

now brings money to her husband, whereas anciently the husband paid money to the family of the wife; as was the case among the *Jewish* patriarchs, the *Greeks,* and the old inhabitants of *Germany.** This alteration has proved of no small advantage to the female sex: for their importance in point of fortune procures to them, in modern times, that assiduity and respect, which are always wanted to compensate for the inferiority of their strength; but which their personal attractions would not always secure.

Our business is with marriage, as it is established in this country. And in treating thereof, it will be necessary to state the terms of the marriage vow, in order to discover:

1. What duties this vow creates.
2. What a situation of mind at the time is inconsistent with it.
3. By what subsequent behaviour it is violated.

The husband promises, on his part, "to love, comfort, honour, and keep, his wife": the wife on hers, "to obey, serve, love, honour, and keep, her husband"; in every variety of health, fortune, and condition: and both stipulate "to forsake all others, and to keep only unto one another, so long as they both shall live." This promise is called the marriage vow; is witnessed before God and the congregation; accompanied with prayers to Almighty God for his blessing upon it; and attended with such circumstances of devotion and solemnity as place the obligation of it, and the guilt of violating it, nearly upon the same foundation with that of oaths.

The parties by this vow engage their personal fidelity expressly and specifically; they engage likewise to consult and promote each other's happiness; the wife, moreover, promises *obedience* to her husband. Nature may have made and left the sexes of the human species nearly equal in their faculties, and perfectly so in their

---

*The ancient *Assyrians* sold their *beauties* by an annual auction. The prices were applied by way of portions to the more homely. By this contrivance, all of both sorts were disposed of in marriage.

rights; but to guard against those competitions which equality, or a contested superiority, is almost sure to produce, the Christian Scriptures enjoin upon the wife that obedience which she here promises, and in terms so peremptory and absolute, that it seems to extend to every thing not criminal, or not entirely inconsistent with the woman's happiness. "Let the wife," says St. Paul, "be subject to her own husband in every thing." "The ornament of a meek and quiet spirit," says the same apostle, speaking of the duty of wives, "is, in the sight of God, of great price." No words ever expressed the true merit of the female character so well as these.

The condition of human life will not permit us to say, that no one can conscientiously marry, who does not prefer the person at the altar to all other men or women in the world: but we can have no difficulty in pronouncing (whether we respect the end of the institution, or the plain terms in which the contract is conceived), that whoever is conscious, at the time of his marriage, of such a dislike to the woman he is about to marry, or of such a subsisting attachment to some other woman, that he cannot reasonably, nor does in fact, expect ever to entertain an affection for his future wife, is guilty, when he pronounces the marriage vow, of a direct and deliberate prevarication; and that, too, aggravated by the presence of those ideas of religion, and of the Supreme Being, which the place, the ritual, and the solemnity of the occasion, cannot fail of bringing to his thoughts. The same likewise of the woman. This charge must be imputed to all who, from mercenary motives, marry the objects of their aversion and disgust; and likewise to those who desert, from any motive whatever, the object of their affection, and, without being able to subdue that affection, marry another.

The crime of falsehood is also incurred by the man who intends, at the time of his marriage, to commence, renew, or continue, a personal commerce with any other woman. And the parity of reason, if a wife be capable of so much guilt, extends to her.

The marriage-vow is violated,

I. By adultery.

II. By any behaviour which, knowingly, renders the life of the other miserable; as desertion, neglect, prodigality, drunkenness, peevishness, penuriousness, jealousy, or any levity of conduct which administers occasion of jealousy.

A late regulation in the law of marriages, in this country, has made the consent of the father, if he be living, of the mother, if she survive the father, and remain unmarried, or of guardians, if both parents be dead, necessary to the marriage of a person under twenty-one years of age. By the Roman law, the consent *et avi et patris* was required so long as they lived. In France, the consent of parents is necessary to the marriage of sons, until they attain to thirty years of age; of daughters, until twenty-five. In Holland, for sons till twenty-five; for daughters, till twenty. And this distinction between the sexes appears to be well founded; for a woman is usually as properly qualified for the domestic and interior duties of a wife or mother at eighteen, as a man is for the world, and the more arduous care of providing for a family, at twenty-one.

The constitution also of the human species indicates the same distinction.*

Chapter 9
OF THE DUTY OF PARENTS

That virtue, which confines its beneficence within the walls of a man's own house, we have been accustomed to consider as little better than a more refined selfishness: and yet it will be confessed, that

*Cùm vis prolem procreandi diutiùs haereat in mare quàm in foeminâ, populi numerus nequaquam minuetur, si seriùs venerem colere inceperint viri.

the subject and matter of this class of duties are inferior to none in utility and importance: and where, it may be asked, is virtue the most valuable, but where it does the most good? What duty is the most obligatory, but that on which the most depends? And where have we happiness and misery so much in our power, or liable to be so affected by our conduct, as in our own families? It will also be acknowledged that the good order and happiness of the world are better upholden whilst each man applies himself to his own concerns and the care of his own family, to which he is present, than if every man, from an excess of mistaken generosity, should leave his own business, to undertake his neighbour's, which he must always manage with less knowledge, conveniency, and success. If, therefore, the low estimation of these virtues be well founded, it must be owing, not to their inferior importance, but to some defect or impurity in the motive. And indeed it cannot be denied, that it is in the power of *association* so to unite our children's interest with our own, as that we shall often pursue both from the same motive, place both in the same object, and with as little sense of duty in one pursuit as in the other. Where this is the case, the judgement above stated is not far from the truth. And so often as we find a solicitous care of a man's own family, in a total absence or extreme penury of every other virtue, or interfering with other duties, or directing its operation solely to the temporal happiness of the children, placing that happiness in amusement and indulgence whilst they are young, or in advancement of fortune when they grow up, there is reason to believe that this is the case. In this way, the common opinion concerning these duties may be accounted for and defended. If we look to the subject of them, we perceive them to be indispensable: If we regard the motive, we find them often not very meritorious. Wherefore, although a man seldom rises high in our esteem who has nothing to recommend him beside the care of his own family, yet we always condemn the neglect of this duty with the utmost severity; both by reason of the manifest and immediate mischief which we see arising from this neglect, and because it argues a want not only of parental affection, but of those moral principles which ought to come in aid of that affection where it is wanting. And if, on the other hand, our praise and esteem of these duties be not proportioned to the good they produce, or to the indignation with which we resent the absence of them, it is for this reason; that virtue is the most valuable, not where it produces the most good, but where it is the most wanted: which is not the case here; because its place is often supplied by instincts, or involuntary associations. Nevertheless, the offices of a parent may be discharged from a consciousness of their obligation, as well as other duties; and a sense of this obligation is sometimes necessary to assist the stimulus of parental affection; especially in stations of life, in which the wants of a family cannot be supplied without the continual hard labour of the father, and without his refraining from many indulgences and recreations which unmarried men of like condition are able to purchase. Where the parental affection is sufficiently strong, or has fewer difficulties to surmount, a principle of duty may still be wanted to direct and regulate its exertions: for otherwise it is apt to spend and waste itself in a womanish fondness for the person of the child; an improvident attention to his present ease and gratification; a pernicious facility and compliance with his humours; an excessive and superfluous care to provide the externals of happiness, with little or no attention to the internal sources of virtue and satisfaction. Universally, wherever a parent's conduct is prompted or directed by a sense of duty, there is so much virtue.

Having premised thus much concerning the place which parental duties hold in the scale of human virtues, we proceed to state and explain the duties themselves.

When moralists tell us, that parents are bound to do *all they can* for their children, they tell us more than is true; for, at that rate, every expense which might have been spared, and every profit omitted which might have been made, would be criminal.

The duty of parents has its limits, like other duties; and admits, if not of perfect precision, at least of rules definite enough for application.

These rules may be explained under the several heads of *maintenance, education,* and *a reasonable provision for the child's happiness in respect of outward condition.*

I. *Maintenance.*

The wants of children make it necessary that some person maintain them: and, as no one has a right to burthen others by his act, it follows, that the parents are bound to undertake this charge themselves. Beside this plain inference, the affection of parents to their children, if it be instinctive, and the provision which nature has prepared in the person of the mother for the sustentation of the infant, concerning the existence and design of which there can be no doubt, are manifest indications of the Divine will.

Hence we learn the guilt of those who run away from their families, or (what is much the same), in consequence of idleness or drunkenness, throw them upon a parish; or who leave them destitute at their death, when, by diligence and frugality, they might have laid up a provision for their support: also of those who refuse or neglect the care of their bastard offspring, abandoning them to a condition in which they must either perish or become burthensome to others; for the duty of maintenance, like the reason upon which it is founded, extends to bastards, as well as to legitimate children.

The Christian Scriptures, although they concern themselves little with maxims of prudence or oeconomy, and much less authorise worldly mindedness or avarice, have yet declared in explicit terms their judgement of the obligation of this duty: "If any provide not for his own, especially for those of his own household, he hath denied the faith, and is worse than an infidel" (1 Tim. v. 8); he hath disgraced the Christian profession, and fallen short in a duty which even infidels acknowledge.

II. *Education.*

Education, in the most extensive sense of the word, may comprehend every preparation that is made in our youth for the sequel of our lives; and in this sense I use it. Some such preparation is necessary for children of all conditions, because without it they must be miserable, and probably will be vicious, when they grow up, either from want of the means of subsistence, or from want of rational and inoffensive occupation. In civilised life, every thing is effected by art and skill. Whence a person who is provided with neither (and neither can be acquired without exercise and instruction) will be useless; and he that is useless, will generally be at the same time mischievous to the community. So that to send an uneducated child into the world, is injurious to the rest of mankind; it is little better than to turn out a mad dog or a wild beast into the streets.

In the inferior classes of the community, this principle condemns the neglect of parents, who do not inure their children betimes to labour and restraint, by providing them with apprenticeships, services, or other regular employment, but who suffer them to waste their youth in idleness and vagrancy, or to betake themselves to some lazy, trifling, and precarious calling: for the consequence of having thus tasted the sweets of natural liberty, at an age when their passion and relish for it are at the highest, is, that they become incapable, for the remainder of their lives, of continued industry, or of persevering attention to any thing; spend their time in a miserable struggle between the importunity of want, and the irksomeness of regular application; and are prepared to embrace every expedient, which presents a hope of supplying their necessities without confining them to the plough, the loom, the shop, or the counting-house.

In the middle orders of society, those parents are more reprehensible, who neither qualify their children for a profession, nor enable them to live without one;* and those in the highest, who, from indolence, indulgence, or avarice, omit to procure their children those liberal attainments which are necessary to make them useful in the stations to which they are destined. A man of fortune, who permits his son to consume the season of education in hunting, shooting, or in frequenting horse-races, assemblies, or other unedifying, if not vicious, diversions, defrauds the community of a benefactor, and bequeaths them a nuisance.

Some, though not the same, preparation for the sequel of their lives, is necessary for youth of every description; and therefore for bastards, as well as for children of better expectations. Consequently, they who leave the education of their bastards to chance, contenting themselves with making provision for their subsistence, desert half their duty.

III. A reasonable provision for the happiness of a child, in respect of outward condition, requires three things: a situation suited to his habits and reasonable expectations; a competent provision for the exigencies of that situation; and a probable security for his virtue.

The first two articles will vary with the condition of the parent. A situation somewhat approaching in rank and condition to the parent's own; or, where that is not practicable, similar to what other parents of like condition provide for their children; bounds the reasonable, as well as (generally speaking) the actual, expectations of the child, and therefore contains the extent of the parent's obligation.

---

*Amongst the *Athenians*, if the parent did not put his child into a way of getting a livelihood, the child was not bound to make provision for the parent when old and necessitous.

Hence, a peasant satisfies his duty, who sends out his children, properly instructed for their occupation, to husbandry or to any branch of manufacture. Clergymen, lawyers, physicians, officers in the army or navy, gentlemen possessing moderate fortunes of inheritance, or exercising trade in a large or liberal way, are required by the same rule to provide their sons with learned professions, commissions in the army or navy, places in public offices, or reputable branches of merchandise. Providing a child with a situation, includes a competent supply for the expenses of that situation, until the profits of it enable the child to support himself. Noblemen and gentlemen of high rank and fortune may be bound to transmit an inheritance to the representatives of their family, sufficient for their support without the aid of a trade or profession, to which there is little hope that a youth, who has been flattered with other expectations, will apply himself with diligence or success. In these parts of the world, public opinion has assorted the members of the community into four or five general classes, each class comprising a great variety of employments and professions, the choice of which must be committed to the private discretion of the parent.* All that can be expected from parents as a *duty*, and therefore the only rule which a moralist can deliver upon the

---

*The health and virtue of a child's future life are considerations so superior to all others, that whatever is likely to have the smallest influence upon these, deserves the parent's first attention. In respect of health, agriculture, and all active, rural, and out-of-door employments are to be preferred to manufactures and sedentary occupations. In respect of virtue, a course of dealings in which the advantage is mutual, in which the profit on one side is connected with the benefit of the other (which is the case in trade, and all serviceable art or labour), is more favourable to the moral character, than callings in which one man's gain is another man's loss; in which what you acquire, is acquired without equivalent, and parted with in distress; as in gaming, and whatever partakes of gaming, and in the predatory profits of war. The following distinctions also deserve notice: A business, like a retail trade, in which the

subject, is that they endeavour to preserve their children in the *class* in which they are born, that is to say, in which others of similar expectations are accustomed to be placed; and that they be careful to confine their hopes and habits of indulgence to objects which will continue to be attainable.

It is an ill-judged thrift, in some rich parents, to bring up their sons to mean employments, for the sake of saving the charge of a more expensive education: for these sons, when they become masters of their liberty and fortune, will hardly continue in occupations by which they think themselves degraded, and are seldom qualified for any thing better.

An attention, in the first place, to the exigencies of the children's respective conditions in the world; and a regard, in the second place, to their reasonable expectations, always postponing the expectations to the exigencies when both cannot be satisfied; ought to guide parents in the disposal of their fortunes after their death. And these exigencies and expectations must be measured by the standard which custom has established: for there is a certain appearance, attendance, establishment, and mode of living, which custom has annexed to the several ranks and orders of civil life (and which compose what is called *decency*), together with a certain

---

profits are small and frequent, and accruing from the employment, furnishes a moderate and constant engagement to the mind, and, so far, suits better with the general disposition of mankind, than professions which are supported by fixed salaries, as stations in the church, army, navy, revenue, public offices, &c. or wherein the profits are made in large sums, by a few great concerns, or fortunate adventures; as in many branches of wholesale and foreign merchandise, in which the occupation is neither so constant, nor the activity so kept alive by immediate encouragement. For security, manual arts exceed merchandise, and such as supply the wants of mankind are better than those which minister to their pleasures. Situations which promise an early settlement in marriage, are, on many accounts, to be chosen before those which require a longer waiting for a larger establishment.

society, and particular pleasures, belonging to each class: and a young person who is withheld from sharing in these for want of fortune, can scarcely be said to have a fair chance for happiness; the indignity and mortification of such a seclusion being what few tempers can bear, or bear with contentment. And as to the second consideration, of what a child may reasonably expect from his parent, he will expect what he sees all or most others in similar circumstances receive; and we can hardly call expectations unreasonable, which it is impossible to suppress.

By virtue of this rule, a parent is justified in making a difference between his children according as they stand in greater or less need of the assistance of his fortune, in consequence of the difference of their age or sex, or of the situations in which they are placed, or the various success which they have met with.

On account of the few lucrative employments which are left to the female sex, and by consequence the little opportunity they have of adding to their income, daughters ought to be the particular objects of a parent's care and foresight; and as an option of marriage, from which they can reasonably expect happiness, is not presented to every woman who deserves it, especially in times in which a licentious celibacy is in fashion with the men, a father should endeavour to enable his daughters to lead a single life with independence and decorum, even though he subtract more for that purpose from the portions of his sons than is agreeable to modern usage, or than they expect.

But when the exigencies of their several situations are provided for, and not before, a parent ought to admit the second consideration, the satisfaction of his children's expectations; and upon that principle to prefer the eldest son to the rest, and sons to daughters: which constitutes the right, and the whole right, of primogeniture, as well as the only reason for the preference of one sex to the other. The preference, indeed, of the first-born has one public good effect, that if the estate were divided equally amongst the sons, it would probably make them all idle; whereas, by the present rule of descent, it makes only one so; which is the less evil of the two. And it must further be observed on the part of the sons, that if the rest of the community make it a rule to prefer sons to daughters, an individual of that community ought to guide himself by the same rule, upon principles of mere equality. For, as the son suffers by the rule, in the fortune he may expect in marriage, it is but reasonable that he should receive the advantage of it in his own inheritance. Indeed, whatever the rule be, as to the preference of one sex to the other, marriage restores the equality. And as money is generally more convertible to profit, and more likely to promote industry, in the hands of men than of women, the custom of this country may properly be complied with, when it does not interfere with the weightier reason explained in the last paragraph.

The point of the children's actual expectations, together with the expediency of subjecting the illicit commerce of the sexes to every discouragement which it can receive, makes the difference between the claims of legitimate children and of bastards. But neither reason will in any case justify the leaving of bastards to the world without provision, education, or profession; or, what is more cruel, without the means of continuing in the situation to which the parent has introduced them; which last is, to leave them to inevitable misery.

After the first requisite, namely, a provision for the exigencies of his situation, is satisfied, a parent may diminish a child's portion, in order to punish any flagrant crime, or to punish contumacy and want of filial duty in instances not otherwise criminal: for a child who is conscious of bad behaviour, or of contempt of his parent's will and happiness, cannot reasonably expect the same instances of his munificence.

A child's vices may be of that sort, and his vicious habits so incorrigible, as to afford much the same reason for believing that he will waste or misemploy the fortune put into his power, as if he were mad or idiotish, in which case a parent may treat him as a madman or an idiot; that is, may deem it sufficient to provide for his support, by an annuity equal to his wants and innocent enjoyments, and which he may be restrained from alienating. This seems to be the only case in which a disinherison, nearly absolute, is justifiable.

Let not a father hope to excuse an inofficious disposition of his fortune, by alleging, that "every man may do what he will with his own." All the truth which this expression contains is, that this discretion is under no control of law; and that his will, however capricious, will be valid. This by no means absolves his conscience from the obligations of a parent, or imports that he may neglect, without injustice, the several wants and expectations of his family, in order to gratify a whim or pique, or indulge a preference founded in no reasonable distinction of merit or situation. Although in his intercourse with his family, and in the lesser endearments of domestic life, a parent may not always resist his partiality to a favourite child (which, however, should be both avoided and concealed, as oftentimes productive of lasting jealousies and discontents); yet, when he sits down to make his will, these tendernesses must give place to more manly deliberations.

A father of a family is bound to adjust his oeconomy with a view to these demands upon his fortune; and until a sufficiency for these ends is acquired, or in due time *probably* will be acquired (for, in human affairs, *probability* ought to content us), frugality and exertions of industry are duties. He is also justified in the declining expensive liberality: for, to take from those who want, in order to give to those who want, adds nothing to the stock of public happiness. Thus far, therefore, and no farther, the plea of "children," of "large families," "charity begins at home," &c. is an excuse for parsimony, and an answer to those who solicit our bounty. Beyond this point, as the use of riches becomes less, the desire of *laying up* should abate proportionably. The truth is, our children gain not so much as we imagine, in the chance of this world's happiness, or even of its external prosperity, by setting out in it with large capitals. Of those who have died rich, a great part began with little. And, in respect of enjoyment, there is no comparison between a fortune which a man acquires by well-applied industry, or by a series of successes in his business, and one found in his possession, or received from another.

A principal part of a parent's duty is still behind, *viz.* the using of proper precautions and expedients, in order to form and preserve his children's virtue.

To us, who believe that, in one stage or other of our existence, virtue will conduct to happiness, and vice terminate in misery; and who observe withal, that men's virtues and vices are, to a certain degree, produced or affected by the management of their youth, and the situations in which they are placed; to all who attend to these reasons, the obligation to consult a child's virtue will appear to differ in nothing from that by which the parent is bound to provide for his maintenance or fortune. The child's interest is concerned in the one means of happiness as well as in the other; and both means are equally, and almost exclusively, in the parent's power.

For this purpose, the first point to be endeavoured after is, to impress upon children the idea of *accountableness*, that is, to accustom them to look forward to the consequences of their actions in another world; which can only be brought about by the parents visibly acting with a view to these consequences themselves. Parents, to do them justice, are seldom sparing of lessons of virtue and religion: in admonitions which cost little, and which profit less; whilst their *example* exhibits a continual contradiction of what they teach.

A father, for instance, will, with much solemnity and apparent earnestness, warn his son against idleness, excess in drinking, debauchery, and extravagance, who himself loiters about all day without employment; comes home every night drunk; is made infamous in his neighbourhood by some profligate connexion; and wastes the fortune which should support, or remain a provision for his family, in riot, or luxury, or ostentation. Or he will discourse gravely before his children of the obligation and importance of revealed religion, whilst they see the most frivolous and oftentimes feigned excuses detain him from its reasonable and solemn ordinances. Or he will set before them, perhaps, the supreme and tremendous authority of Almighty God; that such a Being ought not to be named, or even thought upon, without sentiments of profound awe and veneration. This may be the lecture he delivers to his family one hour; when the next, if an occasion arise to excite his anger, his mirth, or his surprise, they will hear him treat the name of the Deity with the most irreverent profanation, and sport with the terms and denunciations of the Christian religion, as if they were the language of some ridiculous and long-exploded superstition. Now, even a child is not to be imposed upon by such mockery. He sees through the grimace of this counterfeited concern for virtue. He discovers that his parent is acting a part; and receives his admonitions as he would hear the same maxims from the mouth of a player. And when once this opinion has taken possession of the child's mind, it has a fatal effect upon the parent's influence, in all subjects; even those, in which he himself may be sincere and convinced. Whereas a silent, but observable, regard to the duties of religion, in the parent's own behaviour, will take a sure and gradual hold of the child's disposition, much beyond formal reproofs and chidings, which, being generally prompted by some present provocation, discover more of anger than of principle, and are always received with a temporary alienation and disgust.

A good parent's first care is, to be virtuous himself; his second, to make his virtues as easy and engaging to those about him as their nature will admit. Virtue itself offends, when coupled with forbidding manners. And some virtues may be urged to such excess, or brought forward so unseasonably, as to discourage and repel those who observe and who are acted upon by them, instead of exciting an inclination to imitate and adopt them. Young minds are particularly liable to these unfortunate impressions. For instance, if a father's oeconomy degenerate into a minute and teasing parsimony, it is odds but that the son, who has suffered under it, sets out a sworn enemy to all rules of order and frugality. If a father's piety be morose, rigorous, and tinged with melancholy, perpetually breaking in upon the recreation of his family, and surfeiting them with the language of religion on all occasions, there is danger lest the son carry from home with him a settled prejudice against seriousness and religion, as inconsistent with every plan of a pleasurable life; and turn out, when he mixes with the world, a character of levity or dissoluteness.

Something likewise may be done towards the correcting or improving of those early inclinations which children discover, by disposing them into situations the least dangerous to their particular characters. Thus, I would make choice of a retired life for young persons addicted to licentious pleasures; of private stations for the proud and passionate; of liberal professions, and a town-life, for the mercenary and sottish: and not, according to the general practice of parents, send dissolute youths into the army; penurious tempers to trade; or make a crafty lad an attorney; or flatter a vain and haughty temper with elevated names, or situations, or callings, to which the fashion of the world has annexed precedency and distinction, but in which his disposition, without at all promoting his success, will serve both to multiply and exasperate his disappointments. In the same way, that is, with a view to the particular frame and tendency of the

pupil's character, I would make choice of a public or private education. The reserved, timid, and indolent, will have their faculties
called forth and their nerves invigorated by a public education.
Youths of strong spirits and passions will be safer in a private education. At our public schools, as far as I have observed, more literature
is acquired, and more vice; quick parts are cultivated, slow ones are
neglected. Under private tuition, a moderate proficiency in juvenile
learning is seldom exceeded, but with more certainty attained.

Chapter 10
THE RIGHTS OF PARENTS

The rights of parents result from their duties. If it be the duty of a
parent to educate his children, to form them for a life of usefulness
and virtue, to provide for them situations needful for their subsistence and suited to their circumstances, and to prepare them for
those situations; he has a right to such authority, and in support of
that authority to exercise such discipline as may be necessary for
these purposes. The law of nature acknowledges no other foundation of a parent's right over his children, besides his duty towards
them. (I speak now of such rights as may be enforced by coercion.)
This relation confers no property in their persons, or natural
dominion over them, as is commonly supposed.

Since it is, in general, necessary to determine the destination of
children, before they are capable of judging of their own happiness,
parents have a right to elect professions for them.

As the mother herself owes obedience to the father, her authority must submit to his. In a competition, therefore, of commands,
the father is to be obeyed. In case of the death of either, the authority, as well as duty, of both parents, devolves upon the survivor.

These rights, always following the duty, belong likewise to guardians; and so much of them as is delegated by the parents or guardians, belongs to tutors, school-masters, &c.

From this principle, "that the rights of parents result from their duty," it follows that parents have no natural right over the lives of their children, as was absurdly allowed to Roman fathers; nor any to exercise unprofitable severities; nor to command the commission of crimes: for these rights can never be wanted for the purpose of a parent's duty.

Nor, for the same reason, have parents any right to sell their children into slavery. Upon which, by the way, we may observe, that the children of slaves are not, by the law of nature, born slaves: for, as the master's right is derived to him through the parent, it can never be greater than the parent's own.

Hence also it appears, that parents not only pervert, but exceed, their just authority, when they consult their own ambition, interest, or prejudice, at the manifest expense of their children's happiness. Of which abuse of parental power, the following are instances: the shutting up of daughters and younger sons in nunneries and monasteries, in order to preserve entire the estate and dignity of the family; or the using of any arts, either of kindness or unkindness, to induce them to make choice of this way of life themselves; or, in countries where the clergy are prohibited from marriage, putting sons into the church for the same end, who are never likely either to do or receive any good in it, sufficient to compensate for this sacrifice; the urging of children to marriages from which they are averse, with the view of exalting or enriching the family, or for the sake of connecting estates, parties, or interests; or the opposing of a marriage, in which the child would probably find his happiness, from a motive of pride or avarice, of family hostility, or personal pique.

Chapter 11
The Duty of Children

The Duty of Children may be considered,

    I. During childhood.

    II. After they have attained to manhood, but continue in their father's family.

    III. After they have attained to manhood, and have left their father's family.

    I. *During childhood.*

Children must be supposed to have attained to some degree of discretion before they are capable of any duty. There is an interval of eight or nine years between the dawning and the maturity of reason, in which it is necessary to subject the inclination of children to many restraints, and direct their application to many employments, of the tendency and use of which they cannot judge; for which cause, the submission of children during this period must be ready and implicit, with an exception, however, of any manifest crime which may be commanded them.

    II. *After they have attained to manhood, but continue in their father's family.*

If children, when they are grown up, voluntarily continue members of their father's family, they are bound, beside the general duty of gratitude to their parents, to observe such regulations of the family as the father shall appoint; contribute their labour to its support, if required; and confine themselves to such expenses as he shall allow. The obligation would be the same, if they were admitted into any other family, or received support from any other hand.

    III. *After they have attained to manhood, and have left their father's family.*

In this state of the relation, the duty to parents is simply the duty of gratitude; not different *in kind*, from that which we owe to any other benefactor; *in degree*, just so much exceeding other obligations, by how much a parent has been a greater benefactor than any other friend. The services and attentions, by which filial gratitude may be testified, can be comprised within no enumeration. It will show itself in compliances with the will of the parents, however contrary to the child's own taste or judgement, provided it be neither criminal, nor totally inconsistent with his happiness; in a constant endeavour to promote their enjoyments, prevent their wishes, and soften their anxieties, in small matters as well as in great; in assisting them in their business; in contributing to their support, ease, or better accommodation, when their circumstances require it; in affording them our company, in preference to more amusing engagements; in waiting upon their sickness or decrepitude; in bearing with the infirmities of their health or temper, with the peevishness and complaints, the unfashionable, negligent, austere manners, and offensive habits, which often attend upon advanced years: for where must old age find indulgence, if it do not meet with it in the piety and partiality of children?

The most serious contentions between parents and their children are those commonly which relate to marriage, or to the choice of a profession.

A parent has, in no case, a right to destroy his child's happiness. If it be true, therefore, that there exist such personal and exclusive attachments between individuals of different sexes, that the possession of a particular man or woman in marriage be really necessary for the child's happiness; or, if it be true, that an aversion to a particular profession may be involuntary and unconquerable; then it will follow, that parents, where this is the case, ought not to urge their authority, and that the child is not bound to obey it.

The point is, to discover how far, in any particular instance, this *is* the case. Whether the fondness of lovers ever continues with such intensity, and so long, that the success of their desires constitutes, or the disappointment affects, any considerable portion of their happiness, compared with that of their whole life, it is difficult to determine: but there can be no difficulty in pronouncing, that not one half of those attachments, which young people conceive with so much haste and passion, are of this sort. I believe it also to be true, that there are few aversions to a profession, which resolution, perseverance, activity in going about the duty of it, and, above all, despair of changing, will not subdue: yet there are some such. Wherefore, a child who respects his parents' judgement, and is, as he ought to be, tender of their happiness, owes, at least, so much deference to their will, as to try fairly and faithfully, in one case, whether time and absence will not cool an affection which they disapprove; and, in the other, whether a longer continuance in the profession which they have chosen for him may not reconcile him to it. The whole depends upon the experiment being made on the child's part with sincerity, and not merely with a design of compassing his purpose at last, by means of a simulated and temporary compliance. It is the nature of love and hatred, and of all violent affections, to delude the mind with a persuasion that we shall always continue to feel them as we feel them at present; we cannot conceive that they will either change or cease. Experience of similar or greater changes in ourselves, or a habit of giving credit to what our parents, or tutors, or books, teach us, may control this persuasion, otherwise it renders youth very untractable: for they see clearly and truly that it is impossible they should be happy under the circumstances proposed to them, in their present state of mind. After a sincere but ineffectual endeavour, by the child, to accommodate his inclination to his parent's pleasure, he ought not to suffer in his parent's affection, or in his fortunes. The parent, when he has reasonable proof of this, should acquiesce; at all events, the child is *then* at liberty to provide for his own happiness.

Parents have no right to urge their children upon marriages to which they are averse: nor ought, in any shape, to resent the children's disobedience to such commands. This is a different case from opposing a match of inclination, because the child's misery is a much more probable consequence; it being easier to live without a person that we love, than with one whom we hate. Add to this, that compulsion in marriage necessarily leads to prevarication; as the reluctant party promises an affection, which neither exists, nor is expected to take place: and parental, like all human authority, ceases at the point where obedience becomes criminal.

In the above-mentioned, and in all contests between parents and children, it is the parent's duty to represent to the child the consequences of his conduct; and it will be found his best policy to represent them with fidelity. It is usual for parents to exaggerate these descriptions beyond probability, and by exaggeration to lose all credit with their children; thus, in a great measure, defeating their own end.

Parents are forbidden to interfere, where a trust is reposed personally in the son; and where, consequently, the son was expected, and by virtue of that expectation is obliged, to pursue his own judgement, and not that of any other: as is the case with judicial magistrates in the execution of their office; with members of the legislature in their votes; with electors, where preference is to be given to certain prescribed qualifications. The son may assist his own judgement by the advice of his father, or of any one whom he chooses to consult: but his own judgement, whether it proceed upon knowledge or authority, ought finally to determine his conduct.

The duty of children to their parents was thought worthy to be made the subject of one of the Ten Commandments; and, as such, is recognised by Christ, together with the rest of the moral precepts of the Decalogue, in various places of the Gospel.

The same divine Teacher's sentiments concerning the relief of indigent parents, appear sufficiently from that manly and deserved indignation with which he reprehended the wretched casuistry of the Jewish expositors, who, under the name of a tradition, had contrived a method of evading this duty, by converting, or pretending to convert, to the treasury of the temple, so much of their property as their distressed parent might be entitled by their law to demand.

Agreeably to this law of Nature and Christianity, children are, by the law of England, bound to support, as well their immediate parents, as their grandfather and grandmother, or remoter ancestors, who stand in need of support.

Obedience to parents is enjoined by St. Paul to the Ephesians: "Children, obey your parents in the Lord, for this is right"; and to the Colossians: "Children, obey your parents in all things, for this is well-pleasing unto the Lord."*

By the Jewish law, disobedience to parents was in some extreme cases capital: Deut. xxi. 18.

---

*Upon which two phrases, "this is right," and, "for this is well-pleasing unto the Lord," being used by St. Paul in a sense perfectly parallel, we may observe, that moral rectitude, and conformity to the Divine will, were in his apprehension the same.

Book IV
Duties to Ourselves

────────

This division of the subject is retained merely for the sake of *method*, by which the writer and the reader are equally assisted. To the subject itself it imports nothing; for, the obligation of all duties being fundamentally the same, it matters little under what class or title any of them are considered. In strictness, there are few duties or crimes which terminate in a man's self; and so far as others are affected by their operation, they have been treated of in some article of the preceding book. We have reserved, however, to this head the *rights of self-defence;* also the consideration of *drunkenness* and *suicide,* as offences against that care of our faculties, and preservation of our persons, which we account duties, and call *duties to ourselves.*

Chapter 1
THE RIGHTS OF SELF-DEFENCE

It has been asserted, that in a state of nature we might lawfully defend the most insignificant right, provided it were a perfect determinate right, by any extremities which the obstinacy of the aggressor rendered necessary. Of this I doubt; because I doubt whether the general rule be worth sustaining at such an expense; and because, apart from the general consequence of yielding to the attempt, it cannot be contended to be for the augmentation of human happiness, that one man should lose his life, or a limb, rather than another a pennyworth of his property. Nevertheless, perfect rights can only be distinguished by their value; and it is impossible to ascertain the value at which the liberty of using extreme violence begins. The person attacked, must balance, as well as he can, between the general consequence of yielding, and the particular effect of resistance.

However, this right, if it exist in a state of nature, is suspended by the establishment of civil society: because *thereby* other remedies are provided against attacks upon our property, and because it is necessary to the peace and safety of the community, that the prevention, punishment, and redress of injuries, be adjusted by public laws. Moreover, as the individual is assisted in the recovery of his right, or of a compensation for his right, by the public strength, it is no less equitable than expedient, that he should submit to public arbitration the kind, as well as the measure, of the satisfaction which he is to obtain.

There is one case in which all extremities are justifiable; namely, when our life is assaulted, and it becomes necessary for our preservation to kill the assailant. This is evident in a state of nature; unless it can be shown, that we are bound to prefer the aggressor's life to our own, that is to say, to love our enemy *better* than ourselves, which can never be a debt of justice, nor any where appears to be a duty of charity. Nor is the case altered by our living in civil society; because, by the supposition, the laws of society cannot interpose to protect us, nor, by the nature of the case, compel restitution. This liberty is restrained to cases in which no other probable means of preserving our life remain, as flight, calling for assistance, disarming the adversary, &c. The rule holds, whether the danger proceed from a voluntary attack, as by an enemy, robber, or assassin; or from an involuntary one, as by a madman, or person sinking in the water, and dragging us after him; or where two persons are reduced to a situation in which one or both of them must perish; as in a shipwreck, where two seize upon a plank, which will support only one: although, to say the truth, these extreme cases, which happen seldom, and hardly, when they do happen, admit of moral agency, are scarcely worth mentioning, much less discussing at length.

The instance which approaches the nearest to the preservation of life, and which seems to justify the same extremities, is the defence of chastity.

In all other cases, it appears to me the safest to consider the taking away of life as authorized by the law of the land; and the person who takes it away, as in the situation of a minister or executioner of the law.

In which view, homicide, in *England*, is justifiable:

1. To prevent the commission of a crime, which, when committed, would be punishable with death. Thus, it is lawful to shoot a highwayman, or one attempting to break into a house by night; but not so if the attempt be made in the day-time: which particular distinction, by a consent of legislation that is remarkable, obtained also in the Jewish law, as well as in the laws both of Greece and Rome.

2. In necessary endeavours to carry the law into execution, as in suppressing riots, apprehending malefactors, preventing escapes, &c.

I do not know that the law holds forth its authority to any cases besides those which fall within one or other of the above descriptions; or, that, after the exception of immediate danger to life or chastity, the destruction of a human being can be innocent without that authority.

The rights of war are not here taken into the account.

Chapter 2
DRUNKENNESS

Drunkenness is either actual or habitual; just as it is one thing to be drunk, and another to be a drunkard. What we shall deliver upon the subject must principally be understood of a *habit* of intemperance; although *part* of the guilt and danger described, may be applicable to casual excesses; and *all* of it, in a certain degree, foras-much as every habit is only a repetition of single instances.

The mischief of drunkenness, from which we are to compute the guilt of it, consists in the following bad effects:

1. It betrays most constitutions either to extravagances of anger, or sins of lewdness.

2. It disqualifies men for the duties of their station, both by the temporary disorder of their faculties, and at length by a constant incapacity and stupefaction.

3. It is attended with expenses, which can often be ill spared.

4. It is sure to occasion uneasiness to the family of the drunkard.

5. It shortens life.

To these consequences of drunkenness must be added the peculiar danger and mischief of the *example*. Drunkenness is a social festive vice; apt, beyond any vice that can be mentioned, to draw in others by the example. The drinker collects his circle; the circle naturally spreads; of those who are drawn within it, many become the corrupters and centres of sets and circles of their own; every one countenancing, and perhaps emulating the rest, till a whole neighbourhood be infected from the contagion of a single example. This account is confirmed by what we often observe of drunkenness, that it is a *local* vice; found to prevail in certain countries, in certain districts of a country, or in particular towns, without any reason to be given for the fashion, but that it had been introduced by some popular examples. With this observation upon the spreading quality of drunkenness, let us connect a remark which belongs to the several evil effects above recited. The consequences of a vice, like the symptoms of a disease, though they be all enumerated in the description, seldom all meet in the same subject. In the instance under consideration, the age and temperature of one drunkard may have little to fear from inflammations of lust or anger; the fortune of a second may not be injured by the expense; a third may have no family to be disquieted by his irregularities; and a fourth may possess a constitution fortified against the poison of strong liquors. But if, as we always ought to do, we comprehend within the consequences of our conduct the mischief and tendency of the example, the above circumstances, however fortunate for the individual, will be found to vary the guilt of his intemperance less, probably, than he supposes. The moralist may expostulate with him thus: Although the waste of time and of money be of small importance to you, it may be of the utmost to some one or other whom your society corrupts. Repeated or long-continued excesses, which hurt not *your* health, may be fatal to your companion. Although you have neither wife, nor child, nor parent, to lament your absence from home, or expect your return to it with terror; other families, in which husbands and fathers have been invited to share in your ebriety, or encouraged to imitate it, may justly lay their misery or ruin at your door. This will hold good whether the person seduced be seduced immediately by you, or the vice be propagated from you to him through several intermediate examples. All these considerations it is necessary to assemble, to judge truly of a vice which usually meets with milder names and more indulgence than it deserves.

I omit those outrages upon one another, and upon the peace and safety of the neighbourhood, in which drunken revels often end; and also those deleterious and maniacal effects which strong liquors produce upon particular constitutions; because, in general propositions concerning drunkenness, no consequences should be included, but what are constant enough to be generally expected.

Drunkenness is repeatedly forbidden by Saint Paul: "Be not drunk with wine, wherein is excess." "Let us walk honestly as in the day, not in rioting and drunkenness." "Be not deceived: neither fornicators, nor *drunkards*, nor revilers, nor extortioners, shall inherit the kingdom of God." Eph. v. 18; Rom. xiii. 13; 1 Cor. vi. 9, 10.

The same apostle likewise condemns drunkenness, as peculiarly inconsistent with the Christian profession: "They that be drunken, are drunken in the night: but let us, who are of the day, be sober." 1 Thess. v. 7, 8. We are not concerned with the argument; the words amount to a prohibition of drunkenness, and the authority is conclusive.

It is a question of some importance, how far drunkenness is an excuse for the crimes which the drunken person commits.

In the solution of this question, we will first suppose the drunken person to be altogether deprived of moral agency, that is to say, of all reflection and foresight. In this condition, it is evident that he is no more capable of guilt than a madman; although, like him, he may be extremely mischievous. The only guilt with which he is chargeable, was incurred at the time when he voluntarily brought himself into this situation. And as every man is responsible for the consequences which he foresaw, or might have foreseen, and for no other, this guilt will be in proportion to the probability of such consequences ensuing. From which principle results the following rule, *viz.* that the guilt of any action in a drunken man bears the same proportion to the guilt of the like action in a sober man, that the probability of its being the consequence of drunkenness bears to absolute certainty. By virtue of this rule, those vices which are the *known* effects of drunkenness, either in general, or upon particular constitutions, are in all, or in men of such constitutions, nearly as criminal as if committed with all their faculties and senses about them.

If the privation of reason be only partial, the guilt will be of a mixed nature. For so much of his self-government as the drunkard retains, he is as responsible then as at any other time. He is entitled to no abatement beyond the strict proportion in which his moral faculties are impaired. Now I call the guilt of the crime, if a sober man had committed it, the *whole* guilt. A person in the condition we describe, incurs part of this at the instant of perpetration; and by bringing himself into such a condition, he incurred that fraction of the remaining part, which the danger of this consequence was of an integral certainty. For the sake of illustration, we are at liberty to suppose, that a man loses half his moral faculties by drunkenness; this leaving him but half his responsibility, he incurs, when he commits the action, half of the whole guilt. We will also suppose that it was known beforehand, that it was an even chance, or half a certainty, that this crime would follow his getting drunk. This makes him chargeable with half of the remainder; so that altogether, he is responsible in three fourths of the guilt which a sober man would have incurred by the same action.

I do not mean that any real case can be reduced to numbers, or the calculation be ever made with arithmetical precision; but these are the principles, and this the rule by which our general admeasurement of the guilt of such offences should be regulated.

The appetite for intoxicating liquors appears to me to be almost always *acquired*. One proof of which is, that it is apt to return only at particular times and places: as after dinner, in the evening, on the market-day, at the market-town, in such a company, at such a tavern. And this may be the reason that, if a habit of drunkenness be ever overcome, it is upon some change of place, situation, company, or profession. A man sunk deep in a habit of drunkenness will, upon such occasions as these, when he finds himself loosened from the associations which held him fast, sometimes make a plunge, and get out. In a matter of so great importance, it is well worth while, where it is in any degree practicable, to change our habitation and society, for the sake of the experiment.

Habits of drunkenness commonly take their rise either from a fondness for, and connexion with, some company, or some companion, already addicted to this practice; which affords an almost irresistible invitation to take a share in the indulgences which those about us are enjoying with so much apparent relish and delight; or from want of regular employment, which is sure to let in many superfluous cravings and customs, and often this amongst the rest; or, lastly, from grief, or fatigue, both which strongly solicit that relief which inebriating liquors administer, and also furnish a specious excuse for complying with the inclination. But the habit, when once set in, is continued by different motives from those to which it owes its origin. Persons addicted to excessive drinking suffer, in the intervals of sobriety, and near the return of their accustomed indulgence, a faintness and oppression *circa praecordia*, which it exceeds the ordinary patience of human nature to endure. This is usually relieved for a short time by a repetition of the same excess; and to this relief, as to the removal of every long-continued pain, they who have once experienced it, are urged almost beyond the power of resistance. This is not all: as the liquor loses its *stimulus*, the dose must be increased, to reach the same pitch of elevation or ease; which increase proportionably accelerates the progress of all the maladies that drunkenness brings on. Whoever reflects upon the violence of the craving in the advanced stages of the habit, and the fatal termination to which the gratification of it leads, will, the moment he perceives in himself the first symptoms of a growing inclination to intemperance, collect his resolution to this point; or (what perhaps he will find his best security) arm himself with some peremptory rule, as to the times and quantity of his indulgences. I own myself a friend to the laying down of rules to ourselves of this sort, and rigidly abiding by them. They may be exclaimed against as stiff, but they are often salutary. Indefinite resolutions of abstemiousness are apt to yield to *extraordinary* occasions; and *extraordinary* occasions to occur perpetually. Whereas, the stricter the rule is, the more tenacious we grow of it; and many a man will abstain rather than break his rule, who would not easily be brought to exercise the same mortification from higher motives. Not to mention, that when our rule is once known, we are provided with an answer to every importunity.

There is a difference, no doubt, between convivial intemperance, and that solitary sottishness which waits neither for company nor invitation. But the one, I am afraid, commonly ends in the other: and this last in the basest degradation to which the faculties and dignity of human nature can be reduced.

Chapter 3
Suicide

There is no subject in morality in which the consideration of *general consequences* is more necessary than in this of Suicide. Particular and extreme cases of suicide may be imagined, and may arise, of which it would be difficult to assign the particular mischief, or from that consideration alone to demonstrate the guilt; and these cases have been the chief occasion of confusion and doubtfulness in the question: albeit this is no more than what is sometimes true of the most acknowledged vices. I could propose many possible cases even of murder, which, if they were detached from the general rule, and governed by their own particular consequences alone, it would be no easy undertaking to prove criminal.

The true question in this argument is no other than this: May every man who chooses to destroy his life, innocently do so? Limit and distinguish the subject as you can, it will come at last to this question.

For, shall we say, that we are then at liberty to commit suicide when we find our continuance in life become useless to mankind? Any one who pleases, may make himself useless; and melancholy minds are prone to think themselves useless, when they really are not so. Suppose a law were promulgated, allowing each private person to destroy every man he met, whose longer continuance in the world he judged to be *useless;* who would not condemn the latitude of such a rule? who does not perceive that it amounts to a permission to commit murder at pleasure? A similar rule, regulating the rights over our own lives, would be capable of the same extension. Beside which, no one is *useless* for the purpose of this plea, but he who has lost every capacity and opportunity of being useful, together with the possibility of recovering any degree of either; which is a state of such complete destitution and despair, as cannot, I believe, be predicated of any man living.

Or rather, shall we say that to depart voluntarily out of life, is lawful for those alone who leave none to lament their death? If this consideration is to be taken into the account at all, the subject of debate will be, not whether there are any to sorrow for us, but whether their sorrow for our death will exceed that which we should suffer by continuing to live. Now this is a comparison of things so indeterminate in their nature, capable of so different a judgement, and concerning which the judgement will differ so much according to the state of the spirits, or the pressure of any present anxiety, that it would vary little, in hypochondriacal constitutions, from an unqualified licence to commit suicide, whenever the distresses which men felt, or fancied, rose high enough to overcome the pain and dread of death. Men are never tempted to destroy themselves but when under the oppression of some grievous uneasiness: the restrictions of the rule therefore ought to apply to these cases. But what effect can we look for from a rule which proposes to weigh our pain against that of another; the misery that is felt, against that which is only conceived; and in so corrupt a balance as the party's own distempered imagination?

In like manner, whatever other rule you assign, it will ultimately bring us to an indiscriminate toleration of suicide, in all cases in which there is danger of its being committed. It remains, therefore, to inquire what would be the effect of such a toleration: evidently, the loss of many lives to the community, of which some might be useful or important; the affliction of *many* families, and the consternation of *all:* for mankind must live in continual alarm for the fate of their friends and dearest relations, when the restraints of religion and morality are withdrawn; when every disgust which is powerful enough to tempt men to suicide, shall be deemed sufficient to justify it; and when the follies and vices, as well as the inevitable calamities, of human life, so often make existence a burthen.

A second consideration, and perfectly distinct from the former, is this: by continuing in the world, and in the exercise of those virtues which remain within our power, we retain the opportunity of meliorating our condition in a future state. This argument, it is true, does not in strictness prove suicide to be a crime; but if it supply a motive to dissuade us from committing it, it amounts to much the same thing. Now there is no condition in human life which is not capable of some virtue, active or passive. Even piety and resignation under the sufferings to which we are called, testify a trust and acquiescence in the Divine counsels, more acceptable, perhaps, than the most prostrate devotion; afford an edifying example to all who observe them; and may hope for a recompense among the most arduous of human virtues. These qualities are always in the power of the miserable; indeed of none but the miserable.

The two considerations above stated belong to all cases of suicide whatever. Beside which general reasons, each case will be aggravated by its own proper and particular consequences; by the duties that are deserted; by the claims that are defrauded; by the loss, affliction, or disgrace, which our death, or the manner of it, causes our family, kindred, or friends; by the occasion we give to many to suspect the sincerity of our moral and religious professions, and, together with ours, those of all others; by the reproach we draw upon our order, calling, or sect; in a word, by a great variety of evil consequences attending upon peculiar situations, with some or other of which every actual case of suicide is chargeable.

I refrain from the common topics of "deserting our post," "throwing up our trust," "rushing uncalled into the presence of our Maker," with some others of the same sort, not because they are *common* (for that rather affords a presumption in their favour), but because I do not perceive in them much argument to which an answer may not easily be given.

Hitherto we have pursued upon the subject the light of nature alone; taking however into the account, the expectation of a future existence, without which our reasoning upon this, as indeed all reasoning upon moral questions, is vain: we proceed to inquire, whether any thing is to be met with in Scripture, which may add to the probability of the conclusions we have been endeavouring to support. And here I acknowledge, that there is to be found neither any express determination of the question, nor sufficient evidence to prove that the case of suicide was in the contemplation of the law which prohibited murder. Any inference, therefore, which we deduce from Scripture, can be sustained only by construction and implication: that is to say, although they who were authorised to instruct mankind, have not decided a question which never, so far as appears to us, came before them; yet I think, they have left enough to constitute a presumption how they would have decided it, had it been proposed or thought of.

What occurs to this purpose, is contained in the following observations:

1. Human life is spoken of as a *term* assigned or prescribed to us: "Let us run with patience the race that is set before us."—"I have finished my course."—"That I may finish my course with joy."—"Ye have need of patience, that, after ye have done the will of God, ye might receive the promise."—These expressions appear to me

inconsistent with the opinion, that we are at liberty to determine the duration of our lives for ourselves. If this were the case, with what propriety could life be called a *race that is set before us;* or, which is the same thing, "*our course*"; that is, the course set out or appointed to us? The remaining quotation is equally strong: "That, after ye have done the will of God, ye might receive the promise." The most natural meaning that can be given to the words, "after ye have done the will of God," is, after ye have discharged the duties of life so long as God is pleased to continue you in it. According to which interpretation, the text militates strongly against suicide: and they who reject this paraphrase, will please to propose a better.

2. There is not one quality which Christ and his apostles inculcate upon their followers so often, or so earnestly, as that of patience under affliction. Now this virtue would have been in a great measure superseded, and the exhortations to it might have been spared, if the disciples of his religion had been at liberty to quit the world as soon as they grew weary of the ill usage which they received in it. When the evils of life pressed sore, they were to look forward to a "far more exceeding and eternal weight of glory"; they were to receive them, "as chastenings of the Lord," as intimations of his care and love: by these and the like reflections they were to support and improve themselves under their sufferings; but not a hint has any where escaped of seeking relief in a voluntary death. The following text in particular strongly combats all impatience of distress, of which the greatest is that which prompts to acts of suicide: "Consider Him that endured such contradiction of sinners against himself, lest ye be wearied and faint in your minds." I would offer my comment upon this passage, in these two queries: first, Whether a Christian convert, who had been impelled by the continuance and urgency of his sufferings to destroy his own life, would not have been thought by the author of this text "to have been weary," to have "fainted in his mind," to have fallen off from

that example which is here proposed to the meditation of Christians in distress? And yet, secondly, Whether such an act would not have been attended with all the circumstances of mitigation which can excuse or extenuate suicide at this day?

3. The *conduct* of the apostles, and of the Christians of the apostolic age, affords no obscure indication of their sentiments upon this point. They lived, we are sure, in a confirmed persuasion of the existence, as well as of the happiness, of a future state. They experienced in this world every extremity of external injury and distress. To die, was gain. The change which death brought with it was, in their expectation, infinitely beneficial. Yet it never, that we can find, entered into the intention of one of them to hasten this change by an act of suicide; from which it is difficult to say what motive could have so universally withheld them, except an apprehension of some unlawfulness in the expedient.

Having stated what we have been able to collect in opposition to the lawfulness of suicide, by way of direct proof, it seems unnecessary to open a separate controversy with all the arguments which are made use of to defend it; which would only lead us into a repetition of what has been offered already. The following argument, however, being somewhat more artificial and imposing than the rest, as well as distinct from the general consideration of the subject, cannot so properly be passed over. If we deny to the individual a right over his own life, it seems impossible, it is said, to reconcile with the law of nature that right which the state claims and exercises over the lives of its subjects, when it ordains or inflicts capital punishments. For this right, like all other just authority in the state, can only be derived from the compact and virtual consent of the citizens which compose the state; and it seems self-evident, if any principle in morality be so, that no one, by his consent, can transfer to another a right which he does not possess himself. It will be equally difficult to account for the power of the state to commit its subjects to the dangers of war, and to expose their lives without scruple in the field of battle; especially in offensive hostilities, in which the privileges of self-defence cannot be pleaded with any appearance of truth: and still more difficult to explain, how in such, or in any circumstances, prodigality of life can be a virtue, if the preservation of it be a duty of our nature.

This whole reasoning sets out from one error, namely, that the state acquires its right over the life of the subject from the subject's own consent, as a part of what originally and personally belonged to himself, and which he has made over to his governors. The truth is, the state derives this right neither from the consent of the subject, nor through the medium of that consent; but, as I may say, immediately from the donation of the Deity. Finding that such a power in the sovereign of the community is expedient, if not necessary, for the community itself, it is justly presumed to be the will of God, that the sovereign should possess and exercise it. It is this *presumption* which constitutes the right; it is the same indeed which constitutes every other: and if there were the like reasons to authorise the presumption in the case of private persons, suicide would be as justifiable as war, or capital executions. But until it can be shown that the power over human life may be converted to the same advantage in the hands of individuals over their own, as in those of the state over the lives of its subjects, and that it may be intrusted with equal safety to both, there is no room for arguing, from the existence of such a right in the latter, to the toleration of it in the former.

Book V
Duties Towards God

———

Chapter 1
DIVISION OF THESE DUTIES

In one sense, every duty is a duty towards God, since it is his will which makes it a duty: but there are some duties of which God is the object, as well as the author; and these are peculiarly, and in a more appropriated sense, called *duties towards God.*

That silent piety, which consists in a habit of tracing out the Creator's wisdom and goodness in the objects around us, or in the history of his dispensations; of referring the blessings we enjoy to his bounty, and of resorting in our distresses to his succour; may possibly be more acceptable to the Deity than any visible expressions of devotion whatever. Yet these latter (which, although they may be excelled, are not superseded, by the former) compose the only part of the subject which admits of direction or disquisition from a moralist.

Our duty towards God, so far as it is external, is divided into *worship* and *reverence.* God is the immediate object of both; and the difference between them is, that the one consists in action, the other in forbearance. When we go to church on the Lord's day, led thither by a sense of duty towards God, we perform an act of worship: when, from the same motive, we rest in a journey upon that day, we discharge a duty of reverence.

Divine worship is made up of adoration, thanksgiving, and prayer. But, as what we have to offer concerning the two former

may be observed of prayer, we shall make that the title of the
following chapters, and the direct subject of our consideration.

Chapter 2
OF THE DUTY AND OF THE EFFICACY OF PRAYER, SO FAR AS THE SAME APPEAR FROM THE LIGHT OF NATURE

When one man desires to obtain any thing of another, he betakes
himself to entreaty; and this may be observed of mankind in all
ages and countries of the world. Now what is universal, may be
called natural; and it seems probable that God, as our supreme governor, should expect that towards himself, which, by a natural
impulse, or by the irresistible order of our constitution, he has
prompted us to pay to every other being on whom we depend.

The same may be said of thanksgiving.

Prayer likewise is necessary to keep up in the minds of mankind
a sense of God's agency in the universe, and of their own dependency upon him.

Yet, after all, the duty of prayer depends upon its efficacy: for
I confess myself unable to conceive, how any man can pray, or be
obliged to pray, who expects nothing from his prayers; but who is
persuaded, at the time he utters his request, that it cannot possibly
produce the smallest impression upon the being to whom it is
addressed, or advantage to himself. Now the efficacy of prayer
imports that we obtain something in consequence of praying, which
we should not have received without prayer; against all expectation
of which, the following objection has been often and seriously
alleged: "If it be most agreeable to perfect wisdom and justice that
we should receive what we desire, God, as perfectly wise and just,

will give it to us without asking; if it be not agreeable to these attributes of his nature, our entreaties cannot move him to give it us, and it were impious to expect that they should." In fewer words, thus: "If what we request be fit for us, we shall have it without praying; if it be not fit for us, we cannot obtain it by praying." This objection admits but of one answer, namely, that it may be agreeable to perfect wisdom to grant that to our prayers, which it would not have been agreeable to the same wisdom to have given us without praying for. But what virtue, you will ask, is there in prayer, which should make a favour consistent with wisdom, which would not have been so without it? To this question, which contains the whole difficulty attending the subject, the following possibilities are offered in reply:

1. A favour granted to prayer may be more apt, on that very account, to produce good effects upon the person obliged. It may hold in the Divine bounty, what experience has raised into a proverb in the collation of human benefits, that what is obtained without asking, is oftentimes received without gratitude.

2. It may be consistent with the wisdom of the Deity to withhold his favours till they be asked for, as an expedient to encourage devotion in his rational creation, in order thereby to keep up and circulate a knowledge and sense of their dependency upon *him*.

3. Prayer has a natural tendency to amend the petitioner himself; and thus to bring him within the rules which the wisdom of the Deity has prescribed to the dispensation of his favours.

If these, or any other assignable suppositions, serve to remove the apparent repugnancy between the success of prayer and the character of the Deity, it is enough; for the question with the petitioner is not from which, out of many motives, God may grant his petition, or in what particular manner he is moved by the supplications of his creatures; but whether it be consistent with his nature to be moved at all, and whether there be any conceivable motive which may dispose the Divine Will to grant the petitioner what he wants, in consequence of his praying for it. It is sufficient for the petitioner, that he gain his end. It is not necessary to devotion, perhaps not very consistent with it, that the circuit of causes, by which his prayers prevail, should be known to the petitioner, much less that they should be present to his imagination at the time. All that is necessary is, that there be no impossibility apprehended in the matter.

Thus much must be conceded to the objection: that prayer cannot reasonably be offered to God with all the same views, with which we oftentimes address our entreaties to men (views which are not commonly or easily separated from it), *viz.* to inform them of our wants and desires; to tease them out by importunity; to work upon their indolence or compassion, in order to persuade them to do what they ought to have done before, or ought not to do at all.

But suppose there existed a prince, who was known by his subjects to act, of his own accord, always and invariably for the best; the situation of a petitioner, who solicited a favour or pardon from such a prince, would sufficiently resemble ours: and the question with him, as with us, would be, whether, the character of the prince being considered, there remained any chance that he should obtain from him by prayer, what he would not have received without it. I do not conceive that the character of such a prince would necessarily exclude the effect of his subject's prayers; for when that prince reflected that the earnestness and humility of the supplication had generated in the suppliant a frame of mind, upon which the pardon or favour asked would produce a permanent and active sense of gratitude; that the granting of it to prayer would put others upon praying to him, and by that means preserve the love and submission of his subjects, upon which love and submission their own happiness, as well as his glory, depended; that, beside that the memory of the particular kindness would be heightened and prolonged by the anxiety with which it had been sued for, prayer had in other respects so disposed and prepared the mind of the petitioner, as to render capable of future services him who before was unqualified for any: might not that prince, I say, although he proceeded upon no other considerations than the strict rectitude and expediency of the measure, grant a favour or pardon to *this man*, which he did not grant to *another*, who was too proud, too lazy, or too busy, too indifferent whether he received it or not, or too insensible of the sovereign's absolute power to give or to withhold it, ever to ask for it? or even to the *philosopher*, who, from an opinion of the fruitlessness of all addresses to a prince of the character which he had formed to himself, refused in his own example, and discouraged in others, all outward returns of gratitude, acknowledgements of duty, or application to the sovereign's mercy or bounty; the disuse of which (seeing affections do not long subsist which are never expressed) was followed by a decay of loyalty and zeal amongst his subjects, and threatened to end in a forgetfulness of his rights, and a contempt of his authority? These, together with other assignable considerations, and some perhaps inscrutable, and even inconceivable, by the persons upon whom his will was to be exercised, might pass in the mind of the prince, and move his counsels; whilst nothing, in the mean time, dwelt in the petitioner's thoughts, but a sense of his own grief and wants; of the power and goodness from which alone he was to look for relief; and of his obligation to endeavour, by future obedience, to render that person propitious to his happiness, in whose hands, and at the disposal of whose mercy, he found himself to be.

The objection to prayer supposes, that a perfectly wise being must necessarily be inexorable: but where is the proof, that *inexorability* is any part of perfect wisdom; especially of that wisdom which is explained to consist in bringing about the most beneficial ends by the wisest means?

The objection likewise assumes another principle, which is attended with considerable difficulty and obscurity, namely, that upon every occasion there is *one*, and only *one*, mode of acting *for the best;* and that the Divine Will is necessarily determined and confined to that mode: both which positions presume a knowledge of universal nature, much beyond what we are capable of attaining. Indeed, when we apply to the Divine Nature such expressions as these, "God *must* always do what is right," "God *cannot*, from the moral perfection and necessity of his nature, act otherwise than for the best," we ought to apply them with much indeterminateness and reserve; or rather, we ought to confess, that there is something in the subject out of the reach of our apprehension; for, in our apprehension, to be under a necessity of acting according to any rule, is inconsistent with free agency; and it makes no difference which we can understand, whether the necessity be internal or external, or that the rule is the rule of perfect rectitude.

But efficacy is ascribed to prayer without the proof, we are told, which can alone in such a subject produce conviction—the confirmation of experience. Concerning the appeal to experience, I shall content myself with this remark, that if prayer were suffered to disturb the order of second causes appointed in the universe, too much, or to produce its effects with the same regularity that they do, it would introduce a change into human affairs, which in some important respects would be evidently for the worse. Who, for example, would labour, if his necessities could be supplied with equal certainty by prayer? How few would contain within any bounds of moderation those passions and pleasures, which at present are checked only by disease, or the dread of it, if prayer would infallibly restore health? In short, if the efficacy of prayer were so constant and observable as to be relied upon *beforehand*, it is easy to foresee that the conduct of mankind would, in proportion to that reliance, become careless and disorderly. It is possible, in the nature of things, that our prayers may, in many instances, be efficacious, and yet our experience of their efficacy be dubious and obscure. Therefore, if the light of nature instruct us by any other arguments to hope for effect from prayer; still more, if the Scriptures authorise these hopes by promises of acceptance; it seems not a sufficient reason for calling in question the reality of such effects, that our observations of them are ambiguous; especially since it appears probable, that this very ambiguity is necessary to the happiness and safety of human life.

But some, whose objections do not exclude all prayer, are offended with the mode of prayer in use amongst us, and with many of the subjects which are almost universally introduced into public worship, and recommended to private devotion. To pray for particular favours by name, is to dictate, it has been said, to Divine wisdom and goodness: to intercede for others, especially for whole nations and empires, is still worse; it is to presume that we possess such an interest with the Deity, as to be able, by our applications, to bend the most important of his counsels; and that the happiness of others, and even the prosperity of communities, is to depend upon this interest, and upon our choice. Now, how unequal soever our knowledge of the Divine oeconomy may be to the solution of this difficulty, which requires perhaps a comprehension of the entire plan, and of all the ends of God's moral government, to explain satisfactorily, we can understand one thing concerning it: that it is, after all, nothing more than the making of one man the instrument of happiness and misery to another; which is perfectly of a piece with the course and order that obtain, and which we must believe were intended to obtain, in human affairs. Why may we not be assisted by the prayers of other men, who are beholden for our support to their labour? Why may not our happiness be made in some cases to depend upon the intercession, as it certainly does in many upon the good offices, of our neighbours? The happiness and misery of great numbers we see oftentimes at the disposal of one man's choice, or liable to be much affected by his conduct:

what greater difficulty is there in supposing, that the prayers of
an individual may avert a calamity from multitudes, or be accepted
to the benefit of whole communities?

Chapter 3
OF THE DUTY AND EFFICACY OF PRAYER AS
REPRESENTED IN SCRIPTURE

The reader will have observed, that the reflections stated in the
preceding chapter, whatever truth and weight they may be allowed
to contain, rise many of them no higher than to negative arguments in favour of the propriety of addressing prayer to God.
To prove that the efficacy of prayers is not inconsistent with the
attributes of the Deity, does not prove that prayers are actually
efficacious: and in the want of that unequivocal testimony, which
experience alone could afford to this point (but which we do not
possess, and have seen good reason why we are not to expect), the
light of nature leaves us to controverted probabilities, drawn from
the impulse by which mankind have been almost universally
prompted to devotion, and from some beneficial purposes, which,
it is conceived, may be better answered by the audience of prayer
than by any other mode of communicating the same blessings.
The revelations which we deem authentic, completely supply this
defect of natural religion. They require prayer to God as a duty;
and they contain positive assurance of its efficacy and acceptance.
We could have no reasonable motive for the exercise of prayer,
without believing that it may avail to the relief of our wants. This
belief can only be founded, either in a sensible experience of the
effect of prayer, or in promises of acceptance signified by Divine
authority. Our knowledge would have come to us in the former
way, less capable indeed of doubt, but subjected to the abuses and

inconveniences briefly described above; in the latter way, that is, by authorised significations of God's general disposition to hear and answer the devout supplications of his creatures, we are encouraged to pray, but not to place such a dependence upon prayer as might relax other obligations, or confound the order of events and of human expectations.

The Scriptures not only affirm the propriety of prayer in general, but furnish precepts or examples which justify some topics and some modes of prayer that have been thought exceptionable. And as the whole subject rests so much upon the foundation of Scripture, I shall put down at length texts applicable to the five following heads: to the duty and efficacy of prayer in general; of prayer for particular favours by name; for public national blessings; of intercession for others; of the repetition of unsuccessful prayers.

1. Texts enjoining prayer in general: "Ask, and it shall be given you; seek, and ye shall find—If ye, being evil, know how to give good gifts unto your children, how much more shall your Father, which is in heaven, give good things to them that ask him?"—"Watch ye, therefore, and *pray always*, that ye may be accounted worthy to escape all those things that shall come to pass, and to stand before the Son of man."—"Serving the Lord, rejoicing in hope, patient in tribulation, *continuing instant in prayer*."—"Be careful for nothing, but in every thing, *by prayer and supplication*, with thanksgiving, let your requests be made known unto God."—"I will, therefore, that men *pray every where*, lifting up holy hands without wrath and doubting."—"*Pray without ceasing*." Matt. vii. 7. 11; Luke xxi. 36; Rom. xii. 12; Philipp. iv. 6; 1 Thess. v. 17; 1 Tim. ii. 8. Add to these, that Christ's reproof of the ostentation and prolixity of pharisaical prayers, and his recommendation to his disciples, of retirement and simplicity in theirs, together with his dictating a particular form of prayer, all presuppose prayer to be an acceptable and availing service.

2. Examples of prayer for particular favours by name: "For this thing" (to wit, some bodily infirmity, which he calls 'a thorn given

him in the flesh') "I besought the Lord thrice, that it might depart from me."—"Night and day praying exceedingly, that we *might see your face*, and perfect that which is lacking in your faith." 2 Cor. xii. 8; 1 Thess. iii. 10.

3. Directions to pray for national or public blessings: "*Pray for the peace of Jerusalem.*"—"Ask ye of the Lord rain, in the time of the latter rain; so the Lord shall make bright clouds, and give them showers of rain, to every one grass in the field."—"I exhort, therefore, that first of all, supplications, prayers, inter-cessions, and giving of thanks, be made for all men; for kings, and for all that are in authority, that we may lead a quiet and peaceable life, in all godliness and honesty; for this is good and acceptable in the sight of God our Saviour." Psalm cxxii. 6; Zech. x. 1; 1 Tim. ii. 1, 2, 3.

4. Examples of intercession, and exhortations to intercede for others: "And Moses besought the Lord his God, and said, Lord, why doth thy wrath wax hot against thy people? Remember Abra-ham, Isaac, and Israel, thy servants. And the Lord repented of the evil which he thought to do unto his people."—"Peter, therefore, was kept in prison, but prayer was made without ceasing of the church unto God *for him*." "For God is my witness, that without ceasing *I make mention of you always in my prayers*."—"Now I beseech you, brethren, for the Lord Jesus Christ's sake, and for the love of the Spirit, that ye strive together with me, in your *prayers for me*."—"Confess your faults one to another, and *pray one for another*, that ye may be healed: the effectual fervent prayer of a righteous man availeth much." Exod. xxxii. 11; Acts xii. 5; Rom. i. 9, xv. 30; James v. 16.

5. Declarations and examples authorising the repetition of unsuccessful prayer: "And he spake a parable unto them, to this end, that men ought always to pray, and not to faint."—"And he left them, and went away again, and prayed *the third time, saying the*

same words."—"For this thing I besought the Lord *thrice*, that it might depart from me." Luke xviii. 1; Matt. xxvi. 44; 2 Cor. xii. 8.*

Chapter 4
OF PRIVATE PRAYER, FAMILY PRAYER, AND PUBLIC WORSHIP

Concerning these three descriptions of devotion, it is first of all to be observed, that each has its separate and peculiar use; and therefore, that the exercise of one species of worship, however regular it be, does not supersede, or dispense with, the obligation of either of the other two.

I. *Private Prayer* is recommended for the sake of the following advantages:

Private wants cannot always be made the subject of public prayer: but whatever reason there is for praying at all, there is the same for making the sore and grief of each man's own heart the business of his application to God. This must be the office of private exercises of devotion, being imperfectly, if at all, practicable in any other.

Private prayer is generally more devout and earnest than the share we are capable of taking in joint acts of worship; because it affords leisure and opportunity for the circumstantial recollection

---

*The reformed Churches of Christendom, sticking close in this article to their guide, have laid aside prayers for the dead, as authorised by no precept or precedent found in Scripture. For the same reason they properly reject the invocation of saints; as also because such invocations suppose, in the saints whom they address, a knowledge which can perceive what passes in different regions of the earth at the same time. And they deem it too much to take for granted, without the smallest intimation of such a thing in Scripture, that any created being possesses a faculty little short of that omniscience and omnipresence which they ascribe to the Deity.

of those personal wants, by the remembrance and ideas of which the warmth and earnestness of prayer are chiefly excited.

Private prayer, in proportion as it is usually accompanied with more actual thought and reflection of the petitioner's own, has a greater tendency than other modes of devotion to revive and fasten upon the mind the general impressions of religion. Solitude powerfully assists this effect. When a man finds himself alone in communication with his Creator, his imagination becomes filled with a conflux of awful ideas concerning the universal agency, and invisible presence, of that Being; concerning what is likely to become of himself; and of the superlative importance of providing for the happiness of his future existence, by endeavours to please *him* who is the arbiter of his destiny: reflections which, whenever they gain admittance, for a season overwhelm all others; and leave, when they depart, a solemnity upon the thoughts, that will seldom fail, in some degree, to affect the conduct of life.

Private prayer, thus recommended by its own propriety, and by advantages not attainable in any form of religious communion, receives a superior sanction from the authority and example of Christ; "When thou prayest, enter into thy closet; and when thou hast shut the door, pray to thy Father, which is in secret; and thy Father, which seeth in secret, shall reward thee openly."—"And when he had sent the multitudes away, he went up into a mountain *apart to pray.*" Matt. vi. 6: xiv. 23.

II. *Family Prayer.*

The peculiar use of family piety consists in its influence upon servants, and the young members of a family, who want sufficient seriousness and reflection to retire of their own accord to the exercise of private devotion, and whose attention you cannot easily command in public worship. The example also and authority of a father and master act in this way with the greatest force; for his private prayers, to which his children and servants are not witnesses, act not at all upon them as examples; and his attendance upon public worship they will readily impute to fashion, to a care to preserve appearances, to a concern for decency and character, and to many motives besides a sense of duty to God. Add to this, that forms of public worship, in proportion as they are more comprehensive, are always less interesting, than family prayers; and that the ardour of devotion is better supported, and the sympathy more easily propagated, through a small assembly, connected by the affections of domestic society, than in the presence of a mixed congregation.

III. *Public Worship.*

If the worship of God be a duty of religion, public worship is a necessary institution; forasmuch as, without it, the greater part of mankind would exercise no religious worship at all.

These assemblies afford also, at the same time, opportunities for moral and religious instruction to those who otherwise would receive none. In all protestant, and in most Christian countries, the elements of natural religion, and the important parts of the Evangelic history, are familiar to the lowest of the people. This competent degree and general diffusion of religious knowledge amongst all orders of Christians, which will appear a great thing when compared with the intellectual condition of barbarous nations, can fairly, I think, be ascribed to no other cause than the regular establishment of assemblies for divine worship; in which, either portions of Scripture are recited and explained, or the principles of Christian erudition are so constantly taught in sermons, incorporated with liturgies, or expressed in extempore prayer, as to imprint, by the very repetition, some knowledge and memory of these subjects upon the most unqualified and careless hearer.

The two reasons above stated bind all the members of a community to uphold public worship by their presence and example, although the helps and opportunities which it affords may not be necessary to the devotion or edification of all; and to some may be useless: for it is easily foreseen, how soon religious assemblies would fall into contempt and disuse, if that class of mankind who are above seeking instruction in them, and want not that their own piety should be assisted by either forms or society in devotion, were to withdraw their attendance; especially when it is considered, that all who please are at liberty to rank themselves of this class. This argument meets the only serious apology that can be made for the absenting of ourselves from public worship. "Surely (some will say) I may be excused from going to church, so long as I pray at home: and have no reason to doubt that my prayers are as acceptable and efficacious in my closet, as in a cathedral; still less can I think myself obliged to sit out a tedious sermon, in order to hear what is known already, what is better learnt from books, or suggested by meditation." They, whose qualifications and habits best supply to themselves all the effect of public ordinances, will be the last to prefer this excuse, when they advert to the *general consequence* of setting up such an exemption, as well as when they consider the *turn* which is sure to be given in the neighbourhood to their absence from public worship. You stay from church, to employ the sabbath at home in exercises and studies suited to its proper business: your next neighbour stays from church to spend the seventh day less religiously than he passed any of the six, in a sleepy, stupid rest, or at some rendezvous of drunkenness and debauchery, and yet thinks that he is only imitating you, because you both agree in not going to church. The same consideration should over-rule many small scruples concerning the rigorous propriety of some things, which may be contained in the forms, or admitted into the administration, of the public worship of our communion: for it seems impossible that even "two or three should be gathered together" in any act of social worship, if each one require from the rest an implicit submission to his objections, and if no man will attend upon a religious service which in any point contradicts his opinion of truth, or falls short of his ideas of perfection.

Beside the direct necessity of public worship to the greater part of every Christian community (supposing worship at all to be a Christian duty), there are other valuable advantages growing out of the use of religious assemblies, without being designed in the institution, or thought of by the individuals who compose them.

1. Joining in prayer and praises to their common Creator and Governor, has a sensible tendency to unite mankind together, and to cherish and enlarge the generous affections.

So many pathetic reflections are awakened by every exercise of social devotion, that most men, I believe, carry away from public worship a better temper towards the rest of mankind, than they brought with them. Sprung from the same extraction, preparing together for the period of all worldly distinctions, reminded of their mutual infirmities and common dependency, imploring and receiving support and supplies from the same great source of power and bounty, having all one interest to secure, one Lord to serve, one judgement, the supreme object to all of their hopes and fears, to look towards; it is hardly possible, in this position, to behold mankind as strangers, competitors, or enemies; or not to regard them as children of the same family, assembled before their common parent, and with some portion of the tenderness which belongs to the most endearing of our domestic relations. It is not to be expected, that any single effect of this kind should be considerable or lasting; but the frequent return of such sentiments as the presence of a devout congregation naturally suggests, will gradually melt down the ruggedness of many unkind passions, and may generate in time a permanent and productive benevolence.

2. Assemblies for the purpose of divine worship, placing men under impressions by which they are taught to consider their relation to the Deity, and to contemplate those around them with a view to that relation, force upon their thoughts the natural equality of the human species, and thereby promote humility and

condescension in the highest orders of the community, and inspire the lowest with a sense of their rights. The distinctions of civil life are almost always insisted upon too much, and urged too far. Whatever, therefore, conduces to restore the level, by qualifying the dispositions which grow out of great elevation or depression of rank, improves the character on both sides. Now things are made to appear little, by being placed beside what is great. In which manner, superiorities, that occupy the whole field of imagination, will vanish or shrink to their proper diminutiveness, when compared with the distance by which even the highest of men are removed from the Supreme Being; and this comparison is naturally introduced by all acts of joint worship. If ever the poor man holds up his head, it is at church: if ever the rich man views him with respect, it is there: and both will be the better, and the public profited, the oftener they meet in a situation, in which the consciousness of dignity in the one is tempered and mitigated, and the spirit of the other erected and confirmed. We recommend nothing adverse to subordinations which are established and necessary: but then it should be remembered, that subordination itself is an evil, being an evil to the subordinate, who are the majority, and therefore ought not to be carried a tittle beyond what the greater good, the peaceable government of the community, requires.

The public worship of Christians is a duty of Divine appointment. "Where two or three," says Christ, "are gathered together in my name, there am I in the midst of them."* This invitation will want nothing of the force of a command with those who respect the person and authority from which it proceeds. Again, in the Epistle to the Hebrews; "not forsaking the assembling of ourselves together, as the manner of some is":† which reproof seems as

---

*Matt. xviii. 20.
†Heb. x. 25.

applicable to the desertion of our public worship at this day, as to the forsaking the religious assemblies of Christians in the age of the apostle. Independently of these passages of Scripture, a disciple of Christianity will hardly think himself at liberty to dispute a practice set on foot by the inspired preachers of his religion, coeval with its institution, and retained by every sect into which it has been since divided.

Chapter 5
OF FORMS OF PRAYER IN PUBLIC WORSHIP

Liturgies, or preconcerted forms of public devotion, being neither enjoined in Scripture, nor forbidden, there can be no good reason for either receiving or rejecting them, but that of expediency; which expediency is to be gathered from a comparison of the advantages and disadvantages attending upon this mode of worship, with those which usually accompany extemporary prayer.

The advantages of a liturgy are these:

I. That it prevents absurd, extravagant, or impious addresses to God, which, in an order of men so numerous as the sacerdotal, the folly and enthusiasm of many must always be in danger of producing, where the conduct of the public worship is intrusted, without restraint or assistance, to the discretion and abilities of the officiating minister.

II. That it prevents the *confusion* of extemporary prayer, in which the congregation being ignorant of each petition before they hear it, and having little or no time to join in it after they have heard it, are confounded between their attention to the minister and to their own devotion. The devotion of the hearer is necessarily suspended, until a petition be concluded; and before he can assent to it, or properly adopt it, that is, before he can address the same request to God for himself, and from himself, his attention is called off to keep pace with what succeeds. Add to this, that the mind of the hearer is held in continual expectation, and detained from its proper business, by the very novelty with which it is gratified. A congregation may be pleased and affected with the prayers and devotion of their minister, without joining in them; in like manner as an audience oftentimes are with the representation of devotion upon the stage, who, nevertheless, come away without being conscious of having exercised any act of devotion themselves. *Joint* prayer, which amongst all denominations of Christians is the declared design of "coming together," is prayer in which all *join;* and not that which one alone in the congregation conceives and delivers, and of which the rest are merely hearers. This objection seems fundamental, and holds even where the minister's office is discharged with every possible advantage and accomplishment. The labouring recollection, and embarrassed or tumultuous delivery, of many extempore speakers, form an additional objection to this mode of public worship: for these imperfections are very general, and give great pain to the serious part of a congregation, as well as afford a profane diversion to the levity of the other part.

These advantages of a liturgy are connected with two principal inconveniences: first, that forms of prayer composed in one age become unfit for another, by the unavoidable change of language, circumstances, and opinions: secondly, that the perpetual repetition of the same form of words produces weariness and inattentiveness in the congregation. However, both these inconveniences are in their nature vincible. Occasional revisions of a liturgy may obviate the first, and devotion will supply a remedy for the second: or they may both subsist in a considerable degree, and yet be outweighed by the objections which are inseparable from extemporary prayer.

The Lord's Prayer is a precedent, as well as a pattern, for forms of prayer. Our Lord appears, if not to have prescribed, at least to have authorised, the use of fixed forms, when he complied with the request of the disciple, who said unto him, "Lord, teach us to pray, as John also taught his disciples." Luke xi. 1.

The properties required in a public liturgy are, that it be compendious; that it express just conceptions of the Divine Attributes; that it recite such wants as a congregation are likely to feel, and no other; and that it contain as few controverted propositions as possible.

I. That it be compendious.

It were no difficult task to contract the liturgies of most churches into half their present compass, and yet retain every distinct petition, as well as the substance of every sentiment which can be found in them. But brevity may be studied too much. The composer of a liturgy must not sit down to his work with the hope, that the devotion of the congregation will be uniformly sustained throughout, or that every part will be attended to by every hearer. If this could be depended upon, a very short service would be sufficient for every purpose that can be answered or designed by social worship; but seeing the attention of most men is apt to wander and return at intervals, and by starts, he will admit a certain degree of amplification and repetition, of diversity of expression upon the same subject, and variety of phrase and form with little addition to the sense, to the end that the attention, which has been slumbering or absent during one part of the service, may be excited and recalled by another; and the assembly kept together until it may reasonably be presumed, that the most heedless and inadvertent have performed some act of devotion, and the most desultory attention been caught by some part or other of the public service. On the other hand, the too great length of church-services is more unfavourable to piety, than almost any fault of composition can be. It begets, in many, an early and unconquerable dislike to the public worship of their country or communion.

They come to church seldom; and enter the doors, when they do
come, under the apprehension of a tedious attendance, which they
prepare for at first, or soon after relieve, by composing themselves
to a drowsy forgetfulness of the place and duty, or by sending
abroad their thoughts in search of more amusing occupation.
Although there may be some few of a disposition not to be wearied with religious exercises; yet, where a ritual is prolix, and the
celebration of divine service long, no effect is in general to be
looked for, but that indolence will find in it an excuse, and piety
be disconcerted by impatience.

The length and repetitions complained of in our liturgy are
not so much the fault of the compilers, as the effect of uniting
into *one* service what was originally, but with very little regard to
the conveniency of the people, distributed into *three*. Notwithstanding that dread of innovations in religion, which seems to
have become the *panic* of the age, few, I should suppose, would
be displeased with such omissions, abridgements, or change in
the arrangement, as the combination of separate services must
necessarily require, even supposing each to have been faultless in
itself. If, together with these alterations, the Epistles and
Gospels, and Collects which precede them, were composed and
selected with more regard to unity of subject and design; and the
Psalms and Lessons either left to the choice of the minister, or
better accommodated to the capacity of the audience, and the
edification of modern life; the church of England would be in
possession of a liturgy, in which those who assent to her doctrines would have little to blame, and the most dissatisfied must
acknowledge many beauties. The style throughout is excellent;
calm, without coldness; and, though every where sedate, oftentimes affecting. The pauses in the service are disposed at proper
intervals. The transitions from one office of devotion to another,
from confession to prayer, from prayer to thanksgiving, from

thanksgiving to "hearing of the word," are contrived like scenes in the drama, to supply the mind with a succession of diversified engagements. As much variety is introduced also in the form of praying, as this kind of composition seems capable of admitting. The prayer at one time is continued; at another, broken by responses, or cast into short alternate ejaculations: and sometimes the congregation is called upon to take its share in the service, by being left to complete a sentence which the minister had begun. The enumeration of human wants and sufferings in the Litany, is almost complete. A Christian petitioner can have few things to ask of God, or to deprecate, which he will not find there expressed, and for the most part with inimitable tenderness and simplicity.

II. That it express just conceptions of the Divine Attributes.

This is an article in which no care can be too great. The popular notions of God are formed, in a great measure, from the accounts which the people receive of his nature and character in their religious assemblies. An error here becomes the error of multitudes: and as it is a subject in which almost every opinion leads the way to some practical consequence, the purity or depravation of public manners will be affected, amongst other causes, by the truth or corruption of the public forms of worship.

III. That it recite such wants as the congregation are likely to feel, and no other.

Of forms of prayer which offend not egregiously against truth and decency, that has the most merit, which is best calculated to keep alive the devotion of the assembly. It were to be wished, therefore, that every part of a liturgy were personally applicable to every individual in the congregation; and that nothing were introduced to interrupt the passion, or damp the flame, which it is not easy to rekindle. Upon this principle, the *state prayers* in our liturgy should be fewer and shorter. Whatever may be pretended, the congregation do not feel that concern in the subject of these prayers, which must be felt, ere ever prayers be made to God with earnestness. The *state style* likewise seems unseasonably introduced into these prayers, as ill according with that annihilation of human greatness, of which every act that carries the mind to God, presents the idea

IV. That it contain as few controverted propositions as possible.

We allow to each church the truth of its peculiar tenets, and all the importance which zeal can ascribe to them. We dispute not here the right or the expediency of framing creeds, or of imposing subscriptions. But why should every position which a church maintains, be woven with so much industry into her forms of public worship? Some are offended, and some are excluded; this is an evil of itself, at least to *them:* and what advantage or satisfaction can be derived to the *rest*, from the separation of their brethren, it is difficult to imagine; unless it were a duty to publish our system of polemic divinity, under the name of making confession of our faith, every time we worship God; or a sin to agree in religious exercises with those from whom we differ in some religious opinions. Indeed, where one man thinks it his duty constantly to worship a being, whom another cannot, with the assent of his conscience, permit himself to worship at all, there seems to be no place for comprehension, or any expedient left but a quiet secession. All other differences may be compromised by silence. If sects and schisms be an evil, they are as much to be avoided by one side as the other. If sectaries are blamed for taking unnecessary offence, established churches are no less culpable for unnecessarily giving it; they are bound at least to produce a command, or a reason of equivalent utility, for shutting out any from their communion, by mixing with divine worship doctrines which, whether true or false, are unconnected in their nature with devotion.

Chapter 6
OF THE USE OF SABBATICAL INSTITUTIONS

An assembly cannot be collected, unless the time of assembling be fixed and known beforehand: and if the design of the assembly require that it be holden frequently, it is easiest that it should return at stated intervals. This produces a necessity of appropriating set seasons to the social offices of religion. It is also highly convenient that the *same* seasons be observed throughout the country, that all may be employed, or all at leisure, together; for if the recess from worldly occupation be not general, one man's business will perpetually interfere with another man's devotion; the buyer will be calling at the shop when the seller is gone to church. This part, therefore, of the religious distinction of seasons, namely, a general intermission of labour and business during times previously set apart for the exercise of public worship, is founded in the reasons which make public worship itself a duty. But the celebration of divine service never occupies the whole day. What remains, therefore, of Sunday, beside the part of it employed at church, must be considered as a mere rest from the ordinary occupations of civil life: and he who would defend the institution, as it is required by law to be observed in Christian countries, unless he can produce a command for a *Christian sabbath*, must point out the uses of it in that view.

First, then, that interval of relaxation which Sunday affords to the laborious part of mankind contributes greatly to the comfort and satisfaction of their lives, both as it refreshes them for the time, and as it relieves their six days' labour by the prospect of a day of rest always approaching; which could not be said of *casual* indulgences of leisure and rest, even were they more frequent than there is reason to expect they would be if left to the discretion or humanity of interested task-masters. To this difference it may be added, that holidays which come seldom and unexpected, are unprovided, when they do come, with any duty or employment; and the manner of spending them being regulated by no public decency or established usage, they are commonly consumed in rude, if not criminal pastimes, in stupid sloth, or brutish intemperance. Whoever considers how much sabbatical institutions conduce, in this respect, to the happiness and civilization of the labouring classes of mankind, and reflects how great a majority of the human species these classes compose, will acknowledge the utility, whatever he may believe of the origin, of this distinction; and will consequently perceive it to be every man's duty to uphold the observation of Sunday when once established, let the establishment have proceeded from whom or from what authority it will.

Nor is there any thing lost to the community by the intermission of public industry one day in the week. For, in countries tolerably advanced in population and the arts of civil life, there is always enough of human labour, and to spare. The difficulty is not so much to procure, as to employ it. The addition of the seventh day's labour to that of the other six, would have no other effect than to reduce the price. The labourer himself, who deserved and suffered most by the change, would gain nothing.

2. Sunday, by suspending many public diversions, and the ordinary rotation of employment, leaves to men of all ranks and professions sufficient leisure, and not more than what is sufficient, both for the external offices of Christianity, and the retired, but equally necessary duties of religious meditation and inquiry. It is true, that many do not convert their leisure to this purpose; but it is of moment, and is all which a public constitution can effect, that to every one be allowed the opportunity.

3. They, whose humanity embraces the whole sensitive creation, will esteem it no inconsiderable recommendation of a weekly

return of public rest, that it affords a respite to the toil of brutes. Nor can we omit to recount this among the uses which the Divine Founder of the *Jewish* sabbath expressly appointed a law of the institution.

We admit, that none of these reasons show why Sunday should be preferred to any other day in the week, or one day in seven to one day in six, or eight: but these points, which in their nature are of arbitrary determination, being established to our hands, our obligation applies to the subsisting establishment, so long as we confess that some such institution is necessary, and are neither able nor attempt to substitute any other in its place.

Chapter 7
OF THE SCRIPTURE ACCOUNT
OF SABBATICAL INSTITUTIONS

The subject, so far as it makes any part of Christian morality, is contained in two questions:

I. Whether the command, by which the Jewish sabbath was instituted, extends to Christians?

II. Whether any new command was delivered by Christ; or any other day substituted in the place of the Jewish sabbath by the authority or example of his apostles?

In treating of the first question, it will be necessary to collect the accounts which are preserved of the institution in the Jewish history: for the seeing these accounts together, and in one point of view, will be the best preparation for the discussing or judging of any arguments on one side or the other.

In the second chapter of Genesis, the historian, having concluded his account of the six days' creation, proceeds thus: "And on the seventh day God ended his work which he had made; and he rested on the seventh day from all his work which he had made; and God *blessed* the seventh day and *sanctified* it, because that in it he had rested from all his work which God created and made." After this, we hear no more of the sabbath, or of the seventh day, as in any manner distinguished from the other six, until the history brings us down to the sojourning of the Jews in the wilderness, when the following remarkable passage occurs. Upon the complaint of the people for want of food, God was pleased to provide for their relief by a miraculous supply of manna, which was found every morning upon the ground about the camp: "and they gathered it every morning, every man according to his eating; and when the sun waxed hot, it melted: and it came to pass, that on the sixth day they gathered twice as much bread, two omers for one man; and all the rulers of the congregation came and told Moses: and he said unto them, This is that which the Lord hath said, *To-morrow is the rest of the holy sabbath unto the Lord:* bake that which ye will bake to-day, and seethe that ye will seethe; and that which remaineth over, lay up for you, to be kept until the morning. And they laid it up till the morning, as Moses bade; and it did not stink [as it had done before, when some of them left it till the morning], neither was there any worm therein. And Moses said, Eat that to-day: *for to-day is a sabbath unto the Lord;* to-day ye shall not find it in the field. Six days ye shall gather it, but on the seventh day, which is the sabbath, in it there shall be none. And it came to pass, that there went out some of the people on the seventh day for to gather, and they found none. And the Lord said unto Moses, How long refuse ye to keep my commandments and my laws? See, *for that the Lord hath given you the sabbath*, therefore he giveth you on the sixth day the bread of two days: abide ye every man in his place: let no man go out of his place on the seventh day. So the people rested on the seventh day." Exodus xvi.

Not long after this, the sabbath, as is well known, was established with great solemnity, in the fourth commandment.

Now, in my opinion, the transaction in the wilderness above recited, was the first actual institution of the sabbath. For if the sabbath had been instituted at the time of the creation, as the words in Genesis may seem at first sight to import; and if it had been observed all along from that time to the departure of the Jews out of Egypt, a period of about two thousand five hundred years; it appears unaccountable that no mention of it, no occasion of even the obscurest allusion to it, should occur, either in the general history of the world before the call of Abraham, which contains, we admit, only a few memoirs of its early ages, and those extremely abridged; or, which is more to be wondered at, in that of the lives of the first three Jewish patriarchs, which, in many parts of the account, is sufficiently circumstantial and domestic. Nor is there, in the passage above quoted from the sixteenth chapter of Exodus, any intimation that the sabbath, when appointed to be observed, was only the revival of an ancient institution, which had been neglected, forgotten, or suspended; nor is any such neglect imputed either to the inhabitants of the old world, or to any part of the family of Noah; nor, lastly, is any permission recorded to dispense with the institution during the captivity of the Jews in Egypt, or on any other public emergency.

The passage in the second chapter of Genesis, which creates the whole controversy upon the subject, is not inconsistent with this opinion: for as the seventh day was erected into a sabbath, on account of God's resting upon that day from the work of the creation, it was natural enough in the historian, when he had related the history of the creation, and of God's ceasing from it on the seventh day, to add; "And God blessed the seventh day, and sanctified it, because that on it he had rested from all his work which God created and made"; although the blessing and sanctification, *i.e.* the religious distinction and appropriation of that day, were not actually made till many ages afterwards. The words do not assert that God *then* "blessed" and "sanctified" the seventh day, but that he

blessed and sanctified it *for that reason;* and if any ask, why the sabbath, or sanctification of the seventh day, was *then* mentioned, if it
was not *then* appointed, the answer is at hand: the order of connexion, and not of time, introduced the mention of the sabbath, in the
history of the subject which it was ordained to commemorate.

This interpretation is strongly supported by a passage in the
prophet Ezekiel, where the sabbath is plainly spoken of as *given,*
(and what else can that mean, but as *first instituted?*) in the wilderness. "Wherefore I caused them to go forth out of the land of
Egypt, and brought them into the wilderness: and I gave them my
statutes and showed them my judgements, which if a man do, he
shall even live in them: moreover also I *gave them my sabbaths,* to be
a sign between me and them, that they might know that I am the
Lord that sanctify them." Ezek. xx. 10, 11, 12.

Nehemiah also recounts the promulgation of the sabbatical law
amongst the transactions in the wilderness; which supplies another
considerable argument in aid of our opinion: "Moreover thou leddest
them in the day by a cloudy pillar, and in the night by a pillar of fire,
to give them light in the way wherein they should go. Thou camest
down also upon mount Sinai, and spakest with them from heaven,
and gavest them right judgements and true laws, good statutes and
commandments, *and madest known unto them thy holy sabbath,* and
commandedst them precepts, statutes, and laws, by the hand of Moses
thy servant, and gavest them bread from heaven for their hunger, and
broughtest forth water for them out of the rock."* Nehem. ix. 12.

---

* From the mention of the sabbath in so close a connexion with the descent of
God upon mount Sinai, and the delivery of the law from thence, one would be
inclined to believe that Nehemiah referred solely to the fourth commandment.
But the fourth commandment certainly did not first make known the sabbath.
And it is apparent, that Nehemiah observed not the order of events, for he speaks
of what passed upon mount Sinai before he mentions the miraculous supplies of
bread and water, though the Jews did not arrive at mount Sinai till some time after
both these miracles were wrought.

If it be inquired what duties were appointed for the Jewish sab-bath, and under what penalties and in what manner it was observed amongst the ancient Jews; we find that, by the fourth command-ment, a strict cessation from work was enjoined, not only upon Jews by birth, or religious profession, but upon all who resided within the limits of the Jewish state; that the same was to be per-mitted to their slaves and their cattle; that this rest was not to be violated, under pain of death: "Whosoever doeth any work in the sabbath-day, he shall surely be put to death." Exod. xxxi. 15. Beside which, the seventh day was to be solemnised by double sacrifices in the temple: "And on the sabbath-day *two* lambs of the first year without spot, and two tenth-deals of flour for a meat-offering, mingled with oil, and the drink-offering thereof; this is the burnt-offering of every sabbath, beside the continual burnt-offering and his drink-offering." Numb. xxviii. 9, 10. Also *holy convocations*, which mean, we presume, assemblies for the purpose of public worship or religious instruction, were directed to be holden on the sabbath-day: "the seventh day is a sabbath of rest, an holy convo-cation." Levit. xxiii. 3.

And accordingly we read, that the sabbath was in fact observed amongst the Jews by a scrupulous abstinence from every thing which, by any possible construction, could be deemed labour; as from dressing meat, from travelling beyond a sabbath-day's jour-ney, or about a single mile. In the Maccabean wars, they suffered a thousand of their number to be slain, rather than do any thing in their own defence on the sabbath-day. In the final siege of Jerusalem, after they had so far overcome their scruples as to defend their persons when attacked, they refused any operation on the sabbath-day, by which they might have interrupted the enemy in filling up the trench. After the establishment of synagogues (of the origin of which we have no account), it was the custom to assemble in them on the sabbath-day, for the purpose of hearing the law rehearsed and explained, and for the exercise, it is probable, of public devotion: "For Moses of old time hath in every city them that preach him, *being read in the synagogues every sabbath-day.*" The seventh day is *Saturday;* and, agreeably to the Jewish way of computing the day, the sabbath held from six o'clock on the Friday evening, to six o'clock on Saturday evening. These observations being premised, we approach the main question, Whether the command by which the Jewish sabbath was instituted, extend to us?

If the Divine command was actually delivered at the creation, it was addressed, no doubt, to the whole human species alike, and continues, unless repealed by some subsequent revelation, binding upon all who come to the knowledge of it. If the command was published for the first time in the wilderness, then it was immediately directed to the Jewish people alone; and something farther, either in the subject or circumstances of the command, will be necessary to show, that it was designed for any other. It is on this account, that the question concerning the date of the institution was first to be considered. The former opinion precludes all debate about the extent of the obligation; the latter admits, and *primâ facie,* induces, a belief that the sabbath ought to be considered as part of the peculiar law of the Jewish policy.

Which belief receives great confirmation from the following arguments:

The sabbath is described as a sign between God and the people of Israel—"Wherefore the children of Israel shall keep the sabbath, to observe the sabbath throughout their generations for a perpetual covenant; *it is a sign between me and the children of Israel for ever.*" Exodus xxxi. 16, 17. Again: "And I gave them my statutes, and showed them my judgements, which if a man do he shall even live in them; *moreover also I gave them my sabbaths, to be a sign between me and them,* that they might know that I am the Lord that sanctify them." Ezek. xx. 12. Now it does not seem easy to understand how the sabbath could be a *sign* between God and the people of

Israel, unless the observance of it was peculiar to that people, and designed to be so.

The distinction of the sabbath is, in its nature, as much a positive ceremonial institution, as that of many other seasons which were appointed by the Levitical law to be kept holy, and to be observed by a strict rest; as the first and seventh days of unleavened bread; the feast of Pentecost; the feast of tabernacles: and in the twenty-third chapter of Exodus, the sabbath and these are recited together.

If the command by which the sabbath was instituted be binding upon Christians, it must be binding as to the day, the duties, and the penalty; in none of which it is received.

The observance of the sabbath was not one of the articles enjoined by the Apostles, in the fifteenth chapter of Acts, upon them "which, from among the Gentiles, were turned unto God."

St. Paul evidently appears to have considered the sabbath as part of the Jewish ritual, and not obligatory upon Christians as such: "Let no man therefore judge you in meat or in drink, or in respect of an holy day, or of the new moon, or *of the sabbath days*, which are a shadow of things to come, but the body is of Christ." Col. ii. 16, 17.

I am aware of only two objections which can be opposed to the force of these arguments: one is, that the reason assigned in the fourth commandment for hallowing the seventh day, namely, "because God rested on the seventh day from the work of the creation," is a reason which pertains to all mankind; the other, that the command which enjoins the observance of the sabbath is inserted in the Decalogue, of which all the other precepts and prohibitions are of moral and universal obligation.

Upon the first objection it may be remarked, that although in Exodus the commandment is founded upon God's rest from the creation, in Deuteronomy the commandment is repeated with a reference to a different event: "Six days shalt thou labour, and do all thy work; but the seventh day is the sabbath of the Lord thy God; in it thou shalt not do any work; thou, nor thy son, nor thy daughter, nor thy man-servant, nor thy maid-servant, nor thine ox, nor thine ass, nor any of thy cattle, nor the stranger that is within thy gates, that thy man-servant and thy maid-servant may rest as well as thou: and remember that thou wast a servant in the land of Egypt, and that the Lord thy God brought thee out thence, through a mighty hand, and by a stretched-out arm; *therefore* the Lord thy God commanded thee to keep the sabbath-day." It is farther observable, that God's rest from the creation is proposed as the reason of the institution, even where the institution itself is spoken of as peculiar to the Jews: "Wherefore the children of Israel shall keep the sabbath, to observe the sabbath throughout their generations, for a perpetual covenant: it is a sign between me and the children of Israel for ever: *for* in six days the Lord made heaven and earth, and on the seventh day he rested and was refreshed." The truth is, these different reasons were assigned, to account for different circumstances in the command. If a Jew inquired, why the *seventh day* was sanctified rather than the sixth or eighth, his law told him, because God rested on the *seventh day* from the creation. If he asked, why was the same rest indulged to *slaves?* his law bade him remember, that he also was a *slave* in the land of Egypt, and "that the Lord his God brought him out thence." In this view, the two reasons are perfectly compatible with each other, and with a third end of the institution, its being a *sign* between God and the people of Israel; but in this view they determine nothing concerning the extent of the obligation. If the reason by its proper energy had constituted a natural obligation, or if it had been men-tioned with a view to the extent of the obligation, we should sub-mit to the conclusion that all were comprehended by the command who are concerned in the reason. But the sabbatic rest being a duty which results from the ordination and authority of a positive law, the reason can be alleged no farther than as it explains the design of the legislator: and if it appear to be recited with an intentional application to one part of the law, it explains his design upon no other; if it be mentioned merely to account for the choice of the day, it does not explain his design as to the extent of the obligation.

With respect to the second objection, that inasmuch as the other nine commandments are confessedly of moral and universal obligation, it may reasonably be presumed that this is of the same; we answer, that this argument will have less weight when it is considered that the distinction between positive and natural duties, like other distinctions of modern ethics, was unknown to the simplicity of ancient language; and that there are various passages in Scripture, in which duties of a political, or ceremonial, or positive nature, and confessedly of partial obligation, are enumerated, and without any mark of discrimination, along with others which are natural and universal. Of this the following is an incontestable example. "But if a man be just, and do that which is lawful and right; and hath not eaten upon the mountains, nor hath lifted up his eyes to the idols of the house of Israel; neither hath defiled his neighbour's wife, *neither hath come near to a menstruous woman; and* hath not oppressed any, but hath restored to the debtor his pledge; hath spoiled none by violence; hath given his bread to the hungry, and hath covered the naked with a garment; *he that hath not given upon usury, neither hath taken any increase;* that hath withdrawn his hand from iniquity; hath executed true judgement between man and man; hath walked in my statutes, and hath kept my judgements, to deal truly; he is just, he shall surely live, saith the Lord God." Ezekiel xviii. 5–9. The same thing may be observed of the apostolic decree recorded in the fifteenth chapter of the Acts: "It seemed good to the Holy Ghost, and to us, to lay upon you no greater burthen than these necessary things, that ye abstain from

meats offered to idols, and from blood, and from things stran-
gled, and *from fornication:* from which if ye keep yourselves, ye shall
do well."

II. If the law by which the sabbath was instituted was a law only
to the Jews, it becomes an important question with the Christian
inquirer, whether the Founder of his religion delivered any new
command upon the subject; or, if that should not appear to be the
case, whether any day was appropriated to the service of religion by
the authority or example of his apostles.

The practice of holding religious assemblies upon the first day
of the week, was so early and universal in the Christian Church,
that it carries with it considerable proof of having originated from
some precept of Christ, or of his apostles, though none such be
now extant. It was upon the *first* day of the week that the disciples
were assembled, when Christ appeared to them for the first time
after his resurrection; "then the same day at evening, *being the first
day of the week,* when the doors were shut where the disciples were
assembled, for fear of the Jews, came Jesus, and stood in the midst
of them." John xx. 19. This, for any thing that appears in the
account, might, as to the day, have been accidental; but in the 26th
verse of the same chapter we read that "after eight days," that is, on
the *first day* of the week *following,* "*again* the disciples were within";
which second meeting upon the same day of the week looks like
an appointment and design to meet on that particular day. In the
twentieth chapter of the Acts of the Apostles, we find the same
custom in a Christian Church at a great distance from Jerusalem:
"And we came unto them to Troas in five days, where we abode
seven days; and *upon the first day of the week, when the disciples came
together to break bread,* Paul preached unto them." Acts xx. 6, 7.
The manner in which the historian mentions the disciples coming
together to break bread on the *first day* of the week, shows, I think,
that the practice by this time was familiar and established. St. Paul

to the Corinthians writes thus: "Concerning the collection for the saints, as I have given order to the Churches of Galatia, even so do ye; *upon the first day of the week* let every one of you lay by him in store as God hath prospered him, that there be no gathering when I come." 1 Cor. xvi. 1, 2. Which direction affords a probable proof, that the *first* day of the week was already, amongst the Christians both of Corinth and Galatia, distinguished from the rest by some religious application or other. At the time that St. John wrote the book of his Revelation, the first day of the week had obtained the name of the *Lord's day*—"I was in the spirit," says he, "*on the Lord's day*." Rev. i. 10. Which name, and St. John's use of it, sufficiently denote the appropriation of this day to the service of religion, and that this appropriation was perfectly known to the Churches of Asia. I make no doubt that by the *Lord's day* was meant the *first* day of the week; for we find no footsteps of any distinction of days, which could entitle any other to that appellation. The subsequent history of Christianity corresponds with the accounts delivered on this subject in Scripture.

It will be remembered, that we are contending, by these proofs, for no other duty upon the first day of the week, than that of holding and frequenting religious assemblies. A cessation upon that day from labour, beyond the time of attendance upon public worship, is not intimated in any passage of the New Testament; nor did Christ or his apostles deliver, that we know of, any command to their disciples for a discontinuance, upon that day, of the common offices of their professions; a reserve which none will see reason to wonder at, or to blame as a defect in the institution, who consider that, in the primitive condition of Christianity, the observance of a new sabbath would have been useless, or inconvenient, or impracticable. During Christ's personal ministry, his religion was preached to the Jews alone. *They* already had a sabbath, which, as citizens and subjects of that oeconomy, they were obliged to keep;

and did keep. It was not therefore probable that Christ would enjoin another day of rest in conjunction with this. When the new religion came forth into the Gentile world, converts to it were, for the most part, made from those classes of society who have not their time and labour at their own disposal; and it was scarcely to be expected, that unbelieving masters and magistrates, and they who directed the employment of others, would permit their slaves and labourers to rest from their work every seventh day: or that civil government, indeed, would have submitted to the loss of a seventh part of the public industry, and that too in addition to the numerous festivals which the national religions indulged to the people; at least, this would have been an encumbrance, which might have greatly retarded the reception of Christianity in the world. In reality, the institution of a weekly sabbath is so connected with the functions of civil life, and requires so much of the concurrence of civil law, in its regulation and support, that it cannot, perhaps, properly be made the ordinance of any religion, till that religion be received as the religion of the state.

The opinion, that Christ and his apostles meant to retain the duties of the Jewish sabbath, shifting only the day from the seventh to the first, seems to prevail without sufficient proof; nor does any evidence remain in Scripture (of what, however, is not improbable), that the first day of the week was thus distinguished in commemoration of our Lord's resurrection.

The conclusion from the whole inquiry (for it is our business to follow the arguments, to whatever probability they conduct us), is this: The *assembling* upon the first day of the week for the purpose of public worship and religious instruction, is a law of Christianity, of Divine appointment; the *resting* on that day from our employments longer than we are detained from them by attendance upon these assemblies, is to Christians an ordinance of human institution; binding nevertheless upon the conscience of every individual of a country in which a weekly sabbath is established, for the sake of the beneficial purposes which the public and regular observance of it promotes, and recommended perhaps in some degree to the Divine approbation, by the resemblance it bears to what God was pleased to make a solemn part of the law which he delivered to the people of Israel, and by its subserviency to many of the same uses.

Chapter 8
By What Acts and Omissions the Duty of the Christian Sabbath Is Violated

Since the obligation upon Christians to comply with the religious observance of Sunday, arises from the public uses of the institution, and the authority of the apostolic practice, the *manner* of observing it ought to be that which best fulfils *these* uses, and conforms the nearest to *this* practice.

The uses proposed by the institution are;

1. To facilitate attendance upon public worship.

2. To meliorate the condition of the laborious classes of mankind, by regular and seasonable returns of rest.

3. By a general suspension of business and amusement, to invite and enable persons of every description to apply their time and thoughts to subjects appertaining to their salvation.

With the primitive Christians, the peculiar, and probably for some time the only, distinction of the first day of the week, was the holding of religious assemblies upon that day. We learn, however, from the testimony of a very early writer amongst them, that they also reserved the day for religious meditations—*Unusquisque nostrûm* (saith Irenaeus) *sabbatizat spiritualiter, meditatione legis gaudens, opificium Dei admirans.*

WHEREFORE the duty of the day is violated,

1st, By all such employments or engagements as (though dif-fering from our ordinary occupation) hinder our attendance upon public worship, or take up so much of our time as not to leave a sufficient part of the day at leisure for religious reflection; as the going of journeys, the paying or receiving of visits which engage the whole day, or employing the time at home in writing letters, settling accounts, or in applying ourselves to studies, or the read-ing of books, which bear no relation to the business of religion.

2dly, By unnecessary encroachments on the rest and liberty which Sunday ought to bring to the inferior orders of the commu-nity; as by keeping servants on that day confined and busied in preparations for the superfluous elegancies of our table, or dress.

3dly, By such recreations as are customarily forborne out of respect to the day; as hunting, shooting, fishing, public diversions, frequenting taverns, playing at cards or dice.

If it be asked, as it often has been, wherein consists the differ-ence between walking out with your staff or with your gun? between spending the evening at home, or in a tavern? between passing the Sunday afternoon at a game of cards, or in conversation not more edifying, nor always so inoffensive?—to these, and to the same question under a variety of forms, and in a multitude of similar examples, we return the following answer: That the reli-gious observance of Sunday, if it ought to be retained at all, must be upholden by some public and visible distinctions: that, draw the line of distinction where you will, many actions which are situated on the confines of the line, will differ very little, and yet lie on the opposite sides of it: that every trespass upon that reserve which public decency has established, breaks down the fence by which the day is separated to the service of religion: that it is unsafe to trifle with scruples and habits that have a beneficial tendency, although founded merely in custom: that these liberties, however intended,

will certainly be considered by those who observe them, not only
as disrespectful to the day and institution, but as proceeding from
a secret contempt of the Christian faith: that consequently, they
diminish a reverence for religion in others, so far as the authority
of our opinion, or the efficacy of our example, reaches; or rather, so
far as either will serve for an excuse of negligence to those who are
glad of any: that as to cards and dice, which put in their claim to be
considered among the *harmless* occupations of a vacant hour, it may
be observed that few find any difficulty in refraining from *play* on
Sunday, except they who sit down to it with the views and eagerness of gamesters: that *gaming* is seldom innocent: that the anxiety
and perturbations, however, which it excites, are inconsistent with
the tranquillity and frame of temper in which the duties and
thoughts of religion should always both find and leave us: and
lastly, we shall remark, that the example of other countries, where
the same or greater licence is *allowed*, affords no apology for irregularities in our own; because a practice which is tolerated by public usage, neither receives the same construction, nor gives the
same offence, as where it is censured and prohibited.

Chapter 9
OF REVERENCING THE DEITY

In many persons, a seriousness, and sense of awe, overspread the
imagination, whenever the idea of the Supreme Being is presented
to their thoughts. This effect, which forms a considerable security
against vice, is the consequence not so much of reflection, as of
habit; which habit being generated by the external expressions
of reverence which we use ourselves, or observe in others, may
be destroyed by causes opposite to these, and especially by that

familiar levity with which some learn to speak of the Deity, of his attributes, providence, revelations, or worship.

God hath been pleased (no matter for what reason, although probably for this) to forbid the vain mention of his name: "Thou shalt not take the name of the Lord thy God in vain." Now the mention is *vain*, when it is useless; and it is useless, when it is neither likely nor intended to serve any good purpose; as when it flows from the lips idle and unmeaning, or is applied, on occasions inconsistent with any consideration of religion and devotion, to express our anger, our earnestness, our courage, or our mirth; or indeed when it is used at all, except in acts of religion, or in serious and seasonable discourse upon religious subjects.

The prohibition of the third commandment is recognised by Christ, in his sermon upon the mount; which sermon adverts to none but the moral parts of the Jewish law: "I say unto you, Swear not at all: but let your communication be Yea, yea; Nay, nay: for whatsoever is more than these, cometh of evil." The Jews probably interpreted the prohibition as restrained to the name Jehovah, the name which the Deity had appointed and appropriated to himself; Exod. vi. 3. The words of Christ extend the prohibition beyond the *name* of God, to every thing associated with the idea: "Swear not, neither by heaven, for it is God's throne; nor by the earth, for it is his footstool; neither by Jerusalem, for it is the city of the Great King." Matt. v. 35.

The offence of profane swearing is aggravated by the consideration, that in *it* duty and decency are sacrificed to the slenderest of temptations. Suppose the habit, either from affectation, or by negligence and inadvertency, to be already formed, it must always remain within the power of the most ordinary resolution to correct it; and it cannot, one would think, cost a great deal to relinquish the pleasure and honour which it confers. A concern for duty is in fact never strong, when the exertion requisite to vanquish a habit founded in no antecedent propensity, is thought too much, or too painful.

A contempt of positive duties, or rather of those duties for which the reason is not so plain as the command, indicates a disposition upon which the authority of Revelation has obtained little influence. This remark is applicable to the offence of profane swearing, and describes, perhaps, pretty exactly, the general character of those who are most addicted to it.

Mockery and ridicule, when exercised upon the Scriptures, or even upon the places, persons, and forms, set apart for the ministration of religion, fall within the meaning of the law which forbids the profanation of God's name; especially as that law is extended by Christ's interpretation. They are moreover inconsistent with a religious frame of mind: for, as no one ever either feels himself disposed to pleasantry, or capable of being diverted with the pleasantry of others, upon matters in which he is deeply interested; so a mind intent upon the acquisition of heaven, rejects with indignation every attempt to entertain it with jests, calculated to degrade or deride subjects which it never recollects but with seriousness and anxiety. Nothing but stupidity, or the most frivolous dissipation of thought, can make even the inconsiderate forget the supreme importance of every thing which relates to the expectation of a future existence. Whilst the infidel mocks at the superstitions of the vulgar, insults over their credulous fears, their childish errors, or fantastic rites, it does not occur to him to observe, that the most preposterous device by which the weakest devotee ever believed he was securing the happiness of a future life, is more rational than unconcern about it. Upon this subject, nothing is so absurd as indifference—no folly so contemptible as thoughtlessness and levity.

Finally; the knowledge of what is due to the solemnity of those interests, concerning which Revelation professes to inform and

direct us, may teach even those who are least inclined to respect
the prejudices of mankind, to observe a decorum in the style
and conduct of religious disquisitions, with the neglect of which
many adversaries of Christianity are justly chargeable. Serious
arguments are fair on all sides. Christianity is but ill defended by
refusing audience or toleration to the objections of unbelievers.
But whilst we would have freedom of inquiry restrained by no laws
but those of decency, we are entitled to demand, on behalf of
a religion which holds forth to mankind assurances of immortality,
that its credit be assailed by no other weapons than those of sober
discussion and legitimate reasoning: that the truth or falsehood
of Christianity be never made a topic of raillery, a theme for the
exercise of wit or eloquence, or a subject of contention for literary
fame and victory: that the cause be tried upon its merits: that all
applications to the fancy, passions, or prejudices of the reader, all
attempts to pre-occupy, ensnare, or perplex his judgement, by any
art, influence, or impression whatsoever, extrinsic to the proper
grounds and evidence upon which his assent ought to proceed, be
rejected from a question which involves in its determination the
hopes, the virtue, and the repose, of millions: that the controversy
be managed on both sides with sincerity; that is, that nothing be
produced, in the writings of either, contrary to, or beyond, the
writer's own knowledge and persuasion: that objections and difficulties be proposed, from no other motive than an honest and
serious desire to obtain satisfaction, or to communicate information which may promote the discovery and progress of truth: that
in conformity with this design, every thing be stated with integrity,
with method, precision, and simplicity; and above all, that whatever is published in opposition to received and confessedly beneficial persuasions, be set forth under a form which is likely to invite
inquiry and to meet examination. If with these moderate and equitable conditions be compared the manner in which hostilities have

been waged against the Christian religion, not only the votaries of
the prevailing faith, but every man who looks forward with anxiety
to the destination of his being, will see much to blame and to complain of. By *one unbeliever*, all the follies which have adhered, in
a long course of dark and superstitious ages, to the popular creed,
are assumed as so many doctrines of Christ and his apostles, for the
purpose of subverting the whole system by the absurdities which it
is *thus* represented to contain. By *another*, the ignorance and vices
of the sacerdotal order, their mutual dissensions and persecutions,
their usurpations and encroachments upon the intellectual liberty
and civil rights of mankind, have been displayed with no small
triumph and invective; not so much to guard the Christian laity
against a repetition of the same injuries (which is the only proper
use to be made of the most flagrant examples of the past), as to prepare the way for an insinuation, that the religion itself is nothing
but a profitable fable, imposed upon the fears and credulity of the
multitude, and upheld by the frauds and influence of an interested
and crafty priesthood. And yet, how remotely is the character of
the clergy connected with the truth of Christianity! What, after all,
do the most disgraceful pages of ecclesiastical history prove, but
that the passions of our common nature are not altered or excluded
by distinctions of name, and that the characters of men are formed
much more by the temptations than the duties of their profession?
A *third* finds delight in collecting and repeating accounts of wars
and massacres, of tumults and insurrections, excited in almost
every age of the Christian aera by religious zeal; as though the
vices of Christians were parts of Christianity; intolerance and
extirpation precepts of the Gospel; or as if its spirit could be judged
of from the counsels of princes, the intrigues of statesmen, the pretences of malice and ambition, or the unauthorised cruelties of
some gloomy and virulent superstition. By a *fourth*, the succession
and variety of popular religions; the vicissitudes with which sects

and tenets have flourished and decayed; the zeal with which they were once supported, the negligence with which they are now remembered; the little share which reason and argument appear to have had in framing the creed, or regulating the religious conduct, of the multitude; the indifference and submission with which the religion of the state is generally received by the common people; the caprice and vehemence with which it is sometimes opposed; the phrensy with which men have been brought to contend for opinions and ceremonies, of which they knew neither the proof, the meaning, nor the original: lastly, the equal and undoubting confidence with which we hear the doctrines of Christ or of Confucius, the law of Moses or of Mahomet, the Bible, the Koran, or the Shaster, maintained or anathematized, taught or abjured, revered or derided, according as we live on this or on that side of a river; keep within or step over the boundaries of a state; or even in the same country, and by the same people, so often as the event of a battle, or the issue of a negotiation, delivers them to the dominion of a new master—points, I say, of this sort are exhibited to the public attention, as so many arguments against the *truth* of the Christian religion—and with success. For these topics, being brought together, and set off with some aggravation of circum-stances, and with a vivacity of style and description familiar enough to the writings and conversation of free-thinkers, insensi-bly lead the imagination into a habit of classing Christianity with the delusions that have taken possession, by turns, of the public belief; and of regarding it, as what the scoffers of our faith repre-sent it to be, *the superstition of the day*. But is this to deal honestly by the subject, or with the world? May not the same things be said, may not the same prejudices be excited by these representations, whether Christianity be true or false, or by whatever proofs its truth be attested? May not truth as well as falsehood be taken upon credit? May not a religion be founded upon evidence accessible and satisfactory to every mind competent to the inquiry, which yet, by the greatest part of its professors, is received upon authority?

But if the *matter* of those objections be reprehensible, as calculated to produce an effect upon the reader beyond what their real weight and place in the argument deserve, still more shall we discover of management and disingenuousness in the *form* under which they are dispersed among the public. Infidelity is served up in every shape that is likely to allure, surprise, or beguile the imagination; in a fable, a tale, a novel, a poem; in interspersed and broken hints, remote and oblique surmises; in books of travels, of philosophy, of natural history; in a word, in any form rather than the right one, that of a professed and regular disquisition. And because the coarse buffoonery, and broad laugh, of the old and rude adversaries of the Christian faith, would offend the taste, perhaps, rather than the virtue, of this cultivated age, a graver irony, a more skilful and delicate banter, is substituted in their place. An eloquent historian, beside his more direct, and therefore fairer, attacks upon the credibility of Evangelic story, has contrived to weave into his narration one continued sneer upon the cause of Christianity, and upon the writings and characters of its ancient patrons. The knowledge which this author possesses of the frame and conduct of the human mind, must have led him to observe, that such attacks do their execution without inquiry. Who can refute a *sneer?* Who can compute the number, much less, one by one, scrutinize the justice, of those disparaging insinuations which crowd the pages of this elaborate history? What reader suspends his curiosity, or calls off his attention from the principal narrative, to examine references, to search into the foundation, or to weigh the reason, propriety, and force, of every transient sarcasm, and sly allusion, by which the Christian testimony is depreciated and traduced; and by which, nevertheless, he may find his persuasion afterwards unsettled and perplexed?

But the enemies of Christianity have pursued her with poisoned arrows. Obscenity itself is made the vehicle of infidelity. The awful doctrines, if we be not permitted to call them the sacred truths, of our religion, together with all the adjuncts and appendages of its worship and external profession, have been sometimes impudently profaned by an unnatural conjunction with impure and lascivious images. The fondness for ridicule is almost universal: and ridicule to many minds is never so irresistible, as when seasoned with obscenity, and employed upon religion. But in proportion as these noxious principles take hold of the imagination, they infatuate the judgement; for trains of ludicrous and unchaste associations adhering to every sentiment and mention of religion, render the mind indisposed to receive either conviction from its evidence, or impressions from its authority. And this effect being exerted upon the sensitive part of our frame, is altogether independent of argument, proof, or reason; is as formidable to a true religion, as to a false one; to a well-grounded faith, as to a chimerical mythology, or fabulous tradition. Neither, let it be observed, is the crime or danger less, because impure ideas are exhibited under a veil, in covert and chastised language.

Seriousness is not constraint of thought; nor levity, freedom. Every mind which wishes the advancement of truth and knowledge, in the most important of all human researches, must abhor this licentiousness, as violating no less the laws of reasoning, than the rights of decency. There is but one description of men, to whose principles it ought to be tolerable; I mean that class of reasoners who can see *little* in Christianity, even supposing it to be true. To such adversaries we address this reflection. Had Jesus Christ delivered no other declaration than the following—"The hour is coming, in the which all that are in the grave shall hear his voice, and shall come forth: they that have done good, unto the resurrection of life; and they that have done evil, unto the resurrection of damnation"—he had pronounced a message of inestimable importance, and well worthy of that splendid apparatus of prophecy and miracles with which his mission was introduced and attested; a message in which the wisest of mankind would rejoice to find an answer to their doubts, and rest to their inquiries. It is idle to say, that a future state had been discovered already: it had been discovered as the Copernican system was—it was one guess among many. He alone discovers, who *proves;* and no man can prove this point, but the teacher who testifies by miracles that his doctrine comes from God.

Book VI
Elements of Political Knowledge

Chapter 1
OF THE ORIGIN OF CIVIL GOVERNMENT

Government, at first, was either patriarchal or military: *that* of a parent over his family, or of a commander over his fellow-warriors.

I. Paternal authority, and the order of domestic life, supplied the foundation of *civil government*. Did mankind spring out of the earth mature and independent, it would be found perhaps impossible to introduce subjection and subordination among them: but the condition of human infancy prepares men for society, by combining individuals into small communities, and by placing them from the beginning, under direction and control. A family contains the rudiments of an empire. The authority of one over many, and the disposition to govern and to be governed, are in this way incidental to the very nature, and coeval no doubt with the existence, of the human species.

Moreover, the constitution of families not only assists the formation of civil government, by the dispositions which it generates, but also furnishes the first steps of the process by which empires have been actually reared. A parent would retain a considerable part of his authority after his children were grown up, and had formed families of their own. The obedience of which they remembered not the beginning, would be considered as natural;

and would scarcely, during the parent's life, be entirely or abruptly withdrawn. Here then we see the second stage in the progress of dominion. The first was, that of a parent over his young children; this, that of an ancestor presiding over his adult descendants.

Although the original progenitor was the centre of union to his posterity, yet it is not probable that the association would be immediately or altogether dissolved by his death. Connected by habits of intercourse and affection, and by some common rights, necessities, and interests, they would consider themselves as allied to each other in a nearer degree than to the rest of the species. Almost all would be sensible of an inclination to continue in the society in which they had been brought up; and experiencing, as they soon would do, many inconveniences from the absence of that authority which their common ancestor exercised, especially in deciding their disputes, and directing their operations in matters in which it was necessary to act in conjunction, they might be induced to supply his place by a formal choice of a successor; or rather might willingly, and almost imperceptibly, transfer their obedience to some one of the family, who by his age or services, or by the part he possessed in the direction of their affairs during the lifetime of the parent, had already taught them to respect his advice, or to attend to his commands; or lastly, the prospect of these inconveniences might prompt the first ancestor to appoint a successor; and his posterity, from the same motive, united with an habitual deference to the ancestor's authority, might receive the appointment with submission. Here then we have a tribe or clan incorporated under one chief. Such communities might be increased by considerable numbers, and fulfil the purposes of civil union without any other or more regular convention, constitution, or form of government, than what we have described. Every branch which was slipped off from the primitive stock, and removed to a distance from it, would in like manner take root, and grow into a separate clan. Two or three of these clans were frequently, we may suppose, united into one. Marriage, conquest, mutual defence, common distress, or more accidental coalitions, might produce this effect.

II. A second source of personal authority, and which might easily extend, or sometimes perhaps supersede, the patriarchal, is that which results from military arrangement. In wars, either of aggression or defence, manifest necessity would prompt those who fought on the same side to array themselves under one leader. And although their *leader* was advanced to this eminence for the purpose only, and during the operations, of a single expedition, yet his authority would not always terminate with the reasons for which it was conferred. A warrior who had led forth his tribe against their enemies with repeated success, would procure to himself, even in the deliberations of peace, a powerful and permanent influence. If this advantage were added to the authority of the patriarchal chief, or favoured by any previous distinction of ancestry, it would be no difficult undertaking for the person who possessed it to obtain the almost absolute direction of the affairs of the community; especially if he was careful to associate to himself proper auxiliaries, and content to practise the obvious art of gratifying or removing those who opposed his pretensions.

But although we may be able to comprehend how by his personal abilities or fortune one man may obtain the rule over many, yet it seems more difficult to explain how empire became *hereditary*, or in what manner sovereign power, which is never acquired without great merit or management, learns to descend in a succession which has no dependence upon any qualities either of understanding or activity. The causes which have introduced hereditary dominion into so general a reception in the world, are principally the following: the influence of association, which communicates to the son a portion of the same respect which was wont to be paid to the virtues or station of the father; the mutual jealousy of other competitors; the greater envy with which all behold the exaltation of an equal, than the continuance of an acknowledged superiority; a reigning prince leaving behind him many adherents, who can preserve their own importance only by supporting the succession of his children: add to these reasons, that elections to the supreme power having, upon trial, produced destructive contentions, many states would take a refuge from a return of the same calamities in a rule of succession; and no rule presents itself so obvious, certain, and intelligible, as consanguinity of birth.

The ancient state of society in most countries, and the modern condition of some uncivilized parts of the world, exhibit that appearance which this account of the origin of civil government would lead us to expect. The earliest histories of Palestine, Greece, Italy, Gaul, Britain, inform us, that these countries were occupied by many small independent nations, not much perhaps unlike those which are found at present amongst the savage inhabitants of North America, and upon the coast of Africa. These nations I consider as the amplifications of so many single families; or as derived from the junction of two or three families, whom society in war, or the approach of some common danger, had united. Suppose a country to have been first peopled by shipwreck on its coasts, or by emigrants or exiles from a neighbouring country; the new settlers having no enemy to provide against, and occupied with the care of their personal subsistence, would think little of digesting a system of laws, of contriving a form of government, or indeed of any political union whatever; but each settler would remain at the head of his own family, and each family would include all of every age and generation who were descended from him. So many of these families as were holden together after the death of the original ancestor, by the reasons and in the method above recited, would wax, as the individuals were multiplied, into tribes, clans, hordes, or nations, similar to those into which the ancient inhabitants of many countries are known to have been divided, and which are still found wherever the state of society and manners is immature and uncultivated.

Nor need we be surprised at the early existence in the world of some vast empires, or at the rapidity with which they advanced to their greatness, from comparatively small and obscure originals. Whilst the inhabitants of so many countries were broken into numerous communities, unconnected, and oftentimes contending with each other; before experience had taught these little states to see their own danger in their neighbour's ruin; or had instructed them in the necessity of resisting the aggrandisement of an aspiring power, by alliances, and timely preparations; in this condition of civil policy, a particular tribe, which by any means had gotten the start of the rest in strength or discipline, and happened to fall under the conduct of an ambitious chief, by directing their first attempts to the part where success was most secure, and by assuming, as they went along, those whom they conquered into a share of their future enterprises, might soon gather a force which would infallibly over-bear any opposition that the scattered power and unprovided state of such enemies could make to the progress of their victories.

Lastly, our theory affords a presumption, that the earliest governments were monarchies, because the government of families, and of armies, from which, according to our account, civil government derived its institution, and probably its form, is universally monarchical.

Chapter 2
How Subjection to Civil Government Is Maintained

Could we view our own species from a distance, or regard mankind with the same sort of observation with which we read the natural history, or remark the *manners*, of any other animal, there is nothing in the human character which would more surprise us, than the almost universal subjugation of strength to weakness; than to see many millions of robust men, in the complete use and exercise of their personal faculties, and without any defect of courage, waiting upon the will of a child, a woman, a driveller, or a lunatic. And although, when we suppose a vast empire in absolute subjection to one person, and that one depressed beneath the level of his species by infirmities, or vice, we suppose perhaps an extreme case: yet in all cases, even in the most popular forms of civil government, *the physical strength resides in the governed.* In what manner opinion thus prevails over strength, or how power, which naturally belongs to superior force, is maintained in opposition to it; in other words, by what motives the many are induced to submit to the few, becomes an inquiry which lies at the root of almost every political speculation. It removes, indeed, but does not resolve, the difficulty, to say that civil governments are now-a-days almost universally upholden by standing armies; for, the question still returns; How are these armies themselves kept in subjection, or made to obey the commands, and carry on the designs, of the prince or state which employs them?

Now, although we should look in vain for any *single* reason which will account for the general submission of mankind to civil government; yet it may not be difficult to assign for every class and character in the community, considerations powerful enough to dissuade each from any attempts to resist established authority. Every man has his motive, though not the same. In this, as in other instances, the conduct is similar, but the principles which produce it, extremely various.

There are three distinctions of character, into which the subjects of a state may be divided: into those who obey from prejudice; those who obey from reason; and those who obey from self-interest.

I. They who obey from prejudice, are determined by an opinion of right in their governors; which opinion is founded upon *prescription.* In monarchies and aristocracies which are hereditary, the prescription operates in favour of particular families; in republics and elective offices, in favour of particular forms of government, or constitutions. Nor is it to be wondered at, that mankind should reverence authority founded in prescription, when they observe that it is prescription which confers the title to almost every thing else. The whole course, and all the habits of civil life, favour this prejudice. Upon what other foundation stands any man's right to his estate? The right of primogeniture, the succession of kindred, the descent of property, the inheritance of honours, the demand of tithes, tolls, rents, or services, from the estates of others, the right of way, the powers of office and magistracy, the privileges of nobility, the immunities of the clergy, upon what are they all founded, in the apprehension at least of the multitude, but upon prescription? To what else, when the claims are contested, is the appeal made? It is natural to transfer the same principle to the affairs of government, and to regard those exertions of power which have been long exercised and acquiesced in, as so many *rights* in the sovereign; and to consider obedience to his commands, within certain accustomed limits, as enjoined by that rule of conscience, which requires us to render to every man his due.

In hereditary monarchies, the *prescriptive title* is corroborated, and its influence considerably augmented by an accession of religious sentiments, and by that sacredness which men are wont to ascribe to the persons of princes. Princes themselves have not failed to take advantage of this disposition, by claiming a superior dignity, as it were, of nature, or a peculiar delegation from the Supreme Being. For this purpose were introduced the titles of Sacred Majesty, of God's Anointed, Representative, Vicegerent, together with the ceremonies of investitures and coronations, which are calculated not so much to recognise the authority of sovereigns, as to consecrate their persons. Where a fabulous religion permitted it, the public veneration has been challenged by bolder pretensions. The Roman emperors usurped the titles and arrogated the worship of gods. The mythology of the heroic ages, and of many barbarous nations, was easily converted to this purpose. Some princes, like the heroes of Homer, and the founder of the Roman name, derived their birth from the gods, others, with Numa, pretended a secret communication with some divine being; and others, again, like the incas of Peru, and the ancient Saxon kings, extracted their descent from the deities of their country. The Lama of Thibet, at this day, is held forth to his subjects, not as the offspring or successor of a divine race of princes, but as the immortal God himself, the object at once of civil obedience and religious adoration. This instance is singular, and may be accounted the farthest point to which the abuse of human credulity has ever been carried. But in all these instances the purpose was the same—to engage the reverence of mankind, by an application to their religious principles.

The reader will be careful to observe that, in this article, we denominate every opinion, whether true or false, a *prejudice*, which is not founded upon argument, in the mind of the person who entertains it.

II. They who obey from *reason*, that is to say, from conscience as instructed by reasonings and conclusions of their own, are determined by the consideration of the necessity of some government or other; the certain mischief of civil commotions; and the danger of resettling the government of their country better, or at all, if once subverted or disturbed.

III. They who obey from *self-interest*, are kept in order by want of leisure; by a succession of private cares, pleasures, and engagements; by contentment, or a sense of the ease, plenty, and safety, which they enjoy; or lastly, and principally, by fear, foreseeing that they would bring themselves by resistance into a worse situation than their present, inasmuch as the strength of government, each discontented subject reflects, is greater than his own, and he knows not that others would join him.

This last consideration has often been called *opinion of power*.

This account of the principles by which mankind are retained in their obedience to civil government, may suggest the following cautions:

1. Let civil governors learn hence to respect their subjects; let them be admonished, that *the physical strength resides in the governed;* that this strength wants only to be felt and roused, to lay prostrate the most ancient and confirmed dominion; that civil authority is founded in opinion; that general opinion therefore ought always to be treated with deference, and managed with delicacy and circumspection.

2. *Opinion of right*, always following *the custom*, being for the most part founded in nothing else, and lending one principal support to government, every innovation in the constitution, or, in other words, in the custom of governing, diminishes the stability of government. Hence some absurdities are to be retained, and many small inconveniences endured in every country, rather than that the usage should be violated, or the course of public affairs diverted from their old and smooth channel. Even *names* are not indifferent. When the multitude are to be dealt with, there is a *charm* in sounds. It was upon this principle, that several statesmen of those times advised Cromwell to assume the title of king, together with the ancient style and insignia of royalty. The minds of many, they contended, would be brought to acquiesce in the authority of a king, who suspected the office, and were offended with the administration, of a protector. Novelty reminded them of usurpation. The adversaries of this design opposed the measure, from the same persuasion of the efficacy of names and forms, jealous lest the veneration paid to these should add an influence to the new settlement which might ensnare the liberty of the commonwealth.

3. *Government may be too secure.* The greatest tyrants have been those, whose titles were the most unquestioned. Whenever therefore the opinion of right becomes too predominant and superstitious, it is abated by *breaking the custom.* Thus the Revolution broke the *custom of succession,* and thereby moderated, both in the prince and in the people, those lofty notions of hereditary right, which in the one were become a continual incentive to tyranny, and disposed the other to invite servitude, by undue compliances and dangerous concessions.

4. As ignorance of union, and want of communication, appear amongst the principal preservatives of civil authority, it behoves every state to keep its subjects in this want and ignorance, not only by vigilance in guarding against actual confederacies and combinations, but by a timely care to prevent great collections of men of any separate party or religion, or of like occupation or profession, or in any way connected by a participation of interest or passion, from being assembled in the same vicinity. A protestant establishment in this country may have little to fear from its popish subjects, scattered as they are throughout the kingdom, and intermixed with the protestant inhabitants, which yet might think them a formidable body, if they were gathered together into one county. The most frequent and desperate riots are those which break out amongst men of the same profession, as weavers, miners, sailors. This circumstance makes a mutiny of soldiers more to be dreaded than any other insurrection. Hence also one danger of an overgrown metropolis, and of those great cities and crowded districts, into which the inhabitants of trading countries are commonly collected. The worst effect of popular tumults consists in this, that they discover to the insurgents the secret of their own strength, teach them to depend upon it against a future occasion, and both produce and diffuse sentiments of confidence in one another, and assurances of mutual support. Leagues thus formed and strengthened, may

overawe or overset the power of any state; and the danger is greater, in proportion as, from the propinquity of habitation and inter-course of employment, the passions and counsels of a party can be circulated with ease and rapidity. It is by these means, and in such situations, that the minds of men are so affected and prepared, that the most dreadful uproars often arise from the slightest provoca-tions. When the train is laid, a spark will produce the explosion.

Chapter 3
THE DUTY OF SUBMISSION TO CIVIL GOVERNMENT EXPLAINED

The subject of this chapter is sufficiently distinguished from the subject of the last, as the motives which actually produce civil obe-dience, may be, and often are, very different from the reasons which make that obedience a duty.

In order to prove civil obedience to be a moral duty, and an obligation upon the conscience, it hath been usual with many political writers (at the head of whom we find the venerable name of Locke), to state a compact between the citizen and the state, as the ground and cause of the relation between them: which com-pact, binding the parties for the same general reason that private contracts do, resolves the duty of submission to civil government into the universal obligation of fidelity in the performance of promises. This compact is twofold:

First, An *express* compact by the primitive founders of the state, who are supposed to have convened for the declared purpose of settling the terms of their political union, and a future constitution of government. The whole body is supposed, in the first place, to have unanimously consented to be bound by the resolutions of the majority; that majority, in the next place, to have fixed certain fundamental regulations; and then to have constituted, either in one person, or in an assembly (the rule of succession, or appointment, being at the same time determined), a *standing legislature*, to whom, under these preestablished restrictions, the government of the state was thenceforward committed, and whose laws the several members of the convention were, by their first undertaking, thus personally engaged to obey. This transaction is sometimes called the *social compact*, and these supposed original regulations compose what are meant by the *constitution*, the *fundamental laws of the constitution;* and form, on one side, the *inherent indefeasible prerogative of the crown;* and, on the other, the unalienable, inprescriptible *birth-right* of the subject.

Secondly, A *tacit* or *implied* compact, by all succeeding members of the state, who, by accepting its protection, consent to be bound by its laws; in like manner, as whoever *voluntarily enters* into a private society is understood, without any other or more explicit stipulation, to promise a conformity with the rules and obedience to the government of that society, as the known conditions upon which he is admitted to a participation of its privileges.

This account of the subject, although specious, and patronized by names the most respectable, appears to labour under the following objections: that it is founded upon a supposition false in fact, and leading to dangerous conclusions.

No social compact, similar to what is here described, was ever made or entered into in reality: no such original convention of the people was ever actually holden, or in any country could be holden, antecedent to the existence of civil government in that country. It is to suppose it possible to call savages out of caves and deserts, to deliberate and vote upon topics, which the experience, and studies, and refinements, of civil life, alone suggest. Therefore no government in the universe *began* from this original. Some imitation of a social compact may have taken place at a *revolution*. The present age has been witness to a transaction, which bears the nearest resemblance to this political idea, of any of which history has preserved the account or memory: I refer to the establishment of the United States of North America. We saw the *people* assembled to elect deputies, for the avowed purpose of framing the constitution of a new empire. We saw this deputation of the people deliberating and resolving upon a form of government, erecting a permanent legislature, distributing the functions of sovereignty, establishing and promulgating a code of fundamental ordinances, which were to be considered by succeeding generations, not merely as laws and acts of the state, but as the very terms and conditions of the confederation; as binding not only upon the subjects and magistrates of the state, but as limitations of power, which were to control and regulate the future legislature. Yet even here much was presupposed. In settling the constitution, many important parts were presumed to be already settled. The qualifications of the constituents who were admitted to vote in the election of members of congress, as well as the mode of electing the representatives, were taken from the old forms of government. That was wanting, from which every social union should set off, and which alone makes the resolutions of the society the act of the individual—the unconstrained consent of all to be bound by the decision of the majority; and yet, without this previous consent, the revolt, and the regulations which followed it, were compulsory upon dissentients.

But the original compact, we are told, is not proposed as a *fact*, but as a fiction, which furnishes a commodious explication of the mutual rights and duties of sovereigns and subjects. In answer to this representation of the matter, we observe, that the original compact, if it be not a fact, is nothing; can confer no actual authority upon laws or magistrates; nor afford any foundation to rights which are supposed to be real and existing. But the truth is, that in the books, and in the apprehension, of those who deduce our civil rights and obligations *à pactis*, the original convention is appealed to and treated of as a reality. Whenever the disciples of this system speak of the constitution; of the fundamental articles of the constitution; of laws being constitutional or unconstitutional; of inherent, unalienable, inextinguishable rights, either in the prince or in the people; or indeed of any laws, usages, or civil rights, as transcending the authority of the subsisting legislature, or possessing a force and sanction superior to what belong to the modern acts and edicts of the legislature; they secretly refer us to what passed at the original convention. They would teach us to believe, that certain rules and ordinances were established by the people, at the same time that they settled the charter of government, and the powers as well as the form of the future legislature; that this legislature consequently deriving its commission and existence from the consent and act of the primitive assembly (of which indeed it is only the standing deputation), continues subject, in the exercise of its offices, and as to the extent of its power, to the rules, reservations, and limitations, which the same assembly then made and prescribed to it.

"As the first members of the state were bound by express stipulation to obey the government which they had erected; so the succeeding inhabitants of the same country are understood to promise allegiance to the constitution and government they find established, by accepting its protection, claiming its privileges, and acquiescing in its laws; more especially, by the purchase or inheritance of lands, to the possession of which, allegiance to the state is annexed, as the very service and condition of the tenure." Smoothly as this train of argument proceeds, little of it will endure examination. The native subjects of modern states are not conscious of any stipulation with the sovereigns, of ever exercising an election whether they will be bound or not by the acts of the legislature, of any alternative being proposed to their choice, of a promise either required or given; nor do they apprehend that the validity or authority of the law depends at all upon *their* recognition or consent. In all stipulations, whether they be expressed or implied, private or public, formal or constructive, the parties stipulating must both possess the liberty of assent and refusal, and also be conscious of this liberty; which cannot with truth be affirmed of the subjects of civil government as government is now, or ever was, actually administered. This is a defect, which no arguments can excuse or supply: all presumptions of consent, without this consciousness, or in opposition to it, are vain and erroneous. Still less is it possible to reconcile with any idea of stipulation, the practice, in which all European nations agree, of founding allegiance upon the circumstance of nativity, that is, of claiming and treating as subjects all those who are born within the confines of their dominions, although removed to another country in their youth or infancy. In this instance certainly, the state does not presume a compact. Also if the subject be bound only by his own consent, and if the voluntary abiding in the country be the proof and intimation of that consent, by what arguments should we defend the right, which sovereigns universally assume, of prohibiting, when they please, the departure of their subjects out of the realm?

Again, when it is contended that the taking and holding possession of land amounts to an acknowledgement of the sovereign, and a virtual promise of allegiance to his laws, it is necessary to the validity of the argument to prove, that the inhabitants, who first composed and constituted the state, collectively possessed a right to the soil of the country—a right to parcel it out to whom they pleased, and to annex to the donation what conditions they thought fit. How came they by this right? An agreement amongst themselves would not confer it; that could only adjust what already belonged to them. A society of men vote themselves to be the owners of a region of the world—does that vote, unaccompanied especially with any culture, enclosure, or proper act of occupation, make it theirs? does it entitle them to exclude others from it, or to dictate the conditions upon which it shall be enjoyed? Yet this original collective right and ownership is the foundation for all the reasoning by which the duty of allegiance is inferred from the pos session of land.

The theory of government which affirms the existence and the obligation of a social compact, would, after all, merit little discussion, and however groundless and unnecessary, should receive no opposition from us, did it not appear to lead to conclusions unfavourable to the improvement, and to the peace, of human society.

1st. Upon the supposition that government was first erected by, and that it derives all its just authority from, resolutions entered into by a convention of the people, it is capable of being presumed, that many points were settled by that convention, anterior to the establishment of the subsisting legislature, and which the legislature, consequently, has no right to alter, or interfere with. These points are called the *fundamentals* of the constitution: and as it is impossible to determine how many, or what, they are, the suggesting of any such serves extremely to embarrass the deliberations of the legislature, and affords a dangerous pretence for disputing the authority of the laws. It was this sort of reasoning (so far as reasoning of any kind was employed in the question) that produced in this nation the doubt, which so much agitated the minds of men in the reign of the second Charles, whether an Act of Parliament could of right alter or limit the succession of the Crown.

2dly. If it be by virtue of a compact, that the subject owes obedience to civil government, it will follow that he ought to abide by the form of government which he finds established, be it ever so absurd or inconvenient. He is bound by his bargain. It is not permitted to any man to retreat from his engagement, merely because he finds the performance disadvantageous, or because he has an opportunity of entering into a better. This law of contracts is universal: and to call the relation between the sovereign and the subjects a contract, yet not to apply to it the rules, or allow of the effects, of a contract, is an arbitrary use of names, and an unsteadiness in reasoning, which can teach nothing. Resistance to the *encroachments* of the supreme magistrate may be justified upon this principle; recourse to arms, for the purpose of bringing about an amendment of the constitution, never can. No form of government contains a provision for its own dissolution; and few governors will consent to the extinction, or even to any abridgement, of their own power. It does not therefore appear, how despotic governments can ever, in consistency with the obligation of the subject, be changed or mitigated. Despotism is the constitution of many states: and whilst a despotic prince exacts from his subjects the most rigorous servitude, according to this account, he is only holding them to their agreement. A people may vindicate, by force, the rights which the constitution has left them: but every attempt to narrow the prerogative of the crown, by *new* limitations, and in opposition to the will of the reigning prince, whatever opportunities may invite, or success follow it, must be condemned as an infraction of the compact between the sovereign and the subject.

3dly. Every violation of the compact on the part of the governor, releases the subject from his allegiance, and dissolves the government. I do not perceive how we can avoid this consequence, if we found the duty of allegiance upon compact, and confess any analogy between the social compact and other contracts. In private contracts, the violation and non-performance of the conditions, by one of the parties, vacates the obligation of the other. Now the terms and articles of the social compact being nowhere extant or expressed; the rights and offices of the administrator of an empire being so many and various; the imaginary and controverted line of his prerogative being so liable to be over-stepped in one part or other of it; the position, that every such transgression amounts to a forfeiture of the government, and consequently authorises the people to withdraw their obedience, and provide for themselves by a new settlement, would endanger the stability of every political fabric in the world, and has in fact always supplied the disaffected with a topic of seditious declamation. If occasions have arisen, in which this plea has been resorted to with justice and success, they have been occasions in which a revolution was defensible upon other and plainer principles. The plea itself is at all times captious and unsafe.

------◆------

Wherefore, rejecting the intervention of a compact, as unfounded in its principle, and dangerous in the application, we assign for the only ground of the subject's obligation, THE WILL OF GOD AS COLLECTED FROM EXPEDIENCY.

The steps by which the argument proceeds, are few and direct. "It is the will of God that the happiness of human life be promoted"—this is the first step, and the foundation not only of this, but of every, moral conclusion. "Civil society conduces to that end"—this is the second proposition. "Civil societies cannot be upholden, unless, in each, the interest of the whole society be binding upon every part and member of it"—this is the third step, and conducts us to the conclusion, namely, "that so long as the interest of the whole society requires it, that is, so long as the established government cannot be resisted or changed without public inconveniency, it is the will of God (which *will* universally determines our duty) that the established government be obeyed"—and no longer.

This principle being admitted, the justice of every particular case of resistance is reduced to a computation of the quantity of the danger and grievance on the one side, and of the probability and expense of redressing it on the other.

But who shall judge this? We answer, "Every man for himself." In contentions between the sovereign and the subject, the parties acknowledge no common arbitrator; and it would be absurd to refer the decision to *those* whose conduct has provoked the question, and whose own interest, authority, and fate, are immediately concerned in it. The danger of error and abuse is no objection to the rule of expediency, because every other rule is liable to the same or greater: and every rule that can be propounded upon the subject (like all rules indeed which appeal to, or bind the conscience) must in the application depend upon private judgement. It may be observed, however, that it ought equally to be accounted the exercise of a man's own private judgement, whether he be determined by reasonings and conclusions of his own, or submit to be directed by the advice of others, provided he be free to choose his guide.

We proceed to point out some easy but important inferences, which result from the substitution of *public expediency* into the place of all implied compacts, promises, or conventions, whatsoever.

I. It may be as much a duty, at one time, to resist government, as it is, at another, to obey it; to wit, whenever more advantage will, in our opinion, accrue to the community from resistance, than mischief.

II. The lawfulness of resistance, or the lawfulness of a revolt, does not depend alone upon the grievance which is sustained or feared, but also upon the probable expense and event of the contest. They who concerted the Revolution in England, were justifiable in their counsels, because, from the apparent disposition of the nation, and the strength and character of the parties engaged, the measure was likely to be brought about with little mischief or bloodshed; whereas it might have been a question with many friends of their country, whether the injuries then endured and threatened would have authorised the renewal of a doubtful civil war.

III. Irregularity in the first foundation of a state, or subsequent violence, fraud, or injustice, in getting possession of the supreme power, are not sufficient reasons for resistance, after the government is once peaceably settled. No subject of the British empire conceives himself engaged to vindicate the justice of the Norman claim or conquest, or apprehends that his duty in any manner depends upon that controversy. So, likewise, if the house of Lancaster, or even the posterity of Cromwell, had been at this day seated upon the throne of England, we should have been as little concerned to inquire how the founder of the family came there. No civil contests are so futile, although none have been so furious and sanguinary, as those which are excited by a disputed succession.

IV. Not every invasion of the subject's rights, or liberty, or of the constitution; not every breach of promise, or of oath; not every stretch of prerogative, abuse of power, or neglect of duty by the chief magistrate, or by the whole or any branch of the legislative body, justifies resistance, unless these crimes draw after them public consequences of sufficient magnitude to outweigh the evils of civil disturbance. Nevertheless, every violation of the constitution ought to be watched with jealousy, and resented as *such*, beyond what the quantity of estimable damage would require or warrant; because a known and settled usage of governing affords the only security against the enormities of uncontrolled dominion, and because this security is weakened by every encroachment which is made without opposition, or opposed without effect.

V. No usage, law, or authority whatsoever, is so binding, that it need or ought to be continued, when it may be changed with advantage to the community. The family of the prince, the order of succession, the prerogative of the crown, the form and parts of

the legislature, together with the respective powers, office, duration, and mutual dependency, of the several parts, are all only so
many *laws*, mutable like other laws, whenever expediency requires,
either by the ordinary act of the legislature, or, if the occasion
deserve it, by the interposition of the people. These points are
wont to be approached with a kind of awe; they are represented to
the mind as principles of the constitution settled by our ancestors,
and, being settled, to be no more committed to innovation or
debate; as foundations never to be stirred; as the terms and conditions of the social compact, to which every citizen of the state has
engaged his fidelity, by virtue of a promise which he cannot now
recall. Such reasons have no place in our system: to us, if there be
any good reason for treating these with more deference and
respect than other laws, it is either the advantage of the present
constitution of government (which reason must be of different
force in different countries), or because in all countries it is of
importance that the form and usage of governing be acknowledged and understood, as well by the governors as by the governed, and because, the seldomer it is changed, the more perfectly
it will be known by both sides.

VI. As all civil obligation is resolved into expediency, what, it
may be asked, is the difference between the obligation of an
Englishman and a Frenchman? or why, since the obligation of both
appears to be founded in the same reason, is a Frenchman bound
in conscience to bear any thing from his king, which an Englishman would not be bound to bear? Their conditions may differ, but
their *rights*, according to this account, should seem to be equal: and
yet we are accustomed to speak of the *rights* as well as of the happiness of a free people, compared with what belong to the subjects
of absolute monarchies; how, you will say, can this comparison be
explained, unless we refer to a difference in the compacts by which
they are respectively bound? This is a fair question, and the answer

to it will afford a farther illustration of our principles. We admit
then that there are many things which a Frenchman is bound in
conscience, as well as by coercion, to endure at the hands of his
prince, to which an Englishman would not be obliged to submit:
but we assert, that it is for these two reasons alone: *first*, because the
same act of the prince is not the same grievance, where it is agreeable to the constitution, and where it infringes it; *secondly*, because
redress in the two cases is not equally attainable. Resistance cannot be attempted with equal hopes of success, or with the same
prospect of receiving support from others, where the people are
reconciled to their sufferings, as where they are alarmed by innovation. In this way, and no otherwise, the subjects of different states
possess different civil rights; the duty of obedience is defined by
different boundaries; and the point of justifiable resistance placed
at different parts of the *scale* of suffering; all which is sufficiently
intelligible without a social compact.

VII. "The interest of the whole society is binding upon every
part of it." No rule, short of this, will provide for the stability of
civil government, or for the peace and safety of social life. Wherefore, as individual members of the state are not permitted to pursue their private emolument to the prejudice of the community, so
is it equally a consequence of this rule, that no particular colony,
province, town, or district, can justly concert measures for their
separate interest, which shall appear at the same time to diminish
the *sum* of public prosperity. I do not mean, that it is necessary to
the justice of a measure, that it profit each and every part of the
community (for, as the happiness of the whole may be increased,
whilst that of some parts is diminished, it is possible that the conduct of one part of an empire may be detrimental to some other
part, and yet just, provided one part gain more in happiness than
the other part loses, so that the common weal be augmented by
the change): but what I affirm is, that those counsels can never be

reconciled with the obligations resulting from civil union, which cause the *whole* happiness of the society to be impaired for the conveniency of a *part*. This conclusion is applicable to the question of right between Great Britain and her revolted colonies. Had I been an American, I should not have thought it enough to have had it even demonstrated, that a separation from the parent-state would produce effects beneficial to America; my relation to that state imposed upon me a farther inquiry, namely, whether the whole happiness of the empire was likely to be promoted by such a measure: not indeed the happiness of every part; that was not necessary, nor to be expected—but whether what Great Britain would lose by the separation, was likely to be compensated to the joint stock of happiness, by the advantages which America would receive from it. The contested claims of sovereign states and their remote dependencies, may be submitted to the adjudication of this rule with mutual safety. A public advantage is measured by the advantage which each individual receives, and by the number of those who receive it. A public evil is compounded of the same proportions. Whilst, therefore, a colony is small, or a province thinly inhabited, if a competition of interests arise between the original country and their acquired dominions, the former ought to be preferred; because it is fit that, if one must necessarily be sacrificed, the less give place to the greater; but when, by an increase of population, the interest of the provinces begins to bear a considerable proportion to the *entire* interest of the community, it is possible that they may suffer so much by their subjection, that not only theirs, but the whole happiness of the empire, may be obstructed by their union. The rule and principle of the calculation being still the same, the *result* is different: and this difference begets a new situation, which entitles the subordinate parts of the states to more equal terms of confederation, and if these be refused, to independency.

Chapter 4

OF THE DUTY OF CIVIL OBEDIENCE, AS STATED IN THE CHRISTIAN SCRIPTURES

We affirm that, as to the *extent* of our civil rights and obligations, *Christianity* hath left us where she found us; that she hath neither altered nor ascertained it; that the New Testament contains not one passage, which, fairly interpreted, affords either argument or objection applicable to any conclusions upon the subject that are deduced from the law and religion of nature.

The only passages which have been seriously alleged in the controversy, or which it is necessary for us to state and examine, are the two following; the one extracted from St. Paul's Epistle to the Romans, the other from the First General Epistle of St. Peter:

ROMANS xiii. 1–7

"Let every soul be subject unto the higher powers: for there is no power but of God: the powers that be, are ordained of God. Whosoever therefore resisteth the power, resisteth the ordinance of God; and they that resist, shall receive to themselves damnation. For rulers are not a terror to good works, but to the evil. Wilt thou then not be afraid of the power? Do that which is good, and thou shalt have praise of the same: for he is the minister of God to thee for good. But if thou do that which is evil, be afraid; for he beareth not the sword in vain: for he is the minister of God, a revenger to *execute* wrath upon him that doeth evil. Wherefore ye must needs be subject, not only for wrath, but also for conscience sake. For, for this cause pay ye tribute also; for they are God's ministers, attending continually upon this very thing. Render therefore to all their dues; tribute to whom tribute is due, custom to whom custom, fear to whom fear, honour to whom honour."

I PETER ii. 13–18

"Submit yourselves to every ordinance of man, for the Lord's sake; whether it be to the king, as supreme; or unto governors, as unto them that are sent by him for the punishment of evil-doers, and for the praise of them that do well. For so is the will of God, that with well-doing ye may put to silence the ignorance of foolish men: as free, and not using your liberty for a cloak of maliciousness, but as the servants of God."

To comprehend the proper import of these instructions, let the reader reflect, that upon the subject of civil obedience there are two questions: the first, whether to obey government be a moral duty and obligation upon the conscience at all; the second, how far, and to what cases, that obedience ought to extend? that these two questions are so distinguishable in the imagination, that it is possible to treat of the one, without any thought of the other; and lastly, that if expressions which relate to one of these questions be transferred and applied to the other, it is with great danger of giving them a signification very different from the author's meaning. This distinction is not only possible, but natural. If I met with a person who appeared to entertain doubts, whether civil obedience were a moral duty which ought to be voluntarily discharged, or whether it were not a mere submission to force, like that which we yield to a robber who holds a pistol to our breast, I should represent to him the use and offices of civil government, the end and the necessity of civil subjection; or, if I preferred a different theory, I should explain to him the social compact, urge him with the obligation and the equity of his implied promise and tacit consent to be governed by the laws of the state from which he received protection; or I should argue, perhaps, that Nature herself dictated the law of subordination, when she planted within us an inclination to associate with our species, and framed us with capacities so various and unequal. From whatever principle I set out, I should labour to infer from it this conclusion, "That obedience to the state is to be numbered amongst the relative duties of human life, for the transgression of which we shall be accountable at the tribunal of Divine justice, whether the magistrate be able to punish us for it or not"; and being arrived at this conclusion, I should stop, having delivered the conclusion itself, and throughout the whole argument expressed the obedience, which I inculcated, in the most general and unqualified terms; all reservations and restrictions being superfluous, and foreign to the doubts I was employed to remove.

If, in a short time afterwards, I should be accosted by the same person, with complaints of public grievances, of exorbitant taxes, of acts of cruelty and oppression, of tyrannical encroachments upon the ancient or stipulated rights of the people, and should be consulted whether it were lawful to revolt, or justifiable to join in an attempt to shake off the yoke by open resistance; I should certainly consider myself as having a case and question before me very different from the former. I should now define and discriminate. I should reply, that if public expediency be the foundation, it is also the measure, of civil obedience: that the obligation of subjects and sovereigns is reciprocal; that the duty of allegiance, whether it be founded in utility or compact, is neither unlimited nor unconditional; that peace may be purchased too dearly; that patience becomes culpable pusillanimity, when it serves only to encourage our rulers to increase the weight of our burthen, or to bind it the faster; that the submission which surrenders the liberty of a nation, and entails slavery upon future generations, is enjoined by no law of rational morality; finally, I should instruct the inquirer to compare the peril and expense of his enterprise with the effects it was expected to produce, and to make choice of the alternative by which not his own present relief or profit, but the whole and permanent interest of the state, was likely to be best promoted. If any one who had been present at both these conversations should upbraid me with change or inconsistency of opinion, should retort upon me the passive doctrine which I before taught, the large and absolute terms in which I then delivered lessons of obedience and submission, I should account myself unfairly dealt with. I should reply, that the only difference which the language of the two conversations presented was, that I added now many exceptions and limitations, which were omitted or unthought of then: that this difference arose naturally from the two occasions, such exceptions being as necessary to the subject of our present conference, as they would have been superfluous and unseasonable in the former.

Now the difference in these two conversations is precisely the distinction to be taken in interpreting those passages of Scripture, concerning which we are debating. They inculcate the *duty*, they do not describe the *extent* of it. They enforce the obligation by the proper sanctions of Christianity, without intending either to enlarge or contract, without considering indeed, the limits by which it is bounden. This is also the method in which the same apostles enjoin the duty of servants to their masters, of children to their parents, of wives to their husbands: "Servants, be subject to your masters."—"Children, obey your parents in all things."—"Wives, submit yourselves unto your own husbands." The same concise and absolute form of expression occurs in all these precepts; the same silence as to any exceptions or distinctions: yet no one doubts that the commands of masters, parents, and husbands, are often so immoderate, unjust, and inconsistent with other obligations, that they both may and ought to be resisted. In letters or dissertations written professedly upon separate articles of morality, we might with more reason have looked for a precise delineation of our duty, and some degree of modern accuracy in the rules which were laid down for our direction: but in those short collections of practical maxims which compose the conclusion, or some small portion, of a doctrinal or perhaps controversial epistle, we cannot be surprised to find the author more solicitous to impress the duty, than curious to enumerate exceptions.

The consideration of this distinction is alone sufficient to vindicate these passages of Scripture from any explanation which may be put upon them, in favour of an unlimited passive obedience. But if we be permitted to assume a supposition which many commentators proceed upon as a certainty, that the first Christians privately cherished an opinion, that their conversion to Christianity entitled them to new immunities, to an exemption as of *right* (however they might give way to necessity), from the authority of the Roman sovereign; we are furnished with a still more apt and satisfactory interpretation of the apostles' words. The two passages apply with great propriety to the refutation of this error: they teach the Christian convert to obey the magistrate "for the Lord's sake"; "not only for wrath, but for conscience sake"; "that there is no power but of God"; "that the powers that be," even the present rulers of the Roman empire, though heathens and usurpers, seeing they are in possession of the actual and necessary authority of civil government, "are ordained of God"; and, consequently, entitled to receive obedience from those who profess themselves the peculiar servants of God, in a greater (certainly not in a less) degree than from any others. They briefly describe the office of "civil governors, the punishment of evil-doers, and the praise of them that do well"; from which description of the use of government, they justly infer the duty of subjection; which duty, being as extensive as the reason upon which it is founded, belongs to Christians, no less than to the heathen members of the community. If it be admitted, that the two apostles wrote with a view to this particular question, it will be confessed, that their words cannot be transferred to a question totally different from this, with any certainty of carrying along with us their authority and intention. There exists no resemblance between the case of a primitive convert, who disputed the jurisdiction of the Roman government over a disciple of Christianity, and *his* who, acknowledging the general authority of the state over all its subjects, doubts whether that authority be not, in some important branch of it, so ill constituted or abused, as to warrant the endeavours of the people to bring about a reformation by force. Nor can we judge what reply the apostles would have made to this *second* question if it had been proposed to them, from any thing they have delivered upon the *first;* any more than, in the two consultations above described, it could be known beforehand what I would say in the latter, from the answer which I gave to the former.

The only defect in this account is, that neither the Scriptures, nor any subsequent history of the early ages of the church, furnish any direct attestation of the existence of such disaffected sentiments amongst the primitive converts. They supply indeed some circumstances which render probable the opinion, that extravagant notions of the political rights of the Christian state were at that time entertained by many proselytes to the religion. From the question proposed to Christ, "Is it lawful to give tribute unto Caesar?" it may be presumed that doubts had been started in the Jewish schools concerning the obligation, or even the lawfulness, of submission to the Roman yoke. The accounts delivered by Josephus, of various insurrections of the Jews of that and the following age, excited by this principle, or upon this pretence, confirm the presumption. Now, as the Christians were at first chiefly taken from the Jews, confounded with them by the rest of the world, and, from the affinity of the two religions, apt to intermix the doctrines of both, it is not to be wondered at, that a tenet, so flattering to the self-importance of those who embraced it, should have been communicated to the new institution. Again, the teachers of Christianity, amongst the privileges which their religion conferred upon its professors, were wont to extol the "*liberty* into which they were called"—"in which Christ had made them free." This liberty, which was intended of a deliverance from the various servitude, in which they had heretofore lived, to the domination of sinful passions, to the superstition of the Gentile idolatry, or the encumbered ritual of the Jewish dispensation, might by some be interpreted to signify an emancipation from all restraint which was imposed by an authority merely human. At least, they might be represented by their enemies as maintaining notions of this dangerous tendency. To some error or calumny of this kind, the words of St. Peter seem to allude: "For so is the will of God, that with well-doing ye may put to silence the ignorance of foolish men: as free, and not using your liberty for a cloak of maliciousness (*i.e.* sedition), but as the servants of God." After all, if any one think this conjecture too feebly supported by testimony, to be relied upon in the interpretation of Scripture, he will then revert to the considerations alleged in the preceding part of this chapter.

After so copious an account of what we apprehend to be the general design and doctrine of these much-agitated passages, little need be added in explanation of particular clauses. St. Paul has said, "Whosoever resisteth the power, resisteth the ordinance of God." This phrase, "the ordinance of God," is by many so interpreted as to authorise the most exalted and superstitious ideas of the regal character. But surely, such interpreters have sacrificed truth to adulation. For, in the first place, the expression, as used by St. Paul, is just as applicable to one kind of government, and to one kind of succession, as to another—to the elective magistrates of a pure republic, as to an absolute hereditary monarch. In the next place, it is not affirmed of the supreme magistrate exclusively, that *he* is the ordinance of God; the title, whatever it imports, belongs to every inferior officer of the state as much as to the highest. The divine right of *kings* is, like the divine right of other magistrates—the law of the land, or even actual and quiet possession of their office—a right ratified, we humbly presume, by the divine approbation, so long as obedience to their authority appears to be necessary or conducive to the common welfare. Princes are ordained of God by virtue only of that general decree by which he assents, and adds the sanction of his will, to every law of society which promotes his own purpose, the communication of human happiness; according to which idea of their origin and constitution (and without any repugnancy to the words of St. Paul), they are by St. Peter denominated the *ordinance of man*.

Chapter 5
OF CIVIL LIBERTY

Civil Liberty is the not being restrained by any law, but what conduces in a greater degree to the public welfare.

To do what we will, is natural liberty: to do what we will, consistently with the interest of the community to which we belong, is civil liberty; that is to say, the only liberty to be desired in a state of civil society.

I should wish, no doubt, to be allowed to act in every instance as I pleased, but I reflect that the rest also of mankind would then do the same; in which state of universal independence and self-direction, I should meet with so many checks and obstacles to my own will, from the interference and opposition of other men's, that not only my happiness, but my liberty, would be less, than whilst the whole community were subject to the dominion of equal laws.

The boasted liberty of a state of nature exists only in a state of solitude. In every kind and degree of union and intercourse with his species, it is possible that the liberty of the individual may be augmented by the very laws which restrain it; because he may gain more from the limitation of other men's freedom than he suffers by the diminution of his own. Natural liberty is the right of common upon a waste; civil liberty is the safe, exclusive, unmolested enjoyment of a cultivated enclosure.

The definition of civil liberty above laid down, imports that the laws of a free people impose no restraints upon the private will of the subject, which do not conduce in a greater degree to the public happiness; by which it is intimated, 1st, that restraint itself is an evil; 2dly, that this evil ought to be overbalanced by some public advantage; 3dly, that the proof of this advantage lies upon the legislature; 4thly, that a law being found to produce no sensible good effects, is a sufficient reason for repealing it, as adverse and injurious to the rights of a free citizen, without demanding specific evidence of its bad effects. This maxim might be remembered with advantage in a revision of many laws of this country; especially of the game-laws; of the poor-laws, so far as they lay restrictions upon the poor themselves; of the laws against Papists and Dissenters: and, amongst people enamoured to excess and jealous of their liberty, it seems a matter of surprise that this principle has been so imperfectly attended to.

The degree of actual liberty always bearing, according to this account of it, a reversed proportion to the number and severity of the *restrictions* which are either useless, or the utility of which does not outweigh the evil of the restraint, it follows, that every nation possesses some, no nation perfect, liberty: that this liberty may be enjoyed under every form of government: that it may be impaired indeed, or increased, but that it is neither gained, nor lost, nor recovered, by any single regulation, change, or event whatever: that consequently, those popular phrases which speak of a free people; of a nation of slaves; which call one revolution the aera of liberty, or another the loss of it; with many expressions of a like absolute form; are intelligible only in a comparative sense.

Hence also we are enabled to apprehend the distinction between *personal* and *civil* liberty. A citizen of the freest republic in the world may be imprisoned for his crimes; and though his personal freedom be restrained by bolts and fetters, so long as his confinement is the effect of a beneficial public law, his civil liberty is not invaded. If this instance appear dubious, the following will be plainer. A passenger from the Levant, who, upon his return to England, should be conveyed to a lazaretto by an order of quarantine, with whatever impatience he might desire his enlargement, and though he saw a guard placed at the door to oppose his escape, or even ready to destroy his life if he attempted it, would hardly accuse government of encroaching upon his civil freedom; nay, might, perhaps, be all the while congratulating himself that he had at length set his foot again in a land of liberty. The manifest expediency of the measure not only justifies it, but reconciles the most odious confinement with the perfect possession, and the loftiest notions, of civil liberty. And if this be true of the coercion of a prison, that it is compatible with a state of *civil* freedom, it cannot with reason be disputed of those more moderate constraints which the ordinary operation of government imposes upon the will of the individual. It is not the rigour, but the inexpediency of laws and acts of authority, which makes them tyrannical.

There is another idea of civil liberty, which, though neither so simple nor so accurate as the former, agrees better with the signification, which the usage of common discourse, as well as the example of many respectable writers upon the subject, has affixed to the term. This idea places liberty in security; making it to consist not merely in an actual exemption from the constraint of useless and noxious laws and acts of dominion, but in being free from the *danger* of having such hereafter imposed or exercised. Thus, speaking of the political state of modern Europe, we are accustomed to say of Sweden, that she hath lost her *liberty* by the revolution which lately took place in that country; and yet we are assured that the people continue to be governed by the same laws as before, or by others which are wiser, milder, and more equitable. What then have they lost? They have lost the power and functions of their diet; the constitution of their states and orders, whose deliberations and concurrence were required in the formation and establishment of every public law; and thereby have parted with the security which they possessed against any attempts of the crown to harass its subjects, by oppressive and useless exertions of prerogative. The loss of this security we denominate the loss of liberty. They have changed, not their laws, but their legislature; not their enjoyment, but their safety; not their present burthens, but their prospects of future grievances; and this we pronounce a change from the condition of freemen to that of slaves. In like manner, in our own country, the act of parliament, in the reign of Henry the Eighth, which gave to the king's proclamation the force of law, has properly been called a complete and formal surrender of the liberty of the nation; and would have been so, although no proclamation were issued in pursuance of these new powers, or none but what was recommended by the highest wisdom and utility. The security was gone. Were it probable that the welfare and accommodation of the people would be as studiously, and as providently, consulted in the edicts of a despotic prince, as by the resolutions of a popular assembly, then would an absolute form of government be no less free than the purest democracy. The different degree of care and knowledge of the public interest which may reasonably be expected from the different form and composition of the legislature, constitutes the distinction, in respect of liberty, as well between these two extremes, as between all the intermediate modifications of civil government.

The definitions which have been framed of civil liberty, and which have become the subject of much unnecessary altercation, are most of them adapted to this idea. Thus one political writer makes the very essence of the subject's liberty to consist in his being governed by no laws but those to which he hath actually consented; another is satisfied with an indirect and virtual consent; another, again, places civil liberty in the separation of the legislative and executive offices of government; another, in the being governed by *law*, that is, by known, preconstituted, inflexible rules of action and adjudication; a fifth, in the exclusive right of the people to tax themselves by their own representatives; a sixth, in the freedom and purity of elections of representatives; a seventh, in the control which the democratic party of the constitution possesses over the military establishment. Concerning which, and some other similar accounts of civil liberty, it may be observed, that they all labour under one inaccuracy, *viz.* that they describe not so much liberty itself, as the safeguards and preservatives of liberty: for example, a man's being governed by no laws but those to which he has given his consent, were it practicable, is no otherwise necessary to the enjoyment of civil liberty, than as it affords a probable security against the dictation of laws imposing superfluous restrictions upon his private will. This remark is applicable to the rest. The diversity of these definitions will not surprise us, when we consider that there is no contrariety or opposition amongst them whatever: for, by how many different provisions and precautions civil liberty is fenced and protected, so many different accounts of liberty itself, all sufficiently consistent with truth and with each other, may, according to this mode of explaining the term, be framed and adopted.

Truth cannot be offended by a definition, but propriety may. In which view, those definitions of liberty ought to be rejected, which, by making that essential to civil freedom which is unattainable in experience, inflame expectations that can never be gratified, and disturb the public content with complaints, which no wisdom or benevolence of government can remove.

It will not be thought extraordinary, that an idea, which occurs so much oftener as the subject of panegyric and careless declamation, than of just reasoning or correct knowledge, should be attended with uncertainty and confusion; or that it should be found impossible to contrive a definition, which may include the numerous, unsettled, and ever-varying significations, which the term is made to stand for, and at the same time accord with the condition and experience of social life.

Of the two ideas that have been stated of civil liberty, whichever we assume, and whatever reasoning we found upon them, concerning its extent, nature, value, and preservation, this is the conclusion—that *that* people, government, and constitution, is the *freest*, which makes the best provision for the enacting of expedient and salutary laws.

Chapter 6
OF DIFFERENT FORMS OF GOVERNMENT

As a series of appeals must be finite, there necessarily exists in every government a power from which the constitution has provided no appeal; and which power, for that reason, may be termed absolute, omnipotent, uncontrollable, arbitrary, despotic; and is alike so in all countries.

The person, or assembly, in whom this power resides, is called the *sovereign*, or the supreme power of the state.

Since to the same power universally appertains the office of establishing public laws, it is called also the *legislature* of the state.

A government receives its denomination from the form of the legislature; which form is likewise what we commonly mean by the *constitution* of a country.

Political writers enumerate three principal forms of government, which, however, are to be regarded rather as the simple forms, by some combination and intermixture of which all actual governments are composed, than as any-where existing in a pure and elementary state. These forms are,

I. Despotism, or absolute MONARCHY, where the legislature is in a single person.

II. An ARISTOCRACY, where the legislature is in a select assembly, the members of which either fill up by election the vacancies in their own body, or succeed to their places in it by inheritance, property, tenure of certain lands, or in respect of some personal right, or qualification.

III. A REPUBLIC, or democracy, where the people at large, either collectively or by representation, constitute the legislature.

The separate advantages of MONARCHY are, unity of counsel, activity, decision, secrecy, despatch; the military strength and energy which result from these qualities of government; the exclusion of popular and aristocratical contentions; the preventing, by a known rule of succession, of all competition for the supreme power; and thereby repressing the hopes, intrigues, and dangerous ambition, of aspiring citizens.

The mischiefs, or rather the dangers, of MONARCHY are, tyranny, expense, exaction, military domination: unnecessary wars, waged to gratify the passions of an individual; risk of the character of the reigning prince; ignorance, in the governors, of the interests and accommodation of the people, and a consequent deficiency of salutary regulations; want of constancy and uniformity in the rules of government, and, proceeding from thence, insecurity of person and property.

The separate advantage of an ARISTOCRACY consists in the wisdom which may be expected from experience and education—a permanent council naturally possesses experience; and the members who succeed to their places in it by inheritance, will, probably, be trained and educated with a view to the stations which they are destined by their birth to occupy.

The mischiefs of an ARISTOCRACY are, dissensions in the ruling orders of the state, which, from the want of a common superior, are liable to proceed to the most desperate extremities; oppression of the lower orders by the privileges of the higher, and by laws partial to the separate interest of the law-makers.

The advantages of a REPUBLIC are, liberty, or exemption from needless restrictions; equal laws; regulations adapted to the wants and circumstances of the people; public spirit, frugality, averseness to war; the opportunities which democratic assemblies afford to men of every description, of producing their abilities and counsels to public observation, and the exciting thereby, and calling forth to the service of the commonwealth, the faculties of its best citizens.

The evils of a REPUBLIC are, dissension, tumults, faction; the attempts of powerful citizens to possess themselves of the empire; the confusion, rage, and clamour, which are the inevitable consequences of assembling multitudes, and of propounding questions of state to the discussion of the people; the delay and disclosure of public counsels and designs; and the imbecility of measures retarded by the necessity of obtaining the consent of numbers: lastly, the oppression of the provinces which are not admitted to a participation in the legislative power.

A *mixed* government is composed by the combination of two or more of the simple forms of government above described—and in whatever proportion each form enters into the constitution of a government, in the same proportion may both the advantages and evils, which we have attributed to that form, be expected: that is, those are the uses to be maintained and cultivated in each part of the constitution, and these are the dangers to be provided against in each. Thus, if secrecy and despatch be truly enumerated amongst the separate excellencies of regal government, then a mixed government, which retains monarchy in one part of its constitution, should be careful that the other estates of the empire do not, by an officious and inquisitive interference with the executive functions, which are, or ought to be, reserved to the administration of the prince, interpose delays, or divulge what it is expedient to conceal. On the other hand, if profusion, exaction, military domination, and needless wars, be justly accounted natural properties of monarchy, in its simple unqualified form; then are these the objects to which, in a mixed government, the aristocratic and popular part of the constitution ought to direct their vigilance; the dangers against which they should raise and fortify their barriers; these are departments of sovereignty, over which a power of inspection and control ought to be deposited with the people.

The same observation may be repeated of all the other advantages and inconveniences which have been ascribed to the several simple forms of government; and affords a rule whereby to direct the construction, improvements, and administration, of mixed governments—subjected however to this remark, that a quality sometimes results from the conjunction of two simple forms of government, which belongs not to the separate existence of either: thus corruption, which has no place in an absolute monarchy, and little in a pure republic, is sure to gain admission into a constitution which divides the supreme power between an executive magistrate and a popular council.

An *hereditary* MONARCHY is universally to be preferred to an *elective* monarchy. The confession of every writer on the subject of civil government, the experience of ages, the example of Poland, and of the papal dominions, seem to place this amongst the few indubitable maxims which the science of politics admits of. A crown is too splendid a prize to be conferred upon merit: the passions or interests of the electors exclude all consideration of the qualities of the competitors. The same observation holds concerning the appointments to any office which is attended with a great share of power or emolument. Nothing is gained by a popular choice, worth the dissensions, tumults, and interruption of regular industry, with which it is inseparably attended. Add to this, that a king, who owes his elevation to the event of a contest, or to any other cause than a fixed rule of succession, will be apt to regard one part of his subjects as the associates of his fortune, and the other as conquered foes. Nor should it be forgotten, amongst the advantages of an *hereditary* monarchy, that, as plans of national improvement and reform are seldom brought to maturity by the exertions of a single reign, a nation cannot attain to the degree of happiness and prosperity to which it is capable of being carried, unless an uniformity of counsels, a consistency of public measures and designs, be continued through a succession of ages. This benefit may be expected with greater probability where the supreme power descends in the same race, and where each prince succeeds, in some sort, to the aim, pursuits, and disposition of his ancestor, than if the crown, at every change, devolve upon a stranger, whose first care will commonly be to pull down what his predecessor had built up; and to substitute systems of administration, which must, in their turn, give way to the more favourite novelties of the next successor.

Aristocracies are of two kinds. First, where the power of the nobility belongs to them in their collective capacity alone; that is, where, although the government reside in an assembly of the order, yet the members of that assembly separately and individually possess no authority or privilege beyond the rest of the community—this describes the constitution of Venice. Secondly, where the nobles are severally invested with great personal power and immunities, and where the power of the senate is little more than the aggregated power of the individuals who compose it—this is the constitution of Poland. Of these two forms of government, the first is more tolerable than the last: for, although the members of a senate should many, or even all of them, be profligate enough to abuse the authority of their stations in the prosecution of private designs, yet, not being all under a temptation to the same injustice, not having all the same end to gain, it would still be difficult to obtain the consent of a majority to any specific act of oppression which the iniquity of an individual might prompt him to propose: or if the will were the same, the power is more confined; one tyrant, whether the tyranny reside in a single person, or a senate, cannot exercise oppression at so many places, at the same time, as it may be carried on by the dominion of a numerous nobility over their respective vassals and dependants. Of all species of domination, this is the most odious: the freedom and satisfaction of private life are more constrained and harassed by it than by the most vexatious law, or even by the lawless will of an arbitrary monarch, from whose knowledge, and from whose injustice, the greatest part of his subjects are removed by their distance, or concealed by their obscurity.

Europe exhibits more than one modern example, where the people, aggrieved by the exactions, or provoked by the enormities, of their immediate superiors, have joined with the reigning prince in the overthrow of the aristocracy, deliberately exchanging their condition for the miseries of despotism. About the middle of the last century, the commons of Denmark, weary of the oppressions which they had long suffered from the nobles, and exasperated by some recent insults, presented themselves at the foot of the throne with a formal offer of their consent to establish unlimited dominion in the king. The revolution in Sweden, still more lately brought about with the acquiescence, not to say the assistance, of the people, owed its success to the same cause, namely, to the prospect of deliverance that it afforded from the tyranny which their nobles exercised under the old constitution. In England, the people beheld the depression of the barons, under the house of Tudor, with satisfaction, although they saw the crown acquiring thereby a power which no limitations that the constitution had then provided were likely to confine. The lesson to be drawn from such events is this: that a mixed government, which admits a patrician order into its constitution, ought to circumscribe the personal privileges of the nobility, especially claims of hereditary jurisdiction and local authority, with a jealousy equal to the solicitude with which it wishes its own preservation: for nothing so alienates the minds of the people from the government under which they live, by a perpetual sense of annoyance and inconveniency, or so prepares them for the practices of an enterprising prince or a factious demagogue, as the abuse which almost always accompanies the existence of separate immunities.

Amongst the inferior, but by no means inconsiderable advantages of a DEMOCRATIC constitution, or of a constitution in which the people partake of the power of legislation, the following should not be neglected:

I. The direction which it gives to the education, studies, and pursuits, of the superior orders of the community. The share which this has in forming the public manners and national character, is very important. In countries, in which the gentry are excluded from all concern in the government, scarcely any thing is left which leads to advancement, but the profession of arms. They who do not addict themselves to this profession (and miserable must that country be, which constantly employs the military service of a great proportion of any order of its subjects!) are commonly lost by the mere want of object and destination; that is, they either fall, without reserve, into the more sottish habits of animal gratification, or entirely devote themselves to the attainment of those futile arts and decorations which compose the business and recommendations of a court: on the other hand, where the whole, or any effective portion, of civil power is possessed by a popular assembly, more serious pursuits will be encouraged; purer morals, and a more intellectual character, will engage the public esteem; those faculties which qualify men for deliberation and debate, and which are the fruit of sober habits, of early and long-continued application, will be roused and animated by the reward which, of all others, most readily awakens the ambition of the human mind—political dignity and importance.

II. Popular elections procure to the common people courtesy from their superiors. That contemptuous and overbearing insolence, with which the lower orders of the community are wont to be treated by the higher, is greatly mitigated where the people have something to give. The assiduity with which their favour is sought upon these occasions, serves to generate settled habits of condescension and respect; and as human life is more embittered by affronts than injuries, whatever contributes to procure mildness and civility of manners towards those who are most liable to suffer from a contrary behaviour, corrects, with the pride, in a great measure, the evil of inequality, and deserves to be accounted among the most generous institutions of social life.

III. The satisfactions which the people in free governments derive from the knowledge and agitation of political subjects; such as the proceedings and debates of the senate; the conduct and characters of ministers; the revolutions, intrigues, and contentions of parties; and, in general, from the discussion of public measures, questions, and occurrences. Subjects of this sort excite just enough of interest and emotion to afford a moderate engagement to the thoughts, without rising to any painful degree of anxiety, or ever leaving a fixed operation upon the spirits—and what is this, but the end and aim of all those amusements which compose so much of the business of life and of the value of riches? For my part (and I believe it to be the case with most men who are arrived at the middle age, and occupy the middle classes of life,) had I all the money which I pay in taxes to government, at liberty to lay out upon amusement and diversion, I know not whether I could make choice of any in which I could find greater pleasure than what I receive from expecting, hearing, and relating public news; reading parliamentary debates and proceedings; canvassing the political arguments, projects, predictions, and intelligence, which are conveyed, by various channels, to every corner of the kingdom. These topics, exciting universal curiosity, and being such as almost every man is ready to form and prepared to deliver his opinion about, greatly promote, and, I think, improve conversation. They render it more rational and more innocent; they supply a substitute for drinking, gaming, scandal, and obscenity. Now the secrecy, the jealousy, the solitude, and precipitation, of despotic governments, exclude all this. But the loss, you say, is trifling. I know that it is possible to render even the mention of it ridiculous, by representing it as the idle employment of the most insignificant part of the nation, the folly of village-statesmen and coffee-house politicians: but I allow nothing to be a trifle which ministers to the harmless gratification of multitudes; nor any order of men to be insignificant, whose number bears a respectable proportion to the sum of the whole community.

We have been accustomed to an opinion, that a REPUBLICAN form of government suits only with the affairs of a small state: which opinion is founded in the consideration, that unless the people, in every district of the empire, be admitted to a share in the national representation, the government is not, as to them, a republic; that elections, where the constituents are numerous, and dispersed through a wide extent of country, are conducted with difficulty, or rather, indeed, managed by the intrigues and combinations of a few, who are situated near the place of election, each voter considering his single suffrage as too minute a portion of the general interest to deserve his care or attendance, much less to be worth any opposition to influence and application; that whilst we contract the representation within a compass small enough to admit of orderly debate, the interest of the constituent becomes too small, of the representative too great. It is difficult also to maintain any connexion between them. He who represents two hundred thousand, is necessarily a stranger to the greatest part of those who elect him: and when his interest amongst them ceases to depend upon an acquaintance with their persons and character, or a care or knowledge of their affairs; when such a representative finds the treasures and honours of a great empire at the disposal of a few, and himself one of the few; there is little reason to hope that he will not prefer to his public duty those temptations of personal aggrandisement which his situation offers, and which the price of his vote will always purchase. All appeal to the people is precluded by the impossibility of collecting a sufficient proportion of their force and numbers. The factions and the unanimity of the senate are equally dangerous. Add to these considerations, that in a democratic constitution the mechanism is too complicated, and the motions too slow, for the operations of a great empire; whose defence and government require execution and despatch, in proportion to the magnitude, extent, and variety, of its concerns. There is weight, no doubt, in these reasons; but much of the objection seems to be done away by the contrivance of a *federal* republic, which, distributing the country into districts of a commodious extent, and leaving to each district its internal legislation, reserves to a convention of the states the adjustment of their relative claims; the levying, direction, and government, of the common force of the confederacy; the requisition of subsidies for the support of this force; the making of peace and war; the entering into treaties; the regulation of foreign commerce; the equalisation of duties upon imports, so as to prevent the defrauding the revenue of one province by smuggling articles of taxation from the borders of another; and likewise so as to guard against undue partialities in the encouragement of trade. To what limits such a republic might, without inconveniency, enlarge its dominions, by assuming neighbouring provinces into the confederation; or how far it is capable of uniting the liberty of a small commonwealth with the safety of a powerful empire; or whether, amongst co-ordinate powers, dissensions and jealousies would not be likely to arise, which, for want of a common superior, might proceed to fatal extremities; are questions upon which the records of mankind do not authorise us to decide with tolerable certainty. The experiment is about to be tried in America upon a large scale.

Chapter 7
OF THE BRITISH CONSTITUTION

By the CONSTITUTION of a country, is meant so much of its law, as relates to the designation and form of the legislature; the rights and functions of the several parts of the legislative body; the construction, office, and jurisdiction, of courts of justice. The constitution is one principal division, section, or title, of the code of public laws; distinguished from the rest only by the superior importance of the subject of which it treats. Therefore the terms *constitutional* and *unconstitutional*, mean legal and illegal. The distinction and the ideas which these terms denote, are founded in the same authority with the law of the land upon any other subject; and to be ascertained by the same inquiries. In England, the system of public jurisprudence is made up of acts of parliament, of decisions of courts of law, and of immemorial usages; consequently, these are the principles of which the English constitution itself consists, the sources from which all our knowledge of its nature and limitations is to be deduced, and the authorities to which all appeal ought to be made, and by which every constitutional doubt and question can alone be decided. This plain and intelligible definition is the more necessary to be preserved in our thoughts, as some writers upon the subject absurdly confound what is constitutional with what is expedient;

pronouncing forthwith a measure to be unconstitutional, which they adjudge in any respect to be detrimental or dangerous: whilst others, again, ascribe a kind of transcendent authority, or mysterious sanctity, to the constitution, as if it were founded in some higher original than that which gives force and obligation to the ordinary laws and statutes of the realm, or were inviolable on any other account than its intrinsic utility. An act of parliament in England can never be unconstitutional, in the strict and proper acceptation of the term; in a lower sense it may, *viz.* when it militates with the spirit, contradicts the analogy, or defeats the provision, of other laws, made to regulate the form of government. Even that flagitious abuse of their trust, by which a parliament of Henry the Eighth conferred upon the king's proclamation the authority of law, was unconstitutional only in this latter sense.

Most of those who treat of the British constitution, consider it as a scheme of government formally planned and contrived by our ancestors, in some certain aera of our national history, and as set up in pursuance of such regular plan and design. Something of this sort is secretly supposed, or referred to, in the expressions of those who speak of the "principles of the constitution," of bringing back the constitution to its "first principles," of restoring it to its "original purity," or "primitive model." Now this appears to me an erroneous conception of the subject. No such plan was ever formed, consequently no such first principles, original model, or standard, exist: I mean, there never was a date or point of time in our history, when the government of England was to be set up anew, and when it was referred to any single person, or assembly, or committee, to frame a charter for the future government of the country; or when a constitution so prepared and digested, was by common consent received and established. In the time of the civil wars, or rather between the death of Charles the First and the restoration of his son, many such projects were published, but none were carried into execution. The Great Charter, and the Bill of Rights, were wise and strenuous efforts to obtain security against certain abuses of regal power, by which the subject had been formerly aggrieved: but these were, either of them, much too partial modifications of the constitution, to give it a new original. The constitution of England, like that of most countries of Europe, hath grown out of occasion and emergency; from the fluctuating policy of different ages; from the contentions, successes, interests, and opportunities, of different orders and parties of men in the community. It resembles one of those old mansions, which, instead of being built all at once, after a regular plan, and according to the rules of architecture at present established, has been reared in different ages of the art, has been altered from time to time, and has been continually receiving additions and repairs suited to the taste, fortune, or conveniency, of its successive proprietors. In such a building, we look in vain for the elegance and proportion, for the just order and correspondence of parts, which we expect in a modern edifice; and which external symmetry, after all, contributes much more perhaps to the amusement of the beholder, than the accommodation of the inhabitant.

In the British, and possibly in all other constitutions, there exists a wide difference between the actual state of the government and the theory. The one results from the other: but still they are different. When we contemplate the *theory* of the British government, we see the king invested with the most absolute personal impunity; with a power of rejecting laws, which have been resolved upon by both houses of parliament; of conferring by his charter, upon any set or succession of men he pleases, the privilege of sending representatives into one house of parliament, as by his immediate appointment he can place whom he will in the other. What is this, a foreigner might ask, but a more circuitous despotism? Yet, when we turn our attention from the legal extent, to the actual exercise of royal authority in England, we see these formidable prerogatives dwindled into mere ceremonies; and, in their stead, a sure and commanding influence, of which the constitution, it seems, is totally ignorant, growing out of that enormous patronage which the increased territory and opulence of the empire have placed in the disposal of the executive magistrate.

Upon questions of reform, the habit of reflection to be encouraged, is a sober comparison of the constitution under which we live—not with models of speculative perfection, but with the actual chance of obtaining a better. This turn of thought will generate a political disposition, equally removed from that puerile admiration of present establishments, which sees no fault, and can endure no change; and that distempered sensibility, which is alive only to perceptions of inconveniency, and is too impatient to be delivered from the uneasiness which it feels, to compute either the peril or expense of the remedy. Political innovations commonly produce many effects beside those that are intended. The direct consequence is often the least important. Incidental, remote, and unthought-of evil or advantages, frequently exceed the good that is designed, or the mischief that is foreseen. It is from the silent and unobserved operation, from the obscure progress of causes set at work for different purposes, that the greatest revolutions take their rise. When Elizabeth, and her immediate successor, applied themselves to the encouragement and regulation of trade by many wise laws, they knew not, that, together with wealth and industry, they were diffusing a consciousness of strength and independency which would not long endure, under the forms of a mixed government, the dominion of arbitrary princes. When it was debated whether the mutiny act, the law by which the army is governed and maintained, should be temporary or perpetual, little else probably occurred to the advocates of an annual bill, than the expediency of retaining a control over the most dangerous prerogative of the crown—the direction and command of a standing army; whereas, in its effect, this single reservation has altered the whole frame and quality of the British constitution. For since, in consequence of the military system which prevails in neighbouring and rival nations, as well as on account of the internal exigencies of government, a standing army has become essential to the safety and administration of the empire, it enables parliament, by discontinuing this necessary provision, so to enforce its resolutions upon any other subject, as to render the king's dissent to a law which has received the approbation of both houses, too dangerous an experiment any longer to be advised. A contest between the king and parliament, cannot now be persevered in without a dissolution of the government. Lastly, when the constitution conferred upon the crown the nomination to all employments in the public service, the authors of this arrangement were led to it, by the obvious propriety of leaving to a master the choice of his servants; and by the manifest inconveniency of engaging the national council, upon every vacancy, in those personal contests which attend elections to places of honour and emolument. Our ancestors did not observe that this disposition added an influence to the regal office, which, as the number and value of public employments increased, would supersede in a great measure the forms, and change the character, of the ancient constitution. They knew not, what the experience and reflection of modern ages have discovered, that patronage universally is power; that he who possesses in a sufficient degree the means of gratifying the desires of mankind after wealth and distinction, by whatever checks and forms his authority may be limited or disguised, will direct the management of public affairs. Whatever be the mechanism of the political engine, he will guide the motion. These instances are adduced in order to illustrate the proposition which we laid down, that, in politics, the most important and permanent effects have, for the most part, been incidental and unforeseen: and this proposition we inculcate, for the sake of the caution which teaches that changes ought not to be adventured upon without a *comprehensive* discernment of the consequences— without a knowledge as well of the remote tendency, as of the immediate design. The courage of a statesman should resemble that of a commander, who, however regardless of personal danger, never forgets, that, with his own, he commits the lives and fortunes of a multitude; and who does not consider it as any proof of zeal or valour, to stake the safety of *other* men upon the success of a perilous or desperate enterprise.

There is one end of civil government peculiar to a good constitution, namely, the happiness of its subjects; there is another end essential to a good government, but common to it with many bad ones—its own preservation. Observing that the best form of government would be defective, which did not provide for its own permanency, in our political reasonings we consider all such provisions as expedient; and are content to accept as a sufficient ground for a measure, or law, that it is necessary or conducive to the preservation of the constitution. Yet, in truth, such provisions are absolutely expedient, and such an excuse final, only whilst the constitution is worth preserving; that is, until it can be exchanged for a better. I premise this distinction, because many things in the English, as in every constitution, are to be vindicated and accounted for solely from their tendency to maintain the government in its present state, and the several parts of it in possession of the powers which the constitution has assigned to them; and because I would wish it to be remarked that such a consideration is always subordinate to another—the value and usefulness of the constitution itself.

The Government of England, which has been sometimes called a mixed government, sometimes a limited monarchy, is formed by a combination of the three regular species of government: the monarchy residing in the King; the aristocracy, in the House of Lords; and the republic, being represented by the House of Commons. The perfection intended by such a scheme of government is, to unite the advantages of the several simple forms, and to exclude the inconveniencies. To what degree this purpose is attained or attainable in the British constitution, wherein it is lost sight of or neglected; and by what means it may in any part be promoted with better success, the reader will be enabled to judge, by a separate recollection of these advantages and inconveniencies, as enumerated in the preceding chapter, and a distinct application of each to the political condition of this country. We will present our remarks upon the subject in a brief account of the expedients by which the British constitution provides,

1st. For the interest of its subjects.

2dly. For its own preservation.

The contrivances for the first of these purposes, are the following:

In order to promote the establishment of salutary public laws, every citizen of the state is capable of becoming a member of the senate: and every senator possesses the right of propounding to the deliberation of the legislature whatever law he pleases.

Every district of the empire enjoys the privilege of choosing representatives, informed of the interests, and circumstances, and desires of their constituents, and entitled by their situation to communicate that information to the national council. The meanest subject has some one whom he can call upon to bring forward his complaints and requests to public attention.

By annexing the right of voting for members of the House of Commons to different qualifications in different places, each order and profession of men in the community become virtually represented; that is, men of all orders and professions, statesmen, courtiers, country-gentlemen, lawyers, merchants, manufacturers, soldiers, sailors, interested in the prosperity, and experienced in the occupation, of their respective professions, obtain seats in parliament.

The elections, at the same time, are so connected with the influence of landed property, as to afford a certainty that a considerable number of men of great estates will be returned to parliament; and are also so modified, that men the most eminent and successful in their respective professions, are the most likely, by their riches, or the weight of their stations, to prevail in these competitions.

The number, fortune, and quality, of the members; the variety of interests and characters amongst them; above all, the temporary duration of their power, and the change of men which every new election produces; are so many securities to the public, as well against the subjection of their judgements to any external dictation, as against the formation of a junto in their own body, sufficiently powerful to govern their decisions.

The representatives are so intermixed with the constituents, and the constituents with the rest of the people, that they cannot, without a partiality too flagrant to be endured, impose any burthen upon the subject, in which they do not share themselves; nor scarcely can they adopt an advantageous regulation, in which their own interests will not participate of the advantage.

The proceedings and debates of parliament, and the parliamentary conduct of each representative, are known by the people at large.

The representative is so far dependent upon the constituent, and political importance upon public favour, that a member of parliament cannot more effectually recommend himself to eminence and advancement in the state, than by contriving and patronising laws of public utility.

When intelligence of the condition, wants, and occasions, of the people, is thus collected from every quarter; when such a variety of invention, and so many understandings, are set at work upon the subject; it may be presumed, that the most eligible expedient, remedy, or improvement, will occur to some one or other: and when a wise counsel, or beneficial regulation, is once suggested, it may be expected, from the disposition of an assembly so consti- tuted as the British House of Commons is, that it cannot fail of receiving the approbation of a majority.

To prevent those destructive contentions for the supreme power, which are sure to take place where the members of the state do not live under an acknowledged head, and a known rule of suc- cession; to preserve the people in tranquillity at home, by a speedy and vigorous execution of the laws; to protect their interest abroad, by strength and energy in military operations, by those advantages of decision, secrecy, and despatch, which belong to the resolutions of monarchical councils—for these purposes, the constitution has committed the executive government to the administration and limited authority of an hereditary king.

In the defence of the empire; in the maintenance of its power, dignity, and privileges, with foreign nations; in the advancement of its trade by treaties and conventions; and in the providing for the general administration of municipal justice, by a proper choice and appointment of magistrates; the inclination of the king and of the people usually coincides; in this part, therefore, of the regal office, the constitution entrusts the prerogative with ample powers.

The dangers principally to be apprehended from regal govern- ment, relate to the two articles *taxation* and *punishment*. In every form of government, from which the people are excluded, it is the interest of the governors to get as much, and of the governed to give as little, as they can: the power also of punishment, in the hands of an arbitrary prince, oftentimes becomes an engine of extortion, jealousy, and revenge. Wisely, therefore, hath the British constitution guarded the safety of the people, in these two points, by the most studious precautions.

Upon that of *taxation*, every law which, by the remotest construction, may be deemed to levy money upon the property of the subject, must originate, that is, must first be proposed and assented to, in the House of Commons: by which regulation, accompanying the weight which that assembly possesses in all its functions, the levying of taxes is almost exclusively reserved to the popular part of the constitution, who, it is presumed, will not tax themselves, nor their fellow-subjects, without being first convinced of the necessity of the aids which they grant.

The application also of the public supplies, is watched with the same circumspection as the assessment. Many taxes are annual; the produce of others is mortgaged, or appropriated to specific services: the expenditure of all of them is accounted for in the House of Commons; as computations of the charge of the purpose for which they are wanted, are previously submitted to the same tribunal.

In the infliction of *punishment*, the power of the crown, and of the magistrate appointed by the crown, is confined by the most precise limitations: the guilt of the offender must be pronounced by twelve men of his own order, indifferently chosen out of the county where the offence was committed: the punishment, or the limits to which the punishment may be extended, are ascertained, and affixed to the crime, by laws which know not the person of the criminal.

And whereas arbitrary or clandestine confinement is the injury most to be dreaded from the strong hand of the executive government, because it deprives the prisoner at once of protection and defence, and delivers him into the power, and to the malicious or interested designs, of his enemies; the constitution has provided against this danger with double solicitude. The ancient writ of habeas corpus, the habeas-corpus act of Charles the Second, and the practice and determinations of our sovereign courts of justice founded upon these laws, afford a complete remedy for every conceivable case of illegal imprisonment.*

Treason being that charge, under colour of which the destruction of an obnoxious individual is often sought; and government being at all times more immediately a party in the prosecution; the law, beside the general care with which it watches over the safety of the accused, in this case, sensible of the unequal contest in which the subject is engaged, has assisted his defence with extraordinary indulgences. By two statutes, enacted since the Revolution, every person indicted for high treason shall have a copy of his indictment, a list of the witnesses to be produced, and of the jury impanneled, delivered to him ten days before the trial; he is also permitted to make his defence by counsel—privileges which are not allowed to the prisoner, in a trial for any other crime: and, what is of more importance to the party than all the rest, the testimony

---

*Upon complaint in writing by, or on behalf of, any person in confinement, to any of the four courts of Westminster-Hall, in term-time, or to the lord chancellor, or one of the judges, in the vacation; and upon a probable reason being suggested to question the legality of the detention; a writ is issued to the person in whose custody the complainant is alleged to be, commanding him within a certain limited and short time to produce the body of the prisoner, and the authority under which he is detained. Upon the return of the writ, strict and instantaneous obedience to which is enforced by very severe penalties, if no lawful cause of imprisonment appear, the court or judge, before whom the prisoner is brought, is authorised and bound to discharge him; even though he may have been committed by a secretary, or other high officer of state, by the privy council, or by the king in person: so that no subject of this realm can be held in confinement by any power, or under any pretence whatever, provided he can find means to convey his complaints to one of the four courts of Westminster-Hall, or, during their recess, to any of the judges of the same, unless all these several tribunals agree in determining his imprisonment to be legal. He may make application to them, in succession; and if one out of the number be found, who thinks the prisoner entitled to his liberty, that one possesses authority to restore it to him.

of two witnesses, at the least, is required to convict a person of treason: whereas, one positive witness is sufficient in almost every other species of accusation.

We proceed, in the second place, to inquire in what manner the constitution has provided for its own preservation; that is, in what manner each part of the legislature is secured in the exercise of the powers assigned to it, from the encroachments of the other parts. This security is sometimes called the *balance of the constitution:* and the political equilibrium, which this phrase denotes, consists in two contrivances—a balance of power, and a balance of interest. By a balance of power is meant, that there is no power possessed by one part of the legislature, the abuse or excess of which is not checked by some antagonist power, residing in another part. Thus the power of the two houses of parliament to frame laws, is checked by the king's negative: that, if laws subversive of regal government should obtain the consent of parliament, the reigning prince, by interposing his prerogative, may save the necessary rights and authority of his station. On the other hand, the arbitrary application of this negative is checked by the privilege which parliament possesses, of refusing supplies of money to the exigencies of the king's administration. The constitutional maxim, "that the king can do no wrong," is balanced by another maxim, not less constitutional, "that the illegal commands of the king do not justify those who assist, or concur, in carrying them into execution"; and by a second rule, subsidiary to this, "that the acts of the crown acquire not a legal force, until authenticated by the subscription of some of its great officers." The wisdom of this contrivance is worthy of observation. As the king could not be punished, without a civil war, the constitution exempts his person from trial or account; but, lest this impunity should encourage a licentious exercise of dominion, various obstacles are opposed to the private will of the sovereign, when directed to illegal objects. The pleasure of the crown must be

announced with certain solemnities, and attested by certain officers of state. In some cases, the royal order must be signified by a
secretary of state; in others it must pass under the privy seal; and,
in many, under the great seal. And when the king's command is regularly published, no mischief can be achieved by it, without the
ministry and compliance of those to whom it is directed. Now all
who either concur in an illegal order by authenticating its publication with their seal or subscription, or who in any manner assist in
carrying it into execution, subject themselves to prosecution and
punishment, for the part they have taken; and are not permitted to
plead or produce the command of the king in justification of their
obedience.* But farther: the power of the crown to direct the military force of the kingdom, is balanced by the annual necessity of
resorting to parliament for the maintenance and government of
that force. The power of the king to declare war, is checked by the
privilege of the House of Commons, to grant or withhold the supplies by which the war must be carried on. The king's choice of his
ministers is controlled by the obligation he is under of appointing
those men to offices in the state, who are found capable of managing the affairs of his government, with the two houses of parliament. Which consideration imposes such a necessity upon the
crown, as hath in a great measure subdued the influence of

---

*Amongst the checks which parliament holds over the administration of pub-
lic affairs, I forbear to mention the practice of addressing the king, to know by
whose advice he resolved upon a particular measure; and of punishing the authors
of that advice, for the counsel they had given. Not because I think this method
either unconstitutional or improper; but for this reason: that it does not so much
subject the king to the control of parliament, as it supposes him to be already in
subjection. For if the king were so far out of the reach of the resentment of the
House of Commons, as to be able with safety to refuse the information requested,
or to take upon himself the responsibility inquired after, there must be an end of
all proceedings founded in this mode of application.

favouritism; insomuch that it is become no uncommon spectacle in this country, to see men promoted by the king to the highest offices and richest preferments which he has in his power to bestow, who have been distinguished by their opposition to his personal inclinations.

By the *balance of interest*, which accompanies and gives efficacy to the *balance of power*, is meant this—that the respective interests of the three estates of the empire are so disposed and adjusted, that whichever of the three shall attempt any encroachment, the other two will unite in resisting it. If the king should endeavour to extend his authority, by contracting the power and privileges of the Commons, the House of Lords would see their own dignity endangered by every advance which the crown made to independency upon the resolutions of parliament. The admission of arbitrary power is no less formidable to the grandeur of the aristocracy, than it is fatal to the liberty of the republic; that is, it would reduce the nobility from the hereditary share they possess in the national councils, in which their real greatness consists, to the being made a part of the empty pageantry of a despotic court. On the other hand, if the House of Commons should intrench upon the distinct province, or usurp the established prerogative of the crown, the House of Lords would receive an instant alarm from every new stretch of popular power. In every contest in which the king may be engaged with the representative body, in defence of his established share of authority, he will find a sure ally in the collective power of the nobility. An attachment to the monarchy, from which they derive their own distinction; the allurements of a court, in the habits and with the sentiments of which they have been brought up; their hatred of equality and of all levelling pretensions, which may ultimately affect the privileges, or even the existence, of their order; in short, every principle and every prejudice which are wont to actuate human conduct, will determine their choice to the side and support of the crown. Lastly, if the nobles themselves should attempt to revive the superiorities which their ancestors exercised under the feudal constitution, the king and the people would alike remember, how the one had been insulted, and the other enslaved, by that barbarous tyranny. They would forget the natural opposition of their views and inclinations, when they saw themselves threatened with the return of a domination which was odious and intolerable to both.

―――――――

The reader will have observed, that in describing the British constitution, little notice has been taken of the House of Lords. The proper use and design of this part of the constitution, are the following: First, to enable the king, by his right of bestowing the peerage, to reward the servants of the public, in a manner most grateful to them, and at a small expense to the nation: secondly, to fortify the power and to secure the stability of regal government, by an order of men naturally allied to its interests: and, thirdly, to answer a purpose, which, though of superior importance to the other two, does not occur so readily to our observation; namely, to stem the progress of popular fury. Large bodies of men are subject to sudden phrensies. Opinions are sometimes circulated amongst a multitude without proof or examination, acquiring confidence and reputation merely by being repeated from one to another; and passions founded upon these opinions, diffusing themselves with a rapidity which can neither be accounted for nor resisted, may agitate a country with the most violent commotions. Now the only way to stop the fermentation, is to divide the mass; that is, to erect different orders in the community, with separate prejudices and interests. And this may occasionally become the use of an hereditary nobility, invested with a share of legislation. Averse to those prejudices which actuate the minds of the vulgar; accustomed to condemn the clamour of the populace; disdaining to receive laws and opinions from their inferiors in rank; they will oppose resolutions which are founded in the folly and violence of the lower part of the community. Were the voice of the people always dictated by reflection; did every man, or even one man in a hundred, think for himself, or actually consider the measure he was about to approve or censure; or even were the common people tolerably steadfast in the judgement which they formed, I should hold the interference of a superior order not only superfluous, but wrong: for when every thing is allowed to difference of rank and education, which the actual state of these advantages deserves, that, after all, is most likely to be right and expedient, which appears to be so to the separate judgement and decision of a great majority of the nation; at least, that, in general, is right *for them*, which is agreeable to their fixed opinions and desires. But when we observe what is urged as the public opinion, to be, in truth, the opinion only, or perhaps the feigned profession, of a few crafty leaders; that the numbers who join in the cry, serve only to swell and multiply the sound, without any accession of judgement, or exercise of understanding; and that oftentimes the wisest counsels have been thus overborne by tumult and uproar—we may conceive occasions to arise, in which the commonwealth may be saved by the reluctance of the nobility to adopt the caprices, or to yield to the vehemence, of the common people. In expecting this advantage from an order of nobles, we do not suppose the nobility to be more unprejudiced than others; we only suppose that their prejudices will be different from, and may occasionally counteract, those of others.

If the personal privileges of the peerage, which are usually so many injuries to the rest of the community, be restrained, I see little inconveniency in the increase of its number; for it is only dividing the same quantity of power amongst more hands, which is rather favourable to public freedom than otherwise.

The admission of a small number of ecclesiastics into the House of Lords, is but an equitable compensation to the clergy for the exclusion of their order from the House of Commons. They are a set of men considerable by their number and property, as well as by their influence, and the duties of their station; yet, whilst every other profession has those amongst the national representatives, who, being conversant in the same occupation, are able to state, and naturally disposed to support, the rights and interests of the class and calling to which they belong, the clergy alone are deprived of this advantage: which hardship is made up to them by introducing the prelacy into parliament; and if bishops, from gratitude or expectation, be more obsequious to the will of the crown than those who possess great temporal inheritances, they are properly inserted into that part of the constitution, from which much or frequent resistance to the measures of government is not expected.

I acknowledge, that I perceive no sufficient reason for exempting the persons of members of either house of parliament from arrest for debt. The counsels or suffrage of a single senator, especially of one who in the management of his own affairs may justly be suspected of a want of prudence or honesty, can seldom be so necessary to those of the public, as to justify a departure from that wholesome policy, by which the laws of a commercial state punish and stigmatize insolvency. But, whatever reason may be pleaded for their *personal* immunity, when this privilege of parliament is extended to domestics and retainers, or when it is permitted to impede or delay the course of judicial proceedings, it becomes an absurd sacrifice of equal justice to imaginary dignity.

There is nothing in the British constitution so remarkable, as the irregularity of the popular representation. The House of Commons consists of five hundred and fifty-eight members, of whom two hundred are elected by seven thousand constituents; so that a majority of these seven thousand, without any reasonable title to superior weight or influence in the state, may, under certain circumstances, decide a question against the opinion of as many millions. Or, to place the same object in another point of view: If my estate be situated in one county of the kingdom, I possess the ten-thousandth part of a single representative; if in another, the thousandth; if in a particular district, I may be one in twenty who choose two representatives; if in a still more favoured spot, I may enjoy the right of appointing two myself. If I have been born, or dwell, or have served an apprenticeship, in one town, I am represented in the national assembly by two deputies, in the choice of whom I exercise an actual and sensible share of power; if accident has thrown my birth, or habitation, or service, into another town, I have no representative at all, nor more power or concern in the election of those who make the laws by which I am governed, than if I was a subject of the Grand Signior—and this partiality subsists without any pretence whatever of merit or of propriety, to justify the preference of one place to another. Or, thirdly, to describe the state of national representation as it exists in reality, it may be affirmed, I believe, with truth, that about one half of the House of Commons obtain their seats in that assembly by the election of the people, the other half by purchase, or by the nomination of single proprietors of great estates.

This is a flagrant incongruity in the constitution; but it is one of those objections which strike most forcibly at first sight. The effect of all reasoning upon the subject is, to diminish the first impression; on which account it deserves the more attentive examination, that we may be assured, before we adventure upon a reformation, that the magnitude of the evil justifies the danger of the experiment. In a few remarks that follow, we would be understood, in the first place, to decline all conference with those who wish to alter the form of government of these kingdoms. The reformers with whom we have to do, are they who, whilst they change this part of the system, would retain the rest. If any Englishman expect more happiness to his country under a republic, he may very consistently recommend a new-modelling of elections to parliament; because, if the King and House of Lords were laid aside, the present disproportionate representation would produce nothing but a confused and ill-digested oligarchy. In like manner we waive a controversy with those writers who insist upon representation as a *natural* right:* we consider it so far only as a right at all, as it conduces to public utility; that is, as it contributes to the establishment of good laws, or as it secures to the people the just administration of these laws. These effects depend upon the disposition and abilities of the national counsellors. Wherefore, if men the most likely by their qualifications to know and to promote the public interest, be actually returned to parliament, it signifies little who return them. If the properest persons be elected, what matters it by whom they are elected? At least, no prudent statesman would subvert long-established or even settled rules of representation, without a prospect of procuring wiser or better representatives. This then being well observed, let us, before we seek to obtain any thing more, consider duly what we already have. We *have* a House of Commons composed of five hundred and fifty-eight members, in which number are found the most considerable landholders and merchants of the kingdom; the heads of the army, the navy, and the law; the occupiers of great offices in the state;

---

*If this right be *natural*, no doubt it must be equal; and the right, we may add, of one sex, as well as of the other. Whereas every plan of representation that we have heard of, begins by excluding the votes of women; thus cutting off, at a single stroke, one half of the public from a right which is asserted to be inherent in all; a right too, as some represent it, not only universal, but unalienable, and indefeasible, and imprescriptible.

together with many private individuals, eminent by their knowledge, eloquence, or activity. Now if the country be not safe in such hands, in whose may it confide its interests? If such a number of such men be liable to the influence of corrupt motives, what assembly of men will be secure from the same danger? Does any new scheme of representation promise to collect together more wisdom, or to produce firmer integrity? In this view of the subject, and attending not to ideas of order and proportion (of which many minds are much enamoured), but to effects alone, we may discover just excuses for those parts of the present representation which appear to a hasty observer most exceptionable and absurd. It should be remembered, as a maxim extremely applicable to this subject, that no order or assembly of men whatever can long maintain their place and authority in a mixed government, of which the members do not individually possess a respectable share of personal importance. Now whatever may be the defects of the present arrangement, it infallibly secures a great weight of property to the House of Commons, by rendering many seats in that house accessible to men of large fortunes, and to such men alone. By which means those characters are engaged in the defence of the separate rights and interests of this branch of the legislature, that are best able to support its claims. The constitution of most of the small boroughs, especially the burgage tenure, contributes, though undesignedly, to the same effect: for the appointment of the representatives we find commonly annexed to certain great inheritances. Elections purely popular are in this respect uncertain: in times of tranquillity, the natural ascendancy of wealth will prevail; but when the minds of men are inflamed by political dissensions, this influence often yields to more impetuous motives. The variety of tenures and qualifications, upon which the right of voting is founded, appears to me a recommendation of the mode which now subsists, as it tends to introduce into parliament a corresponding mixture of characters and professions.

It has been long observed that conspicuous abilities are most frequently found with the representatives of small boroughs. And this is nothing more than what the laws of human conduct might teach us to expect: when such boroughs are set to sale, those men are likely to become purchasers, who are enabled by their talents to make the best of their bargain. when a seat is not sold, but given by the opulent proprietor of a burgage tenure, the patron finds his own interest consulted, by the reputation and abilities of the member whom he nominates. If certain of the nobility hold the appointment of some part of the House of Commons, it serves to maintain that alliance between the two branches of the legislature which no good citizen would wish to see dissevered: it helps to keep the government of the country in the House of Commons, in which it would not perhaps long continue to reside, if so powerful and wealthy a part of the nation as the peerage compose, were excluded from all share and interest in its constitution. If there be a few boroughs so circumstanced as to lie at the disposal of the crown, whilst the number of such is known and small, they may be tolerated with little danger. For where would be the impropriety or the inconveniency, if the king at once should nominate a limited number of his servants to seats in parliament; or, what is the same thing, if seats in parliament were annexed to the possession of certain of the most efficient and responsible offices in the state? The present representation, after all these deductions, and under the confusion in which it confessedly lies, is still in such a degree popular, or rather the representatives are so connected with the mass of the community by a society of interests and passions, that the will of the people, when it is determined, permanent, and general, almost always at length prevails.

Upon the whole, in the several plans which have been suggested, of an equal or a reformed representation, it will be difficult to discover any proposal that has a tendency to throw more of the business of the nation into the House of Commons, or to collect a set of men more fit to transact that business, or in general more interested in the national happiness and prosperity. One consequence, however, may be expected from these projects, namely, "less flexibility to the influence of the crown." And since the diminution of this influence is the declared and perhaps the sole design of the various schemes that have been produced, whether for regulating the elections, contracting the duration, or for purifying the constitution of parliament by the exclusion of placemen and pensioners; it is obvious to remark, that the more apt and natural, as well as the more safe and quiet way of attaining the same end, would be by a direct reduction of the patronage of the crown, which might be effected to a certain extent without hazarding farther consequences. Superfluous and exorbitant emoluments of office may not only be suppressed for the present; but provisions of law be devised, which should for the future restrain within certain limits the number and value of the offices in the donation of the king.

But whilst we dispute concerning different schemes of reformation, all directed to the same end, a previous doubt occurs in the debate, whether the end itself be good, or safe—whether the influence so loudly complained of can be destroyed, or even much diminished, without danger to the state. Whilst the zeal of some men beholds this influence with a jealousy which nothing but its entire abolition can appease, many wise and virtuous politicians deem a considerable portion of it to be as necessary a part of the British constitution, as any other ingredient in the composition; to be that, indeed, which gives cohesion and solidity to the whole. Were the measures of government, say they, opposed from nothing but principle, government ought to have nothing but the rectitude of its measures to support them: but since opposition springs from other motives, government must possess an influence to counteract these motives; to produce, not a bias of the passions, but a neutrality—it must have some weight to cast into the scale, to set the balance even. It is the nature of power, always to press upon the boundaries which confine it. Licentiousness, faction, envy, impatience of control or inferiority; the secret pleasure of mortifying the great, or the hope of dispossessing them, a constant willingness to question and thwart whatever is dictated or even proposed by another; a disposition common to all bodies of men, to extend the claims and authority of their orders; above all, that love of power, and of showing it, which resides more or less in every human breast, and which, in popular assemblies, is inflamed, like every other passion, by communication and encouragement: these motives, added to private designs and resentments, cherished also by popular acclamation, and operating upon the great share of power already possessed by the House of Commons, might induce a majority, or at least a large party of men in that assembly, to unite in endeavouring to draw to themselves the whole government of the state: or, at least, so to obstruct the conduct of public affairs, by a wanton and perverse opposition, as to render it impossible for the wisest statesman to carry forwards the business of the nation with success or satisfaction.

Some passages of our national history afford grounds for these apprehensions. Before the accession of James the First, or, at least, during the reigns of his three immediate predecessors, the government of England was a government by force; that is, the king carried his measures in parliament by *intimidation*. A sense of personal danger kept the members of the House of Commons in subjection. A conjunction of fortunate causes delivered, at last, the parliament and nation from slavery. That overbearing system which had declined in the hands of James, expired early in the reign of his son. After the Restoration, there succeeded in its place, and, since the Revolution, has been methodically pursued, the more successful expedient of *influence*. Now we remember what passed between the loss of terror, and the establishment of influence. The transactions of that interval, whatever we may think of their occasion or effect, no friend of regal government would wish to see revived. But the affairs of this kingdom afford a more recent attestation to the same doctrine. In the British colonies of North America, the late assemblies possessed much of the power and constitution of our House of Commons. The king and government of Great Britain held no patronage in the country, which could create attachment and influence sufficient to counteract that restless arrogating spirit, which, in popular assemblies, when left to itself, will never brook an authority that checks and interferes with its own. To this cause, excited perhaps by some unseasonable provocations, we may attribute, as to their true and proper original, (we will not say the misfortunes, but) the changes that have taken place in the British empire. The admonition which such examples suggest, will have its weight with those who are content with the general frame of the English constitution; and who consider stability amongst the first perfections of any government.

We protest, however, against any construction, by which what is here said shall be attempted to be applied to the justification of bribery, or of any clandestine reward or solicitation whatever. The very secrecy of such negotiations confesses or begets a consciousness of guilt; which when the mind is once taught to endure without uneasiness, the character is prepared for every compliance; and there is the greater danger in these corrupt practices, as the extent of their operation is unlimited and unknown. Our apology relates solely to that influence, which results from the acceptance or expectation of public preferments. Nor does the influence which we defend, require any sacrifice of personal probity. In political, above all other subjects, the arguments, or rather the conjectures on each side of the question, are often so equally poised, that the wisest judgements may be held in suspense: these I call subjects of *indifference.* But again; when the subject is not *indifferent* in itself, it will appear such to a great part of those to whom it is proposed, for want of information, or reflection, or experience, or of capacity to collect and weigh the reasons by which either side is supported. These are subjects of *apparent indifference.* This indifference occurs still more frequently in personal contests; in which we do not often discover any reason of public utility for the preference of one competitor to another. These cases compose the province of influence: that is, the decision in these cases will inevitably be determined by influence of some sort or other. The only doubt is, what influence shall be admitted. If you remove the influence of the crown, it is only to make way for influence from a different quarter. If motives of expectation and gratitude be withdrawn, other motives will succeed in their place, acting probably in an opposite direction, but equally irrelative and external to the proper merits of the question. There exist, as we have seen, passions in the human heart, which will always make a strong party against the executive power of a mixed government. According as the disposition of parliament is friendly or adverse to the recommendation of the crown in matters which are really or apparently indifferent, as indifference hath been now explained, the business of the empire will be transacted with ease and convenience, or embarrassed with endless contention and difficulty. Nor is it a conclusion founded in justice, or warranted by experience, that because men are induced by views of interest to yield their consent to measures concerning which their judgement decides nothing, they may be brought by the same influence to act in deliberate opposition to knowledge and duty. Whoever reviews the operations of government in this country since the Revolution, will find few even of the most questionable measures of administration, about which the best-instructed judgement might not have doubted at the time; but of which we may affirm with certainty, they were *indifferent* to the greatest part of those who concurred in them. From the success, or the facility, with which they who dealt out the patronage of the crown carried measures like these, ought we to conclude, that a similar application of honours and emoluments would procure the consent of parliaments to counsels evidently detrimental to the common welfare? Is there not, on the contrary, more reason to fear, that the prerogative, if deprived of influence, would not be long able to support itself? For when we reflect upon the power of the House of Commons to extort a compliance with its resolutions from the other parts of the legislature; or to put to death the constitution by a refusal of the annual grants of money to the support of the necessary functions of government—when we reflect also what motives there are, which, in the vicissitudes of political interests and passions, may one day arm and point this power against the executive magistrate; when we attend to these considerations, we shall be led perhaps to acknowledge, that there is not more of paradox than of truth in that important, but much-decried apophthegm, "that an independent parliament is incompatible with the existence of the monarchy."

Chapter 8
OF THE ADMINISTRATION OF JUSTICE

The first maxim of a free state is, that the laws be made by one set of men, and administered by another; in other words, that the legislative and judicial characters be kept separate. When these offices are united in the same person or assembly, particular laws are made for particular cases, springing oftentimes from partial motives, and directed to private ends: whilst they are kept separate, general laws are made by one body of men, without foreseeing whom they may affect; and, when made, must be applied by the other, let them affect whom they will.

For the sake of illustration, let it be supposed, in this country, either that, parliaments being laid aside, the courts of Westminster-Hall made their own laws; or that the two houses of parliament, with the King at their head, tried and decided causes at their bar: it is evident, in the first place, that the decisions of such a judicature would be so many laws; and in the second place, that, when the parties and the interests to be affected by the law were known, the inclinations of the law-makers would inevitably attach on one side or the other; and that where there were neither any fixed rules to regulate their determinations, nor any superior power to control their proceedings, these inclinations would interfere with the integrity of public justice. The consequence of which must be, that the subjects of such a constitution would live either without any constant laws, that is, without any known pre-established rules of adjudication whatever; or under laws made for particular persons, and partaking of the contradictions and iniquity of the motives to which they owed their origin.

Which dangers, by the division of the legislative and judicial functions, are in this country effectually provided against. Parliament knows not the individuals upon whom its acts will operate; it has no cases or parties before it; no private designs to serve; consequently, its resolutions will be suggested by the consideration of universal effects and tendencies, which always produces impartial, and commonly advantageous regulations. When laws are made, courts of justice, whatever be the disposition of the judges, must abide by them; for the legislative being necessarily the supreme power of the state, the judicial and every other power is accountable to that: and it cannot be doubted that the persons who possess the sovereign authority of government will be tenacious of the laws which they themselves prescribe, and sufficiently jealous of the assumption of dispensing and legislative power by any others.

This fundamental rule of civil jurisprudence is violated in the case of acts of attainder or confiscation, in bills of pains and penalties, and in all *ex post facto* laws whatever, in which parliament exercises the double office of legislature and judge. And whoever either understands the value of the rule itself, or collects the history of those instances in which it has been invaded, will be induced, I believe, to acknowledge, that it had been wiser and safer never to have departed from it. He will confess, at least, that nothing but the most manifest and immediate peril of the commonwealth will justify a repetition of these dangerous examples. If the laws in being do not punish an offender, let him go unpunished; let the legislature, admonished of the defect of the laws, provide against the commission of future crimes of the same sort. The escape of one delinquent can never produce so much harm to the community as may arise from the infraction of a rule upon which the purity of public justice, and the existence of civil liberty, essentially depend.

The next security for the impartial administration of justice, especially in decisions to which government is a party, is the independency of the judges. As protection against every illegal attack upon the rights of the subject by the servants of the crown is to be sought for from these tribunals, the judges of the land become not unfrequently the arbitrators between the king and the people, on which account they ought to be independent of either; or, what is the same thing, equally dependent upon both; that is, if they be appointed by the one, they should be removable only by the other. This was the policy which dictated that memorable improvement in our constitution, by which the judges, who before the Revolution held their offices during the pleasure of the king, can now be deprived of them only by an address from both houses of parliament; as the most regular, solemn, and authentic way, by which the dissatisfaction of the people can be expressed. To make this independency of the judges complete, the public salaries of their office ought not only to be certain both in amount and continuance, but so liberal as to secure their integrity from the temptation of secret bribes; which liberality will answer also the farther purpose of preserving their jurisdiction from contempt, and their characters from suspicion; as well as of rendering the office worthy of the ambition of men of eminence in their profession.

A third precaution to be observed in the formation of courts of justice is, that the number of the judges be small. For, beside that the violence and tumult inseparable from large assemblies are inconsistent with the patience, method, and attention, requisite in judicial investigations; beside that all passions and prejudices act with augmented force upon a collected multitude; beside these objections, judges, when they are numerous, *divide* the shame of an unjust determination; they shelter themselves under one another's example; each man thinks his own character hid in the crowd: for which reason, the judges ought always to be so few, as that the conduct of each may be conspicuous to public observation; that each may be responsible in his separate and particular reputation for the decisions in which he concurs. The truth of the above remark has been exemplified in this country, in the effects of that wise regulation which transferred the trial of parliamentary elections from the House of Commons at large to a select committee of that house, composed of thirteen members. This alteration, simply by reducing the number of the judges, and, in consequence of that reduction, exposing the judicial conduct of each to public animadversion, has given to a judicature, which had been long swayed by interest and solicitation, the solemnity and virtue of the most upright tribunals. I should prefer an even to an odd number of judges, and four to almost any other number: for in this number, beside that it sufficiently consults the idea of separate responsibility, nothing can be decided but by a majority of three to one: and when we consider that every decision establishes a perpetual precedent, we shall allow that it ought to proceed from an authority not less than this. If the court be equally divided, nothing is done; things remain as they were; with some inconveniency, indeed, to the parties, but without the danger to the public of a hasty precedent.

A fourth requisite in the constitution of a court of justice, and equivalent to many checks upon the discretion of judges, is, that its proceedings be carried on in public, *apertis floribus;* not only before a promiscuous concourse of by-standers, but in the audience of the whole profession of the law. The opinion of the bar concerning what passes, will be impartial; and will commonly guide that of the public. The most corrupt judge will fear to indulge his dishonest wishes in the presence of such an assembly: he must encounter, what few can support, the censure of his equals and companions, together with the indignation and reproaches of his country.

Something is also gained to the public by appointing two or three courts of concurrent jurisdiction, that it may remain in the option of the suitor to which he will resort. By this means a tribunal which may happen to be occupied by ignorant or suspected judges, will be deserted for others that possess more of the confidence of the nation.

But, lastly, if several courts, co-ordinate to and independent of each other, subsist together in the country, it seems necessary that the appeals from all of them should meet and terminate in the same judicature; in order that one supreme tribunal, by whose final sentence all others are bound and concluded, may superintend and preside over the rest. This constitution is necessary for two purposes: to preserve an uniformity in the decisions of inferior courts, and to maintain to each the proper limits of its jurisdiction. Without a common superior, different courts might establish contradictory rules of adjudication, and the contradiction be final and without remedy; the same question might receive opposite determinations,

according as it was brought before one court or another, and the
determination in each be ultimate and irreversible. A common
appellant jurisdiction, prevents or puts an end to this confusion. For
when the judgements upon appeals are consistent (which may be
expected, whilst it is the same court which is at last resorted to), the
different courts, from which the appeals are brought, will be
reduced to a like consistency with one another. Moreover, if questions arise between courts independent of each other, concerning
the extent and boundaries of their respective jurisdiction, as each
will be desirous of enlarging its own, an authority which both
acknowledge can alone adjust the controversy. Such a power, therefore, must reside somewhere, lest the rights and repose of the
country be distracted by the endless opposition and mutual
encroachments of its courts of justice.

There are two kinds of judicature; the one where the office of
the judge is permanent in the same person, and consequently
where the judge is appointed and known long before the trial; the
other, where the judge is determined by lot at the time of the trial,
and for that turn only. The one may be called a *fixed*, the other a
casual judicature. From the former may be expected those qualifications which are preferred and sought for in the choice of judges,
and that knowledge and readiness which result from experience in
the office. But then, as the judge is known beforehand, he is accessible to the parties; there exists a possibility of secret management
and undue practices; or, in contests between the crown and the
subject, the judge appointed by the crown may be suspected of partiality to his patron, or of entertaining inclinations favourable to
the authority from which he derives his own. The advantage
attending the second kind of judicature, is indifferency; the defect,
the want of that legal science which produces uniformity and justice in legal decisions. The construction of English courts of law,
in which causes are tried by a jury, with the assistance of a judge,

combines the two species with peculiar success. This admirable contrivance unites the wisdom of a fixed with the integrity of a casual judicature; and avoids, in a great measure, the inconveniencies of both. The judge imparts to the jury the benefit of his erudition and experience; the jury, by their disinterestedness, check any corrupt partialities which previous application may have produced in the judge. If the determination were left to the judge, the party might suffer under the superior interest of his adversary: if it were left to an uninstructed jury, his rights would be in still greater danger, from the ignorance of those who were to decide upon them. The present wise admixture of chance and choice in the constitution of the court in which his cause is tried, guards him equally against the fear of injury from either of these causes.

In proportion to the acknowledged excellency of this mode of trial, every deviation from it ought to be watched with vigilance, and admitted by the legislature with caution and reluctance. Summary convictions before justices of the peace, especially for offences against the game laws; courts of conscience; extending the jurisdiction of courts of equity; urging too far the distinction between questions of law and matters of fact—are all so many infringements upon this great charter of public safety.

Nevertheless, the trial by jury is sometimes found inadequate to the administration of equal justice. This imperfection takes place chiefly in disputes in which some popular passion or prejudice intervenes; as where a particular order of men advance claims upon the rest of the community, which is the case of the clergy contending for tithes; or where an order of men are obnoxious by their profession, as are officers of the revenue, bailiffs, bailiffs' followers, and other low ministers of the law; or where one of the parties has an interest in common with the general interest of the jurors, and that of the other is opposed to it, as in contests between landlords and tenants, between lords of manors and the holders of estates under them; or, lastly, where the minds of men are inflamed by political dissensions or religious hatred. These prejudices act most powerfully upon the common people; of which order, juries are made up. The force and danger of them are also increased by the very circumstance of taking juries out of the county in which the subject of dispute arises. In the neighbourhood of the parties, the cause is often prejudged: and these secret decisions of the mind proceed commonly more upon sentiments of favour or hatred—upon some opinion concerning the sect, family, profession, character, connexions, or circumstances of the parties—than upon any knowledge or discussion of the proper merits of the question. More exact justice would, in many instances, be rendered to the suitors, if the determination were left entirely to the judges; provided we could depend upon the same purity of conduct, when the power of these magistrates was enlarged, which they have long manifested in the exercise of a mixed and restrained authority. But this is an experiment too big with public danger to be hazarded. The effects, however, of some local prejudices, might be safely obviated by a law empowering the court in which the action is brought to send the cause to trial in a distant county; the expenses attending the change of place always falling upon the party who applied for it.

There is a second division of courts of justice, which presents a new alternative of difficulties. Either one, two, or a few sovereign courts may be erected in the metropolis, for the whole kingdom to resort to; or courts of local jurisdiction may be fixed in various provinces and districts of the empire. Great, though opposite, inconveniencies attend each arrangement. If the court be remote and solemn, it becomes, by these very qualities, expensive and dilatory: the expense is unavoidably increased when witnesses, parties, and agents, must be brought to attend from distant parts of the country: and, where the whole judicial business of a large nation is collected into a few superior tribunals, it will be found impossible, even if the prolixity of forms which retard the progress of causes were removed, to give a prompt hearing to every complaint, or an immediate answer to any. On the other hand, if, to remedy these evils, and to render the administration of justice cheap and speedy, domestic and summary tribunals be erected in each neighbourhood, the advantage of such courts will be accompanied with all the dangers of ignorance and partiality, and with the certain mischief of confusion and contrariety in their decisions. The law of England, by its circuit, or itinerary courts, contains a provision for the distribution of private justice, in a great measure relieved from both these objections. As the presiding magistrate comes into the county a stranger to its prejudices, rivalships, and connexions, he brings with him none of those attachments and regards which are so apt to pervert the course of justice when the parties and the judges inhabit the same neighbourhood. Again; as this magistrate is usually one of the judges of the supreme tribunals of the kingdom, and has passed his life in the study and administration of the laws, he possesses, it may be presumed, those professional qualifications which befit the dignity and importance of his station. Lastly, as both he, and the advocates who accompany him in his circuit, are employed in the business of those superior courts (to which also their proceedings are amenable), they will naturally conduct themselves by the rules of adjudication which they have applied or learned there; and by this means maintain, what constitutes a principal perfection of civil government, one law of the land in every part and district of the empire.

Next to the constitution of courts of justice, we are naturally led to consider the maxims which ought to guide their proceedings; and, upon this subject, the chief inquiry will be, how far, and for what reasons, it is expedient to adhere to former determinations; or whether it be necessary for judges to attend to any other consideration than the apparent and particular equity of the case before them. Now although to assert that precedents established by one set of judges ought to be incontrovertible by their successors in the same jurisdiction, or by those who exercise a higher, would be to attribute to the sentence of those judges all the authority we ascribe to the most solemn acts of the legislature; yet the general security of private rights, and of civil life, requires that such precedents, especially if they have been confirmed by repeated adjudications, should not be overthrown, without a detection of manifest error, or without some imputation of dishonesty upon the court by whose judgement the question was first decided. And this deference to prior decisions is founded upon two reasons: first, that the discretion of judges may be bound down by positive rules; and secondly, that the subject, upon every occasion in which his legal interest is concerned, may know beforehand how to act, and what to expect. To set judges free from any obligation to conform themselves to the decisions of their predecessors, would be to lay open a latitude of judging with which no description of men can safely be intrusted; it would be to allow space for the exercise of those concealed partialities, which, since they cannot by any human policy be excluded, ought to be confined by boundaries and landmarks. It is in vain to allege, that the superintendency of parliament is always at hand to control and punish abuses of judicial discretion. By what rules can parliament proceed? How shall they pronounce a decision to be wrong, where there exists no acknowledged measure or standard of what is right; which, in a multitude of instances, would be the case, if prior determinations were no longer to be appealed to?

Diminishing the danger of partiality, is one thing gained by adhering to precedents; but not the principal thing. The subject of every system of laws must expect that decision in his own case, which he knows that others have received in cases similar to his. If he expect not this, he can expect nothing. There exists no other rule or principle of reasoning, by which he can foretell, or even conjecture, the event of a judicial contest. To remove therefore the grounds of this expectation, by rejecting the force and authority of precedents, is to entail upon the subject the worst property of slavery—to have no assurance of his rights, or knowledge of his duty. The quiet also of the country, as well as the confidence and satisfaction of each man's mind, requires uniformity in judicial proceedings. Nothing quells a spirit of litigation, like despair of success: therefore nothing so completely puts an end to law-suits, as a rigid adherence to known rules of adjudication. Whilst the event is uncertain, which it ever must be whilst it is uncertain whether former determinations upon the same subject will be followed or not, law-suits will be endless and innumerable: men will commonly engage in them, either from the hope of prevailing in their claims, which the smallest chance is sufficient to encourage; or with the design of intimidating their adversaries by the terrors of a dubious litigation. When justice is rendered to the parties, only half the business of a court of justice is done: the more important part of its office remains—to put an end, for the future, to every fear, and quarrel, and expense, upon the same point; and so to regulate its proceedings, that not only a doubt once decided may be stirred no more, but that the whole train of law-suits, which issue from one uncertainty, may die with the parent-question. Now this advantage can be attained only by considering each decision as a direction to succeeding judges. And it should be observed, that every departure from former determinations, especially if they have been often repeated or long submitted to, shakes the stability of all legal title. It is not fixing a point anew; it is leaving every thing unfixed. For by the same stretch of power by which the present race of judges take upon them to contradict the judgement of their predecessors, those who try the question next may set aside theirs.

From an adherence however to precedents, by which so much is gained to the public, two consequences arise which are often lamented; the hardship of particular determinations, and the intricacy of the law as a science. To the first of these complaints, we must apply this reflection: "That uniformity is of more importance than equity, in proportion as a general uncertainty would be a greater evil than particular injustice." The second is attended with no greater inconveniency than that of erecting the practice of the law into a separate profession; which this reason, we allow, makes necessary: for if we attribute so much authority to precedents, it is expedient that they be known, in every cause, both to the advocates and to the judge: this knowledge cannot be general, since it is the fruit oftentimes of laborious research, or demands a memory stored with long-collected erudition.

———

To a mind revolving upon the subject of human jurisprudence, there frequently occurs this question: Why, since the maxims of natural justice are few and evident, do there arise so many doubts and controversies in their application? Or, in other words, how comes it to pass, that although the principles of the law of nature be simple, and for the most part sufficiently obvious, there should exist nevertheless, in every system of municipal laws, and in the actual administration of relative justice, numerous uncertainties and acknowledged difficulty? Whence, it may be asked, so much room for litigation, and so many subsisting disputes, if the rules of human duty be neither obscure nor dubious? If a system of morality, containing both the precepts of revelation and the deductions of reason, may be comprised within the compass of one moderate volume; and the moralist be able, as he pretends, to describe the rights and obligations of mankind, in all the different relations they may hold to one another; what need of those codes of positive and particular institutions, of those tomes of statutes and reports, which require the employment of a long life even to peruse? And this question is immediately connected with the argument which has been discussed in the preceding paragraph: for, unless there be found some greater uncertainty in the law of nature, or what may be called natural equity, when it comes to be applied to real cases and to actual adjudication, than what appears in the rules and principles of the science, as delivered in the writings of those who treat of the subject, it were better that the determination of every cause should be left to the conscience of the judge, unfettered by precedents and authorities; since the very purpose for which these are introduced, is to give a certainty to judicial proceedings, which such proceedings would want without them.

Now to account for the existence of so many sources of litigation, notwithstanding the clearness and perfection of natural justice, it should be observed, in the first place, that treatises of morality always suppose facts to be ascertained; and not only so, but the intention likewise of the parties to be known and laid bare. For example: when we pronounce that promises ought to be fulfilled in that sense in which the promiser apprehended, at the time of making the promise, the other party received and understood it; the apprehension of one side, and the expectation of the other, must be discovered, before this rule can be reduced to practice, or applied to the determination of any actual dispute. Wherefore the discussion of facts which the moralist supposes to be settled, the discovery of intentions which he presumes to be known, still remain to exercise the inquiry of courts of justice. And as these facts and intentions are often to be inferred, or rather conjectured, from obscure indications, from suspicious testimony, or from a comparison of opposite and contending probabilities, they afford a never-failing supply of doubt and litigation. For which reason, as hath been observed in a former part of this work, the science of morality is to be considered rather as a direction to the parties, who are conscious of their own thoughts, and motives, and designs, to which consciousness the teacher of morality constantly appeals; than as a guide to the judge, or to any third person, whose arbitration must proceed upon rules of evidence, and maxims of credibility, with which the moralist has no concern.

Secondly; there exist a multitude of cases, in which the law of nature, that is, the law of public expediency, prescribes nothing, except that some certain rule be adhered to, and that the rule actually established, be preserved: it either being indifferent what rule obtains, or, out of many rules, no one being so much more advantageous than the rest, as to recompense the inconveniency of an alteration. In all such cases, the law of nature sends us to the law of the land. She directs that either some fixed rule be introduced by an act of the legislature, or that the rule which accident, or custom, or common consent, hath already established, be steadily maintained. Thus, in the descent of lands, or the inheritance of personals from intestate proprietors, whether the kindred of the grandmother, or of the great-grandmother, shall be preferred in the succession; whether the degrees of consanguinity shall be computed through the common ancestor, or from him; whether the widow shall take a third or a moiety of her husband's fortune; whether sons shall be preferred to daughters, or the elder to the younger; whether the distinction of age shall be regarded amongst sisters, as well as between brothers; in these, and in a great variety of questions which the same subject supplies, the law of nature determines nothing. The only answer she returns to our inquiries is, that some certain and general rule be laid down by public authority; be obeyed when laid down; and that the quiet of the country be not disturbed, nor the expectation of heirs frustrated, by capricious innovations. This silence or neutrality of the law of nature, which we have exemplified in the case of intestacy, holds concerning a great part of the questions that relate to the right or acquisition of property. Recourse then must necessarily be had to statutes, or precedents, or usage, to fix what the law of nature has left loose. The interpretation of these statutes, the search after precedents, the investigation of customs, compose therefore an unavoidable, and at the same time a large and intricate, portion of forensic business. Positive constitutions or judicial authorities are, in like manner, wanted to give precision to many things which are in their nature *indeterminate*. The age of legal discretion; at what time of life a person shall be deemed competent to the performance of any act which may bind his property; whether at twenty, or twenty-one, or earlier or later, or at some point of time between these years; can only be ascertained by a positive rule of the society to which the party belongs. The line has not been drawn by nature; the human understanding advancing to maturity by insensible degrees, and its progress varying in different individuals. Yet it is necessary, for the sake of mutual security, that a precise age be fixed, and that what is fixed be known to all. It is on these occasions that the intervention of law supplies the inconstancy of nature. Again, there are other things which are perfectly *arbitrary*, and capable of no certainty but what is given to them by positive regulation. It is fit that a limited time should be assigned to defendants, to plead to the complaints alleged against them; and also that the default of pleading within a certain time should be taken for a confession of the charge: but to how many days or months that term should be extended, though necessary to be known with certainty, cannot be known at all by any information which the law of nature affords. And the same remark seems applicable to almost all those rules of proceeding, which constitute what is called the practice of the court: as they cannot be traced out by reasoning, they must be settled by authority.

Thirdly; in contracts, whether express or implied, which involve a great number of conditions; as in those which are entered into between masters and servants, principals and agents; many also of merchandise, or for works of art; in some likewise which relate to the negotiation of money or bills, or to the acceptance of credit or security; the original design and expectation of the parties was, that both sides should be guided by the course and custom of the country in transactions of the same sort. Consequently, when these contracts come to be disputed, natural justice can only refer to that custom. But as such customs are not always sufficiently uniform or notorious, but often to be collected from the production and comparison of instances and accounts repugnant to one another; and each custom being only that, after all, which amongst a variety of usages seems to predominate; we have *here* also ample room for doubt and contest.

Fourthly; as the law of nature, founded in the very construction of human society, which is formed to endure through a series of perishing generations, requires that the just engagements a man enters into should continue in force beyond his own life; it follows, that the private rights of persons frequently depend upon what has been transacted, in times remote from the present, by their ancestors or predecessors, by those under whom they claim, or to whose obligations they have succeeded. Thus the questions which usually arise between lords of manors and their tenants, between the king and those who claim royal franchises, or between them and the persons affected by these franchises, depend upon the terms of the original grant. In like manner, every dispute concerning tithes, in which an exemption or composition is pleaded, depends upon the agreement which took place between the predecessor of the claimant and the ancient owner of the land. The appeal to these grants and agreements is dictated by natural equity, as well as by the municipal law; but concerning the existence, or the conditions, of such old covenants, doubts will perpetually occur, to which the law of nature affords no solution. The loss or decay of records, the perishableness of living memory, the corruption and carelessness of tradition, all conspire to multiply uncertainties upon this head; what cannot be produced or proved, must be left to loose and fallible presumption. Under the same head may be included another topic of altercation—the tracing out of boundaries, which time, or neglect, or unity of possession, or mixture of occupation, has confounded or obliterated. To which should be added, a difficulty which often presents itself in disputes concerning rights of *way*, both public and private, and of those easements which one man claims in another man's property, namely, that of distinguishing, after a lapse of years, the use of an indulgence from the exercise of a right.

Fifthly; the quantity or extent of an injury, even when the cause and author of it are known, is often dubious and undefined. If the injury consist in the loss of some specific right, the value of the right measures the amount of the injury: but what a man may have suffered in his person, from an assault; in his reputation, by slander; or in the comfort of his life, by the seduction of a wife or daughter; or what sum of money shall be deemed a reparation for damages such as these; cannot be ascertained by any rules which the law of nature supplies. The law of nature commands, that reparation be made; and adds to her command, that, when the aggressor and the sufferer disagree, the damage be assessed by authorised and indifferent arbitrators. Here then recourse must be had to courts of law, not only with the permission, but in some measure by the direction, of natural justice.

Sixthly; when controversies arise in the interpretation of written laws, they for the most part arise upon some contingency which the composer of the law did not foresee or think of. In the adjudication of such cases, this dilemma presents itself: if the laws be permitted to operate only upon the cases which were actually contemplated by the law-makers, they will always be found defective: if they be extended to every case to which the reasoning, and spirit, and expediency, of the provision seem to belong, without any farther evidence of the intention of the legislature, we shall allow to the judges a liberty of applying the law, which will fall very little short of the power of making it. If a literal construction be adhered to, the law will often fail of its end; if a loose and vague exposition be admitted, the law might as well have never been enacted; for this licence will bring back into the subject all the discretion and uncertainty which it was the design of the legislature to take away. Courts of justice are, and always must be, embarrassed by these opposite difficulties; and, as it never can be known beforehand, in what degree either consideration may prevail in the mind of the judge, there remains an unavoidable cause of doubt, and a place for contention.

Seventhly; the deliberations of courts of justice upon every *new* question, are encumbered with additional difficulties, in consequence of the authority which the judgement of the court possesses, as a precedent to future judicatures; which authority appertains not only to the conclusions the court delivers, but to the principles and arguments upon which they are built. The view of this effect makes it necessary for a judge to look beyond the case before him: and, beside the attention he owes to the truth and justice of the cause between the parties, to reflect whether the principles, and maxims, and reasoning, which he adopts and authorises, can be applied with safety to all cases which admit of a comparison with the present. The decision of the cause, were the effects of the decision to stop there, might be easy: but the consequence of establishing the principle which such a decision assumes, may be difficult, though of the utmost importance, to be foreseen and regulated.

Finally; after all the certainty and rest that can be given to points of law, either by the interposition of the legislature or the authority of precedents, one principal source of disputation, and into which indeed the greater part of legal controversies may be resolved, will remain still, namely, "the competition of opposite analogies." When a point of law has been once adjudged, neither that question, nor any which completely, and in all its circumstances, corresponds with *that*, can be brought a second time into dispute: but questions arise, which resemble this only indirectly and in part, in certain views and circumstances, and which may seem to bear an equal or a greater affinity to other adjudged cases; questions which can be brought within any fixed rule only by analogy, and which hold a relation by analogy to different rules. It is by the urging of the different analogies that the contention of the bar is carried on: and it is in the comparison, adjustment, and reconciliation, of them with one another; in the discerning of such distinctions; and in the framing of such a determination, as may either save the various rules alleged in the cause, or if that be impossible, may give up the weaker analogy to the stronger; that the sagacity and wisdom of the court are seen and exercised. Amongst a thousand instances of this, we may cite one of general notoriety, in the contest that has lately been agitated concerning literary property. The personal industry which an author expends upon the composition of his work, bears so near a resemblance to that by which every other kind of property is earned, or deserved, or acquired; or rather there exists such a correspondency between what is created by the study of a man's mind, and the production of his labour in any other way of applying it, that he seems entitled to the same exclusive, assignable, and perpetual, right in both; and that right to the same protection of law. This was the analogy contended for on one side. On the other hand, a book, as to the author's right in it, appears similar to an invention of art, as a machine, an engine,

a medicine: and since the law permits these to be copied, or imitated, except where an exclusive use or sale is reserved to the
inventor by patent, the same liberty should be allowed in the publication and sale of books. This was the analogy maintained by the
advocates of an open trade. And the competition of these opposite
analogies constituted the difficulty of the case, as far as the same
was argued, or adjudged, upon principles of common law. One
example may serve to illustrate our meaning: but whoever takes up
a volume of Reports, will find most of the arguments it contains,
capable of the same analysis: although the analogies, it must be
confessed, are sometimes so entangled as not to be easily unrav-
elled, or even perceived.

Doubtful and obscure points of law are not however nearly so
numerous as they are apprehended to be. Out of the multitude of
causes which, in the course of each year, are brought to trial in the
metropolis, or upon the circuits, there are few in which any point
is reserved for the judgement of superior courts. Yet these few contain all the doubts with which the law is chargeable: for as to the
rest, the uncertainty, as hath been shown above, is not in the law,
but in the means of human information.

———

There are two peculiarities in the judicial constitution of this
country, which do not carry with them that evidence of their propriety which recommends almost every other part of the system.
The first of these is the rule which requires that juries be *unanimous*
in their verdicts. To expect that twelve men, taken by lot out of a
promiscuous multitude, should agree in their opinion upon points
confessedly dubious, and upon which oftentimes the wisest judgements might be holden in suspense; or to suppose that any real

unanimity, or change of opinion, in the dissenting jurors, could be procured by confining them until they all consented to the same verdict; bespeaks more of the conceit of a barbarous age, than of the policy which could dictate such an institution as that of juries. Nevertheless, the effects of this rule are not so detrimental, as the rule itself is unreasonable—in criminal prosecutions, it operates considerably in favour of the prisoner: for if a juror find it necessary to surrender to the obstinacy of others, he will much more readily resign his opinion on the side of mercy than of condemnation: in civil suits, it adds weight to the direction of the judge; for when a conference with one another does not seem likely to produce, in the jury, the agreement that is necessary, they will naturally close their disputes by a common submission to the opinion delivered from the bench. However, there seems to be less of the concurrence of separate judgements in the same conclusion, consequently less assurance that the conclusion is founded in reasons of apparent truth and justice, than if the decision were left to a plurality, or to some certain majority, of voices.

The second circumstance in our constitution, which, however it may succeed in practice, does not seem to have been suggested by any intelligible fitness in the nature of the thing, is the choice that is made of the *House of Lords* as a court of appeal from every civil court of judicature in the kingdom; and the last also and highest appeal to which the subject can resort. There appears to be nothing in the constitution of that assembly; in the education, habits, character, or professions, of the members who compose it; in the mode of their appointment, or the right by which they succeed to their places in it; that should qualify them for this arduous office: except, perhaps, that the elevation of their rank and fortune affords a security against the offer and influence of small bribes. Officers of the army and navy, courtiers, ecclesiastics; young men who have just attained the age of twenty-one, and who have passed their youth in the dissipation and pursuits which commonly accompany the possession or inheritance of great fortunes; country-gentlemen, occupied in the management of their estates, or in the care of their domestic concerns and family interests; the greater part of the assembly born to their station, that is, placed in it by chance; most of the rest advanced to the peerage for services, and from motives, utterly unconnected with legal erudition—these men compose the tribunal, to which the constitution entrusts the interpretation of her laws, and the ultimate decision of every dispute between her subjects. These are the men assigned to review judgements of law, pronounced by sages of the profession, who have spent their lives in the study and practice of the jurisprudence of their country. Such is the order which our ancestors have established. The effect only proves the truth of this maxim—"That when a single institution is extremely dissonant from other parts of the system to which it belongs, it will always find some way of reconciling itself to the analogy which governs and pervades the rest." By constantly placing in the House of Lords some of the most eminent and experienced lawyers in the kingdom; by calling to their aid the advice of the judges, when any abstract question of law awaits their determination; by the almost implicit and undisputed deference, which the uninformed part of the house find it necessary to pay to the learning of their colleagues; the appeal to the House of Lords becomes in fact an appeal to the collected wisdom of our supreme courts of justice; receiving indeed solemnity, but little perhaps of direction, from the presence of the assembly in which it is heard and determined.

These, however, even if real, are minute imperfections. A politician who should sit down to delineate a plan for the dispensation of public justice, guarded against all access to influence and corruption, and bringing together the separate advantages of knowledge and impartiality, would find, when he had done, that he had been transcribing the judicial constitution of England. And it may teach the most discontented amongst us to acquiesce in the government of his country, to reflect, that the pure, and wise, and equal administration of the laws, forms the first end and blessing of social union; and that this blessing is enjoyed by him in a perfection, which he will seek in vain in any other nation of the world.

Chapter 9
OF CRIMES AND PUNISHMENTS

The proper end of human punishment is not the satisfaction of justice, but the prevention of crimes. By the satisfaction of justice, I mean the retribution of so much pain for so much guilt; which is the dispensation we expect at the hand of God, and which we are accustomed to consider as the order of things that perfect justice dictates and requires. In what sense, or whether with truth in any sense, justice may be said to demand the punishment of offenders, I do not now inquire: but I assert, that this *demand* is not the motive or occasion of human punishment. What would it be to the magistrate, that offences went altogether unpunished, if the impunity of the offenders were followed by no danger or prejudice to the commonwealth? The fear lest the escape of the criminal should encourage him, or others by his example, to repeat the same crime, or to commit different crimes, is the sole consideration which authorises the infliction of punishment by human laws. Now that, whatever it be, which is the cause and end of the punishment, ought undoubtedly to regulate the measure of its severity. But this cause appears to be founded, not in the guilt of the offender, but in the necessity of preventing the repetition of the offence: and hence results the reason, that crimes are not by any government punished in proportion to their guilt, nor in all cases ought to be so, but in proportion to the difficulty and the necessity of preventing them. Thus the stealing of goods privately out of a shop may not, in its moral quality, be more criminal than the stealing of them out of a house; yet being equally necessary, and more difficult, to be prevented, the law, in certain circumstances, denounces against it a severer punishment. The crime must be prevented by some means or other; and consequently, whatever means appear necessary to this end, whether they be proportionable to the guilt of the criminal or not, are adopted rightly, because they are adopted upon the principle which alone justifies the infliction of punishment at all. From the same consideration it also follows, that punishment ought not to be employed, much less rendered severe, when the crime can be prevented by any other means. Punishment is an evil to which the magistrate resorts only from its being necessary to the prevention of a greater. This necessity does not exist, when the end may be attained, that is, when the public may be defended from the effects of the crime, by any other expedient. The sanguinary laws which have been made against counterfeiting or diminishing the gold coin of the kingdom might be just until the method of detecting the fraud, by weighing the money, was introduced into general usage. Since that precaution was practised, these laws have slept; and an execution under them at this day would be deemed a measure of unjustifiable severity. The same principle accounts for a circumstance which has been often censured as an absurdity in the penal laws of this, and of most modern nations, namely, that breaches of trust are either not punished at all, or punished with less rigour than other frauds. Wherefore is it, some have asked, that a violation of confidence, which increases the guilt, should mitigate the penalty? This lenity, or rather forbearance, of the laws, is founded in the most reasonable distinction. A due circumspection in the choice of the persons whom they trust; caution in limiting the extent of that trust; or the requiring of sufficient security for the faithful discharge of it; will commonly guard men from injuries of this description; and the law will not interpose its sanctions to protect negligence and credulity, or to supply the place of domestic care and prudence. To be convinced that the law proceeds entirely upon this consideration, we have only to observe, that where the confidence is unavoidable—where no practicable vigilance could watch the offender, as in the case of theft committed by a servant in the shop or dwelling-house of his master, or upon property to which he must necessarily have access—the sentence of the law is not less severe, and its execution commonly more certain and rigorous, than if no trust at all had intervened.

It is in pursuance of the same principle, which pervades indeed the whole system of penal jurisprudence, that the facility with which any species of crimes is perpetrated, has been generally deemed a reason for aggravating the punishment. Thus, sheep-stealing, horse-stealing, the stealing of cloth from tenters or bleaching-grounds, by our laws, subject the offenders to sentence of death: not that these crimes are in their nature more heinous than many simple felonies which are punished by imprisonment or transportation, but because the property, being more exposed, requires the terror of capital punishment to protect it. This severity would be absurd and unjust, if the guilt of the offender were the immediate cause and measure of the punishment; but is a consistent and regular consequence of the supposition, that the right of punishment results from the necessity of preventing the crime: for if this be the end proposed, the severity of the punishment must be increased in proportion to the expediency and the difficulty of attaining this end; that is, in a proportion compounded of the mischief of the crime, and of the ease with which it is executed. The difficulty of discovery is a circumstance to be included in the same consideration. It constitutes indeed, with respect to the crime, the facility of which we speak. By how much therefore the detection of an offender is more rare and uncertain, by so much the more severe must be the punishment when he is detected. Thus the writing of incendiary letters, though in itself a pernicious and alarming injury, calls for a more condign and exemplary punishment, by the very obscurity with which the crime is committed.

From the Justice of God, we are taught to look for a gradation of punishment exactly proportioned to the guilt of the offender: when therefore, in assigning the degrees of human punishment, we introduce considerations distinct from that guilt, and a proportion so varied by external circumstances, that equal crimes frequently undergo unequal punishments, or the less crime the greater; it is natural to demand the reason why a different measure of punishment should be expected from God, and observed by man; why that rule, which befits the absolute and perfect justice of the Deity, should not be the rule which ought to be pursued and imitated by human laws. The solution of this difficulty must be sought for in those peculiar attributes of the Divine nature, which distinguish the dispensations of Supreme Wisdom from the proceedings of human judicature. A Being whose knowledge penetrates every concealment, from the operation of whose will no art or flight can escape, and in whose hands punishment is sure; such a Being may conduct the moral government of his creation, in the best and wisest manner, by pronouncing a law that every crime shall finally receive a punishment proportioned to the guilt which it contains, abstracted from any foreign consideration whatever; and may testify his veracity to the spectators of his judgements, by carrying this law into strict execution. But when the care of the public safety is intrusted to men, whose authority over their fellow-creatures is limited by defects of power and knowledge; from whose utmost vigilance and sagacity the greatest offenders often lie hid; whose wisest precautions and speediest pursuit may be eluded by artifice or concealment; a different necessity, a new rule of proceeding, results from the very imperfection of their faculties. In their hands, the uncertainty of punishment must be compensated by the severity. The ease with which crimes are committed or concealed, must be counteracted by additional penalties and increased terrors. The very end for which human government is established, requires that its regulations be adapted to the suppression of crimes. This end, whatever it may do in the plans of Infinite Wisdom, does not, in the designation of temporal penalties, always coincide with the proportionate punishment of guilt.

There are two methods of administering penal justice.

The first method assigns capital punishment to few offences, and inflicts it invariably.

The second method assigns capital punishment to many kinds of offences, but inflicts it only upon a few examples of each kind.

The latter of which two methods has been long adopted in this country, where, of those who receive sentence of death, scarcely one in ten is executed. And the preference of this to the former method seems to be founded in the consideration, that the selection of proper objects for capital punishment principally depends upon circumstances, which, however easy to perceive in each particular case after the crime is committed, it is impossible to enumerate or define beforehand; or to ascertain however with that exactness which is requisite in legal descriptions. Hence, although it be necessary to fix by precise rules of law the boundary on one side, that is, the limit to which the punishment may be extended; and also that nothing less than the authority of the whole legislature be suffered to determine that boundary, and assign these rules; yet the mitigation of punishment, the exercise of lenity, may without danger be intrusted to the executive magistrate, whose discretion will operate upon those numerous, unforeseen, mutable, and indefinite circumstances, both of the crime and the criminal, which constitute or qualify the malignity of each offence. Without the power of relaxation lodged in a living authority, either some offenders would escape capital punishment, whom the public safety required to suffer; or some would undergo this punishment, where it was neither deserved nor necessary. For if judgement of death were reserved for one or two species of crimes only (which would probably be the case if that judgement was intended to be executed without exception), crimes might occur of the most dangerous example, and accompanied with circumstances of heinous aggravation, which did not fall within *any* description of offences that the laws had made capital, and which consequently could not receive the punishment their own malignity and the public safety required. What is worse, it would be known beforehand, that such crimes might be committed without danger to the offender's life. On the other hand, if to reach these possible cases, the whole class of offences to which they belong be subjected to pains of death, and no power of remitting this severity remain any where, the execution of the laws will become more sanguinary than the public compassion would endure, or than is necessary to the general security.

The law of England is constructed upon a different and a better policy. By the number of statutes creating capital offences, it sweeps into the net every crime which, under any possible circumstances, may merit the punishment of death: but when the execution of this sentence comes to be deliberated upon, a small proportion of each class are singled out, the general character, or the peculiar aggravations, of whose crimes, render them fit examples of public justice. By this expedient, few actually suffer death, whilst the dread and danger of it hang over the crimes of many. The tenderness of the law cannot be taken advantage of. The life of the subject is spared as far as the necessity of restraint and intimidation permits; yet no one will adventure upon the commission of any enormous crime, from a knowledge that the laws have not provided for its punishment. The wisdom and humanity of this design furnish a just excuse for the multiplicity of capital offences, which the laws of England are accused of creating beyond those of other countries. The charge of cruelty is answered by observing, that these laws were never meant to be carried into indiscriminate execution; that the legislature, when it establishes its last and highest sanctions, trusts to the benignity of the crown to relax their severity, as often as circumstances appear to palliate the offence, or even as often as those circumstances of aggravation are wanting which rendered this rigorous interposition necessary. Upon this plan, it is enough to vindicate the lenity of the laws, that *some* instances are to be found in each class of capital crimes, which require the restraint of capital punishment, and that this restraint could not be applied without subjecting the whole class to the same condemnation.

There is however one species of crimes, the making of which capital can hardly, I think, be defended even upon the comprehensive principle just now stated—I mean that of privately stealing from the person. As every degree of force is excluded by the description of the crime, it will be difficult to assign an example, where either the amount or circumstances of the theft place it upon a level with those dangerous attempts to which the punishment of death should be confined. It will be still more difficult to show, that, without gross and culpable negligence on the part of the sufferer, such examples can ever become so frequent, as to make it necessary to constitute a class of capital offences, of very wide and large extent.

The prerogative of pardon is properly reserved to the chief magistrate. The power of suspending the laws is a privilege of too high a nature to be committed to many hands, or to those of any inferior officer in the state. The king also can best collect the advice by which his resolutions should be governed; and is at the same time removed at the greatest distance from the influence of private motives. But let this power be deposited where it will, the exercise of it ought to be regarded, not as a favour to be yielded to solicitation, granted to friendship, or, least of all, to be made subservient to the conciliating or gratifying of political attachments, but as a judicial act; as a deliberation to be conducted with the same character of impartiality, with the same exact and diligent attention to the proper merits and circumstances of the case, as that which the judge upon the bench was expected to maintain and show in the trial of the prisoner's guilt. The questions, whether the prisoner be guilty, and whether, being guilty, he ought to be executed, are equally questions of public justice. The adjudication of the latter question is as much a function of magistracy, as the trial of the former. The public welfare is interested in both. The conviction of an offender should depend upon nothing but the proof of his guilt; nor the execution of the sentence upon any thing beside the quality and circumstances of his crime. It is necessary to the good order of society, and to the reputation and authority of government, that this be known and believed to be the case in each part of the proceeding. Which reflections show, that the admission of extrinsic or oblique considerations, in dispensing the power of pardon, is a crime, in the authors and advisers of such unmerited partiality, of the same nature with that of corruption in a judge.

Aggravations, which ought to guide the magistrate in the selection of objects of condign punishment, are principally these three—repetition, cruelty, combination. The first two, it is manifest, add to every reason upon which the justice or the necessity of rigorous measures can be founded; and with respect to the last circumstance, it may be observed, that when thieves and robbers are once collected into gangs, their violence becomes more formidable, the confederates more desperate, and the difficulty of defending the public against their depredations much greater, than in the case of solitary adventurers. Which several considerations compose a distinction that is properly adverted to, in deciding upon the fate of convicted malefactors.

In crimes, however, which are perpetrated by a multitude, or by a gang, it is proper to separate, in the punishment, the ringleader from his followers, the principal from his accomplices, and even the person who struck the blow, broke the lock, or first entered the house, from those who joined him in the felony; not so much on account of any distinction in the guilt of the offenders, as for the sake of casting an obstacle in the way of such confederacies, by rendering it difficult for the confederates to settle who shall begin the attack, or to find a man amongst their number willing to expose himself to greater danger than his associates. This is another instance in which the punishment which expediency directs, does not pursue the exact proportion of the crime.

Injuries effected by terror and violence, are those which it is the first and chief concern of legal government to repress; because their extent is unlimited; because no private precaution can protect the subject against them; because they endanger life and safety, as well as property; and lastly, because they render the condition of society wretched, by a sense of personal insecurity. These reasons do not apply to frauds which circumspection may prevent; which must wait for opportunity; which can proceed only to certain limits; and by the apprehension of which, although the business of life be incommoded, life itself is not made miserable. The appearance of this distinction has led some humane writers to express a wish, that capital punishments might be confined to crimes of violence.

In estimating the comparative malignancy of crimes of violence, regard is to be had, not only to the proper and intended mischief of the crime, but to the fright occasioned by the attack, to the general alarm excited by it in others, and to the consequences which may attend future attempts of the same kind. Thus, in affixing the punishment of burglary, or of breaking into dwelling-houses by night, we are to consider not only the peril to which the most valuable property is exposed by this crime, and which may be called the direct mischief of it, but the danger also of murder in case of resistance, or for the sake of preventing discovery; and the universal dread with which the silent and defenceless hours of rest and sleep must be disturbed, were attempts of this sort to become frequent; and which dread alone, even without the mischief which is the object of it, is not only a public evil, but almost of all evils the most insupportable. These circumstances place a difference between the breaking into a dwelling-house by day, and by night; which difference obtains in the punishment of the offence by the law of Moses, and is probably to be found in the judicial codes of most countries, from the earliest ages to the present.

Of frauds, or of injuries which are effected without force, the most noxious kinds are—forgeries, counterfeiting or diminishing of the coin, and the stealing of letters in the course of their conveyance; inasmuch as these practices tend to deprive the public of accommodations, which not only improve the conveniencies of social life, but are essential to the prosperity, and even the existence, of commerce. Of these crimes it may be said, that although they seem to affect property alone, the mischief of their operation does not terminate there. For let it be supposed, that the remissness or lenity of the laws should, in any country, suffer offences of this sort to grow into such a frequency, as to render the use of money, the circulation of bills, or the public conveyance of letters, no longer safe or practicable; what would follow, but that every species of trade and of activity must decline under these discouragements; the sources of subsistence fail, by which the inhabitants of the country are supported; the country itself, where the intercourse of civil life was so endangered and defective, be deserted; and that, beside the distress and poverty which the loss of employment would produce to the industrious and valuable part of the existing community, a rapid depopulation must take place, each generation becoming less numerous than the last; till solitude and barrenness overspread the land; until a desolation similar to what obtains in many countries of Asia, which were once the most civilised and frequented parts of the world, succeed in the place of crowded cities, of cultivated fields, of happy and well peopled regions? When therefore we carry forwards our views to the more distant, but not less certain consequences of these crimes, we perceive that, though no living creature be destroyed by them, yet human life is diminished: that an offence, the particular consequence of which deprives only an individual of a small portion of his property, and which even in its general tendency seems to do nothing more than obstruct the enjoyment of certain public conveniencies, may nevertheless, by its ultimate effects, conclude in the laying waste of human existence. This observation will enable those who regard the divine rule of "life for life, and blood for blood," as the only authorised and justifiable measure of capital punishment, to perceive, with respect to the effects and quality of the actions, a greater resemblance than they suppose to exist between certain atrocious frauds, and those crimes which attack personal safety.

In the case of forgeries, there appears a substantial difference between the forging of bills of exchange, or of securities which are circulated, and of which the circulation and currency are found to serve and facilitate valuable purposes of commerce; and the forging of bonds, leases, mortgages, or of instruments which are not commonly transferred from one hand to another; because, in the former case, credit is necessarily given to the signature, and without that credit the negotiation of such property could not be carried on, nor the public utility, sought from it, be attained: in the other case, all possibility of deceit might be precluded, by a direct communication between the parties, or by due care in the choice of their agents, with little interruption to business, and without destroying, or much encumbering, the uses for which these instruments are calculated. This distinction I apprehend to be not only real, but precise enough to afford a line of division between forgeries, which, as the law now stands, are almost universally capital, and punished with undistinguishing severity.

Perjury is another crime, of the same class and magnitude. And, when we consider what reliance is necessarily placed upon oaths; that all judicial decisions proceed upon testimony; that consequently there is not a right that a man possesses, of which false witnesses may not deprive him; that reputation, property, and life itself, lie open to the attempts of perjury; that it may often be committed without a possibility of contradiction or discovery; that the success and prevalency of this vice tend to introduce the most grievous and fatal injustice into the administration of human affairs, or such a distrust of testimony as must create universal embarrassment and confusion: when we reflect upon these mischiefs, we shall be brought, probably, to agree with the opinion of those who contend that perjury, in its punishment, especially that which is attempted in solemn evidence, and in the face of a court of justice, should be placed upon a level with the most flagitious frauds.

The obtaining of money by secret threats, whether we regard the difficulty with which the crime is traced out, the odious imputations to which it may lead, or the profligate conspiracies that are sometimes formed to carry it into execution, deserves to be reckoned amongst the worst species of robbery.

The frequency of capital executions in this country owes its necessity to three causes—much liberty, great cities, and the want of a punishment short of death, possessing a sufficient degree of terror. And if the taking away of the life of malefactors be more rare in other countries than in ours, the reason will be found in some difference in these articles. The liberties of a free people, and still more the jealousy with which these liberties are watched, and by which they are preserved, permit not those precautions and restraints, that inspection, scrutiny, and control, which are exercised with success in arbitrary governments. For example, neither the spirit of the laws, nor of the people, will suffer the detention or confinement of suspected persons, without proofs of their guilt, which it is often impossible to obtain; nor will they allow that masters of families be obliged to record and render up a description of the strangers or inmates whom they entertain; nor that an account be demanded, at the pleasure of the magistrate, of each man's time, employment, and means of subsistence; nor securities to be required when these accounts appear unsatisfactory or dubious; nor men to be apprehended upon the mere suggestion of idleness or vagrancy; nor to be confined to certain districts; nor the inhabitants of each district to be made responsible for one another's behaviour; nor passports to be exacted from all persons entering or leaving the kingdom: least of all will they tolerate the appearance of an armed force, or of military law; or suffer the streets and public roads to be guarded and patrolled by soldiers; or lastly, intrust the police with such discretionary powers, as may make sure of the guilty, however they involve the innocent. These expedients, although arbitrary and rigorous, are many of them effectual: and in proportion as they render the commission or concealment of crimes more difficult, they subtract from the necessity of severe punishment. *Great cities* multiply crimes, by presenting easier opportunities, and more incentives to libertinism, which in low life is commonly the introductory stage to other enormities; by collecting thieves and robbers into the same neighbourhood, which enables them to form communications and confederacies, that increase their art and courage, as well as strength and wickedness; but principally by the refuge they afford to villainy, in the means of concealment, and of subsisting in secrecy, which crowded towns supply to men of every description. These temptations and facilities can only be counteracted by adding to the number of capital punishments. But a *third* cause, which increases the frequency of capital executions in England, is, a defect of the laws, in not being provided with any other punishment than that of death, sufficiently terrible to keep offenders in awe. Transportation, which is the sentence second in the order of severity, appears to me to answer the purpose of example very imperfectly: not only because exile is in reality a slight punishment to those who have neither property, nor friends, nor reputation, nor regular means of subsistence, at home; and because their situation becomes little worse by their crime, than it was before they committed it; but because the punishment, whatever it be, is unobserved and unknown. A transported convict may suffer under his sentence, but his sufferings are removed from the view of his countrymen: his misery is unseen; his condition strikes no terror into the minds of those for whose warning and admonition it was intended. This chasm in the scale of punishment produces also two farther imperfections in the administration of penal justice: the first is, that the same punishment is extended to crimes of very different character and malignancy: the second, that punishments separated by a great interval, are assigned to crimes hardly distinguishable in their guilt and mischief.

The end of punishment is two-fold—*amendment*, and *example*. In the first of these, the *reformation* of criminals, little has ever been effected, and little, I fear, is practicable. From every species of punishment that has hitherto been devised, from imprisonment and exile, from pain and infamy, malefactors return more hardened in their crimes, and more instructed. If there be any thing that shakes the soul of a confirmed villain, it is the expectation of approaching death. The horrors of this situation may cause such a wrench in the mortal organs, as to give them a holding turn: and I think it probable, that many of those who are executed, would, if they were delivered at the point of death, retain such a remembrance of their sensations, as might preserve them, unless urged by extreme want, from relapsing into their former crimes. But this is an experiment that, from its nature, cannot be repeated often.

Of the *reforming* punishments which have not yet been tried, none promises so much success as that of *solitary* imprisonment, or the confinement of criminals in separate apartments. This improvement augments the terror of the punishment; secludes the criminal from the society of his fellow-prisoners, in which society the worse are sure to corrupt the better; weans him from the knowledge of his companions, and from the love of that turbulent, precarious life in which his vices had engaged him: is calculated to raise up in him reflections on the folly of his choice, and to dispose his mind to such bitter and continued penitence, as may produce a lasting alteration in the principles of his conduct.

As aversion to labour is the cause from which half of the vices of low life deduce their origin and continuance, punishments ought to be contrived with a view to the conquering of this disposition. Two opposite expedients have been recommended for this purpose; the one, solitary confinement with hard labour; the other, solitary confinement with nothing to do. Both expedients seek the same end—to reconcile the idle to a life of industry. The former hopes to effect this by making labour habitual; the latter, by making idleness insupportable: and the preference of one method to the other depends upon the question, whether a man is more likely to betake himself, of his own accord, to work, who has been accustomed to employment, or who has been distressed by the want of it. When gaols are once provided for the *separate* confinement of prisoners, which both proposals require, the choice between them may soon be determined by experience. If labour be exacted, I would leave the whole, or a portion, of the earnings to the prisoner's use, and I would debar him from any other provision or supply; that his subsistence, however coarse and penurious, may be proportioned to his diligence, and that he may taste the advantage of industry together with the toil. I would go farther; I would measure the confinement, not by the duration of time, but by quantity of work, in order both to excite industry, and to render it more voluntary. But the principal difficulty remains still; namely, how to dispose of criminals after their enlargement. By a rule of life, which is perhaps too invariably and indiscriminately adhered to, no one will receive a man or woman out of a gaol, into any service or employment whatever. This is the common misfortune of public punishments, that they preclude the offender from all honest means of future support.* It seems incumbent upon the state to secure a maintenance to those who are willing to work for it; and yet it is absolutely necessary to divide criminals as far asunder from one another as possible. Whether male prisoners might not, after the term of their confinement was expired, be distributed in the country, detained within certain limits, and employed upon the public roads; and females be remitted to the overseers of country parishes, to be there furnished with dwellings, and with the materials and implements of occupation—whether by these, or by what other methods, it may be possible to effect the two purposes of *employment* and *dispersion*; well merits the attention of all who are anxious to perfect the internal regulation of their country.

Torture is applied either to obtain confessions of guilt, or to exasperate or prolong the pains of death. No bodily punishment, however excruciating or long-continued, receives the name of torture, unless it be designed to kill the criminal by a more lingering

---

*Until this inconvenience be remedied, small offences had perhaps better go unpunished: I do not mean that the law should exempt them from punishment, but that private persons should be tender in prosecuting them.

death; or to extort from him the discovery of some secret, which is supposed to lie concealed in his breast. *The question by torture* appears to be equivocal in its effects: for since extremity of pain, and not any consciousness of remorse in the mind, produces those effects, an innocent man may sink under the torment, as well as he who is guilty. The latter has as much to fear from yielding, as the former. The instant and almost irresistible desire of relief may draw from one sufferer false accusations of himself or others, as it may sometimes extract the truth out of another. This ambiguity renders the use of torture, as a means of procuring information in criminal proceedings, liable to the risk of grievous and irreparable injustice. For which reason, though recommended by ancient and general example, it has been properly exploded from the mild and cautious system of penal jurisprudence established in this country.

Barbarous spectacles of human agony are justly found fault with, as tending to harden and deprave the public feelings, and to destroy that sympathy with which the sufferings of our fellow-creatures ought always to be seen; or, if no effect of this kind follow from them, they counteract in some measure their own design, by sinking men's abhorrence of the crime in their commiseration of the criminal. But if a mode of execution could be devised, which would augment the horror of the punishment, without offending or impairing the public sensibility by cruel or unseemly exhibitions of death, it might add something to the efficacy of the example: and, by being reserved for a few atrocious crimes, might also enlarge the scale of punishment; an addition to which seems wanting; for, as the matter remains at present, you hang a malefactor for a simple robbery, and can do no more to the villain who has poisoned his father. Somewhat of the sort we have been describing, was the proposal, not long since suggested, of casting murderers into a den of wild beasts, where they would perish in a manner dreadful to the imagination, yet concealed from the view.

Infamous punishments are mismanaged in this country, with respect both to the crimes and the criminals. In the first place, they ought to be confined to offences which are holden in undisputed and universal detestation. To condemn to the pillory the author or editor of a libel against the state, who has rendered himself the favourite of a party, if not of the people, by the very act for which he stands there, is to gratify the offender, and to expose the laws to mockery and insult. In the second place; the delinquents who receive this sentence are for the most part such as have long ceased either to value reputation, or to fear shame; of whose happiness, and of whose enjoyments, character makes no part. Thus the low ministers of libertinism, the keepers of bawdy or disorderly houses, are threatened in vain with a punishment that affects a sense which they have not; that applies solely to the imagination, to the virtue and the pride of human nature. The pillory, or any other infamous distinction, might be employed rightly, and with effect, in the punishment of some offences of higher life; as of frauds and peculation in office; of collusions and connivances, by which the public treasury is defrauded; of breaches of trust; of perjury, and subornation of perjury; of the clandestine and forbidden sale of places; of flagrant abuses of authority, or neglect of duty; and, lastly, of corruption in the exercise of confidential or judicial offices. In all which, the more elevated was the station of the criminal, the more signal and conspicuous would be the triumph of justice.

The *certainty* of punishment is of more consequence than the severity. Criminals do not so much flatter themselves with the lenity of the sentence, as with the hope of escaping. They are not so apt to compare what they gain by the crime with what they may suffer from the punishment, as to encourage themselves with the chance of concealment or flight. For which reason, a vigilant magistracy, an accurate police, a proper distribution of force and intelligence, together with due rewards for the discovery and apprehension of malefactors, and an undeviating impartiality in carrying the laws into execution, contribute more to the restraint and suppression of crimes than any violent exacerbations of punishment. And, for the same reason, of all contrivances directed to this end, those perhaps are most effectual which facilitate the conviction of criminals. The offence of counterfeiting the coin could not be checked by all the terrors and the utmost severity of law, whilst the act of coining was necessary to be established by specific proof. The statute which made possession of the implements of coining capital, that is, which constituted that possession complete evidence of the offender's guilt, was the first thing that gave force and efficacy to the denunciations of law upon this subject. The statute of James the First, relative to the murder of bastard children, which ordains that the concealment of the birth should be deemed incontestable proof of the charge, though a harsh law, was, in like manner with the former, well calculated to put a stop to the crime.

It is upon the principle of this observation, that I apprehend much harm to have been done to the community, by the overstrained scrupulousness, or weak timidity, of juries, which demands often such proof of a prisoner's guilt, as the nature and secrecy of his crime scarce possibly admit of; and which holds it the part of a *safe* conscience not to condemn any man, whilst there exists the minutest possibility of his innocence. Any story they may happen to have heard or read, whether real or feigned, in which courts of justice have been misled by presumptions of guilt, is enough, in their minds, to found an acquittal upon, where positive proof is wanting. I do not mean that juries should indulge conjectures, should magnify suspicions into proofs, or even that they should weigh probabilities in *gold scales:* but when the preponderance of evidence is so manifest as to persuade every private understanding of the prisoner's guilt; when it furnishes the degree of credibility upon which men decide and act in all other doubts, and which experience hath shown that they may decide and act upon with sufficient safety; to reject such proof, from an insinuation of uncertainty that belongs to all human affairs, and from a general dread lest the charge of innocent blood should lie at their doors, is a conduct, which, however natural to a mind studious of its own quiet, is authorised by no considerations of rectitude or utility. It counteracts the care and damps the activity of government; it holds out public encouragement to villainy, by confessing the impossibility of bringing villains to justice; and that species of encouragement which, as hath been just now observed, the minds of such men are most apt to entertain and dwell upon.

There are two popular maxims, which seem to have a considerable influence in producing the injudicious acquittals of which we complain. One is: "That circumstantial evidence falls short of positive proof." This assertion, in the unqualified sense in which it is applied, is not true. A concurrence of well-authenticated circumstances composes a stronger ground of assurance than positive testimony, unconfirmed by circumstances, usually affords. Circumstances cannot lie. The conclusion also which results from them, though deduced by only probable inference, is commonly more to be relied upon than the veracity of an unsupported solitary witness. The danger of being deceived is less, the actual instances of deception are fewer, in the one case than the other. What is called positive proof in criminal matters, as where a man swears to the person of the prisoner, and that he actually saw him commit the crime with which he is charged, may be founded in the mistake or perjury of a single witness. Such mistakes, and such perjuries, are not without many examples. Whereas, to impose upon a court of justice a chain of *circumstantial* evidence in support of a fabricated accusation, requires such a number of false witnesses as seldom meet together; an union also of skill and wickedness which is still more rare; and, after all, this species of proof lies much more open to discussion, and is more likely, if false, to be contradicted, or to betray itself by some unforeseen inconsistency, than that direct proof, which, being confined within the knowledge of a single person, which, appealing to, or standing connected with, no external or collateral circumstances, is incapable, by its very simplicity, of being confronted with opposite probabilities.

The other maxim which deserves a similar examination is this: "That it is better that ten guilty persons escape, than that one innocent man should suffer." If by saying it is *better*, be meant that it is more for the public advantage, the proposition, I think, cannot be maintained. The security of civil life, which is essential to the value and the enjoyment of every blessing it contains, and the interruption of which is followed by universal misery and confusion, is protected chiefly by the dread of punishment. The misfortune of an individual (for such may the sufferings, or even the death, of an innocent person be called, when they are occasioned by no evil intention) cannot be placed in competition with this object. I do not contend that the life or safety of the meanest subject ought, in any case, to be knowingly sacrificed: no principle of judicature, no end of punishment, can ever require *that*.

But when certain rules of adjudication must be persued, when certain degrees of credibility must be accepted, in order to reach the crimes with which the public are infested; courts of justice should not be deterred from the application of these rules, by *every* suspicion of danger, or by the mere possibility of confounding the innocent with the guilty. They ought rather to reflect, that he who falls by a mistaken sentence, may be considered as falling for his country; whilst he suffers under the operation of those rules, by the general effect and tendency of which the welfare of the community is maintained and upholden.

Chapter 10
OF RELIGIOUS ESTABLISHMENTS AND
OF TOLERATION

"A RELIGIOUS establishment is no part of Christianity: it is only the means of inculcating it." Amongst the Jews, the rights and offices, the order, family, and succession of the priesthood, were marked out by the authority which declared the law itself. These, therefore, were *parts* of the Jewish religion, as well as the means of transmitting it. Not so with the new institution. It cannot be proved that any form of church-government was laid down in the Christian, as it had been in the Jewish Scriptures, with a view of fixing a constitution for succeeding ages; and which constitution, consequently, the disciples of Christianity would every where, and at all times, by the very law of their religion, be obliged to adopt. Certainly, no command for this purpose was delivered by Christ himself: and if it be shown that the apostles ordained bishops and presbyters amongst their first converts, it must be remembered that deacons also and deaconesses were appointed by them, with functions very dissimilar to any which obtain in the church at present. The truth seems to have been, that such offices were at first erected in the Christian church, as the good order, the instruction, and the exigencies of the society at that time required, without any intention, at least without any declared design, of regulating the appointment, authority, or the distinction, of Christian ministers under future circumstances. This reserve, if we may so call it, in the Christian Legislator, is sufficiently accounted for by two considerations: First, that no precise constitution could be framed, which would suit with the condition of Christianity in its primitive state, and with that which it was to assume when it should be advanced into a national religion: Secondly, that a particular designation of office or authority amongst the ministers of the new religion, might have so interfered with the arrangements of civil policy, as to have formed, in some countries, a considerable obstacle to the progress and reception of the religion itself.

The authority therefore of a church-establishment is founded in its utility: and whenever, upon this principle, we deliberate concerning the form, propriety, or comparative excellency of different establishments, the single view under which we ought to consider any of them is, that of "a scheme of instruction"; the single end we ought to propose by them is, "the preservation and communication of religious knowledge." Every other idea, and every other end, that have been mixed with this, as the making of the church an engine, or even an *ally*, of the state; converting it into the means of strengthening or diffusing influence; or regarding it as a support of regal in opposition to popular forms of government; have served only to debase the institution, and to introduce into it numerous corruptions and abuses.

The notion of a religious establishment comprehends three things: a clergy, or an order of men secluded from other professions to attend upon the offices of religion; a legal provision for the maintenance of the clergy; and the confining of that provision to the teachers of a particular sect of Christianity. If any one of these three things be wanting, if there be no clergy, as amongst the Quakers; or if the clergy have no other provision than what they derive from the voluntary contribution of their hearers; or if the provision which the laws assign to the support of religion be extended to various sects and denominations of Christians; there exists no national religion or established church, according to the sense which these terms are usually made to convey. He, therefore, who would defend ecclesiastical establishments, must show the separate utility of these three essential parts of their constitution:

1. The question first in order upon the subject, as well as the most fundamental in its importance, is, whether the knowledge and

profession of Christianity can be maintained in a country without a class of men set apart by public authority to the study and teaching of religion, and to the conducting of public worship; and for these purposes secluded from other employments. I add this last circumstance, because in it consists, as I take it, the substance of the controversy. Now it must be remembered, that Christianity is an historical religion, founded in facts which are related to have passed, upon discourses which were holden, and letters which were written, in a remote age, and distant country of the world, as well as under a state of life and manners, and during the prevalency of opinions, customs, and institutions, very unlike any which are found amongst mankind at present. Moreover, this religion, having been first published in the country of Judea, and being built upon the more ancient religion of the Jews, is necessarily and intimately connected with the sacred writings, with the history and polity of that singular people: to which must be added, that the records of both revelations are preserved in languages which have long ceased to be spoken in any part of the world. Books which come down to us from times so remote, and under so many causes of unavoidable obscurity, cannot, it is evident, be understood without study and preparation. The languages must be learned. The various writings which these volumes contain must be carefully compared with one another, and with themselves. What remains of contemporary authors, or of authors connected with the age, the country, or the subject of our Scriptures, must be perused and consulted, in order to interpret doubtful forms of speech, and to explain allusions which refer to objects or usages that no longer exist. Above all, the modes of expression, the habits of reasoning and argumentation, which were then in use, and to which the discourses even of inspired teachers were necessarily adapted, must be sufficiently known, and can only be known at all by a due acquaintance with ancient literature. And lastly, to establish the genuineness and integrity of the canonical Scriptures themselves, a series of testimony, recognising the notoriety and reception of these books, must be deduced from times near to those of their first publication, down the succession of ages through which they have been transmitted to us. The qualifications necessary for such researches demand, it is confessed, a degree of leisure, and a kind of education, inconsistent with the exercise of any other profession. But how few are there amongst the clergy, from whom any thing of this sort can be expected! how small a proportion of their number, who seem likely either to augment the fund of sacred literature or even to collect what is already known! To this objection it may be replied, that we sow many seeds to raise one flower. In order to produce a *few* capable of improving and continuing the stock of Christian erudition, leisure and opportunity must be afforded to great numbers. Original knowledge of this kind can never be universal; but it is of the utmost importance, and it is enough, that there be, at all times, found *some* qualified for such inquiries, and in whose concurring and independent conclusions upon each subject, the rest of the Christian community may safely confide: whereas, without an order of clergy educated for the purpose, and led to the prosecution of these studies by the habits, the leisure, and the object, of their vocation, it may well be questioned whether the learning itself would not have been lost, by which the records of our faith are interpreted and defended. We contend, therefore, that an order of clergy is necessary to perpetuate the evidences of Revelation, and to interpret the obscurity of those ancient writings, in which the religion is contained. But besides this, which forms, no doubt, one design of their institution, the more ordinary offices of public teaching, and of conducting public worship, call for qualifications not usually to be met with amidst the employments of civil life. It has been acknowledged by some, who cannot be suspected of making unnecessary concessions in favour of establishments, "to be barely *possible*, that a person who was never educated for the office should acquit himself with decency as a public teacher of religion." And that surely must be a very defective policy which trusts to *possibilities* for success, when provision is to be made for regular and general instruction. Little objection to this argument can be drawn from the example of the Quakers, who, it may be said, furnish an experimental proof that the worship and profession of Christianity may be upholden without a separate clergy. These sectaries every where subsist in conjunction with a regular establishment. They have access to the writings, they profit by the labours, of the clergy, in common with other Christians. They participate in that general diffusion of religious knowledge, which the constant teaching of a more regular ministry keeps up in the country: with such aids, and under such circumstances, the defects of a plan may not be much felt, although the plan itself be altogether unfit for general imitation.

2. If then an order of clergy be necessary, if it be necessary also to seclude them from the employments and profits of other professions, it is evident they ought to be enabled to derive a maintenance from their own. Now this maintenance must either depend upon the voluntary contributions of their hearers, or arise from revenues assigned by authority of law. To the scheme of voluntary contribution there exists this insurmountable objection, that few would ultimately contribute any thing at all. However the zeal of a sect, or the novelty of a change, might support such an experiment for a while, no reliance could be placed upon it as a general and permanent provision. It is at all times a bad constitution, which presents temptations of interest in opposition to the duties of religion; or which makes the offices of religion expensive to those who attend upon them; or which allows pretences of conscience to be an excuse for not sharing in a public burthen. If, by declining to frequent religious assemblies, men could save their money, at the

same time that they indulged their indolence, and their disinclination to exercises of seriousness and reflection; or if, by dissenting from the national religion, they could be excused from contributing to the support of the ministers of religion; it is to be feared that many would take advantage of the option which was thus imprudently left open to them, and that this liberty might finally operate to the decay of virtue, and an irrecoverable forgetfulness of all religion in the country. Is there not too much reason to fear, that, if it were referred to the discretion of each neighbourhood, whether they would maintain amongst them a teacher of religion or not, many districts would remain unprovided with any; that, with the difficulties which encumber every measure requiring the co-operation of numbers, and where each individual of the number has an interest secretly pleading against the success of the measure itself, associations for the support of Christian worship and instruction would neither be numerous nor long continued? The devout and pious might lament in vain the want or the distance of a religious assembly; they could not form or maintain one, without the concurrence of neighbours who felt neither their zeal nor their liberality.

From the difficulty with which congregations would be established and upheld upon the *voluntary* plan, let us carry our thoughts to the condition of those who are to officiate in them. Preaching, in time, would become a mode of begging. With what sincerity, or with what dignity, can a preacher dispense the truths of Christianity, whose thoughts are perpetually solicited to the reflection how he may increase his subscription? His eloquence, if he possess any, resembles rather the exhibition of a player who is computing the profits of his theatre, than the simplicity of a man who, feeling himself the awful expectations of religion, is seeking to bring others to such a sense and understanding of their duty as may save their souls. Moreover, a little experience of the disposition of the common people will in every country inform us, that it is one thing to edify them in Christian knowledge, and another to gratify their taste for vehement, impassioned oratory; that he, not only whose success, but whose subsistence, depends upon collecting and pleasing a crowd, must resort to other arts than the acquirement and communication of sober and profitable instruction. For a preacher to be thus at the mercy of his audience, to be obliged to adapt his doctrines to the pleasure of a capricious multitude; to be continually affecting a style and manner neither natural to him, nor agreeable to his judgement; to live in constant bondage to tyrannical and insolent directors; are circumstances so mortifying, not only to the pride of the human heart, but to the virtuous love of independency, that they are rarely submitted to without a sacrifice of principle, and a depravation of character—at least it may be pronounced, that a ministry so degraded would soon fall into the lowest hands: for it would be found impossible to engage men of worth and ability in so precarious and humiliating a profession.

If, in deference then to these reasons, it be admitted, that a legal provision for the clergy, compulsory upon those who contribute to it, is expedient; the next question will be, whether this provision should be confined to one sect of Christianity, or extended indifferently to all? Now it should be observed, that this question never *can* offer itself where the people are agreed in their religious opinions; and that it never *ought* to arise, where a system may be framed of doctrines and worship wide enough to comprehend their disagreement; and which might satisfy all, by uniting all in the articles of their common faith, and in a mode of divine worship that omits every subject of controversy or offence. Where such a comprehension is practicable, the comprehending religion ought to be made that of the state. But if this be despaired of; if religious opinions exist, not only so various, but so contradictory, as to render it impossible to reconcile them to each other, or to any one confes-

sion of faith, rule of discipline, or form of worship; if, consequently, separate congregations and different sects must unavoidably continue in the country: under such circumstances, whether
the laws ought to establish one sect in preference to the rest, that
is, whether they ought to confer the provision assigned to the
maintenance of religion upon the teachers of one system of doctrines alone, becomes a question of necessary discussion and of
great importance. And whatever we may determine concerning
speculative rights and abstract proprieties, when we set about the
framing of an ecclesiastical constitution adapted to real life, and to
the actual state of religion in the country, we shall find this question very nearly related to and principally indeed dependent upon
another; namely, "In what way, or by whom, ought the ministers of
religion to be *appointed?*" If the species of patronage be retained to
which we are accustomed in this country, and which allows private
individuals to nominate teachers of religion for districts and congregations to which they are absolute strangers; without some test
proposed to the persons nominated, the utmost discordancy of
religious opinions might arise between the several teachers and
their respective congregations. A popish patron might appoint a
priest to say mass to a congregation of protestants; an episcopal
clergyman be sent to officiate in a parish of presbyterians; or a
presbyterian divine to inveigh against the errors of popery before
an audience of papists. The requisition then of subscription, or any
other test by which the national religion is guarded, may be considered merely as a restriction upon the exercise of private patronage. The laws speak to the private patron thus: "Of those whom we
have previously pronounced to be fitly qualified to teach religion,
we allow you to select one; but we do not allow you to decide what
religion shall be established in a particular district of the country;
for which decision you are no wise fitted by any qualifications
which, as a private patron, you may happen to possess. If it be

necessary that the point be determined for the inhabitants by any other will than their own, it is surely better that it should be determined by a deliberate resolution of the legislature, than by the casual inclination of an individual, by whom the right is purchased, or to whom it devolves as a mere secular inheritance." Wheresoever, therefore, this constitution of patronage is adopted, a national religion, or the legal preference of one particular religion to all others, must almost necessarily accompany it. But, secondly, let it be supposed that the appointment of the minister of religion was in every parish left to the choice of the parishioners; might not this choice, we ask, be safely exercised without its being limited to the teachers of any particular sect? The effect of such a liberty must be, that a papist, or a presbyterian, a methodist, a Moravian, or an anabaptist, would successively gain possession of the pulpit, according as a majority of the party happened at each election to prevail. Now, with what violence the conflict would upon every vacancy be renewed; what bitter animosities would be revived, or rather be constantly fed and kept alive, in the neighbourhood; with what unconquerable aversion the teacher and his religion would be received by the defeated party; may be foreseen by those who reflect with how much passion every dispute is carried on, in which the name of religion can be made to mix itself; much more where the cause itself is concerned so immediately as it would be in this. Or, thirdly, if the state appoint the ministers of religion, this constitution will differ little from the establishment of a national religion; for the state will, undoubtedly, appoint those, and those alone, whose religious opinions, or rather whose religious denominations, agree with its own; unless it be thought that any thing would be gained to religious liberty by transferring the choice of the national religion from the legislature of the country to the magistrate who administers the executive government. The only plan which seems to render the legal maintenance of a clergy practicable, without the legal preference of one sect of Christians to others, is that of an experiment which is said to be attempted or designed in some of the new states of North America. The nature of the plan is thus described: A tax is levied upon the inhabitants for the general support of religion; the collector of the tax goes round with a register in his hand, in which are inserted, at the head of so many distinct columns, the names of the several religious sects that are professed in the country. The person who is called upon for the assessment, as soon as he has paid his quota, subscribes his name and the sum in which of the columns he pleases; and the amount of what is collected in each column is paid over to the minister of that denomination. In this scheme it is not left to the option of the subject, whether he will contribute, or how much he shall contribute, to the maintenance of a Christian ministry; it is only referred to his choice to determine by what sect his contribution shall be received. The above arrangement is undoubtedly the best that has been proposed upon this principle; it bears the appearance of liberality and justice; it may contain some solid advantages; nevertheless, it labours under inconveniences which will be found, I think, upon trial, to overbalance all its recommendations. It is scarcely compatible with that which is the first requisite in an ecclesiastical establishment—the division of the country into parishes of a commodious extent. If the parishes be small, and ministers of every denomination be stationed in each (which the plan seems to suppose), the expense of their maintenance will become too burthensome a charge for the country to support. If, to reduce the expense, the districts be enlarged, the place of assembling will oftentimes be too far removed from the residence of the persons who ought to resort to it. Again: the making the pecuniary success of the different teachers of religion to depend on the number and wealth of their respective followers, would naturally generate strifes and indecent jealousies amongst them; as well as produce a polemical and proselyting spirit, founded in or mixed with views of private gain, which would both deprave the principles of the clergy, and distract the country with endless contentions.

The argument, then, by which ecclesiastical establishments are defended, proceeds by these steps: The knowledge and profession of Christianity cannot be upholden without a clergy; a clergy cannot be supported without a legal provision; a legal provision for the clergy cannot be constituted without the preference of one sect of Christians to the rest: and the conclusion will be conveniently satisfactory in the degree in which the truth of these several propositions can be made out.

If it be deemed expedient to establish a national religion, that is to say, one sect in preference to all others; some *test*, by which the teachers of that sect may be distinguished from the teachers of different sects, appears to be an indispensable consequence. The existence of such an establishment supposes it: the very notion of a national religion includes that of a test.

But this necessity, which is real, hath, according to the fashion of human affairs, furnished to almost every church a pretence for extending, multiplying, and continuing, such tests beyond what the occasion justified. For though some purposes of order and tranquillity may be answered by the establishment of creeds and confessions, yet they are at all times attended with serious inconveniences: they check inquiry; they violate liberty; they ensnare the consciences of the clergy, by holding out temptations to prevarication; however they may express the persuasion, or be accommodated to the controversies or to the fears of the age in which they are composed, in process of time, and by reason of the changes which are wont to take place in the judgement of mankind upon religious subjects, they come at length to contradict the actual opinions of the church, whose doctrines they profess to contain; and they often perpetuate the proscription of sects, and tenets, from which any danger has long ceased to be apprehended.

It may not follow from these objections, that tests and sub-scriptions ought to be abolished: but it follows, that they ought to be made as simple and easy as possible; that they should be adapted, from time to time, to the varying sentiments and circumstances of the church in which they are received; and that they should at no time advance one step farther than some subsisting necessity requires. If, for instance, promises of conformity to the rites, liturgy, and offices of the church, be sufficient to prevent confusion and disorder in the celebration of divine worship, then such prom-ises ought to be accepted in the place of stricter subscriptions. If articles of *peace*, as they are called, that is, engagements not to preach certain doctrines, nor to revive certain controversies, would exclude indecent altercations amongst the national clergy, as well as secure to the public teaching of religion as much of uniformity and quiet as is necessary to edification; then confessions of *faith* ought to be converted into articles of peace. In a word, it ought to be holden a sufficient reason for relaxing the terms of subscription, or for dropping any or all of the articles to be subscribed, that no *present* necessity requires the strictness which is complained of, or that it should be extended to so many points of doctrine.

The division of the country into districts, and the stationing in each district a teacher of religion, forms the substantial part of every church establishment. The varieties that have been intro-duced into the government and discipline of different churches are of inferior importance, when compared with this, in which they all agree. Of these oeconomical questions, none seems more material than that which has been long agitated in the reformed churches of Christendom, whether a parity amongst the clergy, or a distinction of orders in the ministry, be more conducive to the general ends of the institution. In favour of that system which the laws of this country have preferred, we may allege the following reasons: that it secures tranquillity and subordination amongst the clergy themselves; that it corresponds with the gradations of rank in civil life, and provides for the edification of each rank, by stationing in each an order of clergy of their own class and quality; and, lastly, that the same fund produces more effect, both as an allurement to men of talents to enter into the church, and as a stimulus to the industry of those who are already in it, when distributed into prizes of different value, than when divided into equal shares.

After the state has once established a particular system of faith as a national religion, a question will soon occur, concerning the treatment and toleration of those who *dissent* from it. This question is properly preceded by another, concerning the right which the civil magistrate possesses to interfere in matters of religion at all: for, although this right be acknowledged whilst he is employed solely in providing means of public instruction, it will probably be disputed (indeed it ever has been), when he proceeds to inflict penalties, to impose restraints or incapacities, on the account of religious distinctions. They who admit no other just original of civil government, than what is founded in some stipulation with its subjects, are at liberty to contend that the concerns of religion were excepted out of the social compact; that, in an affair which can only be transacted between God and a man's own conscience, no commission or authority was ever delegated to the civil magistrate, or could indeed be transferred from the person himself to any other. We, however, who have rejected this theory, because we cannot discover any actual contract between the state and the people, and because we cannot allow any arbitrary fiction to be made the foundation of real rights and of real obligations, find ourselves precluded from this distinction. The reasoning which deduces the authority of civil government from the will of God, and which collects that will from public expediency alone, binds us to the unreserved conclusion, that the jurisdiction of the magistrate is limited by no consideration but that of general utility: in plainer terms, that whatever be the subject to be regulated, it is lawful for him to interfere whenever his interference, in its general tendency, appears to be conducive to the common interest. There is nothing in the nature of religion, as such, which exempts it from the authority of the legislator, when the safety or welfare of the community requires his interposition. It has been said, indeed, that religion, pertaining to the interests of a life to come, lies beyond the province of civil government, the office of which is confined to the affairs of this life. But in reply to this objection, it may be observed, that when the laws interfere even in religion, they interfere only with temporals; their effects terminate, their power operates only upon those rights and interests, which confessedly belong to their disposal. The acts of the legislature, the edicts of the prince, the sentence of the judge, cannot affect my salvation; nor do they, without the most absurd arrogance, pretend to any such power: but they may deprive me of liberty, of property, and even of life itself, on account of my religion; and however I may complain of the injustice of the sentence by which I am condemned, I cannot allege, that the magistrate has transgressed the boundaries of his jurisdiction; because the property, the liberty, and the life of the subject, *may* be taken away by the authority of the laws, for any reason which, in the judgement of the legislature, renders such a measure necessary to the common welfare. Moreover, as the precepts of religion may regulate all the offices of life, or may be so construed as to extend to all, the exemption of religion from the control of human laws might afford a plea, which would exclude civil government from every authority over the conduct of its subjects. Religious liberty is, like civil liberty, not an immunity from restraint, but the being restrained by no law, but what in a greater degree conduces to the public welfare.

Still it is right "to obey God rather than man." Nothing that we have said encroaches upon the truth of this sacred and undisputed maxim: the right of the magistrate to ordain, and the obligation of the subject to obey, in matters of religion, may be very different; and will be so, as often as they flow from opposite apprehensions of the Divine will. In affairs that are properly of a civil nature, in "the things that are Caesar's," this difference seldom happens. The law authorises the act which it enjoins; Revelation being either silent upon the subject, or referring to the laws of the country, or requiring only that men act by some fixed rule, and that this rule be established by competent authority. But when human laws interpose their direction in matters of religion, by dictating, for example, the object or the mode of divine worship; by prohibiting the profession of some articles of faith, and by exacting that of others, they are liable to clash with what private persons believe to be already settled by precepts of Revelation; or to contradict what God himself, they think, hath declared to be true. In this case, on whichever side the mistake lies, or whatever plea the state may allege to justify its edict, the subject can have none to excuse his compliance. The same consideration also points out the distinction, as to the authority of the state, between temporals and spirituals. The magistrate is not to be obeyed in temporals more than in spirituals, where a repugnancy is perceived between his commands and any credited manifestations of the Divine will; but such repugnancies are much less likely to arise in one case than the other.

When we grant that it is lawful for the magistrate to interfere in religion as often as his interference appears to him to conduce, in its general tendency, to the public happiness; it may be argued, from this concession, that since salvation is the highest interest of mankind, and since, consequently, to advance *that* is to promote the public happiness in the best way, and in the greatest degree, in which it can be promoted, it follows, that it is not only the right, but the duty, of every magistrate invested with supreme power, to enforce upon his subjects the reception of that religion which he deems most acceptable to God; and to enforce it by such methods as may appear most effectual for the end proposed. A popish king, for example, who should believe that salvation is not attainable out of the precincts of the Romish church, would derive a right from our principles (not to say that he would be bound by them) to employ the power with which the constitution intrusted him, and which power, in absolute monarchies, commands the lives and fortunes of every subject of the empire, in reducing his people within that communion. We confess that this consequence is inferred from the principles we have laid down concerning the foundation of civil authority, not without the resemblance of a regular deduction: we confess also that it is a conclusion which it behoves us to dispose of; because, if it really follow from our theory of government, the theory itself ought to be given up. Now it will be remembered, that the terms of our proposition are these: "That it is lawful for the magistrate to interfere in the affairs of religion, whenever his interference appears to him to conduce, by its general tendency, to the public happiness." The clause of "general tendency," when this rule comes to be applied, will be found a very significant part of the direction. It obliges the magistrate to reflect, not only whether the religion which he wishes to propagate amongst his subjects be that which will best secure their eternal welfare; not only, whether the methods he employs be likely to effectuate the establishment of that religion; but also upon this farther question: Whether the kind of interference which he is about to exercise, if it were adopted as a common maxim amongst states and princes, or received as a general rule for the conduct of government in matters of religion, would, upon the whole, and in the mass of instances in which his example might be imitated, conduce

to the fartherance of human salvation. If the magistrate, for
example, should think that, although the application of his power
might, in the instance concerning which he deliberates, advance
the true religion, and together with it the happiness of his people,
yet that the same engine, in other hands, who might assume the
right to use it with the like pretensions of reason and authority that
he himself alleges, would more frequently shut out truth, and
obstruct the means of salvation; he would be bound by this opinion, still admitting public utility to be the supreme rule of his
conduct, to refrain from expedients, which, whatever particular
effects *he* may expect from them, are, in their general operation,
dangerous or hurtful. If there be any difficulty in the subject, it
arises from that which is the cause of every difficulty in morals—
the competition of particular and general consequences; or, what is
the same thing, the submission of one general rule to another rule
which is still more general.

Bearing then in mind, that it is the *general* tendency of the measure, or, in other words, the effects which would arise from the
measure being *generally* adopted, that fixes upon it the character of
rectitude or injustice; we proceed to inquire what is the degree and
the sort of interference of secular laws in matters of religion, which
are likely to be beneficial to the public happiness. There are two
maxims which will in a great measure regulate our conclusions
upon this head. The first is, that any form of Christianity is better
than no religion at all: the second, that, of different systems of faith,
that is the best which is the truest. The first of these positions will
hardly be disputed, when we reflect that every sect and modification of Christianity holds out the happiness and misery of another
life, as depending chiefly upon the practice of virtue or of vice in
this; and that the distinctions of virtue and vice are nearly the same
in all. A person who acts under the impression of these hopes and
fears, though combined with many errors and superstitions, is

more likely to advance both the public happiness and his own, than one who is destitute of all expectation of a future account. The latter proposition is founded in the consideration, that the principal importance of religion consists in its influence upon the fate and condition of a future existence. This influence belongs only to that religion which comes from God. A political religion may be framed, which shall embrace the purposes, and describe the duties of political society perfectly well; but if it be not delivered by God, what assurance does it afford, that the decisions of the Divine judgement will have any regard to the rules which it contains? By a man who acts with a view to a future judgement, the authority of a religion is the first thing inquired after; a religion which wants authority, with him wants every thing. Since then this authority appertains, not to the religion which is most commodious—to the religion which is most sublime and efficacious—to the religion which suits best with the form, or seems most calculated to uphold the power and stability, of civil government—but only to that religion which comes from God; we are justified in pronouncing the *true* religion by its very *truth*, and independently of all considerations of tendencies, aptnesses, or any other internal qualities whatever, to be universally the best.

From the first proposition follows this inference, that when the state enables its subjects to learn *some* form of Christianity, by distributing teachers of a religious system throughout the country, and by providing for the maintenance of these teachers at the public expense; that is, in fewer terms, when the laws *establish* a national religion; they exercise a power and an interference, which are likely, in their general tendency, to promote the interest of mankind: for, even supposing the species of Christianity which the laws patronise to be erroneous and corrupt, yet when the option lies between this religion and no religion at all (which would be the consequence of leaving the people without any public means of instruction, or any regular celebration of the offices of Christianity), our proposition teaches us that the former alternative is constantly to be preferred.

But after the right of the magistrate to establish a particular religion has been, upon this principle, admitted; a doubt sometimes presents itself, whether the religion which he ought to establish, be that which he himself professes, or that which he observes to prevail amongst the majority of the people. Now when we consider this question with a view to the formation of a general rule upon the subject (which view alone can furnish a just solution of the doubt), it must be assumed to be an equal chance whether of the two religions contains more of truth—that of the magistrate, or that of the people. The chance then that is left to truth being equal upon both suppositions, the remaining consideration will be, from which arrangement more efficacy can be expected—from an order of men appointed to teach the people their own religion, or to convert them to another? In my opinion, the advantage lies on the side of the former scheme: and this opinion, if it be assented to, makes it the duty of the magistrate, in the choice of the religion which he establishes, to consult the faith of the nation, rather than his own.

The case also of dissenters must be determined by the principles just now stated. *Toleration* is of two kinds—the allowing to dissenters the unmolested profession and exercise of their religion, but with an exclusion from offices of trust and emolument in the state; which is a *partial* toleration: and the admitting them, without distinction, to all the civil privileges and capacities of other citizens; which is a *complete* toleration. The expediency of toleration, and consequently the right of every citizen to demand it, as far as relates to liberty of conscience, and the claim of being protected in the free and safe profession of his religion, is deducible from the *second* of those propositions which we have delivered as the grounds of our conclusions upon the subject. That proposition asserts truth, and truth in the abstract, to be the supreme perfection of every religion. The advancement, consequently, and discovery of truth, is that end to which all regulations concerning religion ought principally to be adapted. Now, every species of intolerance which enjoins suppression and silence, and every species of persecution which enforces such injunctions, is adverse to the progress of truth; forasmuch as it causes that to be fixed by one set of men, at one time, which is much better, and with much more probability of success, left to the independent and progressive inquiry of separate individuals. Truth results from discussion and from controversy; is investigated by the labours and researches of private persons. Whatever, therefore, prohibits these, obstructs that industry and that liberty, which it is the common interest of mankind to promote. In religion, as in other subjects, truth, if left to itself, will almost always obtain the ascendancy. If different religions be professed in the same country, and the minds of men remain unfettered and unawed by intimidations of law, that religion which is founded in maxims of reason and credibility, will gradually gain over the other to it. I do not mean that men will formally renounce their ancient religion, but that they will adopt into it the more rational doctrines, the improvements and discoveries of the neighbouring sect; by which means the worse religion, without the ceremony of a reformation, will insensibly assimilate itself to the better. If popery, for instance, and protestantism were permitted to dwell quietly together, papists might not become protestants (for the name is commonly the last thing that is changed),* but they would become more enlightened and

---

* Would we let the *name* stand, we might often attract men, without their perceiving it, much nearer to ourselves, than, if they did perceive it, they would be willing to come.

informed; they would by little and little incorporate into their creed many of the tenets of protestantism, as well as imbibe a portion of its spirit and moderation.

The justice and expediency of toleration we found primarily in its conduciveness to truth, and in the superior value of truth to that of any other quality which a religion can possess: this is the principal argument; but there are some auxiliary considerations, too important to be omitted. The confining of the subject to the religion of the state is a needless violation of natural liberty, and is an instance in which constraint is always grievous. Persecution produces no sincere conviction, nor any real change of opinion; on the contrary, it vitiates the public morals, by driving men to prevarication; and commonly ends in a general though secret infidelity, by imposing, under the name of revealed religion, systems of doctrine which men cannot believe, and dare not examine: finally, it disgraces the character, and wounds the reputation of Christianity itself, by making it the author of oppression, cruelty, and bloodshed.

Under the idea of religious toleration, I include the toleration of all books of serious argumentation: but I deem it no infringement of religious liberty, to restrain the circulation of ridicule, invective, and mockery, upon religious subjects; because this species of writing applies solely to the passions, weakens the judgement, and contaminates the imagination, of its readers; has no tendency whatever to assist either the investigation or the impression of truth: on the contrary, whilst it stays not to distinguish between the authority of different religions, it destroys alike the influence of all.

Concerning the admission of dissenters from the established religion to offices and employments in the public service (which is necessary, to render toleration *complete*), doubts have been entertained, with some appearance of reason. It is possible that such religious opinions may be holden, as are utterly incompatible with the necessary functions of civil government; and which opinions consequently disqualify those who maintain them from exercising any share in its administration. There have been enthusiasts who held that Christianity has abolished all distinction of property, and that she enjoins upon her followers a community of goods. With what tolerable propriety could one of this sect be appointed a judge or a magistrate, whose office it is to decide upon questions of private right, and to protect men in the exclusive enjoyment of their property? It would be equally absurd to intrust a military command to a Quaker, who believes it to be contrary to the Gospel to take up arms. This is possible; therefore it cannot be laid down as an universal truth, that religion is not, in its nature, a cause which will justify exclusion from public employments. When we examine, however, the sects of Christianity which actually prevail in the world, we must confess that, with the single exception of refusing to bear arms, we find no tenet in any of them which incapacitates men for the service of the state. It has indeed been asserted that discordancy of religions, even supposing each religion to be free from any errors that affect the safety or the conduct of government, is enough to render men unfit to act together, in public stations. But upon what argument, or upon what experience, is this assertion founded? I perceive no reason why men of different religious persuasions may not sit upon the same bench, deliberate in the same council, or fight in the same ranks, as well as men of various or opposite opinions upon any controverted topic of natural philosophy, history, or ethics.

There are two cases in which test-laws are wont to be applied, and in which, if in any, they may be defended. One is, where two or more religions are contending for establishment; and where there appears no way of putting an end to the contest, but by giving to one religion such a decided superiority in the legislature and government of the country, as to secure it against danger from any other. I own that I should assent to this precaution with many scruples. If the dissenters from the establishment become a majority of the people, the establishment itself ought to be altered or qualified. If there exist amongst the different sects of the country such a parity of numbers, interest, and power, as to render the preference of one sect to the rest, and the choice of that sect, a matter of hazardous success, and of doubtful election, some plan similar to that which is meditated in North America, and which we have described in a preceding part of the present chapter, though encumbered with great difficulties, may perhaps suit better with this divided state of public opinion, than any constitution of a national church whatever. In all other situations, the establishment will be strong enough to maintain itself. However, if a test be applicable with justice upon this principle at all, it ought to be applied in regal governments to the chief magistrate himself, whose power might otherwise overthrow or change the established religion of the country, in opposition to the will and sentiments of the people.

The second case of *exclusion*, and in which, I think, the measure is more easily vindicated, is that of a country in which some disaffection to the subsisting government happens to be connected with certain religious distinctions. The state undoubtedly has a right to refuse its power and its confidence to those who seek its destruction. Wherefore, if the generality of any religious sect entertain dispositions hostile to the constitution, and if government have no other way of knowing its enemies than by the religion which they profess, the professors of that religion may justly be excluded from offices of trust and authority. But even *here* it should be observed, that it is not against the religion that government shuts its doors, but against those political principles, which, however independent they may be of any article of religious faith, the members of that communion are found in fact to hold. Nor would the legislator make religious tenets the test of men's inclinations towards the state, if he could discover any other that was equally certain and notorious. Thus, if the members of the Romish church, for the most part, adhere to the interests, or maintain the right, of a foreign pretender to the crown of these kingdoms; and if there be no way of distinguishing those who do from those who do not retain such dangerous prejudices; government is well warranted in fencing out the whole sect from situations of trust and power. But even in this example, it is not to popery that the laws object, but to popery as the mark of jacobitism; an equivocal indeed and fallacious mark, but the best, and perhaps the only one, that can be devised. But then it should be remembered, that as the connexion between popery and jacobitism, which is the sole cause of suspicion, and the sole justification of those severe and jealous laws which have been enacted against the professors of that religion, was accidental in its origin, so probably it will be temporary in its duration; and that these restrictions ought not to continue one day longer than some visible danger renders them necessary to the preservation of public tranquillity.

After all, it may be asked, Why should not the legislator direct his test against the political principles themselves which he wishes to exclude, rather than encounter them through the medium of religious tenets, the only crime and the only danger of which consist in their presumed alliance with the former? Why, for example, should a man be required to renounce transubstantiation, before he be admitted to an office in the state, when it might seem to be sufficient that he abjure the pretender? There are but two answers that can be given to the objection which this question contains: first, that it is not opinions which the laws fear, so much as inclinations; and that political inclinations are not so easily detected by the affirmation or denial of any abstract proposition in politics, as by the discovery of the religious creed with which they are wont to be united: secondly, that when men renounce their religion, they commonly quit all connexion with the members of the church which they have left; that church no longer expecting assistance or friendship from them: whereas particular persons might insinuate themselves into offices of trust and authority, by subscribing political assertions, and yet retain their predilection for the interests of the religious sect to which they continued to belong. By which means, government would sometimes find, though it could not accuse the individual, whom it had received into its service, of disaffection to the civil establishment, yet that, through him, it had communicated the aid and influence of a powerful station to a party who were hostile to the constitution. These answers however we propose rather than defend. The measure certainly cannot be defended at all, except where the suspected union between certain obnoxious principles in politics, and certain tenets in religion, is nearly universal; in which case, it makes little difference to the subscriber, whether the test be religious or political; and the state is somewhat better secured by the one than the other.

The result of our examination of those general tendencies, by which every interference of civil government in matters of religion ought to be tried, is this: "That a comprehensive national religion, guarded by a few articles of peace and conformity, together with a legal provision for the clergy of that religion; and with a *complete* toleration of all dissenters from the established church, without any other limitation or exception, than what arises from the conjunction of dangerous political dispositions with certain religious tenets; appears to be, not only the most just and liberal, but the wisest and safest system, which a state can adopt; inasmuch as it unites the several perfections which a religious constitution ought to aim at: liberty of conscience, with means of instruction; the progress of truth, with the peace of society; the right of private judgement, with the care of the public safety."

Chapter 11

OF POPULATION AND PROVISION; AND OF AGRICULTURE AND COMMERCE, AS SUBSERVIENT THERETO

The final view of all rational politics is, to produce the greatest quantity of happiness in a given tract of country. The riches, strength, and glory, of nations; the topics which history celebrates, and which alone almost engage the praises and possess the admiration of mankind; have no value farther than as they contribute to this end. When they interfere with it, they are evils, and not the less real for the splendour that surrounds them.

Secondly: although we speak of communities as of sentient beings; although we ascribe to them happiness and misery, desires, interests, and passions; nothing really exists or feels but *individuals*. The happiness of a people is made up of the happiness of single persons; and the quantity of happiness can only be augmented by increasing the number of the percipients, or the pleasure of their perceptions.

Thirdly: notwithstanding that diversity of condition, especially different degrees of plenty, freedom, and security, greatly vary the quantity of happiness enjoyed by the same number of individuals; and notwithstanding that extreme cases may be found, of human beings so galled by the rigours of slavery, that the increase of numbers is only the amplification of misery: yet, within certain limits, and within those limits to which civil life is diversified under the temperate governments that obtain in Europe, it may be affirmed, I think, with certainty, that the quantity of happiness produced in any given district, *so far* depends upon the number of inhabitants, that, in comparing adjoining periods in the same country, the collective happiness will be nearly in the exact proportion of the numbers, that is, twice the number of inhabitants will produce double the quantity of happiness; in distant periods, and different countries, under great changes or great dissimilitude of civil condition, although the proportion of enjoyment may fall much short of that of the numbers, yet still any considerable excess of numbers will usually carry with it a preponderation of happiness; that, at least, it may and ought to be assumed, in all political deliberations, that a larger portion of happiness is enjoyed amongst *ten* persons, possessing the means of healthy subsistence, than can be produced by *five* persons, under every advantage of power, affluence, and luxury.

From these principles it follows, that the quantity of happiness in a given district, although it is possible it may be increased, the number of inhabitants remaining the same, is chiefly and most naturally affected by alteration of the numbers: that, consequently, the decay of population is the greatest evil that a state can suffer; and the improvement of it the object which ought, in all countries, to be aimed at in preference to every other political purpose whatsoever.

The importance of population, and the superiority of *it* to every other national advantage, are points necessary to be inculcated, and to be understood; inasmuch as false estimates, or fantastic notions, of national grandeur, are perpetually drawing the attention of statesmen and legislators from the care of this, which is, at all times, the true and absolute interest of a country: for which reason, we have stated these points with unusual formality. We will confess, however, that a competition can seldom arise between the advancement of population and any measure of sober utility; because, in the ordinary progress of human affairs, whatever, in any way, contributes to make a people happier, tends to render them more numerous.

In the fecundity of the human, as of every other species of animals, nature has provided for an indefinite multiplication.

Mankind have increased to their present number from a single pair; the offspring of early marriages, in the ordinary course of pro-creation, do more than replace the parents: in countries, and under circumstances very favourable to subsistence, the population has been doubled in the space of twenty years; the havoc occasioned by wars, earthquakes, famine, or pestilence, is usually repaired in a short time. These indications sufficiently demonstrate the ten-dency of nature, in the human species, to a continual increase of its numbers. It becomes therefore a question that may reasonably be propounded, what are the causes which confine or check the natu-ral progress of this multiplication? And the answer which first presents itself to the thoughts of the inquirer is, that the popula-tion of a country must stop when the country can maintain no more, that is, when the inhabitants are already so numerous as to exhaust all the provision which the soil can be made to produce. This, however, though an insuperable bar, will seldom be found to be *that* which actually checks the progress of population in any country of the world; because the number of the people have sel-dom, in any country, arrived at this limit, or even approached to it. The fertility of the ground, in temperate regions, is capable of being improved by cultivation to an extent which is unknown; much, however, beyond the state of improvement in any country in Europe. In our own, which holds almost the first place in the knowledge and encouragement of agriculture, let it only be sup-posed that every field in England, of the same original quality with those in the neighbourhood of the metropolis, and consequently capable of the same fertility, were by a like management made to yield an equal produce; and it may be asserted, I believe with truth, that the quantity of human provision raised in the island would be increased five-fold. The two principles, therefore, upon which population seems primarily to depend, the fecundity of the species, and the capacity of the soil, would in most, perhaps in all countries, enable it to proceed much farther than it has yet advanced. The number of marriageable women, who, in each country, remain unmarried, afford a computation how much the agency of nature in the diffusion of human life is cramped and contracted; and the quantity of waste, neglected, or mismanaged surface—together with a comparison, like the preceding, of the crops raised from the soil in the neighbourhood of populous cities, and under a perfect state of cultivation, with those which lands of equal or superior quality yield in different situations—will show in what proportion the indigenous productions of the earth are capable of being farther augmented.

The fundamental proposition upon the subject of *population*, which must guide every endeavour to improve it, and from which every conclusion concerning it may be deduced, is this: "Wherever the commerce between the sexes is regulated by marriage, and a provision for that mode of subsistence, to which each class of the community is accustomed, can be procured with ease and certainty, there the number of the people will increase; and the rapidity, as well as the extent, of the increase, will be proportioned to the degree in which these causes exist."

This proposition we will draw out into the several principles which it contains.

I. First, the proposition asserts the "necessity of confining the intercourse of the sexes to the marriage-union." It is only in the marriage-union that this intercourse is sufficiently prolific. Beside which, family establishments alone are fitted to perpetuate a succession of generations. The offspring of a vague and promiscuous concubinage are not only few, and liable to perish by neglect, but are seldom prepared for or introduced into situations suited to the raising of families of their own. Hence the advantages of marriages. Now nature, in the constitution of the sexes, has provided a stimulus which will infallibly secure the frequency of marriages, with all their beneficial effects upon the state of population, provided the male part of the species be prohibited from irregular gratifications. This impulse, which is sufficient to surmount almost every impediment to marriage, will operate in proportion to the difficulty, expense, danger, or infamy, the sense of guilt, or the fear of punishment, which attend licentious indulgences. Wherefore, in countries in which subsistence is become scarce, it behoves the state to watch over the public morals with increased solicitude: for nothing but the instinct of nature, under the restraint of chastity, will induce men to undertake the labour or consent to the sacrifice of personal liberty and indulgence, which the support of a family, in such circumstances, requires.

II. The second requisite which our proposition states as necessary to the success of population, is, "the ease and certainty with which a provision can be procured for that mode of subsistence to which each class of the community is accustomed." It is not enough that men's *natural* wants be supplied; that a provision adequate to the real exigencies of human life be attainable: habitual superfluities become actual wants; opinion and fashion convert articles of ornament and luxury into necessaries of life. And it must not be expected from men in general, at least in the present relaxed state of morals and discipline, that they will enter into marriages which degrade their condition, reduce their mode of living, deprive them of the accommodations to which they have been accustomed, or even of those ornaments or appendages of rank and station which they have been taught to regard as belonging to their birth, or class, or profession, or place in society. The same consideration, namely, a view to their *accustomed* mode of life, which is so apparent in the superior order of the people, has no less influence upon those ranks which compose the mass of the community. The kind and quality of food and liquor, the species of habitation, furniture, and clothing, to which the common people of each country are

habituated, must be attainable with ease and certainty, before marriages will be sufficiently early and general to carry the progress of
population to its just extent. It is in vain to allege, that a more
simple diet, ruder habitations, or coarser apparel, would be sufficient for the purposes of life and health, or even of physical ease
and pleasure. Men will not marry with this encouragement. For
instance: when the common people of a country are accustomed to
eat a large proportion of animal food, to drink wine, spirits, or
beer, to wear shoes and stockings, to dwell in stone houses, they
will not marry to live in clay cottages, upon roots and milk, with no
other clothing than skins, or what is necessary to defend the trunk
of the body from the effects of cold; although these last may be all
that the sustentation of life and health requires, or that even contribute much to animal comfort and enjoyment.

The ease, then, and certainty, with which the means can be procured, not barely of subsistence, but of that mode of subsisting
which custom hath in each country established, form the point
upon which the state and progress of population chiefly depend.
Now there are three causes which evidently regulate this point: the
mode itself of subsisting which prevails in the country; the quantity of provision suited to that mode of subsistence, which is either
raised in the country or imported into it; and, lastly, the distribution of that provision.

These three causes merit distinct consideration.

I. The mode of living which actually obtains in a country. In
China, where the inhabitants frequent the sea shore, or the banks
of large rivers, and subsist in a great measure upon fish, the population is described to be excessive. This peculiarity arises, not probably from any civil advantages, any care or policy, any particular
constitution or superior wisdom of government; but simply from
hence, that the species of food to which custom hath reconciled
the desires and inclinations of the inhabitants, is that which, of all

others, is procured in the greatest abundance, with the most ease, and stands in need of the least preparation. The natives of Indostan being confined, by the laws of their religion, to the use of vegetable food, and requiring little except rice, which the country produces in plentiful crops; and food, in warm climates, composing the only want of life; these countries are populous, under all the injuries of a despotic, and the agitations of an unsettled government. If any revolution, or what would be called perhaps, refinement of manners, should generate in these people a taste for the flesh of animals, similar to what prevails amongst the Arabian hordes; should introduce flocks and herds into grounds which are now covered with corn; should teach them to account a certain portion of this species of food amongst the necessaries of life; the population, from this single change, would suffer in a few years a great diminution: and this diminution would follow, in spite of every effort of the laws, or even of any improvement that might take place in their civil condition. In Ireland, the simplicity of living alone maintains a considerable degree of population, under great defects of police, industry, and commerce.

Under this head, and from a view of these considerations, may be understood the true evil and proper danger of *luxury*.

LUXURY, as it supplies employment and promotes industry, assists population. But then there is another consequence attending it, which counteracts and often overbalances these advantages. When, by introducing more superfluities into general reception, luxury has rendered the usual accommodations of life more expensive, artificial, and elaborate, the difficulty of maintaining a family conformably with the established mode of living, becomes greater, and what each man has to spare from his personal consumption proportionably less: the effect of which is, that marriages grow less frequent, agreeably to the maxim above laid down, and which must be remembered as the foundation of all our reasoning upon the subject, that men will not marry, to *sink* their place or condition in society, or to forego those indulgences which their own habits, or what they observe amongst their equals, have rendered necessary to their satisfaction. This principle is applicable to every article of diet and dress, to houses, furniture, attendance; and this effect will be felt in every class of the community. For instance: the custom of wearing broad cloth and fine linen repays the shepherd and flax-grower, feeds the manufacturer, enriches the merchant, gives not only support but existence to multitudes of families: hitherto, therefore, the effects are beneficial; and were these the only effects, such elegancies, or, if you please to call them so, such luxuries, could not be too universal. But here follows the mischief: when once fashion hath annexed the use of these articles of dress to any certain class, the middling ranks, for example, of the community, each individual of that rank finds them to be *necessaries* of life; that is, finds himself obliged to comply with the example of his equals, and to maintain that appearance which the custom of society requires. This obligation creates such a demand upon his income, and adds so much to the cost and burden of a family, as to put it out of his power to marry, with the prospect of continuing his habits, or of maintaining his place and situation in the world. We see, in this description, the cause which induces men to waste their lives in a barren celibacy; and this cause, which impairs the very source of population, is justly placed to the account of luxury.

It appears, then, that *luxury*, considered with a view to population, acts by two opposite effects; and it seems probable that there exists a point in the scale, to which luxury may ascend, or to which the wants of mankind may be multiplied with advantage to the community, and beyond which the prejudicial consequences begin to preponderate. The determination of this point, though it assume the form of an arithmetical problem, depends upon circumstances too numerous, intricate, and undefined, to admit of a precise solution. However, from what has been observed concerning the tendency of luxury to diminish marriages, in which tendency the evil of it resides, the following general conclusions may be established:

1st. That, of different kinds of luxury, those are the most innocent, which afford employment to the greatest number of artists and manufacturers; or those, in other words, in which the price of the work bears the greatest proportion to that of the raw material. Thus, luxury in dress or furniture is universally preferable to luxury in eating, because the articles which constitute the one, are more the production of human art and industry, than those which supply the other.

2dly. That it is the *diffusion*, rather than the *degree* of luxury, which is to be dreaded as a national evil. The mischief of luxury consists, as we have seen, in the obstruction which it forms to marriage. Now it is only a small part of the people that the higher ranks in any country compose; for which reason, the facility or the difficulty of supporting the expense of *their* station, and the consequent increase or diminution of marriages among *them*, will influence the state of population but little. So long as the prevalency of luxury is confined to a few of elevated rank, much of the benefit is felt, and little of the inconveniency. But when the imitation of the same manners descends, as it always will do, into the mass of the people; when it advances the requisites of living, beyond what it adds to men's abilities to purchase them; then it is that luxury checks the formation of families, in a degree that ought to alarm the public fears.

3dly. That the condition most favourable to population is that of a laborious, frugal people ministering to the demands of an opulent, luxurious nation; because this situation, whilst it leaves them every advantage of luxury, exempts them from the evils which naturally accompany its admission into any country.

II. Next to the mode of living, we are to consider "the quantity of provision suited to that mode, which is either raised in the country, or imported into it": for this is the order in which we assigned the causes of population, and undertook to treat of them. Now, if we measure the quantity of provision by the number of human bodies it will support in due health and vigour, this quantity, the extent and quality of the soil from which it is raised being given, will depend greatly upon the *kind*. For instance: a piece of ground capable of supplying animal food sufficient for the subsistence of ten persons, would sustain, at least, the double of that number with grain, roots, and milk. The first resource of savage life is in the flesh of wild animals; hence the numbers amongst savage nations, compared with the tract of country which they occupy, are universally small; because this species of provision is, of all others, supplied in the slenderest proportion. The next step was the invention of pasturage, or the rearing of flocks and herds of tame animals: this alteration added to the stock of provision much. But the last and principal improvement was to follow; namely, tillage, or the artificial production of corn, esculent plants, and roots. This discovery, whilst it changed the quality of human food, augmented the quantity in a vast proportion. So far as the state of population is governed and limited by the quantity of provision, perhaps there is no single cause that affects it so powerfully, as the kind and quality of food which chance or usage hath introduced into a country. In England, notwithstanding the produce of the soil has been, of late, considerably increased, by the enclosure of wastes, and the adoption, in many places, of a more successful husbandry, yet we do not observe a corresponding addition to the number of inhabitants; the reason of which appears to me to be, the more general consumption of animal food amongst us. Many ranks of people whose ordinary diet was, in the last century, prepared almost entirely from milk, roots, and vegetables, now require every day a considerable portion of the flesh of animals. Hence a great part of the richest lands of the country are converted to pasturage. Much also of the bread-corn, which went directly to the nourishment of human bodies, now only contributes to it by fattening the flesh of sheep and oxen. The mass and volume of provisions are hereby diminished; and what is gained in the melioration of the soil, is lost in the quality of the produce. This consideration teaches us, that tillage, as an object of national care and encouragement, is universally preferable to pasturage, because the kind of provision which it yields, goes much farther in the sustentation of human life. Tillage is also recommended by this additional advantage, that it affords employment to a much more numerous peasantry. Indeed, pasturage seems to be the art of a nation, either imperfectly civilized, as are many of the tribes which cultivate it in the internal parts of Asia; or of a nation, like Spain, declining from its summit by luxury and inactivity.

The kind and quality of provision, together with the extent and capacity of the soil from which it is raised, being the same; the quantity procured will principally depend upon two circumstances—the *ability* of the occupier, and the *encouragement* which he receives. The greatest misfortune of a country is an indigent tenantry. Whatever be the native advantages of the soil, or even the skill and industry of the occupier, the want of a sufficient capital confines every plan, as well as cripples and weakens every operation, of husbandry. This evil is felt, where agriculture is accounted a servile or mean employment; where farms are extremely subdivided, and badly furnished with habitations; where leases are unknown, or are of short or precarious duration. With respect to the *encouragement* of husbandry; in this, as in every other employment, the true reward of industry is in the price and sale of the produce. The exclusive right to the produce is the only incitement which acts constantly and universally; the only spring which keeps human labour in motion. All therefore that the laws can do, is to secure this right to the occupier of the ground, that is, to constitute such a system of tenure, that the full and entire advantage of every improvement go to the benefit of the improver; that every man work for himself, and not for another; and that no one share in the profit who does not assist in the production. By the *occupier* I here mean, not so much the person who performs the work, as him who procures the labour and directs the management: and I consider the whole profit as *received* by the occupier, when the occupier is benefited by the whole value of what is produced, which is the case with the tenant who pays a fixed rent for the use of land, no less than with the proprietor who holds it as his own. The one has the same interest in the produce, and in the advantage of every improvement, as the other. Likewise the proprietor, though he grant out his estate to farm, may be considered as the *occupier*, insomuch as he regulates the occupation by the choice, superintendency, and encouragement, of his tenants, by the disposition of his lands, by erecting buildings, providing accommodations, by prescribing conditions, or supplying implements and materials of improvement; and is entitled, by the rule of public expediency above mentioned, to receive, in the advance of his rent, a share of the benefit which arises from the increased produce of his estate. The violation of this fundamental maxim of agrarian policy constitutes the chief objection to the holding of lands by the state, by the king, by corporate bodies, by private persons in right of their offices or benefices. The inconveniency to the public arises not so much from the unalienable quality of lands thus holden in perpetuity, as from hence; that proprietors of this description seldom contribute much either of attention or expense to the cultivation of their estates, yet claim, by the rent, a share in the profit of every improvement that is made upon them. This complaint can only be obviated by "long leases at a fixed rent," which convey a large portion of the interest to those who actually conduct the cultivation. The same objection is applicable to the holding of lands by foreign proprietors, and in some degree to estates of too great extent being placed in the same hands.

III. Beside the *production* of provision, there remains to be considered the DISTRIBUTION. It is in vain that provisions abound in the country, unless I be able to obtain a share of them. This reflection belongs to every individual. The plenty of provision produced, the quantity of the public stock, affords subsistence to individuals, and encouragement to the formation of families, only in proportion as it is *distributed*, that is, in proportion as these individuals are allowed to draw from it a supply of their own wants. The *distribution*, therefore, becomes of equal consequence to population with the *production*. Now there is but one principle of distribution that can ever become universal, namely, the principle of "exchange"; or, in other words, that every man have something to give in return for what he wants. Bounty, however it may come in aid of another principle, however it may occasionally qualify the rigour, or supply the imperfection, of an established rule of distribution, can never itself become that rule or principle; because men will not work to give the produce of their labour away. Moreover, the only equivalents that can be offered in exchange for provision are *power* and *labour*. All property is *power*. What we call property in land, is the power to use it, and to exclude others from the use. Money is the representative of *power*, because it is convertible into power: the value of it consists in its faculty of procuring *power* over things and persons. But *power* which results from civil conventions (and of this kind is what we call a man's fortune or estate), is necessarily confined to a few, and is withal soon exhausted: whereas the capacity of *labour* is every man's natural possession, and composes a constant and renewing fund. The hire, therefore, or produce of personal industry, is that which the bulk of every community must bring to market, in exchange for the means of subsistence; in other words, employment must, in every country, be the medium of distribution, and the source of supply to individuals. But when we consider the *production* and *distribution* of provision, as distinct from, and independent of, each other; when, supposing the same quantity to be produced, we inquire in what way, or according to what rule, it may be *distributed*; we are led to a conception of the subject not at all agreeable to truth and reality: for, in truth and reality, though provision must be produced before it be distributed, yet the production depends, in a great measure, upon the distribution. The quantity of provision raised out of the ground, so far as the raising of it requires human art or labour, will evidently be regulated by the demand: the demand, or, in other words, the price and sale, being that which alone rewards the care, or excites the diligence, of the husbandman. But the sale of provision depends upon the number, not of those who want, but of those who have something to offer in return for what they want; not of those who would consume, but of those who can buy; that is, upon the number of those who have the fruits of some other kind of industry to tender in exchange for what they stand in need of from the production of the soil.

We see, therefore, the connexion between population and *employment*. Employment affects population "directly," as it affords the only medium of distribution by which individuals can obtain from the common stock a supply for the wants of their families: it affects population "indirectly," as it augments the stock itself of provision, in the only way by which the production of it can be effectually encouraged—by furnishing purchasers. No man can purchase without an equivalent; and that equivalent, by the generality of the people, must in every country be derived from employment.

And upon this basis is founded the public benefit of *trade*, that is to say, its subserviency to population, in which its only real utility consists. Of that industry, and of those arts and branches of trade, which are employed in the production, conveyance, and preparation, of any principal species of human food, as of the business of the husbandman, the butcher, baker, brewer, corn-merchant, &c. we acknowledge the necessity: likewise of those manufactures which furnish us with warm clothing, convenient habitations, domestic utensils, as of the weaver, tailor, smith, carpenter, &c. we perceive (in climates, however, like ours, removed at a distance from the sun) the conduciveness to population, by their rendering human life more healthy, vigorous, and comfortable. But not one half of the occupations which compose the trade of Europe fall within either of these descriptions. Perhaps two-thirds of the manufacturers in England are employed upon articles of confessed luxury, ornament, or splendour; in the superfluous embellishment of some articles which are useful in their kind, or upon others which have no conceivable use or value but what is founded in caprice or fashion. What can be less necessary, or less connected with the sustentation of human life, than the whole produce of the silk, lace, and plate manufactory? yet what multitudes labour in the different branches of these arts! What can be imagined more capricious than the fondness for tobacco and snuff? yet how many various occupations, and how many thousands in each, are set at work in administering to this frivolous gratification! Concerning trades of this kind (and this kind comprehends more than half of the trades that are exercised), it may fairly be asked, "How, since they add nothing to the stock of provision, do they tend to increase the number of the people?" We are taught to say of trade, "that it maintains multitudes"; but by what means does it *maintain* them, when it produces nothing upon which the support of human life depends? In like manner with respect to foreign commerce; of that merchandise which brings the necessaries of life into a country, which imports, for example, corn, or cattle, or cloth, or fuel, we allow the tendency to advance population, because it increases the stock of provision by which the people are subsisted. But this effect of foreign commerce is so little seen in our own country, that I believe, it may be affirmed of Great Britain, what Bishop Berkley said of a neighbouring island, that, if it were encompassed with a wall of brass fifty cubits high, the country might maintain the same number of inhabitants that find subsistence in it at present; and that every necessary, and even every real comfort and accommodation of human life, might be supplied in as great abundance as they now are. Here, therefore, as before, we may fairly ask, by what operation it is, that foreign commerce, which brings into the country no one article of human subsistence, promotes the multiplication of human life?

The answer of this inquiry will be contained in the discussion of another, *viz.*

Since the soil will maintain many more than it can employ, what must be done, supposing the country to be full, with the remainder of the inhabitants? They who, by the rules of partition (and some such must be established in every country), are entitled to the land; and they who, by their labour upon the soil, acquire a right in its produce; will not part with their property for nothing; or, rather, they will no longer raise from the soil what they can neither use themselves, nor exchange for what they want. Or, lastly, if these were willing to distribute what they could spare of the provision which the ground yielded, to others who had no share or concern in the property or cultivation of it, yet still the most enormous mischiefs would ensue from great numbers remaining unemployed. The idleness of one half of the community would overwhelm the whole with confusion and disorder. One only way presents itself of removing the difficulty which this question states, and which is simply this; that they, whose work is not wanted, nor can be employed, in the raising of provision out of the ground, convert their hands and ingenuity to the fabrication of articles which may gratify and requite those who are so employed, or who, by the division of lands in the country, are entitled to the exclusive possession of certain parts of them. By this contrivance, all things proceed well. The occupier of the ground raises from it the utmost that he can procure, because he is repaid for what he can spare by something else which he wants, or with which he is pleased: the artist or manufacturer, though he have neither any property in the soil, nor any concern in its cultivation, is regularly supplied with the produce, because he gives, in exchange for what he stands in need of, something upon which the receiver places an equal value: and the community is kept quiet, while both sides are engaged in their respective occupations.

It appears, then, that the business of one half of mankind is, to set the other half at work; that is, to provide articles which, by tempting the desires, may stimulate the industry, and call forth the activity, of those upon the exertion of whose industry, and the application of whose faculties, the production of human provision depends. A certain portion only of human labour is, or can be, *productive*; the rest is *instrumental*—both equally necessary, though the one have no other object than to excite the other. It appears also, that it signifies nothing, as to the main purpose of trade, how superfluous the articles which it furnishes are; whether the want of them be real or imaginary; whether it be founded in nature or in opinion, in fashion, habit, or emulation: it is enough that they be actually desired and sought after. Flourishing cities are raised and supported by trading in tobacco; populous towns subsist by the manufactory of ribands. A watch may be a very unnecessary appendage to the dress of a peasant; yet if the peasant will till the ground in order to obtain a watch, the true design of trade is answered: and the watch-maker, while he polishes the case, or files the wheels of his machine, is contributing to the production of corn as effectually, though not so directly, as if he handled the spade or held the plough. The use of tobacco has been mentioned already, not only as an acknowledged superfluity, but as affording a remarkable example of the caprice of human appetite: yet, if the fisherman will ply his nets, or the mariner fetch rice from foreign countries, in order to procure to himself this indulgence, the market is supplied with two important articles of provision, by the instrumentality of a merchandise which has no other apparent use than the gratification of a vitiated palate.

But it may come to pass that the husbandman, landowner, or whoever he be that is entitled to the produce of the soil, will no longer exchange it for what the manufacturer has to offer. He is already supplied to the extent of his desires. For instance, he wants no more cloth; he will no longer therefore give the weaver corn in return for the produce of his looms: but he would readily give it for tea, or for wine. When the weaver finds this to be the case, he has nothing to do but to send his cloth abroad, in exchange for tea or for wine, which he may barter for that provision which the offer of his cloth will no longer procure. The circulation is thus revived: and the benefit of the discovery is, that, whereas the number of weavers, who could find subsistence from their employment, was before limited by the consumption of cloth in the country, that number is now augmented, in proportion to the demand for tea and wine. This is the principle of *foreign* commerce. In the magnitude and complexity of the machine, the principle of motion is sometimes lost or unobserved; but it is always simple and the same, to whatever extent it may be diversified and enlarged in its operation.

The effect of trade upon agriculture, the process of which we have been endeavouring to describe, is visible in the neighbourhood of trading towns, and in those districts which carry on a communication with the markets of trading towns. The husbandmen are busy and skilful; the peasantry laborious; the land is managed to the best advantage; and double the quantity of corn or herbage (articles which are ultimately converted into human provision) raised from it, of what the same soil yields in remoter and more neglected parts of the country. Wherever a thriving manufactory finds means to establish itself, a new vegetation springs up around it. I believe it is true that agriculture never arrives at any considerable, much less at its highest, degree of perfection, where it is not connected with trade, that is, where the demand for the produce is not increased by the consumption of trading cities.

Let it be remembered then, that agriculture is the immediate source of human provision; that trade conduces to the production of provision only as it promotes agriculture; that the whole system of commerce, vast and various as it is, hath no other public importance than its subserviency to this end.

We return to the proposition we laid down, "that employment universally promotes population." From this proposition it follows, that the comparative utility of different branches of national commerce is measured by the number which each branch *employs*. Upon which principle a scale may easily be constructed, which shall assign to the several kinds and divisions of foreign trade their respective degrees of public importance. In this scale, the *first* place belongs to the exchange of wrought goods for raw materials, as of broad-cloth for raw silk; cutlery for wool; clocks or watches for iron, flax, or furs; because this traffic provides a market for the labour that has already been expended, at the same time that it supplies materials for new industry. Population always flourishes where this species of commerce obtains to any considerable degree. It is the cause of employment, or the certain indication. As it takes off the manufactures of the country, it promotes employment; as it brings in raw materials, it supposes the existence of manufactories in the country, and a demand for the article when manufactured. The *second* place is due to that commerce, which barters one species of wrought goods for another, as stuffs for cal-icoes, fustians for cambrics, leather for paper, or wrought goods for articles which require no farther preparation, as for wine, oil, tea, sugar, &c. This also assists employment; because, when the coun-try is stocked with one kind of manufacture, it renews the demand by converting it into another: but it is inferior to the former, as it promotes this end by one side only of the bargain—by what it car-ries out. The *last*, the lowest, and most disadvantageous species of commerce, is the exportation of raw materials in return for wrought goods: as when wool is sent abroad to purchase velvets; hides or peltry, to procure shoes, hats, or linen cloth. This trade is unfavourable to population, because it leaves no room or demand for employment, either in what it takes out of the country, or in what it brings into it. Its operation on both sides is noxious. By its exports, it diminishes the very subject upon which the industry of the inhabitants ought to be exercised; by its imports, it lessens the encouragement of that industry, in the same proportion that it sup-plies the consumption of the country with the produce of foreign labour. Of different branches of *manufactory*, those are, in their nature, the most beneficial, in which the price of the wrought article exceeds in the highest proportion that of the raw material: for this excess measures the quantity of employment, or, in other words, the number of manufacturers, which each branch sustains. The produce of the ground is never the most advantageous article of foreign commerce. Under a perfect state of public oeconomy, the soil of the country should be applied solely to the raising of provisions for the inhabitants, and its trade be supplied by their industry. A nation will never reach its proper extent of population, so long as its principal commerce consists in the exportation of corn or cattle, or even of wine, oil, tobacco, madder, indigo, tim-ber; because these last articles take up that surface which ought to be covered with the materials of human subsistence.

It must be here however noticed, that we have all along considered the inhabitants of a country as maintained by the produce of the country; and that what we have said is applicable with strictness to this supposition alone. The reasoning, nevertheless, may easily be adapted to a different case: for when provision is not produced, but *imported*, what has been affirmed concerning provision, will be, in a great measure, true of that article, whether it be money, produce, or labour, which is exchanged for provision. Thus, when the Dutch raise madder, and exchange it for corn; or when the people of America plant tobacco, and send it to Europe for cloth; the cultivation of madder and tobacco becomes as necessary to the subsistence of the inhabitants, and by consequence will affect the state of population in these countries as sensibly, as the actual production of food, or the manufactory of raiment. In like manner, when the same inhabitants of Holland earn money by the carriage of the produce of one country to another, and with that money purchase the provision from abroad which their own land is not extensive enough to supply, the increase or decline of this carrying trade will influence the numbers of the people no less than similar changes would do in the cultivation of the soil.

The few principles already established will enable us to describe the effects upon population which may be expected from the following important articles of national conduct and oeconomy:

I. Emigration. *Emigration* may be either the overflowing of a country, or the desertion. As the increase of the species is indefinite; and the number of inhabitants which any given tract or surface can support, finite; it is evident that great numbers may be constantly leaving a country, and yet the country remain constantly full. Or whatever be the cause which invincibly limits the population of a country; when the number of the people has arrived at that limit, the progress of generation, beside continuing the succession, will supply multitudes for foreign emigration. In these two cases, emigration neither indicates any political decay, nor in truth diminishes the number of the people; nor ought to be prohibited or discouraged. But emigrants may relinquish their country, from a sense of insecurity, oppression, annoyance, and inconveniency. Neither, again, *here* is it emigration which wastes the people, but the evils that occasion it. It would be in vain, if it were practicable, to confine the inhabitants at home; for the same causes which drive them out of the country, would prevent their multiplication if they remained in it. Lastly; men may be tempted to change their situation by the allurement of a better climate, of a more refined or luxurious manner of living; by the prospect of wealth; or, sometimes, by the mere nominal advantage of higher wages and prices. This class of emigrants, with whom alone the laws can interfere with effect, will never, I think, be numerous. With the generality of a people, the attachment of mankind to their homes and country, the irksomeness of seeing new habitations, and of living amongst strangers, will outweigh, so long as men possess the necessaries of life in safety, or at least so long as they can obtain a provision for that mode of subsistence which the class of citizens to which they belong are accustomed to enjoy, all the inducements that the advantages of a foreign land can offer. There appear, therefore, to be few cases in which emigration can be prohibited, with advantage to the state; it appears also that emigration is an equivocal symptom, which will probably accompany the decline of the political body, but which may likewise attend a condition of perfect health and vigour.

II. Colonisation. The only view under which our subject will permit us to consider *colonisation*, is in its tendency to augment the population of the parent state. Suppose a fertile, but empty island, to lie within the reach of a country in which arts and manufactures are already established; suppose a colony sent out from such a country, to take possession of the island, and to live there under the protection and authority of their native government: the new settlers will naturally convert their labour to the cultivation of the vacant soil, and with the produce of that soil will draw a supply of manufactures from their countrymen at home. Whilst the inhabitants continue few, and lands cheap and fresh, the colonists will find it easier and more profitable to raise corn, or rear cattle, and with corn and cattle to purchase woollen cloth, for instance, or linen, than to spin or weave these articles for themselves. The mother-country, meanwhile, derives from this connexion an increase both of provision and employment. It promotes at once the two great requisites upon which the facility of subsistence, and by consequence the state of population, depend—*production* and *distribution;* and this in a manner the most direct and beneficial. No situation can be imagined more favourable to population, than that of a country which works up goods for others, whilst these others are cultivating new tracts of land for them: for as, in a genial climate, and from a fresh soil, the labour of one man will raise provision enough for ten, it is manifest that, where all are employed in agriculture, much the greater part of the produce will be spared from the consumption; and that three out of four, at least of those who are maintained by it, will reside in the country which receives the redundancy. When the new country does not remit *provision* to the old one, the advantage is less; but still the exportation of wrought goods, by whatever return they are paid for, advances population in that secondary way, in which those trades promote it that are not employed in the production of provision. Whatever prejudice, therefore, some late events have excited against schemes of colonisation, the system itself is founded in apparent national utility; and what is more, upon principles favourable to the common interest of human nature; for it does not appear by what other method newly discovered and unfrequented countries can be peopled, or during the infancy of their establishment be protected or supplied. The error which we of this nation at present lament seems to have consisted not so much in the original formation of colonies, as in the subsequent management; in imposing restrictions too rigorous, or in continuing them too long; in not perceiving the point of time when the irresistible order and progress of human affairs demand a change of laws and policy.

III. MONEY. Where *money* abounds, the people are generally numerous: yet gold and silver neither feed nor clothe mankind; nor are they in all countries converted into provision by purchasing the necessaries of life at foreign markets; nor do they, in any country, compose those articles of personal or domestic ornament which certain orders of the community have learnt to regard as necessaries of life, and without the means of procuring which they will not enter into family-establishments: at least, this property of the precious metals obtains in a very small degree. The effect of money upon the number of the people, though visible to observation, is not explained without some difficulty. To understand this connexion properly, we must return to the proposition with which we concluded our reasoning upon the subject; "that population is chiefly promoted by employment." Now of employment, money is partly the indication, and partly the cause. The only way in which money regularly and spontaneously *flows into* a country, is in return for the goods that are sent out of it, or the work that is performed by it; and the only way in which money is *retained in* a country, is by the country's supplying, in a great measure, its own consumption of manufactures. Consequently, the quantity of money found in a country, denotes the amount of labour and employment: but still, employment, not money, is the cause of population; the accumulation of money being merely a collateral effect of the same cause, or a circumstance which accompanies the existence, and measures the operation, of that cause. And this is true of money, only whilst it is acquired by the industry of the inhabitants. The treasures which belong to a country by the possession of mines, or by the exaction of tribute from foreign dependencies, afford no conclusion concerning the state of population. The influx from these sources may be immense, and yet the country remain poor and ill-peopled; of which we see an egregious example in the condition of Spain, since the acquisition of its South-American dominions.

But, secondly, money may become also a real and an operative *cause* of population, by acting as a stimulus to industry, and by facilitating the means of subsistence. The ease of subsistence, and the encouragement of industry, depend neither upon the price of labour, nor upon the price of provision, but upon the proportion which one bears to the other. Now the influx of money into a country, naturally tends to advance this proportion; that is, every fresh accession of money raises the price of labour before it raises the price of provision. When money is brought from abroad, the persons, be they who they will, into whose hands it first arrives, do not buy up provision with it, but apply it to the purchase and payment of labour. If the state receives it, the state dispenses what it receives amongst soldiers, sailors, artificers, engineers, shipwrights, workmen; if private persons bring home treasures of gold and silver, they usually expend them in the building of houses, the improvement of estates, the purchase of furniture, dress, equipage, in articles of luxury or splendor; if the merchant be enriched by returns of his foreign commerce, he applies his increased capital to the enlargement of his business at home. The money ere long comes to market for provision; but it comes thither through the hands of the manufacturer, the artist, the husbandman, and labourer. Its effect, therefore, upon the price of art and labour, will *precede* its effect upon the price of provision; and during the interval between one effect and the other, the means of subsistence will be multiplied and facilitated, as well as industry be excited by new

rewards. When the greater plenty of money in circulation has produced an advance in the price of provision, corresponding to the
advanced price of labour, its effect ceases. The labourer no longer
gains any thing by the increase of his wages. It is not, therefore, the
quantity of specie collected into a country, but the continual
increase of that quantity, from which the advantage arises to
employment and population. It is only the *accession* of money which
produces the effect, and it is only by money constantly flowing into
a country that the effect can be constant. Now whatever consequence arises to the country from the influx of money, the contrary
may be expected to follow from the diminution of its quantity: and
accordingly we find, that whatever cause drains off the specie of a
country, faster than the streams which feed it can supply, not only
impoverishes the country, but depopulates it. The knowledge and
experience of this effect have given occasion to a phrase which
occurs in almost every discourse upon commerce or politics. The
balance of trade with any foreign nation is said to be against or in
favour of a country, simply as it tends to carry money out, or bring
it in; that is, according as the price of the imports exceeds or falls
short of the price of the exports: so invariably is the increase or
diminution of the specie of a country regarded as a test of the public advantage or detriment which arises from any branch of its
commerce.

IV. TAXATION. As *taxes* take nothing out of a country; as they
do not diminish the public stock, only vary the distribution of it;
they are not necessarily prejudicial to population. If the state exact
money from certain members of the community, she dispenses it
also amongst other members of the same community. They who
contribute to the revenue, and they who are supported or benefited
by the expenses of government, are to be placed one against the
other: and whilst what the subsistence of one part is profited by
receiving, compensates for what that of the other suffers by paying,

the common fund of the society is not lessened. This is true: but it must be observed, that although the sum distributed by the state be always *equal* to the sum collected from the people, yet the gain and loss to the means of subsistence may be very *unequal*; and the balance will remain on the wrong or the right side of the account, according as the money passes by taxation from the industrious to the idle, from the many to the few, from those who want to those who abound, or in a contrary direction. For instance: a tax upon coaches, to be laid out in the repair of roads, would probably improve the population of a neighbourhood; a tax upon cottages, to be ultimately expended in the purchase and support of coaches, would certainly diminish it. In like manner, a tax upon wine or tea distributed in bounties to fishermen or husbandmen would augment the provision of a country; a tax upon fisheries and husbandry, however indirect and concealed, to be converted, when raised, to the procuring of wine or tea for the idle and opulent, would naturally impair the public stock. The effect, therefore, of taxes, upon the means of subsistence, depends not so much upon the amount of the sum levied, as upon the object of the tax and the application. Taxes likewise may be so adjusted as to conduce to the restraint of luxury, and the correction of vice; to the encouragement of industry, trade, agriculture, and marriage. Taxes thus contrived, become rewards and penalties; not only sources of revenue, but instruments of police. Vices indeed themselves cannot be taxed, without holding forth such a conditional toleration of them as to destroy men's perception of their guilt; a tax comes to be considered as a commutation: the materials, however, and incentives of vice may. Although, for instance, drunkenness would be, on this account, an unfit object of taxation, yet public houses and spirituous liquors are very properly subjected to heavy imposts.

Nevertheless, although it may be true that taxes cannot be pronounced to be detrimental to population, by any absolute necessity in their nature; and though, under some modifications, and when urged only to a certain extent, they may even operate in favour of it; yet it will be found, in a great plurality of instances, that their tendency is noxious. Let it be supposed that nine families inhabit a neighbourhood, each possessing barely the means of subsistence, or of that mode of subsistence which custom hath established amongst them; let a tenth family be quartered upon these, to be supported by a tax raised from the nine; or rather, let one of the nine have his income augmented by a similar deduction from the incomes of the rest; in either of these cases, it is evident that the whole district would be broken up: for as the entire income of each is supposed to be barely sufficient for the establishment which it maintains, a deduction of any part destroys that establishment. Now it is no answer to this objection, it is no apology for the grievance, to say, that nothing is taken out of the neighbourhood; that the stock is not diminished: the mischief is done by deranging the distribution. Nor, again, is the luxury of one family, or even the maintenance of an additional family, a recompense to the country for the ruin of nine others. Nor, lastly, will it alter the effect, though it may conceal the cause, that the contribution, instead of being levied directly upon each day's wages, is mixed up in the price of some article of constant use and consumption, as in a tax upon candles, malt, leather, or fuel. This example illustrates the tendency of taxes to obstruct subsistence; and the minutest degree of this obstruction will be felt in the formation of families. The example, indeed, forms an extreme case; the evil is magnified, in order to render its operation distinct and visible. In real life, families may not be broken up, or forced from their habitation, houses be quitted, or countries suddenly deserted, in consequence of any new imposition whatever; but marriages will become gradually less frequent.

It seems necessary, however, to distinguish between the operation of a new tax, and the effect of taxes which have been long established. In the course of circulation, the money may flow back to the hands from which it was taken. The proportion between the supply and the expense of subsistence, which had been disturbed by the tax, may at length recover itself again. In the instance just now stated, the addition of a tenth family to the neighbourhood, or the enlarged expenses of one of the nine, may, in some shape or other, so advance the profits, or increase the employment, of the rest, as to make full restitution for the share of their property of which it deprives them; or, what is more likely to happen, a reduction may take place in their mode of living, suited to the abridgement of their incomes. Yet still the ultimate and permanent effect of taxation, though distinguishable from the impression of a new tax, is generally adverse to population. The *proportion* above spoken of, can only be restored by one side or other of the following alternative: by the people either contracting their wants, which at the same time diminishes consumption and employment; or by raising the price of labour, which necessarily adding to the price of the productions and manufactures of the country, checks their sale at foreign markets. A nation which is burthened with taxes must always be undersold by a nation which is free from them, unless the difference be made up by some singular advantage of climate, soil, skill, or industry. This quality belongs to all taxes which affect the mass of the community, even when imposed upon the properest objects, and applied to the fairest purposes. But abuses are inseparable from the disposal of public money. As governments are usually administered, the produce of public taxes is expended upon a train of gentry, in the maintaining of pomp, or in the purchase of influence. The conversion of property which taxes effectuate, when they are employed in this manner, is attended with obvious evils. It takes from the industrious, to give to the idle; it increases the number of the latter; it tends to accumulation; it sacrifices the conveniency of many to the luxury of a few; it makes no return to the people, from whom the tax is drawn, that is satisfactory or intelligible; it encourages no activity which is useful or productive.

The sum to be raised being settled, a wise statesman will contrive his taxes principally with a view to their effect upon *population*; that is, he will so adjust them as to give the least possible obstruction to those means of subsistence by which the mass of the community is maintained. We are accustomed to an opinion that a tax, to be just, ought to be accurately proportioned to the circumstances of the persons who pay it. But upon what, it might be asked, is this opinion founded; unless it could be shown that such a proportion interferes the least with the general conveniency of subsistence? Whereas I should rather believe, that a tax, constructed with a view to that conveniency, ought to rise upon the different classes of the community, in a much higher ratio than the simple proportion of their incomes. The point to be regarded is, not what men have, but what they can spare; and it is evident that a man who possesses a thousand pounds a year can more easily give up a hundred, than a man with a hundred pounds a year can part with ten; that is, those habits of life which are reasonable and innocent, and upon the ability to continue which the formation of families depends, will be much less affected by the one deduction than the other: it is still more evident, that a man of a hundred pounds a year would not be so much distressed in his subsistence, by a demand from him of ten pounds, as a man of ten pounds a year would be by the loss of one: to which we must add, that the population of every country being replenished by the marriages of the lowest ranks of the society, their accommodation and relief become of more importance to the state, than the conveniency of any higher but less numerous order of its citizens. But whatever be the proportion which public expediency directs, whether the simple, the duplicate, or any higher or immediate, proportion of men's incomes, it can never be attained by any *single* tax; as no single object of taxation can be found, which measures the ability of the subject with suffi-cient generality and exactness. It is only by a system and variety of taxes mutually balancing and equalising one another, that a due proportion can be preserved. For instance: if a tax upon lands press with greater hardship upon those who live in the country, it may be properly counterpoised by a tax upon the rent of houses, which will affect principally the inhabitants of large towns. Distinctions may also be framed in some taxes, which shall allow abatements or exemptions to married persons; to the parents of a certain number of legitimate children; to improvers of the soil; to particular modes of cultivation, as to tillage in preference to pasturage; and in gen-eral to that industry which is immediately *productive*, in preference to that which is only *instrumental;* but above all, which may leave the heaviest part of the burthen upon the methods, whatever they be, of acquiring wealth without industry, or even of subsisting in idleness.

V. EXPORTATION OF BREAD-CORN. Nothing seems to have a more positive tendency to reduce the number of the people, than the sending abroad part of the provision by which they are main-tained; yet this has been the policy of legislators very studious of the improvement of their country. In order to reconcile ourselves to a practice which appears to militate with the chief interest, that is, with the population, of the country that adopts it, we must be reminded of a maxim which belongs to the productions both of nature and art, "that it is impossible to have enough without a superfluity." The point of sufficiency cannot, in any case, be so exactly hit upon, as to have nothing to spare, yet never to want. This is peculiarly true of bread-corn, of which the annual increase is extremely variable. As it is necessary that the crop be adequate to the consumption in a year of scarcity, it must, of consequence, greatly exceed it in a year of plenty. A redundancy therefore will occasionally arise from the very care that is taken to secure the people against the danger of want; and it is manifest that the exportation of this redundancy subtracts nothing from the number that can regularly be maintained by the produce of the soil. Moreover, as the exportation of corn, under these circumstances, is attended with no direct injury to population, so the benefits which indirectly arise to population, from foreign commerce, belong to this, in common with other species of trade; together with the peculiar advantage of presenting a constant incitement to the skill and industry of the husbandman, by the promise of a certain sale and an adequate price, under every contingency of season and produce. There is another situation, in which corn may not only be exported, but in which the people can thrive by no other means; that is, of a newly settled country with a fertile soil. The exportation of a large proportion of the corn which a country produces, proves, it is true, that the inhabitants have not yet attained to the number which the country is capable of maintaining: but it does not prove but that they may be hastening to this limit with the utmost practicable celerity, which is the perfection to be sought for in a young establishment. In all cases except those two, and in the former of them to any greater degree than what is necessary to take off occasional redundancies, the exportation of corn is either itself noxious to population, or argues a defect of population arising from some other cause.

VI. ABRIDGEMENT OF LABOUR. It has long been made a question, whether those mechanical contrivances which *abridge labour*, by performing the same work by fewer hands, be detrimental or not to the population of a country. From what has been delivered in preceding parts of the present chapter, it will be evident that this question is equivalent to another—whether such contrivances diminish or not the quantity of employment. The first and most obvious effect undoubtedly is this; because, if one man be made to do what three men did before, two are immediately discharged: but if, by some more general and remoter consequence, they increase the demand for work, or, what is the same thing, prevent the diminution of that demand, in a greater proportion than they contract the number of hands by which it is performed, the quantity of employment, upon the whole, will gain an addition. Upon which principle it may be observed, first, that whenever a mechanical invention succeeds in one place, it is necessary that it be imitated in every other where the same manufacture is carried on: for, it is manifest that he who has the benefit of a conciser operation, will soon outvie and undersell a competitor who continues to use a more circuitous labour. It is also true, in the second place, that whoever *first* discover or adopt a mechanical improvement, will, for some time, draw to themselves an increase of employment; and that this preference may continue even after the improvement has become general; for, in every kind of trade, it is not only a great but permanent advantage, to have once pre-occupied the public reputation. Thirdly, after every superiority which might be derived from the possession of a secret has ceased, it may be well questioned whether even then any loss can accrue to employment. The same money will be spared to the same article still. Wherefore, in proportion as the article can be afforded at a lower price, by reason of an easier or shorter process in the manufacture, it will either grow into more general use, or an improvement will take place in the quality and fabric, which will demand a proportionable addition of hands. The number of persons employed in the manufactory of stockings has not, I apprehend, decreased since the invention of stocking-mills. The amount of what is expended upon the article, after subtracting from it the price of the raw material, and consequently what is paid for work in this branch of our manufactories, is not less than it was before. Goods of a finer texture are worn in the place of coarser. This is the change which the invention has produced; and which compensates to the manufactory for every other inconveniency. Add to which, that in the above, and in almost every instance, an improvement which conduces to the recommendation of a manufactory, either by the cheapness or the quality of the goods, draws up after it many dependent employments, in which no abbreviation has taken place.

From the reasoning that has been pursued, and the various considerations suggested in this chapter, a judgement may, in some sort, be formed, how far regulations of law are in their nature capable of contributing to the support and advancement of population. I say *how far:* for, as in many subjects, so especially in those which relate to commerce, to plenty, to riches, and to the number of people, more is wont to be expected from laws than laws can do. Laws can only imperfectly restrain that dissoluteness of manners, which by diminishing the frequency of marriages, impairs the very source of population. Laws cannot regulate the wants of mankind, their mode of living, or their desire of those superfluities which fashion, more irresistible than laws, has once introduced into general usage; or, in other words, has erected into necessaries of life. Laws cannot induce men to enter into marriages, when the expenses of a family must deprive them of that system of accommodation to which they have habituated their expectations. Laws, by their protection, by assuring to the labourer the fruit and profit of his labour, may help to make a people industrious; but without industry, the laws cannot provide either subsistence or employment; laws cannot make corn grow without toil and care, or trade flourish without art and diligence. In spite of all laws, the expert, laborious, honest workman will be *employed*, in preference to the lazy, the unskilful, the fraudulent, and evasive: and this is not more true of two inhabitants of the same village, than it is of the people of two different countries, which communicate either with each other, or with the rest of the world. The natural basis of trade is rivalship of quality and price; or, which is the same thing, of skill and industry. Every attempt to *force* trade by operation of law, that is, by compelling persons to buy goods at one market, which they can obtain cheaper and better from another, is sure to be either eluded by the quick-sightedness and incessant activity of private interest, or to be frustrated by retaliation. One half of the commercial laws of many states are calculated merely to counteract the restrictions which have been imposed by other states. Perhaps the only way in which the interposition of law is salutary in trade, is in the prevention of frauds.

Next to the indispensable requisites of internal peace and security, the chief advantage which can be derived to population from the interference of law, appears to me to consist in the encouragement of *agriculture*. This, at least, is the direct way of increasing the number of the people: every other mode being effectual only by its influence upon this. Now the principal expedient by which such a purpose can be promoted, is to adjust the laws of property, as nearly as possible, to the following rules: first, "to give to the occupier all the power over the soil which is necessary for its perfect cultivation"; secondly, "to assign the whole profit of every improvement to the persons by whose activity it is carried on." What we call property in land, as hath been observed above, is power over it. Now it is indifferent to the public in whose hands this power resides, if it be rightly used; it matters not to whom the land belongs, if it be well cultivated. When we lament that great estates are often united in the same hand, or complain that one man possesses what would be sufficient for a thousand, we suffer ourselves to be misled by words. The owner of ten thousand pounds a year, *consumes* little more of the produce of the soil than the owner of ten pounds a year. If the cultivation be equal, the estate in the hands of one great lord, affords subsistence and employment to the same number of persons as it would do if it were divided amongst a hundred proprietors. In like manner we ought to judge of the effect upon the public interest, which may arise from lands being holden by the king, or by the subject; by private persons, or by corporations; by laymen, or ecclesiastics; in fee, or for life; by virtue of office, or in right of inheritance. I do not mean that these varieties make no difference, but I mean that all the difference they do make respects the cultivation of the lands which are so holden.

There exist in this country, conditions of tenure which condemn the land itself to perpetual sterility. Of this kind is the right of *common*, which precludes each proprietor from the improvement, or even the convenient occupation, of his estate, without (what seldom can be obtained) the consent of many others. This tenure is also usually embarrassed by the interference of *manorial* claims, under which it often happens that the surface belongs to one owner, and the soil to another; so that neither owner can stir a clod without the concurrence of his partner in the property. In many manors, the tenant is restrained from granting leases beyond a short term of years; which renders every plan of solid improvement impracticable. In these cases, the owner wants, what the first rule of rational policy requires, "sufficient power over the soil for its perfect cultivation." This power ought to be extended to him by some easy and general law of enfranchisement, partition, and enclosure; which, though compulsory upon the lord, or the rest of the tenants, whilst it has in view the melioration of the soil, and tenders an equitable compensation for every right that it takes away, is neither more arbitrary, nor more dangerous to the stability of property, than that which is done in the construction of roads, bridges, embankments, navigable canals, and indeed in almost every public work, in which private owners of land are obliged to accept that price for their property which an indifferent jury may award. It may here, however, be proper to observe, that although the enclosure of wastes and pastures be generally beneficial to population, yet the enclosure of lands in tillage, in order to convert them into pastures, is as generally hurtful.

But, secondly, agriculture is discouraged by every constitution of landed property which lets in those, who have no concern in the improvement, to a participation of the profit. This objection is applicable to all such customs of manors as subject the proprietor, upon the death of the lord or tenant, or the alienation of the estate, to a fine apportioned to the improved value of the land. But of all institutions which are in this way adverse to cultivation and improvement, none is so noxious as that of *tithes*. A claimant here enters into the produce, who contributed no assistance whatever to the production. When years, perhaps, of care and toil have matured an improvement; when the husbandman sees new crops ripening to his skill and industry; the moment he is ready to put his sickle to the grain, he finds himself compelled to divide his harvest with a stranger. Tithes are a tax not only upon industry, but upon that industry which feeds mankind; upon that species of exertion which it is the aim of all wise laws to cherish and promote; and to uphold and excite which, composes, as we have seen, the main benefit that the community receives from the whole system of trade and the success of commerce. And, together with the more general inconveniency that attends the exaction of tithes, there is this additional evil, in the mode at least according to which they are collected at present, that they operate as a bounty upon pasturage. The burthen of the tax falls with its chief, if not with its whole weight, upon tillage; that is to say, upon that precise mode of cultivation which, as hath been shown above, it is the business of the state to relieve and remunerate, in preference to every other. No measure of such extensive concern appears to me so practicable, nor any single alteration so beneficial, as the conversion of tithes into corn-rents. This commutation, I am convinced, might be so adjusted, as to secure to the tithe-holder a complete and perpetual equivalent for his interest, and to leave to industry its full operation, and entire reward.

Chapter 12
OF WAR, AND MILITARY ESTABLISHMENTS

Because the Christian Scriptures describe wars, as what they are, as crimes or judgements, some have been led to believe that it is unlawful for a Christian to bear arms. But it should be remembered that it may be necessary for individuals to unite their force, and for this end to resign themselves to the direction of a common will: and yet, it may be true that that will is often actuated by criminal motives, and often determined to destructive purposes. Hence, although the origin of wars be ascribed, in Scripture, to the operation of lawless and malignant passion;* and though war itself be enumerated among the sorest calamities with which a land can be visited, the profession of a soldier is nowhere forbidden or condemned. When the soldiers demanded of John the Baptist what they should do, he said unto them, "Do violence to no man, neither accuse any falsely, and be content with your wages."† In which answer we do not find that, in order to prepare themselves for the reception of the kingdom of God, it was required of soldiers to relinquish their profession, but only that they should beware of the vices of which that profession was accused. The precept which follows, "Be content with your wages," supposed them to continue in

*James, iv. 1.
†Luke, iii. 14.

their situation. It was of a Roman centurion that Christ pronounced that memorable eulogy, "I have not found so great faith, no, not in Israel."* The first Gentile convert[†] who was received into the Christian church, and to whom the Gospel was imparted by the immediate and especial direction of Heaven, held the same station: and in the history of this transaction we discover not the smallest intimation, that Cornelius, upon becoming a Christian, quitted the service of the Roman legion; that his profession was objected to, or his continuance in it considered as in any wise inconsistent with his new character.

In applying the principles of morality to the affairs of nations, the difficulty which meets us, arises from hence, "that the particular consequence sometimes appears to exceed the value of the general rule." In this circumstance is founded the only distinction that exists between the case of independent states, and of independent individuals. In the transactions of private persons, no advantage that results from the breach of a general law of justice, can compensate to the public for the violation of the law; in the concerns of empire, this may sometimes be doubted. Thus, that the faith of promises ought to be maintained, as far as is lawful, and as far as was intended by the parties, whatever inconveniency either of them may suffer by his fidelity, in the intercourse of private life, is seldom disputed; because it is evident to almost every man who reflects upon the subject, that the common happiness gains more by the preservation of the rule, than it could do by the removal of the inconveniency. But when the adherence to a public treaty would enslave a whole people; would block up seas, rivers, or harbours; depopulate cities; condemn fertile regions to eternal desolation; cut off a country from its sources of provision, or deprive it of those

*Luke, vii. 9.
[†] Acts, x. 1.

commercial advantages to which its climate, produce, or situation naturally entitle it: the magnitude of the particular evil induces us to call in question the obligation of the general rule. Moral Philosophy furnishes no precise solution to these doubts. She cannot pronounce that any rule of morality is so rigid as to bend to no exceptions; nor, on the other hand, can she comprise these exceptions within any previous description. She confesses that the obligation of every law depends upon its ultimate utility; that, this utility having a finite and determinate value, situations may be feigned, and consequently may possibly arise, in which the general tendency is outweighed by the enormity of the particular mischief: but she recalls, at the same time, to the consideration of the inquirer, the almost inestimable importance, as of other general rules of relative justice, so especially of national and personal fidelity; the unseen, if not unbounded, extent of the mischief which must follow from the want of it; the danger of leaving it to the sufferer to decide upon the comparison of particular and general consequences; and the still greater danger of such decisions being drawn into future precedents. If treaties, for instance, be no longer binding than whilst they are convenient, or until the inconveniency ascend to a certain point (which point must be fixed by the judgement, or rather by the feelings, of the complaining party); or if such an opinion, after being authorised by a few examples, come at length to prevail; one and almost the only method of averting or closing the calamities of war, of either preventing or putting a stop to the destruction of mankind, is lost to the world for ever. We do not say, that no evil can exceed this, nor any possible advantage compensate it; but we say that a loss, which affects *all*, will scarcely be made up to the common stock of human happiness by any benefit that can be procured to a single nation, which, however respectable when compared with any other single nation, bears an inconsiderable proportion to the whole. These, however, are the principles upon which the calculation is to be formed. It is enough, in this place, to remark the cause which produces the hesitation that we sometimes feel, in applying rules of personal probity to the conduct of nations.

As between individuals it is found impossible to ascertain every duty by an immediate reference to public utility, not only because such reference is oftentimes too remote for the direction of private consciences, but because a multitude of cases arise in which it is indifferent to the general interest by what rule men act, though it be absolutely necessary that they act by some constant and known rule or other: and as, for these reasons, certain positive constitutions are wont to be established in every society, which, when established, become as obligatory as the original principles of natural justice themselves; so, likewise, it is between independent communities. Together with those maxims of universal equity which are common to states and to individuals, and by which the rights and conduct of the one as well as the other ought to be adjusted, when they fall within the scope and application of such maxims; there exists also amongst sovereigns a system of artificial jurisprudence, under the name of the *law of nations.* In this code are found the rules which determine the right to vacant or newly discovered countries; those which relate to the protection of fugitives, the privileges of ambassadors, the condition and duties of neutrality, the immunities of neutral ships, ports, and coasts, the distance from shore to which these immunities extend, the distinction between free and contraband goods, and a variety of subjects of the same kind. Concerning which examples, and indeed the principal part of what is called the *jus gentium,* it may be observed, that the rules derive their moral force (by which I mean the regard that ought to be paid to them by the consciences of sovereigns), not from their internal reasonableness or justice, for many of them are perfectly arbitrary, nor yet from the authority

by which they were established, for the greater part have grown
insensibly into usage, without any public compact, formal
acknowledgement, or even known original; but simply from the
fact of their being established, and the general duty of conform-
ing to established rules upon questions, and between parties,
where nothing but positive regulations can prevent disputes, and
where disputes are followed by such destructive consequences.
The first of the instances which we have just now enumerated,
may be selected for the illustration of this remark. The nations of
Europe consider the sovereignty of newly discovered countries as
belonging to the prince or state whose subject makes the discovery; and, in pursuance of this rule, it is usual for a navigator, who
falls upon an unknown shore, to take possession of it, in the name
of his sovereign at home, by erecting his standard, or displaying
his flag, upon a desert coast. Now nothing can be more fanciful,
or less substantiated by any considerations of reason or justice,
than the right which such discovery, or the transient occupation
and idle ceremony that accompany it, confer upon the country of
the discoverer. Nor can any stipulation be produced, by which the
rest of the world have bound themselves to submit to this preten-
sion. Yet when we reflect that the claims to newly discovered
countries can hardly be settled, between the different nations
which frequent them, without some positive rule or other; that
such claims, if left unsettled, would prove sources of ruinous and
fatal contentions; that the rule already proposed, however arbitrary, possesses one principal quality of a rule—determination
and certainty; above all, that it is acquiesced in, and that no one
has power to substitute another, however he might contrive a better, in its place: when we reflect upon these properties of the rule,
or rather upon these consequences of rejecting its authority, we
are led to ascribe to it the virtue and obligation of a precept of natural justice, because we perceive in it that which is the foundation

of justice itself—public importance and utility. And a prince who should dispute this rule, for the want of regularity in its formation, or of intelligible justice in its principle, and by such disputes should disturb the tranquillity of nations, and at the same time lay the foundation of future disturbances, would be little less criminal than he who breaks the public peace by a violation of engagements to which he had himself consented, or by an attack upon those national rights which are founded immediately in the law of nature, and in the first perceptions of equity. The same thing may be repeated of the rules which the law of nations prescribes in the other instances that were mentioned, namely, that the obscurity of their origin, or the arbitrariness of their principle, subtracts nothing from the respect that is due to them, when once established.

***

War may be considered with a view to its *causes* and to its *conduct*.

The *justifying* causes of war are, deliberate invasions of right, and the necessity of maintaining such a balance of power amongst neighbouring nations, as that no single state, or confederacy of states, be strong enough to overwhelm the rest. The objects of just war are, precaution, defence, or reparation. In a larger sense, every just war is a *defensive* war, inasmuch as every just war supposes an injury perpetrated, attempted, or feared.

The *insufficient* causes or *unjustifiable* motives of war, are the family alliances, the personal friendships, or the personal quarrels, of princes; the internal disputes which are carried on in other nations; the justice of other wars; the extension of territory, or of trade; the misfortunes or accidental weakness of a neighbouring or rival nation.

There are *two* lessons of rational and sober policy, which, if it were possible to inculcate them into the councils of princes, would exclude many of the motives of war, and allay that restless ambition which is constantly stirring up one part of mankind against another. The first of these lessons admonishes princes to "place their glory and their emulation, not in extent of territory, but in raising the greatest quantity of happiness out of a given territory." The enlargement of territory by conquest is not only not a just object of war, but in the greater part of the instances in which it is attempted, not even desirable. It is certainly not desirable where it adds nothing to the numbers, the enjoyments, or the security, of the conquerors. What commonly is gained to a nation, by the annexing of new dependencies, or the subjugation of other countries to its dominion, but a wider frontier to defend; more interfering claims to vindicate; more quarrels, more enemies, more rebellions, to encounter; a greater force to keep up by sea and land; more services to provide for, and more establishments to pay? And, in order to draw from these acquisitions something that may make up for the charge of keeping them, a revenue is to be extorted, or a monopoly to be enforced and watched, at an expense which costs half their produce. Thus the provinces are oppressed, in order to pay for being ill-governed; and the original state is exhausted in maintaining a feeble authority over discontented subjects. No assignable portion of country is benefited by the change; and if the sovereign appear to himself to be enriched or strengthened, when every part of his dominion is made poorer and weaker than it was, it is probable that he is deceived by appearances. Or were it true that the grandeur of the prince is magnified by those exploits; the glory which is purchased, and the ambition which is gratified, by the distress of one country without adding to the happiness of another, which at the same time enslaves the new and impoverishes the ancient part of the empire, by whatever names it may be known or flattered, ought to be an object of universal execration; and oftentimes not more so to the vanquished, than to the very people whose armies or whose treasures have achieved the victory.

There are, indeed, two cases in which the extension of territory may be of real advantage, and to both parties. The first is, where an empire thereby reaches to the natural boundaries which divide it from the rest of the world. Thus we account the British Channel the natural boundary which separates the nations of England and France; and if France possessed any countries on this, or England any cities or provinces on that, side of the sea, recovery of such towns and districts to what may be called their natural sovereign, though it may not be a just reason for commencing war, would be a proper use to make of victory. The other case is, where neighbouring states, being severally too small and weak to defend themselves against the dangers that surround them, can only be safe by a strict and constant junction of their strength: here conquest will effect the purposes of confederation and alliance; and the union which it produces is often more close and permanent than that which results from voluntary association. Thus, if the heptarchy had continued in England, the different kingdoms of it might have separately fallen a prey to foreign invasion: and although the interest and danger of one part of the island were in truth common to every other part, it might have been difficult to have circulated this persuasion amongst independent nations; or to have united them in any regular or steady opposition to their continental enemies, had not the valour and fortune of an enterprising prince incorporated the whole into a single monarchy. Here, the conquered gained as much by the revolution, as the conquerors. In like manner, and for the same reason, when the two royal families of Spain were met together in one race of princes, and the several provinces of France had devolved into the possession of a single sovereign, it became unsafe for the inhabitants of Great Britain any longer to

remain under separate governments. The union of England and
Scotland, which transformed two quarrelsome neighbours into
one powerful empire, and which was first brought about by the
course of succession, and afterwards completed by amicable convention, would have been a fortunate conclusion of hostilities, had
it been effected by the operations of war. These two cases being
admitted, namely, the obtaining of natural boundaries and barriers,
and the including under the same government those who have a
common danger and a common enemy to guard against; I know
not whether a third can be thought of, in which the extension of
empire by conquest is useful even to the conquerors.

The second rule of prudence which ought to be recommended
to those who conduct the affairs of nations, is "never to pursue
national *honour* as distinct from national *interest.*" This rule
acknowledges that it is often necessary to assert the honour of a
nation for the sake of its interest. The spirit and courage of a people
are supported by flattering their pride. Concessions which betray
too much of fear or weakness, though they relate to points of mere
ceremony, invite demands and attacks of more serious importance.
Our rule allows all this; and only directs that, when points of honour become subjects of contention between sovereigns, or are
likely to be made the occasions of war, they be estimated with a reference to utility, and not *by themselves.* "The dignity of his crown,
the honour of his flag, the glory of his arms," in the mouth of a
prince, are stately and imposing terms; but the ideas they inspire
are insatiable. It may be always glorious to conquer, whatever be
the justice of the war, or the price of the victory. The dignity of a
sovereign may not permit him to recede from claims of homage
and respect, at whatever expense of national peace and happiness
they are to be maintained; however unjust they may have been in
their original, or in their continuance, however useless to the possessor, or mortifying and vexatious to other states. The pursuit of

honour, when set loose from the admonitions of prudence, becomes in kings a wild and romantic passion: eager to engage, and gathering fury in its progress, it is checked by no difficulties, repelled by no dangers; it forgets or despises those considerations of safety, ease, wealth, and plenty, which, in the eye of true public wisdom, compose the objects to which the renown of arms, the fame of victory, are only instrumental and subordinate. The pursuit of interest, on the other hand, is a sober principle; computes costs and consequences; is cautious of entering into war; stops in time: when regulated by those universal maxims of relative justice, which belong to the affairs of communities as well as of private persons, it is the right principle for nations to proceed by: even when it trespasses upon these regulations, it is much less dangerous, because much more temperate, than the other.

II. The conduct of war. If the cause and end of war be justifiable, all the means that appear necessary to the end are justifiable also. This is the principle which defends those extremities to which the violence of war usually proceeds: for since war is a contest by *force* between parties who acknowledge no common superior, and since it includes not in its idea the supposition of any convention which should place limits to the operations of force, it has naturally no boundary but that in which force terminates—the destruction of the life against which the force is directed. Let it be observed, however, that the licence of war authorises no acts of hostility but what are necessary or conducive to the end and object of the war. Gratuitous barbarities borrow no excuse from this plea: of which kind is every cruelty and every insult that serves only to exasperate the sufferings, or to incense the hatred, of an enemy, without weakening his strength, or in any manner tending to procure his submission; such as the slaughter of captives, the subjecting of them to indignities or torture, the violation of women, the profanation of temples, the demolition of public buildings, libraries, statues, and

in general the destruction or defacing of works that conduce nothing to annoyance or defence. These enormities are prohibited not
only by the practice of civilised nations, but by the law of nature
itself; as having no proper tendency to accelerate the termination,
or accomplish the object of the war; and as containing that which
in peace and war is equally unjustifiable—ultimate and gratuitous
mischief.

There are other restrictions imposed upon the conduct of war,
not by the law of nature primarily, but by the *laws of war* first, and
by the law of nature as seconding and ratifying the laws of war. The
laws of war are part of the law of nations; and founded, as to their
authority, upon the same principle with the rest of that code,
namely, upon the fact of their being established, no matter when or
by whom; upon the expectation of their being mutually observed,
in consequence of that establishment; and upon the general utility
which results from such observance. The binding force of these
rules is the greater, because the regard that is paid to them must be
universal or none. The breach of the rule can only be punished by
the subversion of the rule itself: on which account, the whole mischief that ensues from the loss of those salutary restrictions which
such rules prescribe is justly chargeable upon the first aggressor.
To this consideration may be referred the duty of refraining in war
from poison and from assassination. If the law of nature simply be
consulted, it may be difficult to distinguish between these and
other methods of destruction, which are practised without scruple
by nations at war. If it be lawful to kill an enemy at all, it seems lawful to do so by one mode of death as well as by another; by a dose
of poison, as by the point of a sword; by the hand of an assassin, as
by the attack of an army: for if it be said that one species of assault
leaves to an enemy the power of defending himself against it, and
that the other does not; it may be answered, that we possess at least
the same right to cut off an enemy's defence, that we have to seek

his destruction. In this manner might the question be debated, if there existed no rule or law of war upon the subject. But when we observe that such practices are at present excluded by the usage and opinions of civilised nations; that the first recourse to them would be followed by instant retaliation; that the mutual licence which such attempts must introduce would fill both sides with the misery of continual dread and suspicion, without adding to the strength or success of either; that when the example came to be more generally imitated, which it soon would be, after the sentiment that condemns it had been once broken in upon, it would greatly aggravate the horrors and calamities of war, yet procure no superiority to any of the nations engaged in it; when we view these effects, we join in the public reprobation of such fatal expedients, as of the admission amongst mankind of new and enormous evils without necessity or advantage. The law of nature, we see at length, forbids these innovations, as so many transgressions of a beneficial general rule actually subsisting.

The licence of war then acknowledges *two* limitations: it authorises no hostilities which have not an apparent tendency to effectuate the object of the war; it respects those positive laws which the custom of nations hath sanctified, and which, whilst they are mutually conformed to, mitigate the calamities of war, without weakening its operations, or diminishing the power or safety of belligerent states.

———

Long and various experience seems to have convinced the nations of Europe, that nothing but a *standing army* can oppose a standing army, where the numbers on each side bear any moderate proportion to one another. The first standing army that appeared in Europe after the fall of the Roman legion, was that which was erected in France by Charles VII. about the middle of the fifteenth century: and that the institution hath since become general, can only be attributed to the superiority and success which are every where observed to attend it. The truth is, the closeness, regularity, and quickness, of their movements; the unreserved, instantaneous, and almost mechanical, obedience to orders; the sense of personal honour, and the familiarity with danger, which belong to a disciplined, veteran, and embodied soldiery, give such firmness and intrepidity to their approach, such weight and execution to their attack, as are not to be withstood by loose ranks of occasional and newly levied troops, who are liable by their inexperience to disorder and confusion, and in whom fear is constantly augmented by novelty and surprise. It is possible that a *militia*, with a great excess of numbers, and a ready supply of recruits, may sustain a defensive or a flying war against regular troops: it is also true that any service, which keeps soldiers for a while together, and inures them by little and little to the habits of war and the dangers of action, transforms them in effect into a standing army. But upon this plan it may be necessary for almost a whole nation to go out to war to repel an invader; beside that a people so unprepared must always have the seat, and with it the miseries, of war, at home, being utterly incapable of carrying their operations into a foreign country.

From the acknowledged superiority of standing armies, it follows, not only that it is unsafe for a nation to disband its regular troops, whilst neighbouring kingdoms retain theirs; but also that regular troops provide for the public service at the least possible expense. I suppose a certain quantity of military strength to be necessary, and I say that a standing army costs the community less than any other establishment which presents to an enemy the same force. The constant drudgery of low employments is not only incompatible with any great degree of perfection or expertness in the profession of a soldier, but the profession of a soldier almost always unfits men for the business of regular occupations. Of three inhabitants of a village, it is better that one should addict himself entirely to arms, and the other two stay constantly at home to cultivate the ground, than that all the three should mix the avocations of a camp with the business of husbandry. By the former arrangement, the country gains one complete soldier, and two industrious husbandmen; from the latter, it receives three raw militiamen, who are at the same time three idle and profligate peasants. It should be considered also, that the emergencies of war wait not for seasons. Where there is no standing army ready for immediate service, it may be necessary to call the reaper from the fields in harvest, or the ploughman in seed-time; and the provision of a whole year may perish by the interruption of one month's labour. A standing army, therefore, is not only a more effectual, but a cheaper, method of providing for the public safety, than any other, because it adds more than any other to the common strength, and takes less from that which composes the wealth of a nation—its stock of productive industry.

There is yet another distinction between standing armies and militias, which deserves a more attentive consideration than any that has been mentioned. When the state relies, for its defence, upon a militia, it is necessary that arms be put into the hands of the people at large. The militia itself must be numerous, in proportion to the want or inferiority of its discipline, and the imbecilities or defects of its constitution. Moreover, as such a militia must be supplied by rotation, allotment, or some mode of succession whereby they who have served a certain time are replaced by fresh draughts from the country; a much greater number will be instructed in the use of arms, and will have been occasionally embodied together, than are actually employed, or than are supposed to be wanted, at the same time. Now what effects upon the civil condition of the country may be looked for from this general diffusion of the military character, becomes an inquiry of great importance and delicacy. To me it appears doubtful whether any government can be long secure, where the people are acquainted with the use of arms, and accustomed to resort to them. Every faction will find itself at the head of an army; every disgust will excite commotion, and every commotion become a civil war. Nothing, perhaps, can govern a nation of armed citizens but that which governs an army—despotism. I do not mean that a regular government would become despotic by training up its subjects to the knowledge and exercise of arms, but that it would ere long be forced to give way to despotism in some other shape; and that the country would be liable to what is even worse than a settled and constitutional despotism—to perpetual rebellions, and to perpetual revolutions; to short and violent usurpations; to the successive tyranny of governors, rendered cruel and jealous by the danger and instability of their situation.

The same purposes of strength and efficacy which make a standing army necessary at all, make it necessary, in mixed governments, that this army be submitted to the management and direction of the prince: for however well a popular council may be qualified for the offices of legislation, it is altogether unfit for the conduct of war: in which success usually depends upon vigour and enterprise; upon secrecy, despatch, and unanimity; upon a quick perception of opportunities, and the power of seizing every opportunity immediately. It is likewise necessary that the obedience of an army be as prompt and active as possible; for which reason it ought to be made an obedience of will and emulation. Upon this consideration is founded the expediency of leaving to the prince not only the government and destination of the army, but the appointment and promotion of its officers: because a design is then alone likely to be executed with zeal and fidelity, when the person who issues the order chooses the instruments, and rewards the service. To which we may subjoin, that, in governments like ours, if the direction and *officering* of the army were placed in the hands of the democratic part of the constitution, this power, added to what they already possess, would so overbalance all that would be left of regal prerogative, that little would remain of monarchy in the constitution but the name and expense; nor would these probably remain long.

Whilst we describe, however, the advantages of standing armies, we must not conceal the danger. These properties of their constitution—the soldiery being separated in a great degree from the rest of the community, their being closely linked amongst themselves by habits of society and subordination, and the dependency of the whole chain upon the will and favour of the prince—however essential they may be to the purposes for which armies are kept up, give them an aspect in no wise favourable to public liberty. The danger however is diminished by maintaining, on all occasions, as much alliance of interest, and as much intercourse of sentiment, between the military part of the nation and the other orders of the people, as are consistent with the union and discipline of an army. For which purpose, officers of the army, upon whose disposition towards the commonwealth a great deal may depend, should be taken from the principal families of the country, and at the same time also be encouraged to establish in it families of their own, as well as be admitted to seats in the senate, to hereditary distinctions, and to all the civil honours and privileges that are compatible with their profession: which circumstances of connexion and situation will give them such a share in the general rights of the people, and so engage their inclinations on the side of public liberty, as to afford a reasonable security that they cannot be brought, by any promises of personal aggrandisement, to assist in the execution of measures which might enslave their posterity, their kindred, and their country.

Index

Abraham/Abram, 67, 99, 111, 181

actions, judging. *See* expediency principle

Acts (book of): charity, 143–44; litigation, 159–60; prayer, 242; Sabbath, 265–66; vows to God, 84; war, 457

Adam, 57–58

adoration as duty, 233

adultery, 176–80

adventitious/natural rights, compared, 51–52

advowsons, 121–24

agent responsibilities (commission contracts), 100–102

agricultural production: from colonisation, 440–42; crops *vs.* animals, 425, 428–29; distribution of, 431–32, 436–37; exporting, 437–39, 449–50; incentives, 429–31; laws to encourage, 453–56; and property advantages, 64–65, 430–31; as species right, 56–60. *See also* employment

alienable/unalienable rights, compared, 52–53

allegiance oaths, 118–20

ambition and happiness, 17–19

America (United States), xx, xxi, 293, 303, 349, 403

anger, 149–52

animals/crops. *See* agricultural production

animus imponentis principle, 124

Anti-Jacobin Review, xii

aristocracies, 317–22. *See also* civil government; constitution, British

Aristotle, 11

armies, 322, 329–30, 467–71

Assyria, marriage traditions, 194

balance of interest, 339–40

balance of power, 337–39

balance of trade, defined, 444

benevolence, 25–26

Bentham, Jeremy, xxiii, xxiv–xxv

bribery, 121–24

Britain. *See* constitution, British; England

British constitution. *See* constitution, British

Burke, Edmund, xx–xxi

Caesar, 186

capital punishment: advantages, 377–79; certainty *vs.* severity argument, xxiii–xxiv; frequency of, 384–86; guidelines for exercising, 379–84; public, 389; purpose, 375; state rights, 230–31. *See also* punishment

casual judicature, 356–57

casuistry, defined, 1

charity: defined, 133; habit of, 27; monetary, 144–46; obligation of, xix, 140–44, 147–49; professional assistance as, 138–40; public *vs.* private, 146–47; slavery and, 135–38; toward servants, 134–35

Charles II, 132, 296

Charles VII, 468

children: and divorce, 186; duties of, 212–16; educating, 200–201; employment preparations, 201–7; imperfect rights of, 53; maintaining, 199–200; and parental rights, 210–11; and polygamy, 183; priority of, 196–99; virtue lessons, 207–10

China, 424–25

churches. *See* religious establishments

civil government: and adventitious rights, 51–52; and alienable/unalienable rights, 52–53; allegiance oaths, 118–20; as authority over religion, 404–12; forms of, 316–26; origins, xix–xx, 281–85; and religious toleration, 412–18; and self-

This book is set in Janson Text. Janson was designed not by the Dutch-born, Leipzig-based typefounder Anton Janson (1620–87) whose name it bears, but by Miklos Kis (1650–1702), a Hungarian type designer working in Amsterdam. The typeface was cut some time around 1690.

Printed on paper that is acid-free and meets the requirements of the American National Standard for Permanence of Paper for Printed Library Materials, Z39.48-1992. ∞

Book design by Carl Gross at Quarto, Abington, Pennsylvania
Typography by G&S Typesetters, Austin, Texas
Printed and bound by Worzalla Publishing Company, Stevens Point, Wisconsin